Gubby Allen

Man of Cricket

Gubby Allen

Man of Cricket

E. W. Swanton

Hutchinson / *Stanley Paul*
LONDON MELBOURNE SYDNEY AUCKLAND
JOHANNESBURG

Hutchinson/Stanley Paul & Co. Ltd
An imprint of the Hutchinson Publishing Group
17–21 Conway Street, London W1P 6JP

Hutchinson Publishing Group (Australia) Pty Ltd
16–22 Church Street, Hawthorn, Melbourne,
Victoria 3122

Hutchinson Group (NZ) Ltd
32–34 View Road, PO Box 40–086, Glenfield,
Auckland 10

Hutchinson Group (SA) Pty Ltd
PO Box 337, Bergvlei 2012, South Africa

First published 1985
© E. W. Swanton 1985

Set in Sabon by Tradespools Ltd, Frome
Printed and bound in Great Britain by
Anchor Brendon Ltd, Tiptree, Essex

British Library Cataloguing in Publication Data
Swanton, E. W.
Gubby Allen: man of cricket.
1. Allen, Gubby—England—Biography
I. Title
796.35'8'0924 GV915.A3/
ISBN 0 09 159780 3

Contents

Author's Note

The idea of this biography, and that I should be its author, belongs to Mr R. B. Bloomfield, of Hutchinson. He overcame my initial reluctance, which was based on too close an association and friendship with the subject. How valid my doubts were, the reader must determine. In any event, let me record that Roddy Bloomfield could not have been more encouraging or helpful.

I must express my gratitude to all who have cooperated in various ways in the writing of this book. The first name must be that of Lord Home of the Hirsel, Mr Allen's Eton contemporary, who has not only read the whole ms in typescript and made valuable suggestions but has also found time in a full and busy life to contribute a Foreword which gives the book a highly distinguished Imprimatur. It is surely Gubby in a nutshell. Nor does indebtedness end there, for Lord Home in his opening phrase has coined the apt phrase 'Man of Cricket' which I have 'lifted', with due permission, into my title.

I have had generous help from Mr Allen's sister, Lady Dickson and her husband Marshal of the RAF Sir William Dickson, who also have read the ms and have lent me two books which have been essential to the early part of the story. They are *Early Georgian*, Extracts from the Journal of George Allen (1800–1877) by Dundas Allen, published in Australia in 1958 by Angus and Robertson, and *The Elizabeth Street Cottage*, a record of the firm of Allen, Allen, and Hemsley, by the same author and privately published in 1964. Other help on the family side has come from Mr Allen's cousin, Mr R. H. Allen of Sydney.

Among the many cricketers to whom I have talked and with whom I have corresponded are Sir Donald Bradman, Mr R. E. S. Wyatt, Mr L. E. G. Ames, Mr W. H. V. Levett, Mr F. R. Brown, Sir Leonard Hutton, Mr. R. Aird, Mr W. Wooller, the late Mr J. T. Ikin, Mr P. B. H. May, Mr M. C. Cowdrey and Mr J. P. Mann. The list is not longer for an obvious reason – of the England XI which played in his first Test Match, in 1930 at Lord's, Mr Allen is the only survivor.

Mr S. C. Griffith's recollections of the period between 1964 and 1974 when he as secretary of MCC and Mr Allen as treasurer were so intimately involved in the setting-up of the Cricket Council, the Test and

County Cricket Board and the National Cricket Association have been of much value. I am grateful to the Committee of MCC and to the Secretary, Mr J. A. Bailey, for access to the minutes, and for the ready assistance of Mr S. E. A. Green, the curator. The Right Hon. Denis Howell, who was Minister of Sport at the time of the transfer of authority, has also been helpful in this connection.

Mr M. F. Howard, archivist of the Leys School, has kindly supplied biographical details of the early life of Walter Macarthur Allen, Gubby's father. For information about his preparatory schooldays I am indebted to Mr C. ff. Churchill of Summer Fields, to his contemporary, Mr R. A. K. Jacques, and also to Mr M. J. L. Stow, of Horris Hill. The Vice-Provost of Eton, Mr D. H. Macindoe, has informed me on the somewhat intricate Eton cricket system. Mr B. J. W. Hill has been good enough to allow me to quote from his as yet unpublished *Eton Remembered*.

Mr Simon Frisby, of de Zoete and Bevan, has shed light on my subject as a stockbroker. Mr G. A. Hill has made an estimation of him as a golfer. Mr P. A. Snow, the senior among the representatives of the associate members of the International Cricket Conference, volunteered his impression of Mr Allen as chairman and United Kingdom representative.

This is the third book in my name which has profited greatly from Mr George Plumptre's editorial hand and Mr Humphrey Stone's design. Mr J. D. Coldham, of the Cricket Society, generously offered to read the book in proof. Mrs Jill Chandler, my secretary, has typed the manuscript and laboured cheerfully on its behalf. My wife, Ann, has borne without undue complaint a rationed use of her piano and other domestic dislocations.

I must add an explanation to those who are irritated, as I am, by alterations made to players' initials after their active days are over. A few of these have crept into the scores, including the addition of the unused third initial of Mr Allen himself, and have been noticed too late to justify re-setting. Other scores have been printed according to the practice of the day and the source relied on: for instance the prefix Mr used in *Wisden* in the case of amateurs.

Lastly and chiefly, I am indebted to Mr Allen for the use of his marvellously complete cuttings books, photograph albums, selectorial minutes and other papers; also for much hospitality over a lengthy period. As to the photographs, Mr Patrick Eagar has taken fresh prints of many, and of those still in copyright every effort has been made to determine the identity of the photographers to whom reproduction fees are due.

A select cricket bibliography follows:

Wisden Cricketers' Almanack 1920–1984; *The Cricketer* 1921–1984;

Barclays World of Cricket, The Game from A to Z, Collins, 1980;
Australian Cricket by Jack Pollard, Hodder and Stoughton, 1982; *Lord's
(1787–1945)* by P. F. Warner, Harrap, 1946; *Lord's (1946–1970)* by
Diana Rait-Kerr and Ian Peebles, Harrap, 1971; *Lord's* by Geoffrey
Moorhouse, Hodder and Stoughton, 1983; *Gentlemen v Players* by Sir
Pelham Warner, Harrap, 1950; *Middlesex County Cricket Club 1921–
1947* by N. Haig, 1948; *The Bodyline Controversy* by Laurence Le
Quesne, Secker and Warburg, 1983; *The Wisden Book of Test Cricket
1876–77 to 1977–78*, edited by Bill Frindall, Macdonald and Jane's,
1979.

For some readers it may help to have the following information on
cricket's controlling bodies. When Marylebone Cricket Club set up a
governing structure for the game in 1968 three new bodies were formed.
These are they, with their respective functions:

The Cricket Council is the supreme authority. It comprises representatives from the Test and County Cricket Board, the National Cricket
Association and MCC itself. In practice the Council delegates its powers
in day-to-day affairs to these bodies.

The Test and County Cricket Board, generally known as the TCCB, is
responsible, as its name denotes, for Test Match arrangements as
affecting England and also for all cricket played by the seventeen first-
class counties and the Universities of Oxford and Cambridge.

The National Cricket Association, generally known as the NCA, is
responsible for the administration of all aspects of the game below the
first-class, and the coordination of all ancillary bodies, notably in the
fields of coaching and youth cricket.

The International Cricket Conference or ICC, formed in 1909, is
composed of representatives from all the Test-playing countries, and also
of non-Test-playing countries with recognized governing bodies. These
latter have associate member status. The ICC is responsible for deciding
future Test programmes but has no other mandatory function.

It meets annually at Lord's, and acts as a forum for the discussion of
topical matters, on which it may recommend courses of action to its
members. The president of MCC is by tradition chairman of the ICC in
his year of office, and the secretary of MCC acts in that capacity for the
ICC. The ICC is the focus for suggested amendments in the laws of the
game which are the responsibility of MCC, as they have been since the
formation of the club in 1787.

Foreword

BY LORD HOME OF THE HIRSEL

If there were such an elected title as 'Man of Cricket' the vote with near unanimity would go to Gubby Allen, for he has devoted his life to the game as player, administrator, philosopher and friend. The citation, too, would testify that his influence has been beneficial and added immensely to the prestige of cricket. In one way the verdict would be surprising, for the boy who came to England at the age of six was Australian; ironic, too, that some years later it was in many a contest with the country of his birth that he made his cricketing reputation.

Mr Swanton tells his life story with the knowledge of a fellow-cricketer, and the insight and sympathy of a friend.

As a Commonwealth import, the schoolboy had four early strokes of luck. At Eton College, where the standard of games was high, his naturally competitive spirit was fed. His house-master was C. M. Wells, a man of intellectual stature and an international athlete of renown; his coach was George Hirst who knew everything about seam-bowling; then he found himself the neighbour of 'Plum' Warner who lived nearby, and had a 'net' in his garden. Those three instructed Gubby in the philosophy and lore, the diplomacy and the techniques of cricket for which he had a greedy appetite. Wells, in particular, convinced him that a cricketer who used his brains was more likely to succeed in all departments of the game than one who did not.

In those early days Gubby had the basic requirements of a clear eye and a sense of timing, but it was his dedicated application to translating the theory of batting and bowling into practice which marked him out as one sure to fulfil his ambition, which was to be a really good cricketer.

Early in this book Jim Swanton tells of an exchange between the boy and the then secretary of the MCC. 'If you hold your bat as we suggest you might get into the Eton XI,' and the reply, 'I will get into the Eton XI however I hold my bat.' That might seem rashly cocksure, but I will wager anything that Gubby privately practised the suggested grip until he had proved or disproved it to his own satisfaction. That was his way.

Dedication, application and mental discipline took him steadily up the cricketing ladder, qualifying as batsman, bowler and fielder. It wasn't an easy ascent. At Cambridge his contemporaries included the Ashtons and Percy Chapman; in the Middlesex side there were Hearne and Hendren and Frank Mann and at Test Match level Hobbs and Sutcliffe, Woodfull, Bradman, McCabe and their like.

Sir Robert Menzies, Gubby's great friend, always used to classify score-cards as 'cold statistics', holding that the only way to appreciate cricket was to be at the match. That rule used to hold even during Prime Ministers' Conferences in London. I will therefore skip the statistics with the assurance to the reader that Jim Swanton has made the county and Test Matches, and Gubby's striking performance in them, live again. My favourite is his ten wickets in an innings against Lancashire, where he only bowled at first change because he was late for the start!

There were ups and downs for Gubby, and injury for one of his light physical build was too often just around the corner; but he was a fine pace-bowler – his action was fluent, balanced and poised – and a middle innings batsman of great value to any side.

Interest in this story will inevitably focus on the controversy about Bodyline bowling on the Australian tour of 1932, which brought Anglo–Australian relations to the boil, and from which the resentment simmered on for a very long time.

Gubby has always condemned leg-theory bowling, with a field set accordingly, as bad for the game of cricket, and when Jardine, England's Captain, suggested that Gubby should connive and bowl bumpers he flatly refused to do so. There was no quarrel with Jardine, but he was met with a firm refusal. All sorts of rumours were abroad and accusations made. Jardine was said to have arrived in Australia with a mission to 'hate'. The English selectors were supposed to have hatched a plot whereby pace would be used to intimidate the leading Australian batsmen – the target being the body rather than the stumps. These lurid interpretations of the events are faithfully recorded here.

However Gubby, having opted out of participation, adds a postscript which is authentic and persuasive. He dismisses the plot theory as extravaganza, and attributes the success of bodyline and the fury it evoked to a combination of factors: the adoption of leg theory; the setting of the field with six or seven on the leg-side; the sheer pace of Larwood in particular, and his accuracy which allowed him to follow the movement of the batsman, and bowl at the body rather than the wicket; and finally the uneven bounce of the Australian pitches.

That seems to put the matter in perspective, but it was a sorry affair, and much trouble, friction and recrimination would have been saved if Gubby's protest had been heeded at the time. As it is, the laws have had to be changed, and the helmet is now an unsightly legacy to first-class cricket.

The years when a first-class cricketer is active inevitably attract the public eye, but Jim Swanton is right to allot a large share of Gubby's laurels to the years when he was guiding the committees of the MCC in the administration of the game. There will be a consensus of opinion among cricketers that his influence was beneficial from club cricket through to national and international level.

So how will the reader sum up this man of cricket?

Certainly as a personality in his own right, whose sole test of his own or other people's actions was whether they would contribute to the life and betterment of the game; and one who expected that standard to be accepted by others. He will ask himself why Gubby, with his strong and abrasive opinions, so regularly got his own way. He won't linger long in that speculation because clearly the answer is that so many of his views and conclusions were sheer common sense, and, even when defeated, were seen to be inspired by only one motive – the loyalty and devotion to the well-being of cricket and cricketers. Critics were at once disarmed and convinced by his dedication.

This foreword begins to read like an obituary. It isn't, for Gubby is happily alive and active. Many will find interest and enjoyment in this account of his life.

I

The Very Old Fast Bowler

'I know you – you very old fast bowlah.' The subject of this biography, after filling his venerable but immaculate Bentley a time or two from the same 'quick-wash' garage, was thus addressed by the young West Indian attendant. Once seen never forgotten, one might almost say. For there is nothing whatever ordinary or anonymous about George Oswald Browning Allen.

Let me support this proposition with a brief questionnaire. Who is the only man to have taken all ten wickets at Lord's in a county match? Who is the only famous England cricketer never to have either scored a thousand runs or taken a hundred wickets in a season? Who reversed the natural order of things by being elected first, at a precocious age, to the Committee of MCC, and appointed captain of England afterwards?

Who, after the Second World War, one day asked the MCC Committee, 'What have we ever done to help boys' cricket?' and then proceeded to set the whole national youth movement in train? Who is the only man ever to hold simultaneously the offices of chairman of the Test selectors, chairman of the powerful MCC Cricket Sub-Committee, and chairman of the Umpires' Committee? Who at an Imperial Cricket Conference meeting initiated and led a successful crusade against the dangerous evil of throwing?

Who else? In every facet of his life Gubby has shown, above all, initiative and individuality – and in his many-sided labours for cricket I shall hope to show that his service has been of unique value. Before we go any further, though, why Gubby? Well, the third initial has never been in consistent use, but when it turned up briefly at Eton, boys began to call him Gobby. This soon – and mercifully – became Gubby. In the family he was, and is, always known as Obbie. He was not called George or Oswald or Browning: he was christened George after his grandfather and earlier ancestors, Oswald after a godfather, and Browning after his godmother, who married a relation of the poet. Gubby it is then, and who has ever heard of another?

Most followers of English cricket know that Gubby is Australian by birth, not so many that he was a fourth generation Australian whose great-great-grandmother emigrated to Australia with his great-grand-father aged sixteen in 1816, less than thirty years after the first colonists landed at Sydney. His parents brought him to England at the age of six with an elder brother and a younger sister because his father had such respect for the English system of education. The Allens intended to return to Australia but found English life so much to their taste that they changed their minds and stayed. Gubby, it may be assumed, was thoroughly anglicized long before his schooling at Summer Fields and Eton was complete.

After a happy and successful career at Eton, and three appearances against Harrow at Lord's, Gubby had two years at Cambridge, winning his place as a freshman in Hubert Ashton's powerful 1922 side and taking forty-nine wickets for the University plus twenty-two more for Middlesex in the vacation. The following year he broke down in the University Match (having protested before it that he was not fit), but he had forty-five more wickets for Cambridge, with a further twenty-two later for Middlesex. His physique naturally grew in these two summers wherein he established himself for all to see as an all-round cricketer of high potential. It is from this time that the balance as between batting and bowling utility shifted towards the latter. One wonders how many undergraduate bowlers of genuine pace in modern days have taken ninety-four wickets for a university before their twenty-first birthday.

He was, throughout his days as a cricketer, an amateur in the truest sense. His career came first, he loved playing cricket as he had done from earliest boyhood, and now in his early years in the City the society life of London opened up to him a world, far removed from his upbringing, by which he was greatly attracted. His closest Eton friends had been David Bowes Lyon, David Brand and Willie Hill-Wood.* All doors indeed were open to him, and for a while cricket and the debs were sometimes conflicting attractions. However, when in the late 1920s the chance of playing for England beckoned, the need for practice and complete physical fitness took clear precedence. Between 1930 and 1936 Gubby played in ten Tests at home as well as touring Australia with MCC in the Bodyline tour of 1932–33. Then came the invitation to lead MCC in Australia in 1936–37 for what was hoped, and proved, to be a tour to heal the scars of the one before.

The pattern of Gubby's cricket through the 1920s (as it continued to be after he had won his first England cap in 1930) comprised a mixture of county and club matches. He could seldom get away for more than a week at a time, Middlesex endeavouring to recruit him for their strongest fixtures. Lancashire, for instance, were the reigning champions when on

---

* Bowes Lyon was brother of the future Queen, Brand later to become Viscount Hampden, and Hill-Wood the second son of Sir Samuel Hill-Wood, Bt

a plumb pitch at Lord's in 1929 he took all ten of their wickets for 40 runs. When a year later Larwood was unfit to play for England in the Lord's Test against Australia Gubby was brought in, and although against Bradman on the plumbest of pitches he suffered with the rest, it was a partnership of 125 between A. P. F. Chapman and Allen for the sixth wicket that saved English pride when it had been badly shaken. Gubby in 1931 strengthened his Test credentials, also at Lord's, by making 122 against New Zealand and sharing in a record eighth wicket partnership of 246 with Leslie Ames. In the Second Test he took five for 14.

He played less than usual and with only modest results for Middlesex in 1932, and his choice to go with Douglas Jardine's MCC side to Australia in the winter attracted unfavourable press comment, not on the face of it unreasonable. His contribution to England's victory in the Bodyline series however vindicated the selectors' choice, and thereafter it came to be accepted that he was something of a special case.

No dissenting voices were raised when he was chosen to lead MCC on their next tour of Australia in the winter of 1936–37, for he had just led England to victory in the home Test series against India, and had enjoyed his fullest and most successful all-round season. Though he had never captained either Eton or Cambridge leadership came naturally to him, and the trials and difficulties common to all tours found Gubby in his element. The captain never spared himself, either on the field or off, and though it is inevitably remembered that this was the rubber that England lost after winning the first two Tests the subsequent defeats should be seen more as a triumph for Don Bradman at the height of his powers than as any positive failure on England's part.

On the field Australia 1936–37 marked his peak. Larwood having broken down following the 1932–33 tour, he was when fully attuned the best fast bowler in England. He was, at No 7 or 8 in Test Matches, a valuable bat of orthodox method, and he was a more than ordinarily good close fielder. Now he had shown his leadership qualities both as a tactician and as a tactful and considerate handler of men and situations on tour.

Playing and committee-work coincided for many years on either side of the Second World War. Gubby was elected to the Middlesex Committee in 1931 when he was twenty-nine, and to that of MCC in 1935 at the astonishingly youthful age of thirty-two. There was still plenty of good cricket in him in the early post-war years, and such was the dearth of young players that he was even persuaded to undertake, at the age of forty-five, the leadership of the MCC team to the West Indies. He did not play his last first-class match until just short of his fifty-second birthday in 1954.

The following year he undertook the chairmanship of the Test selectors, and for the next twenty-one years, until he resigned the treasurership of MCC, his involvement in the governance of cricket was unceasing. His chairmanship of the selectors lasted seven, mostly successful, years between 1955 and 1961 inclusive. No International Cricket Conference over more than two decades was complete without him. Between 1964 and 1976 from the focal position of treasurer he guided the affairs of MCC in the tradition of his predecessors in that office, Lord Harris, Lord Hawke and H. S. Altham. He was President of MCC in 1963–64 and the next best thing again eleven years later when in the Duke of Edinburgh's second term in the post he was obliged to delegate most of his duties to the treasurer.

In this latter period Gubby could bring to whatever problem arose a breadth of experience that no one else could match. In committee he has always been definite in his views and often trenchant in his expression of them. Though he has been known to alter his opinion – the change of the LBW Law which, like most other people, he at first favoured, and, also like many others, now deplores is an example – he is not easy to convince, and he can cling like a limpet when a major issue is at stake. The recent change in the constitution of the Cricket Council (which led him to resign as a matter of principle) is a characteristic instance. Once he was convinced, by photographic and other evidence, of the gravity of the throwing crisis, especially in regard to Anglo-Australian relations, he never rested until he had recruited Sir Donald Bradman to the cause. Between them they found the answer.

Strong men have been worn down by his tenacity in argument, especially when they have had trains to catch and they have known that for Gubby home is the other side of the flint wall that flanks the Harris Garden behind the pavilion at Lord's. Perfectionists are not always easy people to live with, and Gubby has always been a perfectionist, whether in the Committee Room at Lord's, or on the golf course, re-writing the MCC Coaching Book, tending his car or his roses, ordering his dinner, or even describing in close anatomical detail his latest strain or his last hip operation. (He has undergone five, as a legacy of his bowling, and today in his eighties, though he needs a buggy to get round the golf course, is walking better than for years, and without pain.)

Considering his forthrightness of speech on most cricket matters it says much that those holding contrary views have not as a rule taken offence. This is because of his complete sincerity, and because he is no respecter of persons. If he may give small change to the heavyweight the young are sure of his consideration – and any help they choose to ask for. He has been a good friend to any number of young cricketers.

There is moreover one important department of his labour for cricket in which he has shown a much less assertive aspect of his personality than in others. This is his capacity as a selector, wherein all who served under him give the picture of a quietly judicial chairman, taking infinite trouble to ascertain the views of others, and so ensure that the claims of every likely player were carefully assessed as well as every factor of pitch and weather taken into account concerning the coming match. This impression by his colleagues is amply confirmed by the minutes taken. Gubby's guiding principle in selection was 'when in doubt, go for class'. Hence the choice for Australia of the twenty-one-year-old Colin Cowdrey: hence the successful recalls in successive Tests in 1956 of Cyril Washbrook, David Sheppard and Denis Compton which enabled England to retain the Ashes.

Although he had always played a certain amount of golf to a single-figure handicap it was not until Gubby gave up playing club cricket and took on the selector's mantle at the age of fifty-two that he gave the game his serious, concentrated attention: and the adjectives are not chosen lightly. It is a general supposition among golfers that their friends are keenly interested in their last round, their last extraordinary incident, crowning misfortune, or whatever. He was anything but an exception to this common trend, and it is recorded how one of his Stock Exchange partners and old friend, Denis Hill-Wood, was known to interrupt the flow of reminiscence on a Monday morning and rule: 'One hole, Gubby, one hole!'

G. A. Hill, a Walker Cup golfer and another old friend, recalls how Gubby, playing with him at Muirfield, holed his second stroke at the first hole, which is 449 yards from the medal tee, with a five iron. He thinks the wind must have been behind. The second measures 349 yards. He played his second with an eight iron. Again the pitch was dead straight. It hit the pin, ran round the rim of the hole and finished an inch or two away. Alec describes him as 'for a short period in middle age damn good'. He also tells how when they were travelling together Gubby qualified some anecdote by adding, 'But that was before I became good.' Alec laughed so much he had to stop the car. Gubby was inclined to make remarks like this, tongue in cheek. Who was mocking whom, we wonder. Gubby was elected late in life to the Oxford and Cambridge Golfing Society, that exclusive company largely confined to blues. At the time he was playing off a handicap of four and at the age of fifty-nine he represented the Old Etonians in the Halford-Hewitt Cup. Just as at cricket he developed a sound batting method and a technically correct bowling action, so at golf he practised hard to perfect a good swing. He was perhaps unique in being convinced that he could still improve his game when in his sixties.

I venture another golf story since it is so characteristic both of Gubby and his old crony, the legless Sir Douglas Bader. Playing Royal St

George's one day in a strong wind off the sea Douglas on the high tee at the seventh was hit by a gust at the top of the back-swing, lost this balance and fell. Gubby stepped forward to pick him up whereat Douglas, who hated being helped and invariably declined to be, lying on the ground, struck out at him with his driver. His opponent jumped clear but was not amused, saying, 'I'll never try and help you again.'

Years passed and they were playing the Berkshire. At the fourteenth hole on the Blue Course the great airman hooked into the trees, found a difficult lie, and as he played his stroke somehow got his legs crossed and capsized. Whereat there followed:

'Gubby, come and pull me up, will you?'

'No, get yourself up.'

'I can't.'

'If you don't get up you lose the match.'

Impasse. One couple went through them, then another. Then:

'I'll help you up if you apologize for striking at me at Sandwich.'

'All right, damn you.'

In the club-house afterwards those who had passed through and asked what had been going on were told 'We were only having a discussion.' Neither incident was referred to again until a month or so before Douglas died when they were playing the same hole. He asked Gubby if he remembered, adding 'You know I never meant to hit you.' The memory of this touches Gubby, who had become very fond of him. But talk about an irresistible force meeting an immovable object!

There are other aspects of Gubby's life which will merit attention as his story unfolds in detail. He had, not least, a highly interesting and responsible war service, starting as a Territorial soldier, being attached to the RAF, and gravitating later to the War Office where he worked in Military Intelligence liaising with the Americans in the field of enemy anti-aircraft defence. He had flown at his own request on a bombing mission over Germany at a time in 1941 when this was a particularly testing exercise. His job at the time was the briefing of pilots on enemy 'flak' and he wanted to see things at first hand. At Bomber Group he met and formed a friendship with 'Bomber' Harris. He visited Italy at the Americans' request, and watched the battle for Monte Cassino over a tête-à-tête luncheon on a hill-top with 'Alex', a friend of pre-war days and now the Commander-in-Chief. To his horror the great man spread a white tablecloth. 'What about aircraft?' Gubby asked. 'Oh, don't bother about them.' It is in Gubby's nature to enjoy being 'in the know', and luckily for him his liaison aptitude was made good use of. He ended the war as a Lieut-Colonel, decorated by the Americans with the Legion of Merit.

It is inevitable that so strong a personality, having held so many positions of authority from boyhood to old age, will have aroused dislike in some, perhaps a reluctant tolerance in others. In earlier years, when he was making his mark as a cricketer and simultaneously working hard to earn a living, there were contemporaries and rivals who resented his having been, or at least seeming to be, the favoured son of Lord's, and in particular the protégé of Plum Warner, who between the wars was the most influential figure in the councils of MCC. Warner had known Gubby's cricket from his Eton schooldays, and the fact that his belief in Gubby was almost invariably justified by results did not disarm those with other axes to grind. There has always been, too, a certain ambivalence in county cricket circles in respect of 'Lord's'. For some people and at some periods 'love-hate' perhaps describes the feeling – and for all his adult life the name of G. O. Allen has in the mind of followers of cricket of every degree personified Lord's and MCC.

He is a man to whom no one reacts negatively. He has always been surrounded by a circle of fond friends who have encouraged his reminiscences, pulled his leg, and told stories about him probably adding a bit of spice for good measure. They have been and still are, of all ages and from all walks of life, eminent or humble. Then there are those still very close to cricket with whom he has worked both in the coaching field under the banner of the National Cricket Association (of which he was the virtual founder) and in the administration of Middlesex. No one ever seeks his advice in vain, or gets it in other than very precise terms.

No general sketch would be complete without mention of Gubby as a reminiscer and raconteur. There he sits in the committee room in the right-hand chair with the television nearby, conversing on every aspect of cricket which he or others may initiate and finding an apt story from his own experience wherein he may well be the central figure. Is he too modest, when encouraged to tell of his many moments of glory with bat and ball? Well, frankly no, and his hearers don't expect him to be. To steer the talk into likely channels is all part of the game – of which he is well aware. Are not most reminiscent artists apt to dwell on the stories of their successes, anyway? And if as the tale unfolds we recognize that we've heard this one before, what matter? It is well told, and the narrator is obviously getting much pleasure from the recounting. Moreover if he talks a lot – something common to most bachelors – he can also be a sympathetic listener to anyone who gains his respect. Lord Home, a friend since boyhood, underlines this among his virtues. 'A good listener,' he says, adding, 'once he starts!'

The house in Grove End Road the other side of the Harris Garden at first gives no clue to the abiding interest of its owner. Some coloured prints of Eton decorate the ground-floor rooms. A photograph on a side-table of Sir Robert Menzies, splendidly arrayed in the robes of the Order of the Thistle and with an affectionate inscription, adds distinction to the drawing-room. An oil painting of his father looks benignly from the stairs, dressed as the Commandant of the Special Constabulary. A print of Weaver's latest painting of Lord's, the mount signed by fellow England captains, hangs on the first-floor landing.

Only on admission to Gubby's bedroom is there some evidence to support the comment of his sister, Lady Dickson, that in his later years he became 'married to cricket'. He is photographed with Percy Chapman, going out after lunch to continue their great partnership against Australia. There are the team groups of the two tours of Australia. He and Leslie Ames are marching forth to continue their record partnership against New Zealand. There is that best of all action photographs, of Gubby airborne just after delivery to Stan McCabe. And there is a frame which shows two scenes from the Brisbane Test: of Gubby jumping out to O'Reilly, and Don Bradman after having been caught off him in the slips for o. 'Funny,' he says, 'that it should have taken a famous golfer, Roger Wethered, to make the point that not many people in the same match can have hit the best bowler in the world for six and got out the world's best batsman for a duck.'

Noteworthy indeed, but scarcely more so than to see, below these pictorial reminders of great days past, on the top of a book-shelf running the whole breadth of the room, in neat piles assembled the agendae and minutes of countless Lord's meetings, all dressed from the left in correct date order.

When I once, in the sort of bantering exchange only possible among old friends, told him he was a hypochondriacal megalomaniac he seemed rather tickled with the phrase and perhaps even set about living up to it. If there are elements of conceit in his make-up there are also streaks of modesty and self-criticism. Though he is naturally a member of all the best cricket clubs he will only rarely wear even an MCC tie, and seems to reserve the England tie for Test Matches. He was always a quiet dresser. The members of the Eton Society, the exclusive institution known as Pop, were and are still conspicuous by a traditional finery including gorgeous brocaded waistcoats and sponge-bag trousers. Photographs show him with a sober waistcoat above dark trousers. He thought the full rig was too much of a good thing. He is far from being ostentatious, and has little time for those who can be so described. Though he has spent so much time in the limelight it's fair to say he has never sought it.

When the television coverage turns, by the way, to racing Gubby is all attention. It is yet another unusual thing about him that he is a close and regular follower of racing who now never has a bet. A betting book exists to prove he used to have more than an occasional flutter – but the last entry is dated 1935!

On 31 July 1982 came Gubby's eightieth birthday, an occasion which the MCC Committee decided should be celebrated by a dinner in the Long Room after the pattern of the only other known to have been held there in honour of an individual. It was given for Plum Warner back in 1953. Gubby's was, literally, a glittering affair illumined by the picture-lights and the candles on the round tables. Groups of friends were seated together. An illustrious array of Test cricketers of all generations attended. The cricket establishment, naturally, was fully represented.

The toast of the evening was proposed in a characteristically light, whimsical vein by Lord Home, the guest of honour replying with becoming modesty. The company enjoyed the slightly different versions of a chance allegedly given in the Eton–Winchester of 1921 off Gubby's bowling to Alec at first slip by John Guise, who went on to make 278. The blame, we listeners felt, lay rather between Mervyn Hill, still fiddling with his gloves, and the bowler who ran up before the wicket-keeper was ready rather than with the fielder whose despairing dive just touched the ball as it flew for 4. Never mind, Eton, despite Guise's historic innings, won in the end quite easily – and Gubby with nine for 94 had a splendid match. The Long Room echoed to much laughter, that night, and for a company to whom the fellowship traditional to cricket came as second nature it was a party the memory of which would lighten the days ahead.

There was an admirable television interview during the tea interval of the Lord's Test against Pakistan a few days later wherein Peter West drew out of his subject a singularly modest version of the high points in his playing career. Then they talked of administration: what was his most influential contribution? Gubby said that his part in starting, just after the war, the national movement to help and encourage the young was the thing that had brought him most pride. His chief regret? Undoubtedly his support for the change in the old LBW Law. Whatever picture cricket-loving viewers looking in that day might have imagined of the men of power in cricket, this octogenarian seemed to be the antithesis of the cartoonist's idea of the reactionary old Lord's member. The eightieth milestone for some might have been the moment to bow out from active involvement. But not for Mr Cricket. There were major issues to be resolved, as well as scripts for new coaching films to be written, the Middlesex 2nd XI to keep an eye on, and much else. Rather, it seemed that the affectionate regard surrounding the birthday gave him a fresh impetus.

Lastly, so far as this opening sketch is concerned, yes, he is a bachelor. He has always enjoyed feminine company and made a number of lasting friendships. As for romantic attachments the family tell of several of which they had high hopes. In one or two otherwise favourable cases maybe the lady was not available. Or was it that in the end the perfectionist in him took over? Did anyone quite measure up? There are scraps of evidence in the pages that follow. But to any gentle probing on this an enigmatic smile is the only answer.

2
Australian Roots

Enough has emerged already, I would hope, of what might be termed the essential Allen to make it wholly unsurprising to discover that his ancestors were, for the most part, men not only of initiative and ability but of notably independent spirit.

The first of the Allen family of whom there is positive record is George, who died in Coolatore, County Wexford in 1663. Dundas Allen, a descendant writing a century later, wrote that this George Allen was a member of 'an ancient and respectable family seated in the reign of Charles I on the borders of Sherwood Forest, Nottinghamshire, but in consequence of opposing Oliver Cromwell ... fled to Wexford, Ireland for an asylum during the Civil Wars, and abandoned a good estate which has never been recovered.' The probability is then that George Allen of Coolatore was born in England.

An earlier and surely conclusive English link concerns the crest and coat of arms which has been used by the Allen family for two centuries and more. There are tombs in the Essex churches of Thaxted and Hatfield Peveril with fifteenth- and sixteenth-century dates which show the identical bearings of, in armorial terms, a demi-lion holding a rudder in its paw, and a cross potent on a shield. On these tombs the name is spelt both as Allen and Alleyne. So the probable though unprovable procession of the Allens passes from Essex to Sherwood Forest to County Wexford and thence, as we shall see, to London, then across the world (for all but a century) to New South Wales, and finally, so far as Gubby's branch are concerned, back to England.

George Allen of Coolatore had two grandsons – Dundas Allen does not identify the parents – George, born in 1713, and Joseph, born two years later. George graduated at Trinity College, Dublin, and in due course took holy orders, becoming rector of Kilmanagh and Prebend of Monomolin. This is Gubby's great-great-great grandfather. Nothing of his character has come to light, but a strong Puritan strain will in due course be noted in his great grandfather, the Prebendary's redoubtable grandson.

But it is the Prebendary's cousin, Joseph, who played an important part in the family story and so now claims attention. After being apprenticed to a Dr Wigram of Wexford, Joseph at the age of 25 sailed as surgeon's first mate in the flagship of Lord Anson, the commander of a squadron of eight ships under orders to attack Spanish trade and colonies in the Pacific, and in particular a galleon which plied between the west coast of America and the Philippines. The galleon was eventually captured and the prize-money for the whole voyage came to nearly half a million sterling. Joseph Allen's share, it was said, set him up in life, as did the friendship he formed with Lord Anson and others.

He was quickly elected, first, Warden and then Master of Dulwich College, thus providing another unresolved clue in family relationships since it was Edward Alleyne, the actor, who had founded the College in 1619. Joseph ruled Dulwich for thirty years, and 'though he had not been in great accord with his Fellows during his Mastership' they did him proud on his retirement, commissioning Romney to paint his portrait, which he left to the College at his death. It hangs in Dulwich Gallery.

But back to the main stream; Prebendary Allen had one son, Richard, born in 1744, who, like his uncle, became a doctor, and, also like his uncle, made his way in the world. He came to London, had four children by Mary Piery, on whose death he married Mary Lickfold, she being twenty-two and he forty-seven. Of the second marriage there were seven children, rapidly produced, of whom George, the youngest, was born in November, 1800, and they lived in Southwark.

When Joseph Allen died, in 1796, he left two-thirds of a tidy fortune of £24,000 to his nephew, Richard, who at some stage of his medical career became one of the Prince Regent's doctors. This attachment, by family report and on the evidence at his death, gave Richard a taste for high living. The Prince held extravagant court at Brighton, whither at his command Richard was summoned, travelling in luxury and living in great style. In 1806 Dr Richard Allen, Gubby's great-great grandfather, died at Brighton, and was buried in Southwark Cathedral.

One would like to know more of this son of the Rectory, but the hard fact was that he left his wife, with five surviving children to look after, almost penniless, apart from 'my leasehold house, No. 74 Oxford Street, County Middlesex, to carry on the business of vending medecines with the help of my daughter Elizabeth.' The profits from this subsidiary enterprise were to be divided among his many children. Elizabeth was one of his first wife Mary's family.

Enter now the skeleton in the cupboard. Richard Allen had employed to manage his chemist's shop in Oxford Street one Thomas Collicot, who had been a surgeon's mate in the Navy. Poor Mary Allen and Collicot, who was a widower with three children, ran the shop for three years together, and thereupon were married, he promising to provide for her and the combined family. This was in December 1809, Mary being forty and Collicot forty-two. Mary bore one Collicot child which died in infancy.

This at least was a mercy, for in late 1814 or thereabouts Collicot was arrested and tried for defrauding the revenue. Stamp duty in those days was payable on the sale of medicine, and each bottle had to be stamped. On hearing of her husband's arrest Mary hurried to the shop and stamped all the bottles, so that when the police made a search next day all was in order. Notwithstanding this, Collicot was convicted, and – almost impossible as it is to believe – was sentenced to be hanged. Presumably Gubby's great-great grandmother was lucky in that her brave, pathetic gesture did not land her in the dock beside her husband!

As it was, she got to work and in her extremity adopted the sound principle of going straight to the top – in fact to the Duke of Kent, the Prince Regent's younger brother (and father of the future Queen Victoria), who had known Richard Allen from his days at Brighton. The Duke intervened, and the sentence was duly commuted to transportation to New South Wales.

What now for Mary? Naturally enough she sought aid once more and was again deservedly successful. Robert Wigram, a grandson of the doctor to whom Joseph Allen had been apprenticed in Wexford, had come to London with £200 and a letter from his mother to Joseph. He prospered as a merchant, and later became a close friend of Richard's. He proved a friend in need to Mary, giving her the passage-money for herself and the Allen and Collicot children, and an invaluable letter to Lachlan Macquarie, Governor of New South Wales. She sailed with three of her own children and three of Collicot's from 'a southern port' in the Mary Rose, on 26 July 1815, just a month after the Battle of Waterloo, and landed at Sydney Cove on 19 January 1816. The dates come from the journal of George, her youngest and Gubby's great grandfather, who kept this at times fascinating record from his arrival, not yet sixteen, until shortly before his death at seventy-seven.

Thus with her numerous brood Mary stepped ashore into the first Australian penal settlement – founded less than thirty years before – to join the husband who had travelled, presumably in more basic circumstances, some months ahead of her. Her one crucial asset was the letter to Governor Macquarie – who, for his part, had a man-size job on his hands. Though Captain Cook had discovered the eastern seaboard in 1770 it was 1788 before Captain Phillip, with his squadron of eleven ships, established the first settlements at Sydney and Botany Bay.

As the late Robert Menzies was inclined to point out, the American War of Independence made in effect not one nation but two, for Britain, no longer able, after 1776, to use North America as a dumping-ground for criminals, bankrupts, and other undesirables thought thus to colonize what soon became New South Wales. 'From this somewhat murky origin has grown a nation of life, character and purpose.' Thus wrote Australia's greatest Prime Minister.

When Mary Collicot arrived in January 1816, Macquarie had not long preceded her. He had been sent to bring a humane and sensible administration in place of the corrupt rule of the original convict guards. He found a settlement of around 12,000 in Sydney, and about as many again scattered on the banks of the Murray River or up and down the coast to the north and south. Macquarie received Mary and her young family kindly. He gave the eldest Collicot 200 acres of land, and four cows, promised to reward the two Allen boys similarly in due course and arranged for George to be apprenticed to the Government Printer.

Mary and Thomas Collicot were reunited, and by 1819 were Master and Matron respectively of a Female Orphan Institution at Paramatta on the river of that name. George Allen therefore had now to fend for himself in the rough world of Sydney, with financial help from his stepfather. In many cases, including that of Collicot, transportation itself was considered punishment meet to fit the crime, and the evidence that exists suggests he did his duty by his wife and family.

In such a society past records were no bar to progress. Indeed Howe, the Government Printer, George's first employer, had arrived as a convict, and had had time to found Australia's first newspaper, the *Sydney Gazette*, before drinking himself to death, a not uncommon end. From his vantage-point in the Government Solicitors' Office, young George Allen kept well abreast of what was going on in the courts and beyond: smuggling, robbery, murder – Sydney was rife with crime. The gallows were generally busy – and seen to be busy – on Fridays.

As one who was to become one of the leading citizens of the fast-growing city of Sydney, and also as the founder of the Allen fortunes, George's early progress as extracted from his journal by Dundas Allen deserves some further notice. Governor Macquarie duly granted him 300 acres around Breakfast Creek on his undertaking to employ three transported convicts. Though he never lived on the property, in due course he exchanged it at a profit. At the age of twenty-one he became the first solicitor who had served the whole time of his articles there, to be admitted in New South Wales, and he duly set up in Macquarie Street and began to practise. The following year he wooed and won Jane Bowden, the daughter, not yet sixteen, of a Wesleyan clergyman who had arrived with his wife as free settlers from Devonshire in 1811. George had had first to wear down some disapproval from the Bowdens on account of his uncertain prospects rather than any conceivable doubt of his religious principles.

For at the age of twenty, young George had been attracted by the

Wesleyan Methodist missions to New Zealand and the Pacific Islands, the headquarters of which were in Sydney, and had joined the Methodist Society. He was at first strongly attracted to go as a missionary to Tonga – or, as it was then known, Tongataboo.

He forswore drink and smoking – and, after quite a struggle, even snuff! As for dancing, his journal entry after 'a grand Ball on board the Dauntless sloop of war' is nothing if not explicit:

> 24 July 1821. What are the miseries attending a drunken fit are too well known to need any comment – such there appears to have been at the Ball last night. I have known the time when I should have enjoyed the pleasures of a Ball room, but thanks be to God for His unspeakable mercy in snatching me as a Brand from Hell, and for giving me a relish for things of much greater importance.

His journal is full of the narrowest moralizing, from which not even his mother, away at Parramatta, removed from his influence, altogether escaped. Having explained why he felt he could not in conscience stand godfather to the child of a friend because he disapproved of the way the established Church baptized its children, he decided on a serious religious letter to his mother. Notwithstanding that 'she attends the means of Grace very regularly, receives the Sacrament and attends to all the ordinances of religious Worship, but I am afraid she does not experience true religion.' Mary Collicot's reply is not recorded.

George purchased an estate at Surry Hills, despite a financial scare when the Bank of New South Wales, in which he held a £100 proprietorial share, was all but ruined by a fraudulent cashier. Then the Allens moved to Elizabeth Street, his practice duly expanding with the growth of Sydney. On 17 May 1824 came the first of no fewer than fourteen children, a boy, christened out of gratitude to the family benefactor, George Wigram Allen. He was destined to be Gubby's grandfather.

By 1831 George had built, on ninety-six acres of land purchased from St Phillip's Glebe (just south of Rozelle Bay) a comely and substantial residence called Toxteth Park, which henceforth was the family home. Gubby's father was born at Toxteth. It is today a listed building still in perfect order, in the care of a Roman Catholic religious order as a large girls' school. The Mother Superior recently entertained there Dick Allen, Gubby's cousin, and his son and grandson, the fourth, fifth, and sixth Allen generations. The architect, John Verge, built also Camden Park, the family home of the Stanhams, where cricket has long been played in charming surroundings akin, as many an English visiting club will attest, to country-house cricket at home.

George's pious outpourings can be explained in part no doubt by his being brought into continual touch professionally with the seamy side of life. At one moment he is lamenting that of ninety-eight prisoners due for trial at the criminal court twenty-one are accused of murder; in the next he is 'glad to hear that the poor unhappy persons who suffered this day the vengeance of the Law died penitently, and one or two of them, it is said, died very happy.' Savage as the law was even by the standards of the day, George was prepared to take 'my man John Crawley' before the Bench for pretending to be deaf in order to avoid work, and merely notes that the twenty-five lashes received by the poor wretch were well deserved. What a baffling thing was Victorian morality, whether English or Colonial!

Dundas Allen's researches in his book *Early Georgian* (published in 1958 by Angus & Robertson) peter out in the mid-1840s, but by this time George Allen had already become mayor of the now city of Sydney, and chairman of committees in the New South Wales Legislative Council. He was on the governing body of Sydney College, later to become Sydney Grammar School, and a member of the Senate of Sydney University. He was president of the Bank of New South Wales. As to his life-long zeal in humanitarian works Gubby's great grandfather was president of the Total Abstinence Society, and an avid promoter of such causes as 'The Reclamation of Prostitutes and the Spiritual Nourishment of Seamen'. He was a leading lay preacher and – as light relief, no doubt – was president of the Floral Society. He retained a fervent interest in Wesleyan missionary work, and though he is not recorded as having ever gone there the family papers include a letter of touching affection from King George of Tonga. All in all, it adds up to a remarkable weight of achievement.

A great moment came when in 1847 his eldest, George Wigram, having served his articles, was admitted as a solicitor. The brass plate now proclaimed the firm as Allen and Son. Gradually old George handed over to young Wigram, as he was known, the former, it is a relief to read, mellowing with age, and rejoicing in family gatherings at Toxteth where as many as thirty or forty children sat down at table. When he died there in 1877 the Lieutenant-Governor and the Chief Justice headed the list of pall-bearers.

Wigram seems to have inherited many of his father's virtues – and, we may assume, a character reflecting his more prosperous start in life. Altogether an easier man to live with! He was elected to parliament, and during the 1870s became successively Minister of Justice and Speaker of the House. He, too, was a pillar of the university and of the Bank of New South Wales, and the old man lived just long enough to take pride in his son being knighted. Wigram likewise bred a large family, including Gubby's father, Walter, the tenth of eleven. Wigram became KCMG shortly before his sudden death aged sixty-one in 1885.

In Wigram's time the family firm, now Allen and Allen, expanded with the growth of Sydney, but though all six of his sons entered the law only three of them became partners in it, and of these only one, Reginald, had served his articles at the time of his father's untimely death. Accordingly experienced lawyers outside the family were sought as partners, and in 1894 an Englishman, A. M. Hemsley, joined the firm which thereupon adopted the title by which it is still known, Allen, Allen and Hemsley. Founded by George Allen in 1822, it is, of course, the oldest law firm in Australia, wherein five generations of Allens have served. Moreover by a happy chance when new and larger premises were sought in the 1960s they were found in Elizabeth Street, the very one in which George Allen had started business 140-odd years before.

Gubby's father, Walter, was one of the three who were all called to the bar but did not practise and spent most of their lives in England. Of those brothers who joined the firm the most notable personality was Reginald, the first of the Allens to make his name as a sportsman. 'Uncle Reggie' played for Australia in the second of the two Tests against Shaw and Shrewsbury's team of 1886–87. He batted at No. 4 and in a low-scoring match at Sydney which England won made 14 and 30. He was, it seems, more interested in bloodstock breeding and racing than the law and was for forty-nine years a member of the committee of the Australian Jockey Club.

Walter Macarthur Allen was born at Toxteth in 1870 and had his early schooling in Sydney, just where is not known but probably at Sydney College, founded by his grandfather. However, shortly after his father's death he was brought, aged sixteen, by his mother to England where George Boyce Allen, his eldest brother and fourteen years his senior, had long settled. Even in 1886 it cannot have been easy to find a suitable public school for a boy of that age, but he was accepted by the Leys School, Cambridge, which had been founded by leading Methodists on the outskirts of the town ten years earlier. These included two McArthur brothers who established an export business with Australia, and the younger of whom, Alexander, was on such close terms with the Allens that Gubby's father had been christened Walter MacArthur (the spelling varies). Alexander McArthur, on returning to England, became MP for Leicester, and acted *in loco parentis* to the youngster during his school and undergraduate days in England. Five of Alexander's sons were sent to the Leys, the younger of them overlapping Walter Allen's time there.

Walter had three summers in the Leys XI, averaging 40 in his last year and being described as 'the best bat we have ever had'. Going up to Trinity Hall he captained the college cricket side and got as near the university team as playing for the next XVI against the First XII.

On the evidence of the great C. M. Wells, who was up at the same time, he was a dangerous forcing bat, who might have got a blue if he had fully exerted himself. These were halcyon days for Cambridge cricket with heroes such as F. S. Jackson, Gregor MacGregor, S. M. J. Woods, 'Ranji', and Wells himself drawing the crowds to Fenner's. So father was within distance of a noble company.

There seems little doubt that Walter Allen, in marked contrast to his father and grandfather – and indeed to his younger son – took life very much as it came. Though he passed his legal examinations, ate the statutory dinners admitting him to the Inner Temple, and could call himself a barrister-at-law, he did not join the family firm on returning to Australia, and never went into practice. He made many friends in his undergraduate days and earned himself at Cambridge a popularity among Englishmen which he never lost.

In 1896 Walter Allen married in Sydney, Marguerite Julie (Pearl) Lamb, whose ancestry is at least as intriguing as that of the Allens though unfortunately less precisely documented. Overshadowing it is a momentous question-mark which, despite research by the Allen family, including Gubby's brother, Geoffrey, is unlikely now ever to be resolved. Pearl Lamb's grandfather was John Lamb, a naval officer from Westmorland who as a midshipman had first seen the great natural harbour and emerging town of Sydney in 1813 – three years in fact before Gubby's paternal great grandfather. John seemingly liked what he saw and on his retirement from the Navy emigrated to Sydney with his wife (née Emma Trant Robinson) and family, having received a grant of land in lieu of pension – in those days a not uncommon arrangement. John Lamb's family eventually numbered fifteen, of whom Edward, Pearl's father, was the second.

John Lamb had his own merchant vessel, was (likewise with George Allen) a member of the first Legislative Council of New South Wales, and was chosen to present to the Governor a petition urging that there should be an end to the sending of convicts. He died in 1862. Thus both sides of Gubby's family played leading parts in the early administration and expansion of New South Wales.

Edward Lamb married in 1853 at Port Macquarie Julie Clemence Beaufils Lamonnerie di Fattorini, daughter of Jean Baptiste de la Monnerie di Fattorini and Clemence Beaufils.

The mystery surrounds the origins of this Jean Baptiste etc. It is known that he studied medicine under Dr Abernethy of Edinburgh, married in France, emigrated to Australia and practised at Port Macquarie where, having outlived his wife by thirteen years, he died in 1853, shortly before his daughter's marriage. The names and dates are as recorded on a joint tombstone in Port Macquarie cemetery. Fact ends here and legend now takes over.

Who was Edward Lamb's father-in-law? Well, he emigrated from

France to Australia in the 1830s. He was a medical man of some repute in Port Macquarie, known only as Dr Fattorini. The story passed on in letters and by word of mouth in the Lamb family was that he was educated at the court of the Empress Josephine and at the Paris military academy. His mother's name was thought to have been de la Monnerie, in which case it is feasible that he should have sought a fresh identity under the Italian – or Corsican – name of Di Fattorini.

Lady Dickson, Gubby's sister, says that her grandfather, Edward Lamb, was told by the old Roman Catholic priest who attended Fattorini at the last that he said when dying: 'Napoleon educated me and said he was my father': to which the priest added: 'No one lies in making his last confession.' The priest said also that Fattorini told him he had left France, because he was known to be a Bonapartist, at the time of certain plots against King Louis Philippe. He was born in 1787, according to the tomb-stone, and in 1785 and 1786 Napoleon was stationed at Valence, the French equivalent of the former RMA, the gunner academy at Woolwich. In 1786 Napoleon was seventeen, so the dates at least fit the possibility of an illicit liaison. The imposing tomb at Fort Macquarie, guarded by two cypress trees at the highest point of the cemetery, bears (or did bear) the Napoleonic crown. The *Sydney Morning Herald* mentioned the crown and the legend of the Napoleonic blood in an article on the historic church and graveyard of Port Macquarie at the time of the visit of Gubby's MCC team in 1936–37. Treading this delicate ground no further, I would merely offer the thought that the singular determination of purpose which was evident in the earlier Allens, and which runs so conspicuously through Gubby's life, *may* be also an inheritance with the most illustrious roots from his mother.

According to Lady Dickson, 'My father said there might have been proof if Aunt Clemmie, Mum's eldest sister, hadn't been so addicted to spring-cleaning and burnt all the family letters and records.'

A final intriguing and in this case definite note on antecedents, involves the marriage of Gubby's sister, Patricia, to the distinguished airman, now Marshal of the RAF Sir William Dickson (whose last active appointment in 1958–59 was Chief of the Defence Staff). It is established that Admiral Lord Nelson had his daughter Horatia by Lady Hamilton. Horatia's children included Sir William's grandfather on his mother's side, Nelson Ward. The Dicksons had no sons but there is a surviving daughter, Susanna Margaret. The possibility at least exists therefore that in the veins of this daughter, Mrs Susanna Vedel, and of her children there flows the martial blood of two of the great antagonists of history, Nelson and Napoleon.

3
English Boyhood

Gubby was born on 31 July 1902 in the house built by his father in Victoria Road, Bellevue Hill, only a ten-minute drive from the heart of Sydney. Thaxted is a substantial house with a suberb view over the harbour, and Gubby spent the first six years of his life there until his parents decided to take their children to England for their schooling.

Drama had attended the voyage of Gubby's great grandfather to Australia, and drama of a different kind marked the return to England of his branch of the family nearly a century later. Walter Allen had booked them all on the SS *Waratah*, which was due to sail from Sydney via the Cape. However Oswald Watt, returning on the *Waratah* after a visit to England on its maiden voyage, sent a cable while at sea saying 'Don't like this ship, suggest you re-book.' Considering that the *Waratah* belonged to the Blue Anchor line, of which Watt was a director, Walter Allen had no hesitation in taking his friend's advice. Watt, so the family story has it, decided that the ship was unstable when one night it rolled so far that the water went out of his bath. His cable was a mercy indeed, for on its next journey, on which the Allens had been booked, the *Waratah* encountered a hurricane in the Indian Ocean between Durban and the Cape and sank with all hands. This ranks as one of the great unsolved mysteries of the sea. Not a spar or a lifeboat was ever found, the commonest theory being that when completely battened down she turned turtle.

Accordingly on 30 January 1909 Mr and Mrs W. M. Allen (and maid), Master G., Master O. and Miss Patricia Allen sailed for England from Sydney on the SS *Pericles*. So says the list of saloon passengers which, as with most of the other documentation of a long life, is preserved in the first of Gubby's many scrap-books. His brother's christian names, by the way, were Geoffrey Thornton Macarthur; hence Gubby was designated, no doubt for the only time in his life, by his second initial. There is a certain grim aptness in this, since but for his godfather, Oswald, after whom he was named, he would have perished as a child at sea. Happily for the game of cricket destiny had other plans.

Gubby dimly recalls playing cricket on the lawn with his brother, father and uncles, one of whom, Reggie, had played for Australia. His earliest memories centre also round two great friends of his father, and of each other, Oswald Watt, known as Toby, and Leslie Wilson, ultimately Sir Leslie, who served a record fourteen years as Governor of Queensland. They never tired of playing with the children when they came to Thaxted. For Toby Watt Gubby formed an undying admiration and affection. Gubby's birthplace, a little short of Royal Sydney Golf Club as one approaches Rose Bay, is regularly pointed out to English cricketing visitors. It was with pre-Australian seventeenth-century family history in mind that Walter Allen named the house Thaxted.

Wilson was an Englishman who came first to Australia as ADC to the Governor of New South Wales. Toby Watt, an Aussie through and through, sounds a devil of a fellow. He was a pioneer aeronaut, and in July 1914, having bought a Blériot monoplane, he found himself in Egypt. Thinking that England would not come into the approaching war, on an impulse he flew to France and enlisted. He was decorated by General Joffre with the Military Cross of the Legion of Honour, the first Australian to be so rewarded, and became so celebrated as to give authenticity to this family legend redolent of the chivalry of earlier days: he was shot down between the French and German lines. The Germans shelled him for half-an-hour, after which came a loud-speaker message from the German trenches saying 'If Captain Watt is still alive he may return to the French lines.' Whereat he emerged from a shell-hole, saluted both lines, amid cheers, and marched back to safety. When the Australian Air Force came to England later in the war the French released him, and he commanded the original Australian squadron. He flew in their first attack, earning himself a reprimand (being over age) and a CB. What a hero to thrill a schoolboy!

The Allens lived first in a London flat in Sloane Street, but they soon moved into the country, to the first of several houses in the attractive Thames-side village of Datchet. It was there when he was slightly older that Gubby's affection for Watt took expression in a passion for model aeroplanes. He and his cousin, Dick, made and flew these aeroplanes endlessly, and thereby formed a friendship with a boy from the bicycle shop in Windsor called Sydney Camm which had important consequences.

Walter Allen was so impressed by young Camm that after a while he sent him with an introduction to his friend Tommy Sopwith, an aeronaut just beginning to make his subsequent great fame as an aircraft designer. Camm took his chance so well that in due course he, too, won fame as a designer of many types of aircraft including the Hurricane. When Gubby's sister, Pat, met Sir Sydney Camm late in his life she was naturally thrilled when he said he owed his success in life to the introduction to Sopwith (later Sir Thomas) given him by her father.

Gubby supplies a whimsical postscript regarding Toby Watt. He used to maintain he was not well off, and his godson was therefore pleased to get a legacy of £1000 after the poor man, on a morning swim, came to an untimely end by drowning. Years later, on tour with MCC and playing at Sydney University, Gubby saw a portrait of Watt and asked what it was doing there. He was told he was one of the largest benefactors to the University, having left it £356,000.

Gubby's education was entrusted for two years or more to a governess, but a little before his tenth birthday he was sent to Summer Fields, one of the leading preparatory schools then as now, agreeably situated just north of Oxford up the Banbury Road. It has never been suggested that even as a child Gubby lacked self-assurance. Nevertheless his first term at school in the summer of 1912 must have been the pleasanter for the presence there already of three of his Allen cousins, Bruce, Lawrence and Dick. Being the youngest Gubby was accordingly known as Allen iv.

It was in the summer holidays of 1912 that Allen iv was taken by his father to see his first Test Match. It was at the Oval between England and South Africa, and they went because Reggie Spooner, one of the legendary sporting heroes of the day, and a great friend of Walter and Pearl Allen, was playing. Everyone must recall watching his first Test Match, and Gubby, who was just ten, had two special reasons for doing so. The game had not long started when a ball from Sydney Barnes stood up straight off the wet pitch and hit the wicket-keeper, E. J. Smith — for ever known as 'Tiger' — full in the mouth. Gubby asked his father what they were picking up and was told, 'I'm afraid they're his teeth.' Thereupon Spooner, while 'Tiger' was having his lip stitched, kept wicket.

Early in the afternoon South Africa were bowled out for 95 (Barnes five for 28, Woolley five for 41), and Hobbs and Rhodes were opening the England innings in reply. Wilfred Rhodes was out for a duck, whereupon, according to *Wisden*, 'Hobbs and Spooner soon put their side in a flattering position, the batting, while they were together being very fine indeed.'

Gubby was going to become very fond of Jack Hobbs whom he was seeing for the first time; but now his hero was, of course, Reggie Spooner — and what boy could have had a finer? The partnership added a 'brilliant' 61, at which point came the day's second memorable episode. For Spooner was caught at square-leg — and Gubby burst into tears. Gubby, according to family legend, was chided by his father at such a public display of emotion. 'Old boy, I don't think you ought to cry just because a friend of yours got out,' to which came the precocious comment: 'It wasn't because he got out but because he played such a terrible stroke.' It had been a full-pitch!

Note the names of Hobbs (whose 68 was easily top score in the match) and Woolley. Gubby's first Test at Lord's in 1930 was the last Test appearance there of both these great cricketers, and he and Frank were on the same side in the latter's last Test of all, at the Oval against Australia in August 1934, twenty-two years on.

The ten-year-old at his first Test that day was due to play with or against several others on the England side – 'Young Jack' Hearne, of course, over many summers with Middlesex, Bill Hitch, that dynamic Surrey cricketer, Rhodes and 'Tiger' Smith. There was always a rapport with 'Tiger', who was one of the best umpires during Gubby's prime as a player, before he settled in, so to speak, as the resident patriarch of Edgbaston. He died, aged ninety-three, only in 1979, and for many years Gubby had been the only man living who saw 'my teeth knocked out at the Oval'.

To return to Summer Fields, Allen iv in his second summer, 1913, made the 2nd XI, and in his remaining two years there graced the XI, of which in 1915 he was captain. From these years one has the evidence not only of the school magazines but of a leather-bound note-book wherein – in a handwriting very similar to today's – Gubby wrote down his performances, with batting and bowling averages, of every match he played in while at school. Thus we know that in what is described as the Jubilee Match the Sons beat the Fathers in what was something of an Allen benefit, Walter Allen, going in No 8 for the Fathers, making 52 out of a total of 93, and Allen iv, with his usual flair for the occasion, taking six for 41.

The needle match in those days – and needle was clearly the word – was Summer Fields v Horris Hill. In 1914 there was a singular encounter between the two schools, this apart from a retrospective view showing an England captain on each side, Allen for Summer Fields, Jardine for Horris Hill. The match was played at Oxford, and the home side, *having been put in by Jardine*, batted on and on and on until when the declaration came at 112 for nine only twenty minutes' batting time remained. Jardine took seven for 30, including the wicket of Allen, lbw for 2. He then contributed 2 not out to the Horris Hill total of 19 for two!

The Summer Fields magazine blandly disposes of the matter reporting that 'on account of the goodness of the bowling, and the difficulty of moving the ball on the slow ground, nine wickets fell for only 112 before the innings could be closed. . . . Hollis and Davis made a nice stand towards the end.' It added that Jardine 'bowled with great command over the ball and a variety of pace; his swerve also induced three batsmen to stop the ball with their pads.'

Gubby, not yet twelve at the time, remembers Mr Alington, the cricket master, known as 'The Bear', but recalls little about the match, and certainly nothing of the prevailing tensions. However, more sinister and more plausible first-hand evidence comes from the late Christopher Hollis, a member of that Summer Fields team, who, writing about his passion for cricket despite his lack of skill at it, in his book *Oxford in the Twenties* describes 'my most notable, though not perhaps most creditable performance on the cricket field' as having in this innings batted for two hours late in the afternoon for 18 on the instruction of the games-master. (The score-book says 17 not out.) Hollis recalls that 'Up till then we had that season remained unbeaten, but it was well known that Horris Hill's team was greatly stronger than ours. The master who was in charge of our games therefore devised a plan that if we won the toss we should bat all day and thus make a draw of the match. So it worked out ... Thus the match drawn and our faith unfaithful kept falsely true.'

Hollis goes on to say that when they met half a century later, and shortly before Jardine died, the latter 'vividly remembered this match at Summer Fields in the summer of 1914 and still bitterly resented the conduct in it of Mr Alington, our cricket master.' What must have made the affair no doubt doubly galling for Jardine was the fact that he had unwittingly played into his opponents' hands by putting them in. There was an extraordinary maturity about Jardine from his earliest years, and it is not over-stretching it surely to suppose that this infuriating early experience may have helped to determine his unyielding philosophy as a cricketer and captain.

On the face of it the facts of this game of long ago redound little to the credit of Summer Fields, but I can carry the saga further thanks to the memory of M. J. L. Stow, lately headmaster of Horris Hill, as his father J. L., widely known as 'Daddy', had been before him. Confirming the facts of the 1914 match, he writes that Summer Fields may have been getting their own back. This was the background which he had from his father, and which I can do no better than record verbatim:

Maybe this was revenge for an incident which my father told me about. He was in charge of the 1st XI as he was for the Jardine match, but this happened a year or two earlier. H.H. had a fastish bowler and a Summer Fields batsman, trying to avoid a short ball, ducked, but not low enough and was hit on the head. Cries of horror from the boundary and the bearded Summer Fields head-master, accompanied by the matron in full uniform came on the field to render first aid to the stricken boy. After a three minute interval the boy said he would continue and returned to the crease to general applause and cries of 'brave boy!' from the bearded H.M. But Horris Hill had a barrack-room lawyer type on the side and, to my father's horror (he was of course umpiring), this small boy approached the captain with a whispered message that the ball had been straight and low. Just as the bowler was about to bowl the next ball the captain approached my father and appealed for lbw. Up went my father's hand. Cries of 'disgraceful' etc. from the boundary!! – so perhaps the Jardine incident was S.F. revenge. Those were the days!

The final thought, provoked by Mr Stow's hilarious picture, is that 'the barrack-room lawyer type' *may* have been little Jardine. Whether or not this was so, one can at least record that, while still lacking nothing in keenness, prep school exchanges are distinctly more civilized now than then.

In the team 'characters' Gubby is identically and with disappointing brevity described in both years as 'promising with both bat and ball'. He was an average athlete as a prep school boy, and had his colours for football as an inside-right.

The star sportsman contemporary with Gubby at Summer Fields and also at Eton was, however, I. J. (now Sir James) Pitman, later Chairman of Sir Isaac Pitman, a director of the Bank of England, Chairman of the Royal Society of Teachers, and for twenty years Conservative MP for Bath. At Oxford Jim Pitman won blues for rugger, athletics and skiing. He also played on the wing for England v Scotland at Twickenham – the only Etonian, incidentally, to win a rugby football cap for England.

During Gubby's time at Summer Fields it was arranged for him to go on to Haileybury. Geoffrey had been sent to Haileybury and was enjoying life there, and Gubby adored his elder brother. However fate stepped in in the formidable person of his father's friend at Cambridge, C. M. Wells. Walter Allen met Wells again playing golf at Datchet, practically on Eton's doorstep. Wells was a house-master, and when he heard that young Gubby was at Summer Fields and a promising cricketer the schools grapevine was brought into operation. By a happy coincidence, it seems, Wells had a last-minute vacancy, and could offer the boy a place. This, of course, is the age-old ploy of successful house-masters in schools world over. Wells no doubt kept a place or two up his sleeve for just such as situation.

Gubby stresses that it meant some financial sacrifice on his father's part to send his second son to Eton, for there was not very much money. Walter Allen, being too old for military service, had joined the Metropolitan Special Constabulary at the outbreak of war as an Assistant Staff Officer to the Commandant, Sir Edward Ward. By the end of it he had been awarded the OBE and in 1920, now a CBE, rose to be Commandant of the force. This involved regular, if not arduous, work at New Scotland Yard, and an honorarium insignificant compared with what might have accrued had he followed a career at the bar.

The picture of Walter Allen is of a benevolent and much-loved father, a good-looking natural sportsman, and accordingly hopeful that his younger son would make a cricketer. Lord Home remembers getting to know the Allens first when practising in the net Plum Warner had at Datchet. In the Allen's garden there was both a net and a tennis court, Walter being a good and keen player.

There is no record, by the way, of any sporting proclivities in Pearl Allen. She had in common with her husband unusual good looks but little compatibility of temperament. She kept at a discreet distance a string of admirers, of whom Plum was not the least.

At all events Walter Allen said 'Eton', and so it was. It can have made the decision no easier that Gubby was hostile to the idea, and 'charming little boy' though he no doubt was, as family and friends agree in remembering him, it has never been suggested that he was anything but firm-willed. This time for once he lost the argument, and, despite tears at the time, has been for ever grateful that he did. 'Eton made me,' he says, and it was an Eton wherein his house-master was going to be his tutor, counsellor and friend.

4
Eton

It took Gubby all that first 1915–16 winter to come to terms with Eton. He hadn't wanted to go, and at first he was miserable. He was placed in Middle Fourth which was higher than Summer Fields expected, and he was perhaps overplaced. And the first master he was 'up to', Hubert Brinton, with whose son he later became friends, gave him no peace. Worse were the attentions of two bullies. One of them was soon superannuated, to the relief of all the small boys in the house. The other had his come-uppance in the manner of the best school stories. There is a week-end task at Eton consisting of a divinity essay known as Sunday Questions. Bully number two asked to see Gubby's Sunday Questions and promptly tore them up. Gubby picked up a fountain-pen lying on a desk beside him, squirted its ink full into his face, and followed up by hitting him with clenched fist in the same place as hard as he could. 'It is the only time I ever struck anyone except about four times with the cane as captain of the house, and only one of those seriously.'

His first Eton friendship was as deep as any. He and David Bowes Lyon arrived at Wells's on the same day, and found themselves in adjacent rooms – two rather frightened small boys facing this strange, bewildering school world together.

By the summer of 1916, the first of his six Eton summers, Gubby began to enjoy life, as he continued to do thereafter. He batted and bowled respectably in the junior house matches, and was among the choices for Lower Sixpenny, a club which in those days (but not now) depended on a boy's age and position in the school.

In these darkest days of the First World War a young boy's memories are of the expressive face of his house-master at breakfast and dinner. The news from the front told perpetually of the loss of Old Etonians, all too often former members of the house, or of young cricketers Wells had bowled to in the XI nets a few years or even months before. Gubby and his friends adopted the practice of reading through the newspaper casualty lists early, and if they came upon a familiar Eton name, as they so often did, they gave Wells the widest berth possible. In his moments of black grief he could be fierce to a degree.

Gubby had his own special anxiety since brother Geoffrey was with the BEF. A surviving letter from him tells of a narrow escape:

> Two days ago we had pieces of an anti-aircraft shell ('Archies') fall down within a yard of our tent as the Huns were firing at our observation balloons. I am back at the Transport with a bad foot at present, so did not go up the line again.

The date was September 1917 and since he later assuredly went 'up the line' often enough before the Armistice he was lucky indeed as an infantry subaltern to survive.

To read the *Eton College Chronicle* of the First World War years is to be reminded both of the vast scale of the fighting – so much greater than the British were called upon to endure in the Second World War – and of the idealistic spirit in which the sacrifice was made. There is a poignancy in the obituary tributes which flowed through every issue of the *Chronicle* that rends the heart at a remove of all but seventy years.

Gubby recalls the war-time black-out and that, despite compulsory allotment digging, Eton's war-time food was fairly meagre. He was luckier, though, than most in that on Sundays he and his cousin, Dick, could walk the couple of miles or so to Datchet for replenishment and home comforts. Dick, six months older than Gubby, had been at Summer Fields with him, and entered A. B. Ramsay's house a half ahead, also through the friendly intervention of Wells. Since Dick's father had taken the ship to Australia in 1914 and been prevented from returning by the outbreak of war, Datchet was a holiday home for Dick, and there naturally grew up between the cousins a close friendship which was continued at Cambridge, and still exists today.

The clearest of all early Eton memories for Gubby was how on the announcement of the Armistice on 11 November 1918, the school as one man decided to proceed to Windsor Castle. They found H. K. Marsden, then Master-in-College, the ultimate stickler for rules and regulations, commanding Windsor Bridge with cries of 'Go back, go back.' However on hearing shouts of 'Throw him in the river' the unarmed Horatius deemed prudence the wiser part and retreated. Maybe Marsden reflected as he withdrew that with the cessation of hostilities he could get back to his life's work at Eton, undistracted by his curious form of war service which, it was said, consisted of regulating railway time-tables.

Celebration, it seems, at first outran discipline, but, according to the *Chronicle*, 'within two days a prompt application of Georgic One, and in some cases, we hear, threats of expulsion, stopped any excessive demonstration of emotion.'

The last *Chronicle* of the Michaelmas half of 1918 records that 5610 Etonians had been engaged on active service. Of these 1124 lost their lives, and 1068 were wounded. Eton's decorations included 13 Victoria

Crosses, 51 CBs, 121 CMGs, 407 DSOs, 554 MCs, 1331 Mentioned in Dispatches. There were 398 Foreign Decorations. In bald figures such was the scale of Eton's service and sacrifice.

The number of boys in the school was '1077 plus 7 Belgians – another record.' The record presumably lay in the total, irrespective of the handful of Belgians who had been given sanctuary.

In May 1919 (with details of late casualties still demanding space) the front page of the *Chronicle* shone with the top-boots and Sam Brownes of a group of eighteen Etonian generals who had accepted 'to meet the School and receive its thanks for the services you have rendered to the Empire in the war.' Thirty-one generals had received invitations. The line had to be drawn there since the number of mere brigadier-generals was 165! The array included three of the five army commanders at the war's end, Sir Herbert Plumer (2nd Army), Sir Henry Rawlinson (4th Army) and Sir Julian Byng (3rd Army). There were speeches in School Yard, with the generals and the school dignitaries assembled on the Chapel steps. The Provost and Fellows entertained their distinguished guests to luncheon in School Hall, and finally came the inspection and march-past of the Eton OTC Battalion, 600 strong.

Cadet Allen was on parade, but foremost no doubt in his thoughts was the chance that was coming his way later that same afternoon when he was due to play in a trial called The Twelve and Eight wherein the First XII were tested by the best of the rest strengthened by the professional and several masters. A good performance here would give him a distinct lift up the ladder that led to Lord's.

At this pregnant point, though, it is worth briefly retracing our steps to note Gubby's cricket since his Summer Fields days – which is possible thanks to the meticulous factual records he kept and subsequently transferred in his neat rounded hand to the small leather-bound book. In this his sporting career is preserved in the utmost detail from his entry into Summer Fields in May 1912 down to and including the summer holidays after his last year in the Eton XI, 1921.

In his first Eton summer half, 1916, C. M. Wells's won the first ten of their junior matches before being thoroughly beaten, I note, by the house of my wife's father, R. H. de Montmorency. Young Allen had creditable all-round figures in these junior house matches considering that, still just short of his fourteenth birthday, he was playing with boys who might have been two full years older. Characteristically, the leather book reveals not only the date, the opponents, each side's scores, and Gubby's batting contribution and full bowling analysis, but even exactly where on the various subsidiary grounds the games were played: thus Dutchman's four, Triangle, Lower Sixpenny three, Mesopotamia two. Can any youthful cricketer's achievement have been more minutely recorded?

The following summer of 1917, still short of his fifteenth birthday, Gubby one glorious afternoon in a junior house match took nine for 52, and almost at once established himself in the rarified atmosphere of Upper Sixpenny. Willie Hill-Wood, his life-long friend, and he were the scourges of the junior house matches and saw Wells's to a narrow victory in the final of the Junior House Cup.

Gubby's first appearances in public date from the summer holidays of 1917, by which time he had just had his fifteenth birthday. C. F. Tufnell, who had played for Kent in the dark ages, collected a team of small boys against one found by another benevolent enthusiast, O. R. Borradaile. There were two matches, one at the Oval and one at Lord's, G. O. Allen being bowled for nought in the first but at Lord's making his very first mark by scoring 16 and taking four for 64 in 20 overs. 'Allen played a very stylish innings, and more will be heard of him,' forecast *The Sportsman*. 'He bowled, too, very well....' An auspicious first press mention!

Still a junior for house purposes in 1918, Gubby was now captain of Wells's and stood out as quite a terror, with 647 runs at an average of 40 (more than double the next boy's) and a bag of 75 wickets *at 4.70 each*. One unforgettable afternoon on Dutchman's six he made his first-ever hundred, declared at 176 for three, then took six for 11 to bowl out E. W. Stone's luckless juniors for 54.

His 1919 season began with the Lord's Easter classes and a precocious rejoinder to the secretary of MCC as to his grip on the bat. The background to this had been a contretemps in the nets with Major E. G. Wynyard who at the time had charge of the classes, over which perhaps he exercised something of a military sway. Teddy Wynyard, an able player, does not come through in cricket history as a sympathetic character, and when from the back of the net he ordered an adjustment of the grip the young shaver told him he proposed to continue as taught at school by Mr Wells. The exchange ended with Gubby thanking Harry White, the groundsman who had been bowling to him, saying that he had had enough and walking out of the net. Hence a no doubt indignant report to the secretary and Gubby being called to his office.

His first chance on returning to Eton came in the Twelve and Eight which followed the great affair of the generals' inspection. Gubby's chief memory of that first trial on Upper Club is of his being bowled *at* very short by the school fast bowler. The latter was roundly ticked off by the captain, Clem Gibson, who then took him off and himself knocked Gubby's castle over for nine.

Came the first post-war Fourth of June and, amid the celebrations, the annual matches against Eton Ramblers. Gubby was chosen for the 2nd XI, went in No 4 to join Ronny Aird and was promptly run out, responding to the latter's call, by half the length of the pitch. The victim vividly recalls the conversation when his friend and rival eventually returned to the Upper Club pavilion having made 72.

R.A. 'You must admit that that was bad luck.'
G.O.A. 'I don't know about bad luck.'
R.A. 'Oh, you must run to a chap in brown suede shoes.'

What neither knew was that the suede-shod cover-point, no doubt recently home from France, was Eddie Campbell, a distinguished Eton cricketer of the 1912 vintage who had played for the Public Schools at Lord's and was rated one of the best fielders in England.

Thereafter things continued to go none too well. In the first place Gubby strained intercostal muscles in the left side – a trouble that was to plague him for four years – and so could not bowl; nor did he make many runs. He played his first match for the XI against RMC Sandhurst and scored 13, and against the Free Foresters was bowled out, as might anyone be, man or boy, by Michael Falcon for 6. Against MCC, going in first with Hill-Wood, he made a more promising 29 (c. Lee, b. Kidd) but in his next match, at Charterhouse, facing in-swingers and Raymond Robertson-Glasgow for the first time, he edged his first ball for 4, was all but bowled by the third and was caught behind by Ivor Gilliat off the fourth. His opening partner, Hill-Wood, did little better but had taken four wickets. Moreover though the match was first thought to be a tie the Eton scorer called for a recount, after which it was amicably agreed that four byes had escaped calculation and Eton were therefore declared the winners.

With only the rarest exceptions Gubby declined through his cricket career to expose himself unless completely satisfied about his fitness. He was chosen to play against Winchester, a fixture of almost parallel prestige and antiquity, if not public interest to the Eton and Harrow, but he persuaded Wells he was not fit, thereby lessening his prospect of winning his colours.

Following Eton v Winchester (won by Winchester after a spirited match by 69 runs) there was one final trial before Lord's, the I Zingari match. He was picked for that, and again Hill-Wood and Allen opened and both got blobs, Gubby st. Twining b. Henley. The ball was down the leg-side and bounced back to the stumps off the wicket-keeper's pads: more than a bit unlucky! Willie's place as an all-rounder had been secure all the half, but Gubby's rival in a rain-ruined match, J. S. Scott, had made the top score of 39.

It looked as though Wynyard and Lacey, the MCC secretary whose advice as to his grip of the bat he had rejected, were going to have the last laugh, but when Gubby saw the team against Harrow posted in Spottiswoode's window he could scarcely believe his eyes, for there was his name, seventh on the list. Looking back, he thinks his house-master must have advised his inclusion, not out of favouritism but because he saw the potential. The captain may have been still hoping he could bowl.

So the great day dawned, fine and warm, Lord's was full to bursting, frock-coats and high fashion abounding as though the 1914 match was but a year away; the captains were presented to the King; and Eton won the toss. As Hill-Wood and Allen walked out to bat Gubby said: 'Now, Willie, you must admit you're feeling a bit nervous today.' 'Nonsense,' came the reply, 'never felt better in my life.' Hill-Wood faced the first ball, a huge out-swinger from Billy Collins, the Harrow captain. He aimed to leg, and it passed by well outside the off-stump. Next ball, same again. To the third ball an identical stroke sent a dolly catch to square-leg. The fielder, R. H. Baucher, at first apparently mesmerized by the occasion, at length rushed in, took the ball on the half-volley and threw down the stumps, while the batsmen, thinking a catch inevitable, were going merely through the motions of running. Gubby was out by yards. The *Chronicle* briskly disposed of the matter: 'Allen ran himself out in the first over.' Gubby's admirable captain said: 'Don't worry. You'll have plenty more chances' — just the sort of kind words a boy remembers.

At this distance it looks a case of nerves all round. But imagine the parental agony, and the ultimate frustration of being run out without having faced a ball! Gubby's clearest memory is of his idol, Reggie Spooner, having given an encouraging word as he walked out through the Long Room, and of his waiting at the pavilion door to say with feeling on his return a couple of minutes later, 'I'll *never* wish anyone luck again as they go out to bat.'

Eton made only 176 (Hill-Wood 43, David Brand 50*) and Harrow, with 76 for five, were making something like a respectable reply when, according to the *Chronicle*, 'claret-cup came out at four forty-five and Gibson was immediately irresistible.' In a few overs the last five wickets fell without another run scored, so that Eton found themselves in the totally unexpected position of being able to force the follow-on. Claret indeed!

However they preferred to bat again, and so Hill-Wood and Allen in late afternoon were again facing the music. Again Eton's first pair were separated without a run scored. This time it was Willie who made the duck and Gubby who shaped up to the banana-swingers of Collins. My future publisher, who did not make many mistakes in a long and successful career, chose to post only two slips with two gulleys, and Gubby well remembers edging his first ball at catching height just where third slip would, and no doubt should, have been. So instead of collecting the most ignominious possible pair he gratefully ran three. Moreover, though Eton were 75 for six at the close he was still there, not out 34. His

ETON v HARROW

At Lord's, 11 and 12 July 1919

ETON

W. W. Hill-Wood c Richards b Miles	43	– b Ramsay	0
G. O. Allen run out	0	– not out	69
C. H. Gibson lbw b W. A. R. Collins	1	– c Richards b Ramsay	4
W. R. Shirley c Bennett b Ramsay	0	– c Gold b Ramsay	3
R. Aird c Gold b Ramsay	7	– b W. A. R. Collins	4
R. S. Chance c Murly-Gotto b Miles	8	– c Richards b Ramsay	13
Hon. D. F. Brand not out	50	– c Richards b Miles	8
C. T. W. Mayo c Geaves b Miles	0	– st Richards b Geaves	9
G. J. Yorke c Bennett b Ramsay	14	– b Geaves	0
J. P. Dewhurst b Miles	15	– lbw b Geaves	7
G. H. B. Fox c Miles b Ramsay	23	– not out	11
B 11, l-b 2, w 1, n-b 1	15	B 4, l-b 6, w 5	15
	176	**(9 wkts., dec.)**	**143**

Bowling: *First Innings* – W. Collins 20–6–50–1; Ramsay 22.1–6–46–4; Geaves 5–0–15–0; Miles 15–3–33–4; Baucher 2–0–5–0; I. G. Collins 3–1–12–0. *Second Innings* – W. Collins 23–8–40–1; Ramsay 21–7–37–4; Geaves 6–0–18–3; Miles 12–1–30–1; Baucher 1–0–3–0.

HARROW

C. T. Bennett b Gibson	21	– c and b Hill-Wood	3
H. J. Enthoven c and b Hill-Wood	2	– st Aird b Hill-Wood	7
P. H. Gold lbw b Hill-Wood	16	– b Gibson	12
H. T. Murly-Gotto c and b Hill-Wood	1	– c Gibson b Hill-Wood	4
I. G. Collins c Allen b Gibson	3	– b Gibson	1
F. S. Geaves lbw b Gibson	19	– c Chance, b Gibson	3
R. H. Baucher c Aird b Hill-Wood	4	– b Hill-Wood	0
R. O. Ramsay b Gibson	0	– c and b Hill-Wood	0
W. A. R. Collins b Gibson	0	– not out	3
E. J. Richards not out	0	– c Mayo b Hill-Wood	6
W. S. Miles b Gibson	0	– st Aird b Hill-Wood	2
B 5, l-b 3, n-b 2	10		
	76		**41**

Bowling: *First Innings* – Gibson 17.4–11–18–6; Hill-Wood 18–2–40–4; Brand 3–3–0–0; Shirley 3–0–8–0. *Second Innings* – Gibson 10–5–12–3; Hill-Wood 9.4–1–29–7.

Umpires: W. A. J. West and J. Moss.

Eton won by 202 runs.

first big day at Lord's had given Gubby a valuable illustration of the changes and chances inseparable from cricket, as well as an introduction to the charged atmosphere that only a large crowd and a traditional occasion combine to produce.

When next day after a lengthy rain delay Eton declared with nine wickets down, he 'took out his bat' for 69. At the first time of asking he had shown, as he generally did throughout his cricket career, that the bigger the occasion the better he liked it.

Harrow were set 244 to win – and on the slow pitch were ignominiously dismissed for 41. The control and life of Gibson (a bowler of classic action, as the Australians discovered to their cost two years later) coupled with the guile of Hill-Wood were altogether too much for the

Harrovians, Gibson taking nine wickets in the match and Hill-Wood eleven. The latter's constant pace-change, modelled on the bowling of Wells, his house-master, was accompanied more by the threat than the reality of leg-spin. The *Chronicle* reports, unsigned but strongly suggesting in their caustic wit and unashamed partisanship the hand of George Lyttelton, still make amusing reading. Hill-Wood's bowling is described as having 'a reptilian fascination'.

What is most striking in the newspaper coverage is its inordinate length and the sympathetic tone in which the mostly anonymous reporters write about the young gentlemen's efforts. In the *Daily Mail* H. J. Henley — a fond colleague of mine in later years — wrote that 'Mr Allen alone obtained any mastery of the attack. He showed every care but his method was engagingly stylish and easy, and he exploited a wide array of strokes.' Note the *Mail*'s prefix, Mr. The reports of the match in Gubby's cuttings-book, embellished by cartoons and photographs, run to almost 200 column inches and all of them had words of praise and encouragement for his second innings.

Did such extravagant publicity tend to make schoolboys too pleased with themselves? In fact, of course, the far greater accent on games at all public schools as compared with today, and consequent hero-worship of 'the bloods', contributed to a different public school ethos, from late Victorian days up to the Second World War.

The *Eton College Chronicle* spread house, as well as school cricket scores liberally over its pages, but so did the magazines of other schools, even if the cachet of the match at Lord's, with its central place in the London season, put Eton and Harrow on something of a pinnacle, elevating them, it might be added, to a position not always justified by the quality of their play.

That Gubby was lucky in having such a wise (and peculiar) old bird as a house-master may be inferred by this small anecdote remembered sixty-five years afterwards. The match with Harrow in those days was part of Long Leave which lasted until the Monday evening. Gubby and Willie reported back to Wells's study together, confident of a good reception for they had both performed with great success. Wells (who could not pronounce his Rs) did not look up from his desk as he remarked 'Vewy disappointing match.' Nonplussed, they said that Eton hadn't done too badly. 'No, we only won by 202 wuns. If that chap hadn't leaned over the pavilion wails and stopped the ball with his newspaper, Hawwow would have been bowled out for 39. Good night.' That was all. His boys were not going to get swollen heads if he could help it.

In fact Wells must have been particularly gratified by the wholesale victory, to which his own two boys had made such important contributions, because this was to be the last of his twenty-two summers as master-in-charge of Eton cricket. He was getting on for fifty, and he had taken over at a low ebb in Eton's cricket fortunes for which his predecessor's over-long tenure was held accountable. Besides, there was a Test cricketer on the staff well qualified to succeed him in R. A. Young.

Wells had followed in 1898 the famous R. A. H. Mitchell, who was rated the best amateur batsman in England immediately previous to the epochal arrival (in 1865) of W. G. Grace. Mitchell himself had taken a very personal, intimate charge of the cricket on coming down from Oxford. Wells's approach to the job was quite otherwise. He encouraged the boys to run their own show, to the extent that it required an invitation from the captain of the XI *each day* to secure his presence in the nets. No invitation, no Wells.

Wells arrived at Eton from Dulwich and Cambridge in 1893 as a classical scholar and sportsman of high repute, an all-round cricketer who had distinguished himself at Lord's for his University, Middlesex and the Gentlemen, and a Harlequin stand-off half who had been instrumental in a great English victory over Scotland. There is no doubting either his success as a coach or the affection aroused by this highly unusual, wholly unemotional man of dry wit and deep understanding of boys.

His interest did not extend to women. Pat Dickson recalls him as grumpy towards her sex, and Lord Home illustrates his misogyny by relating how when Mrs Alington came to dinner he put the clock on an hour 'so that when the ladies left the dining-room his male guests had time to savour his incomparable port and put an end to the whole business in reasonable time.' His idiosyncrasy fascinated all who knew him. He was a famous authority on red wine, though when one of his obituarists sent a draft of his effort to a distinguished and equally fastidious colleague of Wells, A. S. F. Gow, concluding with the words: 'As all his friends will remember, C. M. Wells was a great judge of claret, burgundy, and port', the manuscript was returned with the word 'burgundy' deleted. Perhaps they had had a difference of view as to the respective merits of a Côte de Nuits and Côte de Beaune. His stamp collection was second only to that of King George V, the two of them comparing their respective acquisitions. He was an expert on the stock market, reputedly reading the *Financial Times* from end to end. He was a passionate fisherman, who according to Alec Home on his annual visits to Norway killed more salmon of forty pounds or more than anyone before or since. In *The Way the Wind Blows* (Collins 1976) is a splendid story which I hope I may be forgiven for lifting piecemeal:

> Once when he was over ninety he fell into the river Test and found it difficult to get out. His fellow anglers insisted that he should in

future be accompanied by a ghillie. A friend a year later enquired whether he had fallen into the Test again. 'Yes,' he said, 'I did so the other day. I thought that I must give that fellow something to do.'

Wells was prone to bursts of irritation for which his boys were much on the look-out. Gubby and he were one day watching a house match. George Lyttelton was one of the umpires, and after he had given a batsman out, perhaps dubiously, Dr Alington, the headmaster, walking his dog round the boundary, went across to talk to him. Wells said: 'Allen, go over and ask the headmaster to leave the field at once. I will not have him interfewing in a game in which my pupils are engaged.' 'I'm afraid I can't do that, sir,' said Gubby, whereupon Wells, furious, jumped on his bicycle and rode away. That evening Gubby heard with disquiet the unmistakable footfall approaching his room. Wells just poked his head round the door and said, 'You were quite wight, Allen. Good night.' He called him Allen, by the way, with the stress on the second syllable, to the end of his life. No wonder Gubby held for his house-master from his schooldays on, an affectionate reverence not untinged with awe.

To return to the over-strong accent on games, and especially cricket, in Gubby's time, Lord Home, when asked whether there was altogether too much of a good thing, answered that that was certainly not so in his case and recalled that on Sundays – when, of course, there was no organized cricket – he used to spend hours on the slip-catching machine. But he does think that for some the proverbial public school diet of 'cricket and the classics' was rather too rich.

Wells's retirement as master in charge of cricket was simultaneous with that of Matt Wright, another and truly venerable Eton institution since he had completed thirty-five years of service as the school professional. Wright, a north-countryman by birth and cricket up-bringing, had been at Eton eleven years before Buckinghamshire in 1896 entered a side in the Minor Counties' Championship. For several years thereafter he was their mainstay with bat and ball, and without ever being a top-class cricketer he taught the rudiments with perennial cheerfulness, and was rewarded with the affection of many Eton generations. He, too, was 'a character', one of whose remarks Lord Home recalls. After he had been poking about and achieving little, Wright called out from the bowling end of the net, 'If you must miss, sir, do it in style.' He kept his sports shop long after his retirement as coach, and was still bowling away in the nets and dropping them on a length when he was past seventy.

After Wells and Wright there followed in the summer of 1920 two personalities of a quite different sort in Young and Hirst. Dick Young was an outstanding school and university cricketer in the halcyon days for both Repton and Cambridge between 1901 and 1908. He went with MCC to Australia, in 1907–08 as batsman and reserve wicket-keeper, and it was unfortunate for his reputation that he used to be cited as a prime example of the unwisdom of attempting to strengthen a side's batting at the cost of playing an inferior wicket-keeper. In a tight Test at Sydney, lost by England by two wickets, he dropped three catches, and was reputedly at sea with Len Braund's leg-breaks and googlies. 'It's no good, Braund,' he called in his distress, 'I can't read you.' Though he played in thick-lensed spectacles from school-days on he could still bat well enough in 1921 to make 124 for Sussex against the Australians, with Gregory and McDonald. I recall playing club cricket with him in the 1930s and being amused by his theories. One, in order to help rectify the balance between bat and ball, was to put at captains' disposal a stated small quantity of water with which at their discretion – and presumably either before play or at an interval – they could judiciously refresh the pitch! Whether they were to get a daily allowance or would have had to make do with one per match I cannot remember. Not everyone responded to Young's coaching, though Gubby liked and got along with him very well.

Wells's coaching greatly helped his batting. The man who did more for Gubby's bowling than anyone was, however, the immortal Yorkshireman, George Hirst, who after thirty years' service to his county was now at the start of what proved to be nineteen years of coaching at Eton. Gubby started the season poorly, unable to get any runs and being so plagued by his sore side that, after the opening match, he bowled in constant distress and with little reward.

Midway through the half he decided that he couldn't go on with his bowling. He thought that he could make a decent batsman and would concentrate on that. This was his state of mind when Hirst, who lived in the summer in a cottage on the ground at Agar's Plough, said that he'd like him next Sunday to come to tea. When Gubby arrived Hirst said he'd heard he was thinking of giving up bowling. He knew what he was going through because he'd seen the pain in his face. 'What I want to say to you is that I think you'd be making a mistake. You must obviously get your trouble right. But, if you can, you've got certain things which I wish I'd had – a perfect rhythm and copy-book action, and you make the ball bustle off the ground. Very few people have both the rhythm and the pace off the pitch. If you go on with your bowling I think you might one day be a great fast bowler. All I'm saying is, just think it over.'

Gubby said, 'Well, George, if you put it like that I suppose I must try and stick it out.' He adds today: 'But for what George said I might easily have given up bowling. He was the nicest, kindest man in the world, and I think that talk with him made my cricket career.'

What the boy of seventeen had received that afternoon from George was not only a judgement by a famous cricketer and a plea for perseverance but an illustration in modesty which he did not fail to take to heart. There were things Hirst 'wished he'd got'; this from one of the great all-rounders of history, a man with 2700 wickets to his name and 36,000 runs.

The most dramatic bowling performance of Gubby's schooldays quickly followed his visit to George's cottage. At Winchester alongside the water-meadows, after the home side had won the toss, he was put on to bowl second change with one wicket down for about 60 and proceeded to take the remaining nine in 19.1 overs for 34 runs, out of a total of 242. Seven of the nine were clean bowled, mostly, the hero remembers, with in-swingers. The ball generally moves in the air at Winchester, and Gubby's natural ball has always been the away-swinger. Perhaps that was what the Wykehamists were looking for. However, there is no accounting for these things as every bowler knows. The critics were unanimous in their praise, as they also were in their condemnation of the Eton fielding as compared with Winchester's.

When Winchester went in again 14 runs in front Gubby, getting the new ball this time, bowled down the first two wickets, but on the second afternoon the challenge of making 240 to win was altogether too much, Eton being bowled out for a feeble 108. This was the first and last time Eton lost against either Harrow or Winchester during Hirst's time at Eton. But he must have been not a little consoled by the achievement of his young hopeful.

This was the oft-quoted occasion of the blunt rejoinder to Willie Hill-Wood, the Eton captain. The story helps to illustrate Hirst's qualities as a coach as described by George Lyttelton in the Eton chapter of the admirable book edited by W. N. Roe, *Public Schools Cricket 1901–1950*:

> From him they learnt how the game should be played in every sense, and his geniality, wisdom, and quiet force of character impressed all who knew him. A grand man to meet when you had been bowled first ball – and when you had made a hundred, and your head was in the sky. He restored your balance with the kindliest twinkle and a few direct but never harsh words. 'How did that happen, George?' asked the captain after an unexpected defeat. 'Well, sir, you bowled too long' – a pause – 'and you bowled too bad.' Who could resent that? Not this captain who was a cricketer. He grinned, and a fortnight later scattered Harrow wickets like chaff.

Hill-Wood in fact not only took four for 23 in eighteen overs in

WINCHESTER v ETON

At Winchester, 25 and 26 June 1920

WINCHESTER

J. E. Frazer b Allen	59	– run out		16
J. L. Guise c Egerton b Bridgman	7	– b Allen		27
C. T. Ashton b Allen	25	– c and b Brand		49
T. B. Raikes b Allen	0	– b Allen		10
D. A. W. Thesiger b Allen	0	– b Hill-Wood		49
B. Pinney c and b Allen	10	– c Dewhurst b Bridgman		1
R. T. D. Hornby c Brand b Allen	55	– not out		33
R. C. Huband b Allen	4	– c Hill-Wood		22
D. A. S. Sladen b Allen	56	– b Brand		0
M. N. E. Macmullen b Allen	3	– c Allen b Hill-Wood		7
J. P. A. Graham not out	6	– st Hill b Hill-Wood		0
Byes, etc.	17	Byes, etc.		11
	242			**225**

Bowling: *First Innings* – Hill-Wood 17–2–86–0; Bridgman 15–2–42–1; Brand 10–0–45–0; Allen 19.1–6–34–9; Egerton 2–0–9–0; Dewhurst 3–0–9–0. *Second Innings* – Hill-Wood 23.4–4–78–4; Bridgman 4–1–25–1; Brand 13–0–36–2; Allen 21–2–57–2; Dewhurst 3–0–18–0.

ETON

W. W. Hill-Wood c Huband b Guise	27	– b Ashton		28
Hon. D. F. Brand c Pinney b Raikes	50	– c Pinney b Raikes		5
R. Aird b Sladen	49	– c Huband b Ashton		11
J. P. Dewhurst b Raikes	32	– run out		5
G. O. Allen st Huband b Raikes	2	– c Huband b Ashton		4
C. T. W. Mayo c Raikes b Sladen	0	– b Raikes		15
W. U. B. Egerton c and b Raikes	12	– lbw b Raikes		2
M. Ll. Hill run out	6	– c Fraser b Ashton		11
G. J. Yorke c Fraser b Ashton	24	– b Raikes		15
K. E. M. Tufnell not out	4	– lbw b Raikes		1
M. R. Bridgman b Ashton	4	– not out		8
Byes, etc.	18	Byes, etc.		3
	228			**108**

Bowling: *First Innings* – Ashton 18–2–65–2; Graham 9–2–39–0; Raikes 24–7–55–4; Guise 9–1–35–1; Sladen 6–1–16–2. *Second Innings* – Ashton 21.1–7–35–4; Raikes 22–3–55–5; Sladen 2–0–15–0.

Winchester won by 131 runs.

Harrow's first innings at Lord's, but brought his captaincy to a fitting conclusion by making, in that peculiar but effective crouching style, 75 not out of the 121 that Eton needed to win. Gubby's was the only wicket to fall, and though he bowled twenty-two economical overs in the match he took only two wickets. It had been a disappointing season for him apart from that one glorious day at Winchester. His left side had been a constant worry.

He recalls one other 1920 match, though, for a sufficient reason apart from an unusual sequel. MCC brought down, as always, a side full of distinguished names including Arthur Fielder, of Kent and England. Only just the wrong side of forty, Fielder's pace was still distinctly brisk, and Hill-Wood and Allen took the brunt of his early overs. He twice hit

Gubby in the box, the second time knocking it inside out so that repairs had to be made on the spot – with the bat handle. Nevertheless he made 39 (his top score of the season) before Fielder bowled him out.

Many years later at Lord's Gubby saw a charming-looking grey-haired chap talking in the Tavern to some youngsters on the ground-staff and was told it was Fielder. Gubby introduced himself and said, 'Did you once go down and play cricket at Eton?' Old Fielder said, 'Yes, I did, and I did an awful thing. A little pink-and-white boy came in first and I hit him badly two or three times, and I was so ashamed of myself.' Gubby replied, 'I'm glad you were because I was the boy.' Whereupon, of course, the two fast bowlers fell to reminiscing, and with this glamorous bond in common, that they were (as they still are) the only men since the dark ages to have taken all ten wickets at Lord's. Fielder did it for the Players in 1906, the pink-and-white boy, as has been told, twenty-three years later.

The summer of 1921 was a golden one for cricket, if one can keep in perspective the desperately one-sided Test series against Warwick Armstrong's Australians. Gubby's last half began with the reassuring news from the Admissions Tutor of Trinity College Cambridge – not that in those days it was very much more than a formality – that his entry had been approved. 'You did well in mathematics, and not too badly in two languages.' A boy with no academic propensities whatever must have been well satisfied with that, his house-master likewise. The Eton captain was the Hon D. F. Brand (who became Viscount Hampden). It was the third year in the XI for Brand, Aird, and Allen who had progressed in that order of seniority. David Brand, who was and remained always a great friend, was an all-round cricketer of much talent, as he showed a year later in the only first-class cricket he ever played, with A. C. MacLaren's MCC side in New Zealand and Australia.

At the start of the season Gubby went in first and had the new ball, but after a couple of ducks he moved down the order. His side was still a nagging trouble, and in any case he was not strong enough to open both the batting and bowling. Reading the voluminous reports in the *Eton Chronicle* and the press, one concludes that if he had concentrated on one department his performance on paper would probably have been a good deal more impressive. Luckily – in the long term – he did not. Just how much he enjoyed his cricket for Eton is a moot point, for he did not take failure lightly. Lord Home (then Lord Dunglass) won his place in the XI this year, and, fielding first slip, recalls that he didn't soon forget a dropped catch. If things did not go well he blamed all concerned, not excluding himself. There were no doubt unworthy suspicions, both at Eton and at other times in his cricket life, that some of the aches and pains were inclined to come on at convenient moments.

ETON v WINCHESTER

At Eton, 24 and 25 June 1921

WINCHESTER

J. L. Guise c Sheldon b Bridgman...........	8	– run out	278
R. C. Huband c Hill b Allen	15	– b Bridgman	0
B. Pinney c Cox b Bridgman	4	– b Coventry	21
T. B. Raikes c Barber b Allen	1	– b Sheldon	2
A. R. V. Barker c Sheldon b Allen..........	0	– c Brand b Dunglass...............	13
E. H. F. Fuller b Sheldon	5	– lbw b Allen	6
M. N. Macmullen b Allen...................	1	– c Bridgman b Allen...............	9
G. C. W. Dicker b Allen.....................	0	– b Aird	5
D. H. Macpherson c Aird b Sheldon	10	– c Dunglass b Allen	9
F. C. Mallett c Hill b Sheldon...............	2	– b Allen	0
G. E. Brown not out........................	8	– not out	0
B.....................................	3	B 30, l-b 5, w 3..............	38
	57		381

Bowling: *First Innings* – Allen 8–2–20–5; Sheldon 3–1–7–3; Bridgman 8–2–22–2; Brand 3–1–5–0. *Second Innings* – Allen 27–7–74–4; Sheldon 7–2–30–1; Bridgman 14–0–76–1; Brand 16–1–72–0; Coventry 8–1–32–1; Dunglass 3–2–8–1; Cox 7–0–37–0; Aird 3–1–14–1.

ETON

Hon D. F. Brand c Barker b Macpherson..	6	– b Guise	12
G. O. Allen b Macpherson	11		
R. Aird c Guise b Raikes	5	– not out	112
P. E. Lawrie st Huband b Guise	92	– c Macmullen b Raikes	42
T. C. Barber b Raikes.......................	21	– not out	1
G. K. Cox c Brown b Raikes................	64		
M. Ll. Hill b Raikes	6		
Lord Dunglass not out.......................	25		
Hon. J. B. Coventry c Fuller b Raikes......	1		
H. D. Sheldon lbw b Raikes.................	11		
M. R. Bridgman c Brown b Raikes.........	0		
B 3, l-b 5, n-b 5	13	B 11, l-b 3, w 1, n-b 2	17
	255	(2 wkts.)	184

Bowling: *First Innings* – Raikes 27.2–5–92–7; Macpherson 11–2–44–2; Guise 17–3–63–1; Brown 7–0–31–0; Mallett 2–0–12–0. *Second Innings* – Raikes 19–5–58–1; Macpherson 8–1–45–0; Guise 11.4–2–50–1; Brown 5–2–14–0.

Eton won by 8 wickets.

What redeemed his last summer was Eton's success in both the great schools matches and Gubby's own part therein. The Winchester match, played on Agar's Plough on a fast wicket and in what Warner in the *Morning Post* described as tropical heat, has an assured place in cricket history because it contained the highest innings ever played by a schoolboy. But no less extraordinary than J. L. Guise's 278 for Winchester were the surrounding circumstances. For Winchester were bowled out on the first morning in little more than an hour for 57 (Allen five for 20). After Eton had replied with 255, Winchester, going in again in the late afternoon 198 behind, performed no better – save for Guise. They made 381, the next highest score being 38 extras. The other 21 Winchester innings in the match mustered a beggarly hundred between them. And, when the tired Eton side were set to make 184 to win, a cavalier 112 not out by Aird brought them victory after all – with scarcely a qualm and by eight wickets. In *The Boys' Own Paper* this would have been rated a tall story.

Brand is credited with using Gubby's bowling judiciously in the heat (27–7–74–4), but was accounted slow to baulk Guise's penchant for the leg-side. At last the hero was run out by an extra fielder recently placed there, and when Brand was taxed with this tardy re-disposition he made a remark which has since been credited to other captains in a variety of contexts: 'Oh, I was just lulling him into a false sense of security.'

Gubby, with twenty wickets in two years against Winchester behind him, began his last Eton and Harrow by clean bowling the first three Harrovians, C. T. Bennett, H. J. Enthoven and L. G. Crawley (all, by the way, future blues). At this point he was rested in favour of the Hon J. B. Coventry (captain of Worcestershire in 1929 and 1930) who polished off the tail, taking four for 9! Harrow were bowled out for 64, and though they redeemed themselves in their second innings, wherein Leonard Crawley made a powerful hundred, the leeway was too great, Eton winning by seven wickets, the same margin as against Winchester. Gubby, going in five places lower than on his first appearance two years earlier, scored a valuable 34, and took two tail-end wickets in the second innings.

The most significant happening so far as he was concerned was something he only heard about some years later. The University Match had ended in an innings victory for Cambridge earlier in the week, and Hubert Ashton, due to follow his brother, Gilbert, in the Cambridge captaincy, called at Lord's to collect his bag and watch some cricket. His visit coincided with Gubby's first fine fast spell, and its quality was duly registered. It proved a lucky chance for both of them.

The weather was of the best 1921 vintage, Lord's was crowded, the focus as usual of fashion and Society, and the press coverage was as usual greater than now obtains for a Test Match. Going through the cuttings, one is struck by the warmth and generosity of the reporting and by the light and friendly spirit of the many cartoons. Here were these sprigs of *jeunesse dorée* exposed to an altogether exaggerated limelight, and not a hint of inverted snobbery apparent anywhere.

Gubby topped the Eton bowling in this last summer with twenty-seven wickets, averaged 19 with the bat and was chosen to play at Lord's for Lord's Schools against The Rest. The pick of these two teams, the first being confined to the eight schools who enjoyed the honour of playing there, Eton, Harrow, Rugby, Marlborough, Clifton, Tonbridge, Cheltenham and Haileybury, then represent the Public Schools against the Army. However Gubby at the end-of-term OTC camp ('very boring') was smitten by sunstroke (contracted while asleep on his face!) and was therefore obliged to withdraw. (I assume that he belongs to an extremely select company to have suffered sun-stroke when sleeping.) However consolation was at hand before the summer ended.

Were there in Gubby's schooldays academic successes to go hand in hand with games? I have not been encouraged to pursue enquiries. Nor, it seems, has his subsequent formidable form in the Committee Room owed anything to early training in the Debating Society. Gubby enjoyed his duties as Captain of House, and won the privilege of Eton Society membership for six terms. He admits to having been very lazy at school, and has never ceased regretting the fact. He was interested only, it seems, in mathematics and geography.

In the winter he played with fair success all the four varieties of football that Eton offered: their own unique specialities of the Field and Wall games as well as rugger and soccer. In 1920–21 he represented the school in the Field, in matches necessarily confined to OEs. At the Wall, a form of exercise beyond any non-Etonian's comprehension, he distinguished himself by getting the first goal for twelve years! In the annual show-piece on St Andrew's Day between Collegers and Oppidans he was on the winning side.

He played for two years in the rugger XV, whose fixtures in those days were confined to the Lent Half. This system put Eton out of the main stream since all other schools played almost all their matches in the Michaelmas term. However Gubby in his last year was on the winning side against both Beaumont and Wellington. He played scrum-half in 1920 in his first Schools' match against Beaumont, and in one of the five reports faithfully recorded he is scoring 'a clever but unconventional try' against Beaumont, the only one, since Eton were beaten 4–3. Gubby developed a half-back partnership with the future international, Pitman, which often earned favourable mention, though Eton were generally beaten.

In his second and last rugger season Gubby was moved up to stand-off half. He had something of a field day against Beaumont, who were beaten 36–nil. Eton even won by a single point, 11–10, at Wellington who hitherto had lost only one match the whole season. This victory produced a short homily in *The Sportsman* from a gnarled old Fleet Street character called Arthur Podmore, whose office, as I recall, seemed to be the saloon bar of Anderton's Hotel, long demolished, and whose complexion matched the cerise of his Old Haileyburian tie. Deploring recent 'incidents' in the first-class game, he remarks: '"When the money comes in, the sport goes out" is a saying which has been testified to for all time, and it is important that the schools should hold their own in a game which is essentially theirs.' This from a thirsty old journalist in 1921! Gubby enjoyed the Rugby Union game, and played at Cambridge for his college, Trinity. The fact that he aimed no higher was probably because as an undergraduate he was somewhat light and brittle for the hurly-burly.

Gubby left Eton with much to be thankful for, and has been ever-conscious of his debt. It broadened the life of a young Australian to a degree otherwise unimaginable, and, of course, his cricket as well as his friendships broadened his experience and outlook. In the Easter holidays, for instance, he stayed with David Brand's parents, the Hampdens, at The Hoo in Hertfordshire for coaching at the hands of J. T. Hearne. Similarly, with the Vivian-Smiths at Squerries in Kent, the boys were coached by Frank Woolley. (Thus, incidentally, did he come in contact with the world of professional cricket, as represented by these two distinguished and admirable ornaments of it.) Cricket would not itself have introduced him to the society in which he moved after his school-days. Such an unusually long membership of Pop points to a wide popularity and a full measure of youthful charm.

Lord Home crystallized his own feelings in answer to the question: 'What did Eton give to me? An introduction to life in a large and various company; a sniff of the value of independence; tolerance; self-discipline accepted as infinitely superior to orders; responsibility shouldered lightly; to feel, but not to wear one's feelings on one's sleeve; a perception of the fun of living; a recognition that power and authority must be exercised with restraint.' Gubby's experience at Eton was somewhat more restricted. Nor could he express himself so articulately. Yet he would subscribe completely to the philosophy of this one life-long friend among many made during those adolescent years, 1915 to 1921.

5
Salad Days

Early in August, 1921, just after his nineteenth birthday, Gubby received a wire sent while Middlesex were playing in the Canterbury Week:

> If qualification all right very pleased if you will play for county against Somerset and Warwickshire on August 17th and 20th – Mann

Apart from the qualification clause the interest in this invitation lies today in the fact of Frank Mann committing himself a fortnight ahead to giving a couple of trials to a schoolboy when the Champion County were pressing hard to retain their title. It was not that he was short of players for, augmenting the distinguished professional nucleus of five (Hearne, Hendren, Lee, Murrell, and Durston) and the two regular amateurs (Haig and himself) there were a dozen amateurs of experience, some of whom would certainly have been available. It was no unusual thing for counties to blood boys who had just left, or occasionally even had another year at school. Two others of the 1921 Eton side, Ronny Aird and Mervyn Hill, were given games for Hampshire and Somerset respectively, but neither county had such ambitions as Middlesex, who not only played Gubby at Lord's against Somerset but also a Wellington boy, P. N. Durlacher.

Gubby kept in form in those preceding August days with some good club cricket, and in particular with a two-day match for Eton Ramblers against Eastbourne on the Saffrons – due before the month was out to be the scene of the Australians' historic first defeat against A. C. MacLaren's XI. Most of the Eastbourne side (as was not unusual between the wars) had had first-class experience, so Gubby cannot have been displeased to make 17 and 53, and to take four good wickets for 48. What gratified him especially was that after he had found an almost unplayable one, pitching middle-stump and hitting off, to bowl out Ernest Smith, who had played as an all-rounder in his day for Oxford, Yorkshire and the Gentlemen, Smith had gone out of his way to congratulate him and to prophesy a rosy future, 'if you can go on bowling a few of those'. Outwardly assured though he might seem to be, Gubby then as always needed to have his self-confidence nourished by the older generation.

Geoffrey Cuthbertson, soon to become a close friend, added, 'Don't worry about your batting at Cambridge – there's plenty of that – concentrate on your bowling.'

On the morning of his first match for Middlesex he had the encouraging word which he then most valued, from Plum Warner, regretting he could not be at Lord's, wishing him all good luck and adding: 'If you fail, don't mind (I made one and four against Somerset too, in my first match, and you have an additional weapon in your bowling) ... May you have a long and prosperous career with the best of all counties, and if Middlesex cricket brings you one half the happiness it brought me you will be a fortunate man.'

Gubby was put on first change against Somerset after Durston and Haig, and late in the innings bowled out the veteran all-rounder Ernest Robson when the latter was making up for lost time after rain. He was bowled off his pads by Jack White, the famous slow left-armer, for three. Still, to have confined Somerset to 39 runs off seventeen overs in the drawn match was a not inauspicious beginning. At Edgbaston he took one for 32, the wicket being that of the No 11, Harry Howell, the England fast bowler; and, going in last but one, made nought not out. Middlesex won by an innings, then defeated Kent in a magnificent finish, and, in the final clash against Surrey at Lord's only less famous than Plum Warner's Match of the previous year which had brought Middlesex the Championship, pulled off a splendid win against the odds and so, amid great excitement and with the gates closed, held on to it.

As a fully-fledged Middlesex player Gubby came down to London from Cambridge early in his first term to the dinner commemorating the winning of the Championship, at the Prince's Restaurant, Piccadilly. There were ten courses, washed down by Veuve Cliquot 1911, with Offleys 1890 port and Prince's best brandy Grande Fine 1865, to fortify the company while they were addressed in turn by the High Sheriff of Middlesex and the Lords Harris, Dewar, and Dalziell. All Gubby recalls is that because Harris spoke for fifty minutes he and Cuthbertson missed the last train which enabled undergraduates to get into their college or 'digs' before midnight. Geoff Cuthbertson – better off than most – hired a car.

There was an unexpected sequel to Gubby's first appearances. During the following winter the county were surprised to receive a query as to his residential qualification – and the Allens to learn that it emanated from Walter's old friend, Lord Hawke. They certainly had a house at Datchet, which meant a bona fide qualification for Bucks. But likewise there was a flat near Victoria regularly used by father and frequently by son. Walter much resented the fact that Hawke had not established the facts personally rather than making the matter official, and for a while the two

were not on speaking terms. The authenticity of the qualification was
soon established, but relations were distinctly frosty until Gubby, a while
afterwards, jumping into a railway carriage bound for the north
discovered, when the only other occupant lowered his newspaper, that it
was Lord Hawke. The ice was broken and the breach healed. Gubby, by
the way, was on his way to York to stay with the parents of Cosmo and
Aidan Crawley, whose father, Canon A. S., was then Chaplain to the
Archbishop. This is one of the comparatively few references to the
Church in his scrap-books and diaries. The fact is that although he has
had friends among the clergy he has never shown interest in matters
ecclesiastical, nor been a communicating member of a parish church. It
might be said of him, as of many others similarly scrupulous in all their
dealings and who would never descend from the highest principles, that
they live by Christian values without feeling any obligation towards
public worship.

Gubby was lucky enough to be given his first chance by Middlesex
before ever he set foot in Cambridge. It was however at the university
during his two-year residence that the greater opportunities came his
way, and it was thence that he emerged as a cricketer not only of high
potential but considerable performance. He went up, of course, at a
vintage time. Of G. E. C. Wood's 1920 Cambridge side five afterwards
played for England, Arthur Gilligan and Percy Chapman being captains.
The 1921 side under Gilbert Ashton won nine matches including
thumping victories over full Yorkshire, Lancashire, Somerset and Warwickshire sides, the latter twice. They lost only to the Australians and
were accounted the best Cambridge side since 1878.

In 1922 a query hung over the attack for only Graham Doggart of the
bowlers remained. However three newcomers swiftly made their mark in
P. A. Wright, from Wellingborough, already noticed by Northants,
F. B. R. Browne, from Eastbourne, known as Tishy from the habit of
crossing his legs in a perilous-looking way after a racehorse with a similar
peculiarity, and Gubby. If the results were less spectacular, the Cambridge of 1922, led by the second of the Ashtons, Hubert, turned out to
be scarcely less formidable than that of 1921, finally, as their predecessors had done, defeating Oxford by an innings. Gubby's batting at No
9 was not needed in the University Match: nor was that of M. D. (Dar)
Lyon, who twelve months later, going in first wicket down, made a
hundred at Lord's against the Players. Batsmen welcomed by their
counties such as T. C. Lowry, W. W. Timms and Cuthbertson could not
find places.

In the Freshman's Match Gubby did very little, and is inclined to say he
was saving himself somewhat since he was due next day to play against
the university for Middlesex. I wonder! Anyway, history is on his side
for, coming on first change after Ashton had decided to bat on a softish

pitch and Haig had accounted for the first two wickets, he took six for 29. First he bowled out the captain with a snorter, and after lunch had the wickets of Doggart, Lyon, 'Joe' Shelmerdine, Wright and Browne. Thus he confirmed with some emphasis the impression formed by Ashton at Lord's on the occasion of the Eton and Harrow. The ball to which Ashton succumbed, in theory impossible to bowl, the out-swinger which on pitching breaks back, has been produced by Gubby just a few times in his career. This was one. Cuthbertson was soon to get one, and Stan McCabe, unluckily for him, received two.

The several surviving photographs of this first bowling feat against his own university show Joe Murrell standing back — which is interesting in that when asked when he began really to concentrate on pace Gubby says it was at this time because Murrell declined to come up to the stumps. Gubby felt he had to press a bit to make sure of reaching him.

It was on the evidence of his bowling in his first summer that, extraordinary to relate, a single doubt on the validity of his action appeared in the annual review of Cambridge cricket in the 1923 *Wisden*. The anonymous author wrote:

> A word of warning to Allen. Now and then when he tried to get on a little extra speed, his delivery looked, to say the least, very dubious. Otherwise, there was no fault to be found with him and he had days of startling success.

This is a strange imputation in itself, made by someone impossible now to trace. That it was (almost) a lone voice can be fairly assumed since until long after his retirement from playing Gubby never even knew of its existence. I believe it may have been Don Bradman who with humorous mischief pointed out the stray comment at the time of the throwing crisis of 1960. There was also a lone remark in an unsigned *Morning Post* report of the Middlesex-Kent match later that season which while pooh-poohing the idea, acknowledges its existence in someone's mind. Perhaps it was the hallucination of some rheumy-eyed old journalist — who contributed the Cambridge review — and never got further than the press-box. The *Morning Post* passage read:

> Allen also sent down many a good over. One hears murmurs about his action; but we like Allen's bowling immensely. If his action is hurried as he puts down the extra fast one, it looks fair enough. There is little to choose between him and A. E. R. Gilligan as the best fast bowler of the day.

Could Gubby too, just once at Fenner's, delivering from the edge of the crease and trying to bowl the in-swinger, straining for the extra yard, have lost his rhythm, and, without in the least meaning to do so, approached the delivery stride open-chested with elbow bent? Let me add, he does not encourage the possibility – or give it the slightest credence!

It looks from cuttings and reports as though after he had demolished the university batting for Middlesex Gubby was set fair for a blue. Still not yet twenty however, he needed encouragement and still remembers, after he had bowled sixteen wicketless overs against Lancashire in his first match for the university, his captain saying as they walked off the field: 'Don't worry – you'll often bowl worse and take five.' In the second innings he got rid of Makepeace and Hallows, while Bill Wright in seven overs took five for 5, and the university won comfortably. There were five wickets for Allen in another easy win against Warwickshire, three against Yorkshire, and, to silence any argument, five in each innings against Sussex, ten for 65 in the match.

Gubby's most poignant memory of that first happy summer term at Fenner's contains something of a cricket moral. Perambulators v Etceteras in those days was a full-scale three-day trial match, the sides captained by the university captain and secretary. Gubby and his friend Cuthbertson, the latter a candidate for one of the opening batting places, were on opposite sides. Both reckoned this might be Cuthbertson's last chance, and the very last thing Gubby wanted to do was to nip it in the bud. Facing Cuthbertson he accordingly gripped the new ball across the seam (thus in theory ensuring that it would not swing), and promptly shattered the stumps with what in fact was a brute of a ball that might have bowled anyone.

In the second innings therefore poor Cuthbertson faced a pair of spectacles. Gubby, trying again to be helpful, bowled a ball on the pads, and it was struck off the bat's full face, whereupon leg-slip threw himself sideways and made the catch of a lifetime. So the victim 'collected them', as the saying is. Somehow cricket is inclined to resent attempts at manipulation.

Gubby was given his blue in May Week when, following the end of term and with examinations over, the college balls were held, and girls in profusion descended on what in those days was otherwise, of course, a male bastion. Gubby's party of eight first saw the Footlights revue and altogether made a night of it, he next morning pulling his trousers on over his pyjamas and just getting in time to Fenner's, where the university were playing the Free Foresters. The situation was not lost on Hubert Ashton who said, 'Right, you'll have a damn good bowl,' and gave him twenty-one overs.

Hubert no doubt had in his mind the corresponding match two years before when the captain, George Wood, with an abundance of talent at hand, had given him just one early trial and played him in May Week against the Foresters only because an old blue was unavailable. Having made nothing in the first innings, the second of the Ashtons reckoned his chance of a blue was now nil, drowned his sorrows, and arrived next morning at Fenner's not having been to bed. He then went in and played a scintillating innings of 236 not out in four hours. Thereafter there was no stopping him. In 1921, averaging 50 in seven innings against the Australians, he proved himself one of the best bats in England, and was rated highly unlucky not to play in a Test Match.

Now here he was having succeeded his brother, Gilbert, moulding together another powerful university side. Gubby was lucky in his first captain, for 'I suppose that at times I was difficult.' Surely not? Well, there was a match against the Army (quite a strong side in those days) when Gubby, coming in No 10 and being told by his captain, who was still in with about 150 to his name, to keep his end up, rushed up the pitch and got bowled. No 10 indeed!

Gubby had much regard for Hubert, who must have seen this mettlesome freshman as a potential match-winner on the big day. There was another future Test captain in the Cambridge of 1922, Percy Chapman no less, whom no sane captain would have thought of dropping, for he had amply proved himself the preceding two years, and in any case was worth anything up to twenty or thirty runs as a fielder. In a dozen matches before Lord's he made only a couple of fifties. But against Oxford he excelled himself with a sparkling 102 not out and a week later, likewise at Lord's, he was hitting the Players' bowling for 160.

Cambridge were strong favourites for the University Match, and the fact that the weather favoured them settled it. On the first day Willie Hill-Wood, who had won the last place in the side, opening the innings, obstructed Oxford in his own peculiarly effective way for four and three quarter hours for 81 on a slow, unresponsive pitch. Hubert Ashton and Chapman more than made up for lost time on the second morning, and the captain would probably have made his second hundred in successive years against Oxford if bad light followed by rain had not caused a stoppage when he was 90 not out. He declared over lunch at 403 for four, whereupon Oxford, on a pitch growing ever less morbid, after a creditable performance that afternoon, melted away on the third day. Following on, they were 17 for seven before being bowled out a second time for 81 and losing by an innings and 100. The rot started on the last morning when Hubert Ashton — whose fielding at short-leg was likened at various times to that of Bill Hitch and A. O. Jones — made a remarkable diving catch off Gubby to dispose of Oxford's top-scorer, the gifted Lionel Hedges.

In the *Daily Mail* H. J. Henley decided that 'the match should live in the annals of University cricket as G. O. Allen's match.' Gubby thinks

GOA's mother, Marguerite Julie (Pearl) Allen (née Lamb), 1873-1962, *c* 1900

GOA's father, Walter Macarthur Allen, KBE 1870-1943. He was Commandant, Metropolitan Special Constabulary for eighteen years; knighted in 1926

First photograph. GOA and brother Geoffrey, aged about three and six

A cricketer! GOA aged nine: positively his only appearance as a wicket-keeper

Toxteth Park, built by GOA's great grandfather in 1831 and for two generations the family home. Lying south of Rozelle Bay in Sydney's suburbia, it is now a girls' school run by an order of Roman Catholic nuns

Thaxted, built by his father and GOA's birthplace, commands a superb view of Rose Bay and Sydney Harbour. The Allens had 16th century roots in Thaxted, Essex

First captaincy. The Summer Fields XI of 1915: back row, A. B. Robinson, F. L. Slater, G. P. Murray, R. A. K. Jacques, W. J. Ponsonby, H. M. Finlay. Sitting, J. N. B. Alexander, GOA, I. J. Pitman. Front row, C. E. Bleck, D. J. V. H. H-Miller

GOA with sister Pat and cousin Dick at Datchet: a summer Sunday out from Eton

C. M. Wells, cricketer, classicist and man of many parts

Back row, Major-Gen. J. Ponsonby, Major-Gen. R. L. Mullens, Major-Gen. E. J. Montagu-Stuart-Wortley, Major-Gen. H. S. Jeudwine, Major-Gen. A. E. Sandbach, Lt.-Gen. S. W. T. D'O Snow, Lt.-Gen. Sir W. P. Pulteney, Major-Gen. H. G. Davies. Middle row, Major-Gen. C. R. R. McGrigor, Major-Gen. C. F. Romer, Lt.-Gen. Sir W. T. Furse, Lt.-Gen. Sir F. J. Davies, Dr. Butler, Sir H. Babington-Smith, A. B. Ramsay, Major-Gen. Hon. Sir W. Lambton, Lt.-Gen. The Earl of Cavan, Lt.-Gen. Sir C. Fergusan. Sitting, Sir Gen. Sir H. S. Rawlinson, Dr. James (Provost), Gen. Sir H. C. O. Plumer, Dr. Alington (H.M.), Gen. Sir J. H. G. Byng, F. H. Rawlins, Esq. (Vice-Provost)

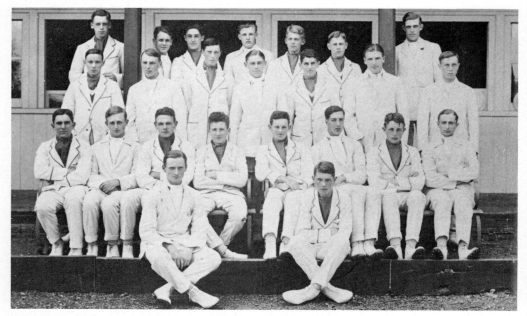

Winchester v. Eton, 1920. Defeat for Eton, a triumph (nine for 34) for GOA. At Back, R. T. D. Hornby, W. I. E. B. Egerton, J. L. Guise, C. T. W. Mayo, B. Pinney, M. N. E. Macmullen, K. E. M. Tufnell. 2nd Row, J. P. P. Graham, M. Ll. Hill, D. A. S. Sladen, GOA, R. C. Huband, J. P. Dewhurst, M. R. Bridgeman. Sitting, T. B. Raikes, Hon. D. F. Brand, J. E. Fraser, W. W. Hill-Wood (Captain), C. T. Ashton (Captain), G. J. Yorke, D. A. W. Thesiger, R. Aird. At bottom, 12th men, Hon. J. B. Coventry, A. F. Robertson.

Four enduring friendships: *top*, Willie Hill-Wood and David Bowes Lyon; *below* David Brand, afterwards Lord Hampden, and Alec Dunglass, now Lord Home of the Hirsel

July, 1919: GOA's first Eton and Harrow, the scene at the luncheon interval

The Eton XI, 1919. From the left, J. P. Dewhurst, G. H. B. Fox, R. Aird, G. J. Yorke, W. R. Shirley, C. H. Gibson (captain), W. W. Hill-Wood, Hon. D. F. Brand, G. O. Allen, R. S. Chance, C. T. W. Mayo

GOA when a Cambridge freshman; a copy-book picture at the delivery stride, head behind a good front arm, back foot nearly square with the bowling crease.

H. Ashton b Allen 7. GOA, playing for Middlesex v. Cambridge, finds the 'unplayable' ball for the University captain, an out-swinger that came back off the pitch. Note the position of Murrell, the wicket-keeper

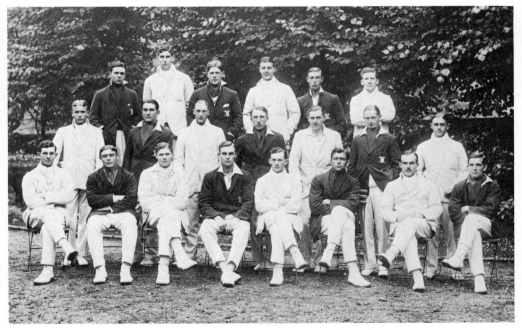

Oxford v. Cambridge, 1922: back row, L. P. Hedges, F. B. R. Browne, M. Patten, G. O. Shelmerdine, F. H. Barnard, W. W. Hill-Wood. Middle row, P. A. Wright, T. B. Raikes, C. A. Fiddian-Green, B. H. Lyon, M. D. Lyon, C. H. Knott, G. O. Allen. Sitting, C. T. Ashton, V. R. Price, A. P. F. Chapman, G. T. S. Stevens, H. Ashton (Captain), R. H. Bettington, A. G. Doggart, R. L. Holdsworth

The Hon. David Bowes Lyon married Rachel Spender-Clay at St Margaret's, Westminster on 6 February 1929. GOA was best man

Middlesex in 1926; standing, H. W. Lee, J. W. Hearne, T. J. Durston, A. R. Tanner, H. R. Murrell, E. Hendren; sitting, Hon. C. N. Bruce, N. Haig, F. T. Mann (Captain), G. T. S. Stevens, G. O. Allen

this is too high a rating since he had so much help from the pitch.
Nevertheless nine for 78 in the match was a feather in his cap, and it brought
his total for the university season to forty-nine wickets at 15 runs each.
Browne took fifty and Gubby's new-ball partner, 'Bill' Wright, fifty-two.

Graham Doggart, father of Hubert, grandfather of Simon, who made
71, contributed what Plum Warner considered the best innings on the

OXFORD v CAMBRIDGE

At Lord's, 10–12 July 1922

CAMBRIDGE

Mr C. A. Fiddian-Green (Leys) b Raikes....	23
Mr W. W. Hill-Wood (Eton) c Lyon b Raikes	81
Mr A. G. Doggart (Bishop's Stortford)	
b Raikes	71
Mr H. Ashton (Winchester) not out.........	90
Mr G. O. Shelmerdine (Cheltenham)	
c Stevens b Bettington	13
Mr A. P. F. Chapman (Uppingham) not out	
	102
B 15, l-b 4, w 1, n-b 3	23
(4 wkts., dec.)	403

Mr C. T. Ashton (Winchester), Mr M. D. Lyon (Rugby), Mr G. O. Allen (Eton), Mr P. A.
Wright (Wellingborough) and Mr F. B. R. Browne (Eastbourne) did not bat.

Bowling: *First Innings* – Raikes 44–19–65–3; Price 17–6–61–0; Robertson-Glasgow
43.1–18–97–0; Bettington 44–11–92–1; Stevens 19–3–65–0.

OXFORD

Mr R. H. Bettington (New South Wales)			
lbw b Browne	21	– lbw b Wright......................	1
Mr F. H. Barnard (Charterhouse) c Doggart			
b Wright....................................	22	– b Wright...........................	5
Mr R. L. Holdsworth (Repton) c H. Ashton			
b Browne...................................	10	– b Allen............................	4
Mr B. H. Lyon (Rugby) c C. T. Ashton			
b Browne...................................	0	– b Allen............................	0
Mr L. P. Hedges (Tonbridge) c H. Ashton			
b Allen.....................................	44	– lbw b Wright......................	0
Mr G. T. S. Stevens (University College			
School) b Wright...........................	41	– b Browne.........................	29
Mr C. H. Knott (Tonbridge) b Allen.........	13	– b Allen............................	4
Mr V. R. Price (Bishop's Stortford) b Allen .	1	– lbw b Allen........................	0
Mr M. Patten (Winchester) c Lyon b Allen..	8	– c Allen b Hill-Wood	3
Mr R. C. Robertson-Glasgow			
(Charterhouse) c H. Ashton b Allen.......	5	– not out............................	11
Mr T. B. Raikes (Winchester) not out	19	– b Hill-Wood......................	12
B 21, l-b 17...........................	38	B 9, l-b 3	12
	222		81

Bowling: *First Innings* – Allen 33.1–17–60–5; Wright 30–14–41–2; Browne 34–19–
35–3; Hill-Wood 16–7–36–0; Doggart 6–5–2–0; C. T. Ashton 3–0–10–0. *Second
Innings* – Allen 9–4–18–4; Wright 11–6–13–3; Browne 6–1–18–1; Hill-Wood 2.1–
0–3–2; Doggart 5–0–17–0.

Umpires: W. A. J. West and J. Moss.

Cambridge won by an innings and 100 runs.

first day. Cambridge's declaration at 403 for four meant that Claude, the youngest Ashton, Lyon and Allen, who were due to make around thirty first-class hundreds between them, never got to the wicket.

Gubby adds a significant recollection which escaped the match reporters. The going-off for light on the second morning which brought the Ashton-Chapman stand to an end came in answer to an appeal by the Oxford captain, Greville Stevens. He remembers no other instance of the fielding captain making a successful light appeal, and nor do I — though I recall an occasion in utter murk at Dover when Kent might almost justifiably have done so to prevent lethal injury from the bat of Gary Sobers.

After the University Match Gubby played the rest of the season for Middlesex. Batting at No 9 or even 10 he scarcely had the opportunity of playing an innings of any substance, but with some not outs averaged 16. With Haig and Durston getting the new ball and Jack Hearne and Stevens to provide the spin Gubby in small doses picked up 22 wickets and actually headed the Middlesex averages. The impression is of a young player being carefully steered through his initiation into county cricket by Frank Mann.

The Mann family recall that during a match played in a heat-wave Frank received a wire from Pearl Allen asking him to make sure her son wore a hat — remember the sun-stroke at camp! The picture emerges of Mann as an amused and fond avuncular figure so far as Gubby was concerned, himself handicapped in his mobility as the result of shrapnel wounds in foot and knee and arm, listening indulgently to tales of aches and pains. 'He was not a malingerer — but toes sometimes grew sore at convenient moments,' is the verdict of a playing contemporary.

Whatever minor ills of the flesh may have hampered him in 1922, Gubby, aged twenty, ended his first summer for Cambridge and Middlesex 9th in the national averages, behind only Rhodes, F. B. R. Browne, Parker, Richmond, Freeman, Macaulay, Kilner and J. C. White, with seventy-one wickets at 15 runs apiece. (Alas, many will be thinking, for the departed age when spin ruled the roost!)

As with so much else in life, Gubby was fortunate in his first captains of both university and county. Hubert Ashton, who had spent the last two years of the war in France, where he had won the MC, was a man who earned everyone's respect — a mature undergraduate and a splendid cricketer. F. T. M. — 'Efty Mann, they called him — was a big fellow in every way, by inclination a legendary hitter who could nevertheless adapt his game to whatever needs arose. He was no great theorist or tactician but a conventional captain who ruled Middlesex in the spirit of benevolent autocracy characteristic of his time. Before the war his speed and formidable physique had earned him a rugger blue to add to the one he won for cricket – a considerable achievement in that he came from Malvern, a soccer school.

Back at Cambridge for the Michaelmas term in the autumn of 1922 Gubby had an important letter from Hubert Ashton saying that Willie Hill-Wood, whom he had hoped would accept the secretaryship of the CUCC for 1923, would not be in residence after all. Would Gubby therefore take it on? Now the secretaryship by no means led always to the captaincy, but it did so more often than not. Gubby's appointment therefore put him potentially in line of succession.

As it happened, Percy Chapman, secretary in 1922, did not, after all, stay up a fourth year, and the 1923 elected captain was therefore to be Claude, youngest of the Ashton brotherhood, who thereby emulated the Studds, G.B., C.T., and J. E. K., in 1882–84 inclusive and equalled a surely unbeatable record by leading Cambridge in three successive years.

During the winter Gubby's horizons were broadened and life made much more congenial by the purchase of a car. He had been left by Godfather Watt a legacy of £1000 which was to be his on his twenty-first birthday due at the end of July 1923. On this security his father advanced him the money to buy for £178.10.0 a new snub-nosed Morris-Cowley. Gubby's earliest recollection of this car is amusing to recall, though to him it was anything but a joke at the time. In February 1923 England played Ireland at Leicester, and he drove there from Cambridge his friends, W. W. (subsequently Lord) Wakefield, almost a legend already as a fast, fierce, and formidable back-row forward, and A. T. Young, the university scrum-half, not yet an International but travelling as reserve scrum-half to the great C. A. Kershaw.

There being the usual Rugby Union dinner after the match, Gubby whiled the evening away at a movie before his passengers were free to leave. When they did so dear little Arthur Young was so palpably tight that Wavell Wakefield relegated him to the bitter cold of the open dicky seat behind the hood. As luck would have it, and in those days it often did have it, one of the tyres sprang a puncture – involving, of course, getting the spare and the tool-kit from the dicky or boot. These being extracted, Arthur grew somewhat playful, bowling the spare wheel down the road like a hoop. Since they had stopped on a hill, he promptly lost control of the wheel which careered out of sight into the darkness. The owner thinks they might have been searching for an hour before, with the aid of headlights, the wheel was located in a field several hundred yards away. By that time Wakefield was in the mood for murder, and had to be dissuaded from leaving the little so-and-so to walk back to Cambridge.

As befell J. E. K. Studd before him, the third of the Ashton trinity could not match the success of his brothers in beating Oxford. He had only Allen and Wright left of the 1922 side, and on these two and the captain fell the brunt of the bowling. Batsmen were less hard to find than change bowlers, but though Tom Lowry had a marvellously good season containing four hundreds there was no replacing the class of Hubert Ashton or Chapman. Moreover as the term proceeded Gubby and his captain found it increasingly difficult to see eye to eye on matters of selection and tactics.

Gubby, playing against a touring side for the first time, helped the University start the season well by beating the West Indies by nine wickets inside two days. Thus he first met young Learie Constantine (who did not make any great mark — except in the field — until his next tour), George Challenor, the model for West Indian batsmen in those days, and others who showed themselves to be fine cricketers when the weather improved later on. Because of the war there had been no West Indian visit since 1906, and of the side that came in 1923 the only survivors were Challenor and the captain, who had also led the 1906 side, H. B. G. Austin.

Harold Austin, son of a former bishop of the West Indies, might fairly be called the father of West Indian cricket, just as Challenor was the first of their great batsmen. They were white Barbadians both and men of a substance and stature recognized throughout the islands. Challenor is recalled by Gubby for his correctness of method — which brought him 1500 runs and an average of 51 on this tour which paved the way for the admission of West Indies to the Test circle five years later.

In the Middlesex match at Fenner's a year earlier Gubby, playing for the county, had bowled himself into the university side. Now, against the county, going in No 9, he scored his first first-class fifty, putting on 120 in an hour and forty minutes with R. C. Huband, a reserve wicket-keeper who reached 61 not out in the first of his only two appearances in first-class cricket. Gubby followed by bowling thirty-four overs, taking six for 89, the six including the immortals, Hearne and Hendren, Mann and H. L. Dales. The Middlesex captain must have been encouraged — the boy was coming along well.

Even better was to come: eight, including Holmes and Sutcliffe, for 77 in thirty-one overs against a full Yorkshire side. Allen and Wright bowled unchanged and the county were bowled out for 139 — a remarkable performance notwithstanding help from the pitch and even if the university could make only 63 in reply. Fenner's in those days was apt to be difficult after rain.

Playing on tour against Essex Gubby recalls a rather surprising lapse by the admirable batsman (and future selector) Peter — or Percy — Perrin. Some called him one name, some another, and there were under-graduates at Colchester who may have called him something else when he stood there having been caught a foot off the ground in the gulley, got

away with it and went on to make 70. Taxed with this years later, the old
rascal said: 'Yes, I shouldn't have done it against the 'Varsity.'

Lord's as usual brought out Gubby's best – ten wickets in the match
against MCC and 48 runs. Young Reg Sinfield, a groundstaff product
before he gravitated to Gloucestershire, took a pair, bowled Allen each
time with dead shooters – which he remembered ever after. The *Daily
Telegraph* correspondent thought that apart from a spell by J. W. H. T.
Douglas, Allen had produced 'about the best bout of fast bowling I have
seen this season'.

It was agreed that the opening bowlers should be rested from the final
game before the all-important one, but at the last minute Gubby was
called upon to play against Shrimp Leveson Gower's XI at Eastbourne,
the understanding being that he shouldn't bowl. He did not, but, as ill-
luck would have it, with only three days to go before the University
Match he pulled the always-suspect side-muscle when throwing in. A try-
out in the Lord's nets on the morning of the match ended with Gubby
pronouncing himself unfit. Nevertheless he was persuaded to play,
whereupon Ashton lost the toss and Oxford went in on a very hot day
and on a perfect wicket.

The match was an unmitigated disaster for Cambridge. Gubby
according to Plum Warner in the *Morning Post* was 'quite unable to
show his true form', and Oxford's innings ended close on time for 422.
That night there broke over London the worst thunderstorm, wrote one
of the experts, 'since the one preceding the Derby of 1911'. The ground
nevertheless was fit for play by noon – surely umpires were not so fussy
in those days? – and Cambridge had been bowled out twice by quarter
past five for 59 and 136. Oxford's margin of victory, an innings and 227
runs, was (and remains) the widest in the history of the Match.

Reg Bettington, the Oxford captain from Australia, took eleven
wickets with his leg-breaks and googlies, Stevens, by nature of a similar
type but under orders to revert to orthodox off-spinning, seven. The
pitch however was so difficult that Cambridge were simply ensnared, and
the feat of the match was undoubtedly C. H. Taylor's hundred for
Oxford, the first ever made at Lord's by a freshman of either side.

Gubby's contribution was an analysis, bowling half-pace in short
spells, of nought for 37 in 15 overs, and scores of 8 and 28, the latter the
highest Cambridge innings of the match. But from the otherwise
disastrous occasion came an unexpected and permanent bonus. At the
luncheon interval on the first day he took a friend's advice and made
what was no doubt termed 'a dramatic dash' by taxi to the consulting-
rooms in the City of a well-known osteopath named Blake. Blake
diagnosed that, in lay terms, an intercostal muscle had been caught
between two ribs. He manipulated, strapped up the affected part and

advised his patient not to bowl any more that summer. Gubby bowled again as best he could that afternoon, then took a month's rest before, in an emergency, taking the field for Middlesex – and never experienced that particular affliction again. Blake specialized in sporting injuries. He was frowned on, inevitably, by the medical profession, applied a means test to his patients, and died in his forties, it was said from over-work.

When Gubby took part in the ill-starred University Match of 1923 he had known for some weeks that he was to be rusticated from Trinity. He in no way resented this, for he had done no work, and even in those days a minimum was called for. When the blues met after the Match to elect their 1924 captain they knew his position, but knew also that if they plumped for Gubby another college would have happily received him as an undergraduate. Claude Ashton, the captain, however, at the meeting nominated as his successor not Gubby (who as secretary and therefore captain-designate was not present) but the 'Colonial', Tom Lowry, and Lowry was elected.

When Ashton and Gubby had talked the matter over beforehand Gubby had said words to the effect that if Ashton felt he wanted to put up someone else as captain he would not take it amiss. At the meeting, however, according to Leonard Crawley, who was present, Ashton said, 'Gubby would be quite happy not to be appointed' – a very distinct difference of emphasis. Leonard, incidentally, favoured a free vote in camera rather than in cold blood round a table since 'no one likes to vote against a friend in public, even though he may not consider him a suitable candidate.' As all know, Gubby later in life showed himself an admirable captain. Whether the burdens of university captaincy would have matured him sufficiently at the age of twenty-one, coming up to twenty-two, is a moot point, on which there are few survivors to give a view.

Looking back to those distant days Gubby harbours no hard feelings at having been passed over. He was spared the decision as between a natural desire to be captain and the fairly urgent necessity of getting down to earning a living. He only remarks wryly that whereas the Ashtons had never appreciated Lowry – who had been up since 1921 and distinguishing himself for Somerset – he had rated it a first priority as secretary to make him welcome in the side and persona grata with the captain. (As it happened Lowry's side of 1924 redeemed a poor season by beating Oxford handsomely, and when New Zealand came first to England in 1927 they did so under his leadership.)

Gubby went down from Cambridge in the summer of 1923, having made many new friends as well as keeping up with old ones. His interests had been wholly social and sporting. He had played rugger for Trinity in the winter and began what has proved a life-long interest in racing through meeting those Newmarket trainers who found time to enjoy the cricket at Fenner's. There were the Jarvises, Jack and Basil, 'Boxer' Cannon and the Leaders. Gubby took cricket sides to Newmarket: hence the formation of a cheerful club which played occasional games called The Tramps.

Early in August Gubby, whose family used to take a house there, was playing lawn tennis in the Isle of Wight Championships, 'and had beaten one of the favourites in the first round' when out of the blue came a wire from Mann asking him to play for Middlesex at Canterbury. Hearne, it turned out, was unfit to play and Haig to bowl. The same might well have been said of Gubby since he had not turned his arm over since the University Match, and here he was pitched suddenly into the Canterbury Week, and very soon facing Woolley, the Pride of Kent, obviously with a taste for runs. (Back on the island he got a slating from the local press for scratching from the tennis tournament!)

This was a historic match as can be imagined from the scores: Kent 445 (Woolley 270) and 159 (Guise four for 20); Middlesex 457 and 148 for three. Frank Woolley played what was then the highest innings ever for Kent, and yet was on the losing side. On the third day the game looked to be heading for a sure draw when, according to Nigel Haig, the historian of Middlesex over this period, Mann, 'with no very hostile intentions, put Guise on to bowl; the result was miraculous, Guise taking the wickets of J. L. Bryan, Seymour, Woolley and Ashdown in four overs, for 9 runs, and Stevens quickly accounted for the remainder.' Middlesex had little trouble knocking off the runs. Guise, playing as a batsman, bowled innocent-looking stuff with perhaps a hint of flight. He never did anything like this again, though in the first innings, in five expensive overs when all the accredited bowlers had had enough, he had had Woolley and Kent's captain, Lionel Troughton, caught on the boundary.

In the circumstances Gubby came at least as well as could be expected from the onslaught with 28–3–83–2, the two being good ones, Bill Ashdown and Lionel Hedges. Moreover it was he who made a fine running catch at deep mid-wicket to dispose of Woolley. He was fielding under a tree which was then at the top of the field, and the batsman (who, if the truth be told, was inclined in private to attribute his dismissals to the intervention of Providence or some lapse by an umpire) maintained he hadn't seen him there because he was in the shade!

Gubby, not himself inclined to forget when fate has run against him, recalls another incident from this game of sixty years ago. Bryan, who came in first, aimed to hook him early in the day and hit a towering catch to R. H. Hill, fielding at deep mid-on. Richard Hill, who never looked like catching it, in fact failed to get a touch, and as the batsman ran down to the bowler's end Bryan remarked jocularly to the fielder, 'I always put a bit of cut on those.' Reminiscing together recently on a Greek cruise

Gubby found the victim who escaped word perfect on that missed catch.

In four further matches for Middlesex at the summer's end Gubby was often in the picture, taking seven wickets and making 45 not out in the blood match against Surrey at Lord's. Profiting from a more respectable place in the order, he reached 70 against Warwickshire, his highest score so far.

Then came his first Scarborough Festival, a memorable occasion for a young cricketer in those days. It was likewise, of course, his first appearance for the Gentlemen, and he had a good match with four wickets, those of Sutcliffe, Roy Kilner and Rhodes, the latter bowled out twice, and innings of 23 and 53. Wilfred Rhodes's second dismissal was curious, and earned a long explanatory paragraph in *The Times*. The great man hit the ball on to his foot whence it rolled back on to the stumps. By one of those very occasional freaks both bails were shaken out of their sockets but both remained lodged, one with one end on top of the off-stump, the other with one end stuck against the middle-stump below the socket. Frank Gilligan, the wicket-keeper, drew attention to this, whereupon Wilfred suggested gruffly that they should 'get on with the game'. There had been a recent instruction to umpires on this point, and Frank Chester, after walking up the pitch to make sure, gave Rhodes out. It is, incidentally, the law today that 'the wicket is down if a bail in falling lodges between two of the stumps'.

At the end of the season Gubby's figures in the national averages attested his all-round potential — he had taken sixty-six wickets at 19 runs each, and averaged 24 with the bat. But ill-luck had struck again in his last match, for MCC at Scarborough against Yorkshire. His first and great hero, Reggie Spooner, was playing also for MCC in what proved to be his last first-class match. Going in first he made only 10 but in his own elegant, wristy style. He was also still swift in the pick-up at cover-point, and there is a sad irony in the fact that in backing up a throw of Spooner's Gubby fell painfully on the point of his left shoulder, an injury that gave him trouble late in life.

Gubby's first City job with Royal Exchange Assurance in the marine underwriting room, begun in the autumn of 1923, luckily enabled him to play as much first-class cricket in 1924 as in 1923 — and as much as he was to play in any subsequent summer: seventeen Championship matches out of Middlesex's twenty-two.

It was a wet summer, wherein runs were often hard to come by and spin rather had it over speed. His figures accordingly, though boosted by two match-winning efforts, were steady rather than spectacular. Fifty wickets at 17 runs each and 500-odd runs, average 21. However he had the thrill of helping Middlesex in a notable race for the Championship, won in the last few days of the season by Yorkshire, and he ended with a fine flourish at Scarborough.

Gubby's first wicket of the 1924 season was that of a youngster coming in first for Gloucestershire who had begun to attract notice the year before. Walter Hammond played on to Allen bowling fast down a strong wind from the Nursery, and *The Times* thought that 'his stance at the wicket is not one of which any old-fashioned player can approve'. The young man was apparently two-shouldered, and *The Cricketer* thought that he looked a better bowler than a batsman. The critics – and the Middlesex XI – were soon to have evidence that spoke otherwise.

Early in the summer Gubby was a witness from the dressing-room balcony of the most fabulous of Frank Mann's hitting feats in the Middlesex-Yorkshire match at Lord's. The anonymous *Times* reporter must have been F. B. Wilson, for he later described the four sixes in question, all off Rhodes, in almost identical tems under his own name in *The Cricketer*. Of the first two successive hits which landed on the top of the pavilion one was a ballooner, the second almost a skimmer, each falling within 12 feet of one another. These must have been the hits which, so Ian Peebles used to tell, persuaded an elderly member that he was under personal attack whereupon he picked up his umbrella and departed, possibly (like John Willes of earlier memory) shaking the dust of Lord's from his feet for ever. A third hit was a low drive 'which was fortunately steered clear of one of the large windows on the ground floor'. 'The last was a sliced drive, almost a mis-hit. It hit the railings which guard the top of the pavilion.... If Mr Mann had hit that ball properly it would never have been seen again, like the famous arrow in a contest described by Virgil, if one remembers correctly, it might have caught fire.'

In old age one must never trust one's memory, as we all discover to our cost. By a strange quirk Gubby for years described these hits, adding that he was the non-striker at the time, and even offered to bet Greville Stevens £100 shortly before the latter's death when he maintained that it was he who was batting. The scoreboard discloses that G. O. Allen had gone in No 3, no doubt because Hearne and Hendren were playing for England, and it is clear that Mann's partner was indeed Stevens. Gubby, by the way, maintains that the very best straight hit he ever saw at Lord's was Kim Hughes's on to the top of the pavilion off Chris Old in the 1980 Centenary Test.

There was more astonishing cricket in the offing at Lord's, Middlesex catching it hot and strong from what for some weeks was the all-conquering combination of Arthur Gilligan and Maurice Tate. On an admittedly 'false' pitch – a favourite word of Warner's – these two bowled out Middlesex for 104 and 41. Gubby's 43 not out in the first innings with Hendren's 15 and 17 were the only double figure scores. In three weeks the slinging speed of Gilligan coupled with the pace off the pitch and late swing of Tate were irresistible: eighty-five wickets they took between them in eleven completed innings, including the bowling out of South Africa for 30 in the First Test at Edgbaston. What a lucky discovery Gilligan made when, taking out a new ball to the nets and asking the hitherto slow-medium off-breaker, Tate, to whistle a few down, he brought to light the latent power of those heavy shoulders and brawny arms! And how cruel that no sooner was the lethal combination established than the accident to Gilligan impaired it for evermore!

The story is well known how Arthur very soon afterwards was hit over the heart while batting at the Oval in the Gents and Players. Thinking little of it, he next day, batting at No 10, scored 112 in an hour and a half. But lasting damage had been done. Though leading England in two more Tests at home and throughout the MCC tour of Australia, that winter little but Gilligan's superb fielding at mid-off remained. Tate soldiered on gallantly, rarely with adequate support, the best fast-medium bowler of his generation. Gubby's time was coming – but not for a while yet.

Using a spare day to go down to Eton, he accounted for nine of the boys, who were bowled out for 59 – rather a letting of the fox into the farm-yard, but it was rated, strangely perhaps, by *The Times* as 'about the best thing that could have happened to them'.

Next Gubby (though he has little detailed memory of events) was engaged in very much sterner things. How stern was known not from the Yorkshire-Middlesex match reports but in a subsequently published exchange of letters between MCC (who had been requested by Yorkshire to investigate critical reports by the umpires, Butt and Reeves) and the Yorkshire Committee regarding the return match between them at Sheffield. The discipline of Yorkshire on the field under the easy-going Geoffrey Wilson had earned unfavourable comment on the cricket circuit around this time. On this occasion trouble seems to have been started by the Bramall Lane crowd and even, it was said, by some of the Yorkshire members who, according to Middlesex, murmured about 'bloody southern umpires' before a ball was bowled. There had been rain, and Wilson put Middlesex in, as the reports say Mann would have done to Yorkshire had the toss gone his way.

The start was extraordinary in that Stevens and Horace Dales, the Middlesex opening pair, whose partnerships were usually marked by stodginess rather than sparkle, scored 65 together in the first half-hour. When the crowd began to barrack, Stevens sat down, and declined to continue batting until the row stopped. This is rarely a helpful gesture, and although some sort of order was restored, the crowd – which on the first day numbered 20,000 – continued to barrack intermittently and noisily throughout the match. 'Under such conditions,' says *Wisden*, 'cricket could not be played in a proper spirit. Some fine work was done by both sides, but no one enjoyed the match.' On the field Abe Waddington was named by Harry Butt as having behaved particularly badly. It will be noted that Yorkshire asked MCC to examine the case, and it was to the secretary of MCC that Waddington wrote a letter of regret. This was not however the end of the matter, for Middlesex stated during the summer that they were not prepared to play against Yorkshire the following year. At that, Yorkshire deputed the famous Rockley Wilson (no relation) to represent them at a meeting at Lord's. According to family legend he announced that 'if you drop us for one year we'll drop you for fifty'. This seems to have brought everyone to their senses, and Middlesex eventually withdrew their threat.

In the *Wisden* review of the season the matter is finally rounded off thus: 'With stronger leadership all trouble would probably have been avoided. Mr Geoffrey Wilson did his best as captain, but he had not the force of will and character to control the discordant element in his team, and when the season was over he resigned his post.'

Few games stick in the mind like those wherein a side wins after having to follow on. Such a one came next when Middlesex moved down from Sheffield to Trent Bridge. Notts, batting first on a plumb wicket, made 462, bowled out Middlesex for 253, and at the close of the second day had two more Middlesex men out for 53. Gubby recalls an incident that evening which might have had a bearing on the result and is an instance of the rough justice he was prepared to hand out when he deemed it called for. Batting No 3 (Hearne and Hendren being away at a Test Match) he moved out of his ground, well after having made a stroke which involved no question of a run, and indulged in a bit of gardening.

Suddenly the ball was thrown in hard at the stumps by John Gunn. Fortunately Ben Lilley, the keeper, caught it just before it broke the wicket with Gubby yards down the pitch. He said, 'You shouldn't do that, Mr Allen, when John's around.' 'Really,' said Gubby, 'well if that's so he's not going to enjoy his second innings.' John Gunn – never held in anything like the same esteem as brother George – had made a hundred in the first innings. No doubt forewarned when he came in again, he promptly got what Gubby intended to be a fast bouncer, ducked and the ball skidded through low and bowled him for one.

But that item of by-play aside, what a third day was this! Middlesex, with eight second innings wickets to fall, were 156 behind when it started, and soon the Hon C. N. Bruce was retiring with a damaged hand. Against the full Notts attack Middlesex began to play their way forcefully out of trouble. John Guise led the counter-attack with a

NOTTINGHAMSHIRE v MIDDLESEX

At Trent Bridge, 12–14 July 1924

NOTTINGHAMSHIRE

G. Gunn b Durston	55	– b Haig	38
W. Whysall lbw b Haig	36	– c Lee b Allen	32
J. Gunn st Murrell b Haig	113	– b Allen	1
Mr A. W. Carr c Guise b Lee	134	– b Haig	2
W. Payton c Moffat b Durston	65	– c Durston b Allen	1
B. Lilley c Murrell b Guise	19	– b Allen	0
W. Flint c Guise b Haig	13	– lbw b Durston	23
S. J. Staples c Murrell b Durston	4	– c Durston b Haig	1
F. Barratt b Haig	2	– b Allen	1
F. C. Matthews run out	2	– b Allen	0
L. Richmond not out	0	– not out	14
B 9, l-b 8, w 2	19	B 4, l-b 5	9
	462		122

Bowling: *First Innings* – Haig 42–5–134–4; Durston 25.4–2–83–3; Allen 16–2–68–0; Lee 15–0–61–1; Guise 15–1–64–1; Fowler 7–0–33–0. *Second Innings* – Haig 19–5–49–3; Durston 5.5–0–33–1; Allen 13–1–31–6.

MIDDLESEX

Mr H. L. Dales b Staples	13	– c Carr b Matthews	5
H. W. Lee lbw b Richmond	38	– c Flint b Matthews	51
Mr G. O. Allen lbw b Barratt	21	– c and b Staples	22
Hon. C. N. Bruce c G. Gunn b Flint	26	– st Whysall b Richmond	58
Mr F. T. Mann lbw b Barratt	0	– b Barratt	0
Mr J. L. Guise c Flint b Barratt	1	– c Carr b Flint	100
Mr N. Haig b Matthews	17	– b Matthews	29
Mr N. J. D. Moffat not out	55	– lbw b Matthews	6
H. R. Murrell b Matthews	2	– c Whysall b Flint	44
T. J. Durston c and b Flint	45	– lbw b Richmond	28
A. Fowler b Richmond	4	– not out	4
B 16, l-b 11, w 2, n-b 2	31	B 2, l-b 4, w 1, n-b 4	22
	253		358

Bowling: *First Innings* – Barratt 22–4–61–3; Matthews 10–3–33–2; Staples 14–3–49–1; Flint 13–3–26–2; Richmond 16.5–4–53–2. *Second Innings* – Barratt 22–6–62–1; Matthews 24–3–98–4; Staples 9–0–45–1; Flint 22–4–80–2; Richmond 17.2–1–48–2; J. Gunn 3–0–14–0.

Umpires: W. A. Buswell and W. Phillips.

Middlesex won by 27 runs.

priceless hundred in two and three quarter hours, and with eight wickets down and his side now 74 runs ahead Clarence Bruce returned to continue his innings, using only his right hand. He then batted as only a strong-wristed racquets player could, while Jack Durston and Archie Fowler both played their parts. In forty minutes 75 runs were put on before Bruce was stumped for 58, in the course of which he hit eight fours, 'chiefly drives'. Neither Gubby nor I ever remember seeing a man play an innings of any significance using literally one hand. (Lionel Tennyson is sometimes credited with having made 63 in a 1921 England-Australia Test with one hand, but though gravely handicapped with thumb and first finger strapped together, he was able at least to guide or steady the bat with his left hand.)

Finally George Gunn and Whysall, with their side needing 150 to win in two and a half hours, on a pitch as good as new, in three quarters of an hour made 72 together before Gubby accounted for Whysall and then in the circumstances already recorded, sent back John Gunn. Nigel Haig next clean bowled both George and Arthur Carr. There was now no stopping either of them. Notts in fact were 95 for nine before the last pair made half the 55 still needed. Middlesex won however by 27 runs, and Gubby 'bowling fast and making the ball come quickly off the wicket' came in with the thrilling figures of 13–1–31–6. Perhaps J. Gunn had helped unwittingly to provide the spur.

Soon afterwards the game against Somerset at Weston-super-Mare provided our subject with a spur of a different sort. Although Gubby had announced himself unfit to play before the University Match of 1923 there were those who thought he had thrown in the towel. Tom Lowry was apparently among them, and Gubby told his captain that he hoped he might be given the opportunity to show whether he tried or not. Well, the end of the story is not too hard to predict; Lowry's middle-stump was soon sent cart-wheeling and he was one of seven wickets which fell to Gubby for 32 runs: Somerset all out 82. Subsequently let it be added that the expatriate Australian and the New Zealander became firm friends!

Such were some of the purple points in Gubby's Middlesex season of 1924, but the match at Bristol which, if they had won it, would probably have brought the Championship south again must be briefly noted. On a drying pitch on the first day Gloucestershire made only 31, to which Middlesex replied with 74. The pitch remained difficult throughout the game, yet while no one else on either side reached more than 42 Hammond in just under four hours made 174 not out, out of a total of 294 for nine declared. Charlie Parker achieved his second hat-trick of the match (Gubby being involved in both) before Middlesex succumbed by 61 runs. Wally Hammond's skill on bad wickets became legendary – but this was his second season and he was only twenty-one.

Through his cricket life the strongest opposition was inclined to bring the best out of Gubby, and of this Scarborough 1924 was a fair example. Chosen as in the previous year for the Gentlemen, and coming on second change, he took five of the first six Players' wickets (those of Holmes, Hearne, Hendren, Tyldesley and Whysall) for 40 runs and made 33 in a game subsequently spoiled by rain. Gubby recalls being helped by a sea-mist, which must have made him a highly uncomfortable proposition with the ball swinging about all over the place.

The South Africans' visit to Scarborough to play against a C. I. Thornton's XI of next to England strength brought the season to a fitting close. Making 143 and 273 against the scratch side's 461 for six declared, the South Africans were beaten on the stroke of time by an innings and 41 runs. Getting the new ball this time, Gubby's match figures were 49–7–118–10. He dismissed the cream of the South African team in one innings or the other, clean bowling six, having another caught behind and another lbw.

There was even a post-season suggestion in the *Evening Standard* that G. O. Allen might well be chosen to go with MCC to Australia that winter. He always had his press backers, and when things went well, with that beautiful action there were not lacking those (besides Plum Warner) who saw an England cap round the corner. The prospect was evident, but there was no lack of capable and experienced cricketers still ahead of him in the queue.

6

Cricket and the City

The mid-1920s, as has been indicated, saw Gubby finding his feet in a world quite new to him as regards both his business and private life. He enjoyed his job with the Royal Exchange Assurance well enough, apart from the continuing difficulty of making ends meet. They paid him a meagre salary, and his financial stringency was made more acute by his having taken a friend's advice and gambled on margins in the rubber market. Thus he lost not only the balance of the Toby Watt £1000 legacy but as much again besides. The brokers concerned were 'very good about it', but the last of the debt was not paid off for several years. Gubby learned his lesson, and has been extremely careful in money matters ever since. As an attractive and (except financially) eligible young bachelor, he was soon on the hostesses' lists and finding that one deb dance led to another.

In the summer he played all the cricket he could, for Middlesex when he could get away, and otherwise at week-ends for MCC, Eton Ramblers, IZ, and the other wandering clubs. There was country-house cricket as well. He began to play some squash, and so kept reasonably fit, but thinks that during his earlier London years parties and late nights took their toll.

'Whilst many think cricket was always my obsession,' he says, 'it was to this new social world I encountered on coming down from Cambridge that I was most attracted. Some might say it was due to snobbery, I think it was novelty and excitement. I was playing cricket for fun and enjoying life in a big way. It was some years later when I returned from France in 1929 and was very disappointed at not being chosen for England that summer that I really began to think in terms of playing for England.'

The only abiding cloud in the sky of the Allen family was the absence on service in India of Gubby's and Pat's dearly-loved brother, Geoffrey. On leaving Haileybury, Geoffrey had been commissioned via Sandhurst into the Royal Fusiliers, and had been posted to Ireland. After a while it was judged that Geoffrey was a marked man by Sinn Fein, and he was therefore transferred to the RF's other battalion in India.

Gubby's first cuttings entry for 1925 shows the programme for the England-All Blacks match at Twickenham when C. J. Brownlie was sent off the field and the Prince of Wales at half-time made an unavailing effort to secure his return. Gubby recalls buying the evening paper on his way to the ground, and the exhilaration of all at the news that, in reply to Australia's first innings of 600, Hobbs and Sutcliffe had batted the hot Melbourne day through and were still together with 283 runs on the board.

Gubby's cricket in 1925 followed what was to be the usual mixture of cricket and the City. He made one break-through this summer in getting his first first-class hundred, for the Gentlemen at the Oval, and another when, arising from that, he was chosen for the first time for the much more prestigious match against the Players at Lord's.

Before Gubby's scrap-book number three records, the Oval Gentlemen and Players is the only entry of its kind in his complete collection – three pasted-in pages from a score-book. The match was between the Royal Artillery and the Quidnuncs, played at Woolwich on 22 and 23 June. Gubby was the match-manager and likewise, of course, the captain of the Quidnuncs, a Cambridge club of great antiquity, membership of which was confined to blues and near blues. It had (and still has) very few fixtures, and it must have been almost impossible, even in the 1920s, for them to find a side of members for a two-day match on a Monday and Tuesday. Gunner cricket was pretty strong about this time – they had just beaten a good-looking MCC side at Lord's, for instance, by ten wickets – and it got to Gubby's ears before the start that one member of the opposition was openly criticizing the quality of the XI he had got together. He was even reported as having said of the Quidnuncs captain 'He's nothing like so good as he thinks he is.' Right! They had better be shown otherwise.

The Gunners batted first and were bowled out exclusively by Gubby for 106: G. O. A. 12.5 overs, ten for 25, including the hat-trick. He then went in first, and made 101 out of the Quidnunc total of 198. So much for the first day. In the second innings the enemy acquitted themselves even more lamentably, though their tormentor was marginally less devastating. They made 87, Allen seven for 27, and so were beaten by an innings and five runs. Over the two Gunner innings 48 byes made the biggest contributions.

One confesses to a certain sympathy for them. Basil Hill-Wood was the only possible other Quidnunc member playing. He made 41, and promptly scotched the prospect of Gubby getting all ten a second time by taking the first wicket in the second innings. The fact was that Gubby was obliged to collect a side from all and sundry. Of course, on his day he was much too fast for any cricketer short of first-class. All in all, though, one is left wondering what might have happened if that chap had not opened his mouth too wide before the game began – or, perish the thought, if the

ROYAL ARTILLERY v QUIDNUNCS

At Woolwich, 22 and 23 June 1925

ROYAL ARTILLERY

W. M. Leggatt b Allen	2	– b Allen	5
Capt. C. O. Olliver b Allen	1	– c Crewdson b Allen	7
H. S. Garrett b Allen	5	– c Le Blanc Smith b Allen	6
Major C. D. Rawson c Le Blanc Smith b Allen	41	– c and b Allen	4
G. C. Cooke b Allen	1	– not out	12
Capt. A. B. Van Straubenzee b Allen	0	– b Allen	4
Lieut.-Col. C. A. Lyon b Allen	0	– b Antrobus	2
F. E. Hugonin c Crewdson b Allen	12	– b Allen	10
Capt. R. O Skinner b Allen	0	– b Hill-Wood	3
H. H. Merton not out	17	– b Allen	0
Major Lambert b Allen	0	– st Crewdson b Antrobus	1
Extras	27	Extras	33
	106		87

QUIDNUNCS

M. N. Kenyon lbw b Rawson	7
G. O. Allen lbw b Lyon	101
R. Poore c Hugonin b Rawson	1
R. A. G. Tilney c Olliver b Merton	2
Col. W. J. L. Poston c Lambert b Rawson	1
B. S. Hill-Wood b Cooke	48
T. E. Le Blanc Smith c Lyon b Cooke	10
Major W. T. Crewdson run out	3
F. O. G. Lloyd b Coke	0
M. R. Bridgeman c Olliver b Cooke	11
C. J. Antrobus not out	0
Extras	14
	198

Quidnuncs won by an innings and 5 runs.

hero had pulled an early muscle!

Throughout all his life Gubby has always been a dangerous man to provoke. The cricket correspondent of *The Times* wrote afterwards naming two men who (in matches of less moment) had made hundreds and taken all ten, but without a hat-trick thrown in. So be it still, as far as my knowledge goes, in 1984.

And now to more serious matters. The tradition of Gents and Players at the Oval was always that no claims for inclusion were made in the case of those whose counties had a coinciding match, and that the fixture-list was kept down so that reputable sides should be chosen from those available. In 1925 Surrey, Middlesex, Sussex, Hampshire and Warwickshire were among the seven counties unengaged – which enabled the Players to start a formidable order with Hobbs and Sandham, followed by Hearne, Hendren, Bowley and Jack Parsons. Likewise their attack included Tate, Howell, Kennedy and Hearne. The Gentlemen had five who were or became Test cricketers. When on the second morning they went in against the Players' overnight score of 403 for eight declared Tate (then at his peak) had the first five out for just over 100. Gubby batted No 8 and was joined by Haig at 217 for eight, with only Mervyn Hill, the wicket-keeper, to follow. Would they make the 37 to save the follow-on? Yes, they did, and Hobbs tried all possible changes to no effect. On they went, playing ever more fluently and well until – to quote my old friend and *Daily Telegraph* predecessor, Colonel Philip Trevor, CBE (this full appellation was invariably used) – 'there was a hurricane of cheering when, at a quarter past six, the Players total was passed . . . and the two batsmen were accorded a magnificent ovation that continued for several minutes.'

But there is another significant item connected with Gubby's innings that day. The social life of London which he found on coming down from Cambridge exerted in his salad days a strongish pull, as has been noted. Nevertheless it would have needed something special to keep him up late in the middle of an important match. As it happened there was something special, the coming-out ball of Mary Martin-Smith. Gubby was already a close enough friend to be asked to the Martin-Smith's preceding dinner-party. Cricket was not going to spoil a night like this, and it didn't. He danced it through, and got to bed at six. Friendship ripened into affection in the following years, and, looking back, Gubby considers, without presuming to know the answer if he had done so, that it was probably the biggest mistake of his life that he never proposed. At that time he was not thinking of marriage, and though he was relatively speaking penniless he is honest enough to say that an element of selfishness likewise held him back. In December 1932 ('on the first day of the Sydney Test') Mary Martin-Smith married Denis Hill-Wood, a younger brother of Willie's and a future partner of Gubby's on the Stock Exchange. Needless to say they have always been devoted friends.

And now – getting back to Gents and Players – Gubby had to face at breakfast the wrath of his father, who was so cross at his burning the candle at both ends that he declared he would not go to the Oval to see the continuation of the match. Instead his son's surmise is that he followed the progress of the game – and his score – on the tape machine of his club, perhaps growing even crosser at missing the performance.

So much Gubby recalls, and with it another item, an aside with Jack Hobbs as the latter crossed from cover-point to cover-point. Could he lend Gubby a couple of match-sticks, he wanted to know, and when asked why said, 'To keep your eyes open.' Jack and G. O., as he called him, were on terms of this sort. True enough, says G.O., his lack of sleep caught up with him towards the close. The stand of 193 for the ninth wicket was ended when Haig was out for 98. Gubby ending the day 93 not out with No 11 at the wicket. Mervyn Hill proved such a good partner next morning that Gubby's first first-class hundred swelled to

GENTLEMEN v PLAYERS

At the Oval, 8–10 July 1925

PLAYERS

J. B. Hobbs (Capt.) b Calthorpe	5	– run out	51
A. Sandham c Hill b Fender	50		
J. W. Hearne b Allen	103	– not out	65
E. Hendren b Haig	59	– c Tennyson b Calthorpe	31
E. H. Bowley lbw b Bettington	12	– b Bettington	39
J. H. Parsons c Hill b Fender	72	– lbw b Calthorpe	14
A. S. Kennedy not out	59	– c Fender b Tennyson	15
M. W. Tate b Allen	7	– lbw b Calthorpe	5
F. Edwards b Fender	8	– c Bettington b Tennyson	10
H. Strudwick not out	4	– not out	7
B 5, l-b 17, n-b 2	24	B 12, n-b 3	15
(8 wkts., dec.)	**403**	**(7 wkts., dec.)**	**252**

H. Howell did not bat.

Bowling: *First Innings* – Allen 23–4–81–2; Calthorpe 27–6–71–1; Haig 26–5–56–1; Bettington 17–1–86–1; Fender 27–4–85–3. *Second Innings* – Allen 3–1–9–0; Calthorpe 17–0–59–3; Haig 18–3–64–0; Bettington 17–1–64–1; Fender 9–3–19–0; Tennyson 4–0–22–2.

GENTLEMEN

Hon. F. S. G. Calthorpe c Parsons b Tate	63	– b Tate	11
C. H. Titchmarsh c Strudwick b Tate	21	– run out	15
R. Aird c Strudwick b Tate	8	– not out	31
G. R. Jackson b Tate	5	– c Hobbs b Kennedy	14
Hon. C. N. Bruce lbw b Tate	7	– b Kennedy	36
Hon. L. H. Tennyson c Strudwick b Tate	69	– st Strudwick b Tate	28
P. G. H. Fender b Edwards	21	– b Tate	12
G. O. Allen b Howell	130		
R. H. Bettington b Kennedy	8		
N. Haig c Strudwick b Tate	98	– not out	51
M. L. Hill not out	6		
B 15, l-b 6, n-b 1	22	L-b 2	2
	458	**(6 wkts.)**	**200**

Bowling: *First Innings* – Tate 42–9–148–7; Howell 28–0–119–1; Kennedy 23–4–64–1; Hearne 10–3–31–0; Edwards 23–3–55–1; Bowley 11–2–19–0. *Second Innings* – Tate 12–0–80–3; Howell 6–0–31–0; Kennedy 9.3–0–59–2; Bowley 5–0–28–0.

Umpires: F. Parris and W. Phillips.

The Gentlemen won by four wickets.

130. The Players declared in mid-afternoon at 252 for seven: setting a generous target of 198 in one and three quarter hours and this the Gentlemen achieved by four wickets. It was, of course, far from being a straight victory, but rather one in the spirit of the fixture: much good cricket, nothing given away, and ample pleasure enjoyed all round.

And so to Lord's for the classic of the year which, played in glorious weather and on the plumbest of pitches, went very much the Players' way though they were unable to press their advantage fully home. That they could not do so on the last day was due in the first place to Greville Stevens's second admirable innings in the match (75 and 129 and four for

72 was his contribution) and in the second to a confident, unbeaten 52 by Gubby. The Gentlemen had been highly likely to lose until he and Fender, batting 'freely and well', put on 70 for the seventh wicket on the last afternoon.

On paper anyway Gubby up to that point had not had a great match. He had made 11 in the Gentlemen's first innings when he was out lbw to Macaulay, and on returning to the dressing-room encountered the deity of Lord's himself. The exchange and its consequences have been told before. 'Satisfied, young man?' enquired Lord Harris. Not inclined to mask his feelings, irrespective of age or rank, Gubby replied: 'Satisfied that I hit it hard enough to be heard all round the ground.' His Lordship grunted and, reputedly, made off for the cricket office where without more ado he struck out the name of W. A. J. West from the umpires' list.

This dictatorial upshot (difficult to comprehend in these days of individual captains' reports, and a studied appreciation at the end of the season by all concerned) upset Gubby, who liked old Bill West and wouldn't have spoken so vehemently if he had had an inkling of the consequences. (In fact West was coming up to 63. He officiated until the end of the season and then, as Wisden put it, 'dropped out'.)

On the Gentlemen going into the field Gubby was preparing to bowl the first over to Hobbs from West's end when West said, 'Oh, Mr Allen, I'm sorry – they tell me you hit that one.' Somewhat embarrased, Gubby said something like, 'Oh, Bill, I did, but forget it,' adding in, as he thought, a lighter tone: 'Just you give them out when we shout.' A moment later, sure enough, Hobbs got a very thick outside edge. Bowler, wicket-keeper Sherwell and all the slips 'went up', and to their astonishment West said, 'not out'.

When Hobbs got down to the bowler's end Gubby said: 'Jack, you old so-and-so, you practically hit that one for four': to which the reply came, 'G.O., I did no such thing.' Hobbs went on to make 140 before he hooked a short one, 'Allen bringing off a fine catch at forward short-leg.' The scene moves to a later occasion in the season where Gubby again taxes the Master with having hit it. 'Of course, I did, but you're very young, G.O. I couldn't let the umpire down by saying so in his presence, could I? Besides' – with a twinkle – 'he might give me out next time!'

What emerges from this story, remembered in detail by Gubby, is that in his early twenties he was indeed still somewhat naïve: also perhaps that old West probably was a bit 'past it'.

Jack was very much in the centre of the stage in that summer of 1925, for he was growing rapidly closer to W. G.'s massive tally of 126 first-class hundreds. When the summer began he had made 113 hundreds, and he started in May in prime form with several more on the blameless Oval wicket. No one in history had ever made more than thirteen in a season, yet his 140 at Lord's in mid-July was his eleventh, and 124th in all, and in the next match at Blackheath on 20 July came his 125th.

All the public now took it for granted that the magic 126 would be achieved any day. But, of course, cricket, even for a Hobbs or a Bradman, is not like that. Hobbs began to score like an ordinary mortal. A young miner of Notts whom he had not seen before, bowling pretty quick, Larwood by name, had him caught behind at the Oval for one. The posters began to proclaim when he had made only 40 or 50, 'Hobbs fails again'. Naturally he got caught up in the general excitement. When Middlesex came to the Oval for the first half of the 'London Derby', 20,000-odd turned up, but Hobbs was marvellously caught by Murrell down the leg-side off Durston for 49, and it was young Allen who took the honours with five wickets for 40. It was exactly four weeks after that 125th hundred when down at Taunton, in front of a large holiday crowd and with Pathé News film cameras as well as the press there in force W. G.'s magic 126 was reached. Whereupon 'the media' departed, sporting England relaxed, and Hobbs promptly made it 127, incidentally so winning the game for Surrey on the last afternoon. Before the end of the season he reached 3000 runs for the only time in his life and brought his hundreds to sixteen, a figure then unapproached and since bettered only by Denis Compton.

Gubby's scrap-books, naturally enough, are personal records, of games and other happenings in which he took part, but there are cuttings of really big events such as Coronations, and in this case is a press photograph covering half a page showing Jack Hobbs the hero of the hour standing beside the oil of W. G., full of beard and wearing an MCC cap, painted by an unknown artist, which hangs now in Lord's pavilion.

The 1925 cricket content of the scrap-book ends abruptly here in mid-August, for Gubby was suddenly struck down not by another sporting injury but, if you please, by a gnat-sting, sustained over the week-end of the Notts match at Lord's while staying down on the river at Datchet with the Warners. The victim is sure this was the only time in his career when 'absent ill' appeared against his name on the score-sheet. Needless to say this was no ordinary insect which prompted a two-column headline in the *Evening News* entitled 'Beware of the – Gnat'. Gubby's publicity-attracting personality has been noted already. We read of '*two* nurses applying fomentations at frequent intervals'. There is a photograph of Mr G. O. Allen and some words of warning to the public from Sir William Simpson, a great authority on health in tropical countries. The wet summer, it seemed, had encouraged a scourge of gnats and mosquitoes. Gubby's gnat gave him a bite on the shin, the mark of which is (on request) visible to this day. It kept him three days in hospital and put paid to his cricket for the summer.

All that remained was for the critics to review the season, chiefly from the view-point of England's chances against Australia in England in 1926. Following three disastrous post-war rubbers there was a general advocacy of youth, and a universal regret at the paucity of speed. However, both Gubby and Harold Larwood, in that order, are discussed as possibles by G. L. Jessop in the *Evening News*. Jack Hobbs in the *Daily Mail*, and an anonymous correspondent in *The Observer*. My future colleague on the *Evening Standard*, little J. A. H. Catton, went to town with a whole column in praise of Gubby: 'I can tell the reader this – that cricketers of far less ability have been included in an Eleven of England.'

The first matter to engage Gubby's attention as the 1926 season began was the General Strike. By now his father was Commandant of the Metropolitan Special Constabulary, and Gubby, having stubbed his toe, was recruited on to the staff at the then headquarters, Scotland House.

The strike over, Gubby had only limited opportunity to advertise his claims for a Test place. He made no great mark in the Whitsuntide match against Sussex, but, batting at No 4, helped Middlesex win at Worcester with innings of 66 and 55, and three wickets. Next the Australians came to Lord's to play Middlesex, and batted all Saturday for 357 for four, Allen (coming on second change) bowling well but without taking a wicket.

When the Test Trial sides were announced over the week-end however, there was his name for England, with Larwood's for the Rest. 'Why G. O. Allen should be given a place no man can say,' wrote an anonymous correspondent in one of the Monday papers. Gubby throughout his career was inclined to answer criticism with performance, as he did now by taking five of the last six Australian wickets to fall, four of them in eleven balls, all clean bowled with the stumps uprooted each time. Certainly there were a lot of runs on the board, but only the last of the five was a rabbit. The point was that, for once, Mann gave him the new ball, which was usually monopolized by Durston and Haig.

Monty Noble, the great Australian captain of Edwardian days, wrote kindly of Gubby's performance and likewise of Greville Stevens's whose 149, going in first against the speed of Gregory, was accounted by Warner a great innings. 'Sydney Man English Bowling Hope', announced the *Sydney Morning Herald* in a banner headline. Gubby was described as the 'real Cotter', and it was pointed out that, though the Australian selectors in the circumstances would never pick him, Gubby was eligible for both sides.

Nineteen at the time, I recall very well the vast interest in the Australian visit of 1926 – this was only the third Test series in England, after all, since 1912. There were 31,000 at Lord's on the first day of the *Trial* Match when on a slow pitch Gubby's only success was to bowl out

Fender – who tended rather to be his rabbit. His memory is of the kindness of old Dick Burrows to a fellow-bowler, umpiring at his end and warning him about no-balls rather than calling him. 'It's only a Trial Match, but be careful.' Despite this encouragement Gubby's recollection is of bowling poorly and batting well. He made 44, second top score to Hobbs and 16 not out in a drawn match. Young Larwood (twenty-one and a half and in only his second season) came distinctly the better out of a comparison with Gubby, taking five good wickets in the match for 79 runs.

However for the First Test at Trent Bridge – wherein there was scarcely any play – and for the Second at Lord's the selectors, despite the protestations about youth, found something of an elderly dark horse as Tate's opening bowling partner in Fred Root of Worcestershire. The argument was that his in-swing would be new and unfamiliar to the Australians, and with four major wickets in the two innings of a high-scoring drawn match Root justified the experiment. Though Root then fell out of the selectors' reckoning, Larwood however had been blooded at Lord's, and done well enough to deserve a further chance, which duly came to him in the culminating Test at the Oval wherein the Ashes were recovered. As things turned out Gubby, though at one point in 1929 he sniffed selection against South Africa, had to wait four more years for his first Test cap.

There was one considerable distinction, however, for the Allen family to enjoy that summer of 1926 in the King's Honours, for Walter Macarthur Allen, after having served for six years as Commandant-in-Chief of the Metropolitan Special Constabulary, was raised from CBE to a knighthood. He continued in the post until ill-health caused his retirement in 1940.

An extraordinary – perhaps even unique – incident happened that summer when Yorkshire came to Lord's. Gubby was bowling to Sutcliffe early in their innings when the wicket-keeper and all the close fielders joined Gubby himself in an appeal for a catch behind the wicket. To their astonishment Frank Chester said 'not out'. At the end of the over that greatest of umpires walked down the pitch, and pointed to a distinct red mark on the outside of the off-stump. 'As I thought,' he remarked. As he might have said it was no doubt 'Elementary, my dear Watson,' granted that exceptional speed of reaction and degree of self-confidence. It was typical of Sutcliffe, Middlesex must have thought, that he was the batsman concerned, for he was generally regarded as not only a formidable player but also a very lucky one. One can imagine him leaning on his bat and surveying Chester's inspection, superbly aloof. As it happened what should have been Gubby's wicket was taken comparatively cheaply by that very occasional bowler Harry Lee; Sutcliffe c.

Hendren, b. Lee 44.

As an example of Chester's virtuosity the decision has passed into cricket lore. I don't recall hearing or reading of a parallel instance.

Among Gubby's recollections are of his getting within sight of his first county hundred in a long stand with Hearne at Bradford: of how when he had made 80 he 'just missed the damn thing' and was lbw to Edgar Oldroyd of all people, who only took thirty-nine wickets in a long career, and of his being upbraided by J. W. for his carelessness. Then there was another palpitating match at Trent Bridge, specially significant after Middlesex's historic victories here in the two preceding years. This time Middlesex were set to make 369 in the fourth innings, Gubby being sent in No 3. Now did come that first county hundred, and an admirable one it was from all accounts, made in two hours, forty minutes, and with nineteen fours. Mann, who was going well at the other end, said at this auspicious moment, 'Come on, you can go quietly now and we'll get these runs.' Alas, a young man is vulnerable after achieving a notable target, and this one had something of a rush of blood to the head and was promptly caught at the wicket. He made the widest possible detour on his return to the pavilion past his captain, but the greatest hitter of the day stalked him menacingly. 'You bloody little fool,' rang in Gubby's ears as he made his way through the applauding Nottingham members. Middlesex, almost inevitably, lost wickets in the chase against the clock, and in the end were beaten by 14 runs just three minutes from time. Getting the new ball for once, Gubby took four wickets in the Notts first innings, and so altogether the 'bloody little fool' had, personally, a very good match.

He followed with another, at Lord's against Gloucestershire, taking seven for 30 in one innings and making 53 in another. Finally in the local Derby at Lord's which Surrey won by an innings he shared the punishment suffered by the seven Middlesex bowlers used while Hobbs exceeded by one run the 315 not out with which Holmes had broken the old Lord's record the previous year. For seven hours the Master batted. He dealt mortal injury to a sparrow in flight, said *The Times*, but seemed to give no chance. *The Times* cluck-clucked a bit on this 'modern mania' of going for 'records' in inverted commas, and thought that Mr Fender would at least have declared when, immediately on Hobbs reaching 300 (just sixteen short!), Mr Jardine was dismissed for 103. Next day it had to be admitted that Mr Fender had been proved right in the end — but then Middlesex had batted *very* disappointingly in both innings.

In these last days of the summer of 1926 all cricket was played in a spirit of euphoria, engendered by the great Ashes victory at the Oval. The story possessed all the ingredients of drama, the promotion of the youthful Percy Chapman to the captaincy, the success of Harold Larwood, the fast bowling discovery so long awaited, the last curtain-call of the veteran, Wilfred Rhodes, and, above all, the great stand of Hobbs and Sutcliffe on the ruined wicket which determined the result.

The *Morning Post* had erected a giant score-board at their office in the Aldwych. Great crowds followed the play thereby, watching for hours at a time. And then just after six o'clock came 'the fateful figures announcing England's victory. Even as the board turned in the crowd sensed the news. A mighty cheer rang out, to swell and set the echoes rolling down the Strand to the west, down Fleet Street to the east, and to the north up Kingsway.' Subtract a little, if you will, from the *Morning Post*'s glowing 'House Ad.' and shed a tear maybe for the old paper destined a decade later to be absorbed quietly into the *Daily Telegraph*. Still there remains a picture of an England glowing in the one sporting victory that counted above all others, that over those former 'Colonials' from Down Under.

Gubby's cricket was due soon to be frustratingly interrupted, but in the winter of 1926–27 he had a lovely bonus in the shape of an MCC tour to South America. Cricket is deep-rooted in Argentina, planted there by expatriate Britons early in the nineteenth century, and it was played also, then more than today, in Uruguay, Chile, and Peru. The serious cricket took place in Argentina, whose Cricket Association had issued the invitation to MCC, but the tour opened in Montevideo, and, at its end the team crossed the Andes to show the flag in Valparaiso and Lima before returning home via the Panama Canal.

In the MCC's wholly amateur side was a wide assortment both of age and skills. Plum Warner, the captain, was fifty-three, and Gerry Weigall, asked perhaps for the certainty of good enertainment value, three years older. At the other end of the scale were three in their early twenties, Alec Pilkington, Lord Dunglass (as Lord Home then was) and Gubby. There were four serving soldiers – Captains T. O. Jameson, R. T. Stanyforth, the wicket-keeper, due the following winter to take MCC to South Africa, and L. C. R. Isherwood, and a subaltern, H. P. Miles – and three county captains, Guy Jackson of Derbyshire, Maurice Jewell of Worcestershire, and Jack White of Somerset.

Though he was thirty-five, and had been the pillar of his county for years, White's fame as a Test cricketer lay ahead. He, Tommy Jameson, of Hampshire, and Gubby, as all-rounders, formed the backbone of the side. It approximated, I suppose, to a strong Free Forester side such as might at that time have given a good game at Oxford or Cambridge. The point was, it was just about adequate for its purpose on the field, and no doubt even better equipped off it. T. H. Carlton Levick, a kindly chap and devoted MCC member, went along as honorary manager – a highly necessary adjunct on an expedition of this sort.

Apart from an occasional club match at home this, of course, was

Gubby's only experience of Warner as a captain, and on the evidence of it he rates him the best he ever played under. Plum's record since he led the first-ever MCC team overseas – to Australia in 1903–04 – proclaimed him as a considerate leader for whom men enjoyed playing, and who got the utmost out of them. But it was especially as a tactician that he so impressed Gubby. Though he could have previously seen none of the opposition, except Clem Gibson who captained Argentina in the four 'Tests', he summed them all up so quickly, for the benefit of his bowlers. Steeped in cricket all his life he spotted strengths and weaknesses in an over or two – a quality which naturally served him well as a selector.

The hospitality received from the British community everywhere was in accord with the lavish standards of the day. When they travelled up-country the team lived in a luxurious train with marble baths and sitting-rooms which had been built for the Prince of Wales's tour a few years before. No pioneer hardship was involved! The only drawback to a perfect holiday was, at its worst, the heat. For Gubby the tour cemented the friendship with Alec Home which began at Eton. They shared cabins on the boats each way – a test of virtue in itself. The only fly in the ointment for Home was a grumbling appendix which kept him out of several matches and sent him to hospital.

Jack White thought he had found an infallible system for roulette, so a syndicate was formed which at first did well. However the day came when it all went wrong and both Home and Allen remember the latter (not himself a member of the syndicate) being deputed to visit the sick-bed and bear the sad news that they'd lost the lot. Then there was the poker school and the game in the train as they crossed the Andes. Farmer White had two full houses, aces high – if memory is to be trusted – but was twice beaten by Jameson with royal straight flushes. Whereupon White in mock disgust threw the only pack of cards out of the window. Yes, Gubby can see it now, just as they were passing Aconcagua, looming snow-clad on the right. The atlas indeed shows Aconcagua (22,834 ft.) as the highest mountain in the Andean chain, and the railway does cross east and west to the south of it. The Guinness Book of Records notes that it is more than 40,000 feet above the Pacific Abyssal Plain, and, for that matter, 42,834 above the Peru-Chile Trench 180 miles out to sea – none of which, even if he had known it, can have been of much interest or comfort to Farmer White. However he was soon laughing again, and indeed spent the tour laughing, even when they missed catches off his bowling.

There was one (military) culprit who never caught anything. White would turn away, and say 'Tell me when he's dropped it.' This was an attitude likely to be remembered by Gubby whose equanimity was apt to be tested by dropped catches. At first slip to him, at school, on this tour, and often in club cricket, Alec Home is as well placed to know as most. He may forgive, but he doesn't forget. After which I had better add that Gubby rates our cricketing Prime Minister as having been a distinctly good slipper, as well as a useful away-swing medium-pacer and a determined bat.

Opening the bowling and batting when it mattered at No 3, Gubby was generally in the thick of it. MCC won two of the four three-day games in Argentina, and lost one on a crumbling pitch by twenty-nine runs. Rain ruined the other.

At Valparaiso Gubby was bowling when there was an earth tremor which shook off the bails – whereupon one of the expatriates, of whom all the oppositions were comprised, hooked his next ball for six on to the race-track. In the last match at Lima Gubby took twelve wickets for a handful – which earned him the congratulations of President Leguia of Peru: 'How fine, how splendid!' They lurched home through a hurricane in an old tub called the *Orita*, our hero spending most of the ten days horizontal in his cabin, going through the ship's library of Edgar Wallace.

For Gubby there was not much more splendour due for a while on the cricket front, for a job in France was in the offing. However, before he went off to Trouville in mid-June to learn the language – and just to refresh the selectors' memory – he had an excellent match for MCC against the first-ever New Zealand team to England, brought by Tom Lowry, making 38 and 104 not out in a match evenly drawn, and taking ten wickets in the two innings.

Though otherwise unsuccessful as a bowler in half-a-dozen matches for Middlesex, he took five for 99 against Notts, made memorable by a fiery pitch on which Dick Twining was gravely hurt and several others less seriously. Twining was knocked unconscious by a good length ball from Larwood which hit him under the heart. It was said that if his heart had been on the 'other' beat at that precise second the blow might have killed him.

Middlesex had just followed on 242 behind when the accident happened. However, far from crumpling, Lee (102), Hendren (56) and Allen (74) batted with much courage, while Haig, 'giving it room' and using his wrists as he was wont to do against speed, reached 50. According to Warner, Gubby played Larwood better than anyone. 'He got well on top of the rising balls, flinging his arms well up, and dropping his wrists at the moment of playing the ball ... It was in every respect the innings of a "class" batsman.'

Larwood, who took nine for 122 in the match and made 67 not out in the first innings, also came in for high praise from Plum who thought it was 'the most bouncing wicket we have seen at Lord's since 1910'. There was no suggestion, by the way, that at this stage of his career at any rate Larwood was being encouraged by his captain, Arthur Carr, to bowl short. Notts owed a notable victory chiefly to him.

Gubby's last cricket memory in 1927 is of watching Tom Enthoven play the innings of his life for Middlesex at Lord's against Lancashire, the county champions. After making a sedate first 50, and with his side in the direst trouble, Enthoven suddenly began an onslaught on the bowling, and especially that of the formidable McDonald. 'In a manner worthy of Gilbert Jessop', *Wisden* tells us, he scored 89 more runs in fifty-five minutes, most of them with Fred Price, the No 11, holding fast at the other end. Hence the nickname that stuck through his playing days, 'Gibraltar' Price. Never a great cricketer, Enthoven was very much the man for a crisis.

And so to France. Obviously this hiatus in Gubby's cricket career retarded his progress. But his business career had to come first, and here seemed an opportunity more attractive than the world of insurance. Hugh Vivian-Smith, father of two boys in Wells's house with Gubby, an eminent City figure, and among many other things Chairman of Royal Exchange Assurance, in company with Sir Frederick Richmond, Chairman of the Debenham's group, had a financial interest in a silk-manufacturing firm in Lyons. They offered Gubby the chance of learning about the silk trade at first hand, and after a six-weeks' refresher in French, down he went to Lyons for what proved a stay of eighteen months. He knew no one, and after London life the sense of isolation is not hard to imagine. There was however quite a good golf course, and Gubby dined frequently with the French steward and his wife. He thinks he must have got his handicap down to about eight or ten (equivalent to a bit more, of course, under the modern handicap system), and in the summer of 1928 he won the South of France Handicap, beating a Jap in the final.

Golf – and fishing! One week-end Gubby went fishing with a French fellow-employee, who, growing expansive as the day wore on and the wine sank in, confided that he thought that the firm was financially far from what was supposed. Gubby was sufficiently impressed to return home and report the matter to his superiors. Vivian-Smith enjoyed helping people, especially the young, but he had the reputation of being quick-tempered. His protégé was sent back to France with something like a flea in his ear, but was told to keep his eyes open.

Not long afterwards, in early 1929, enquiries having been made meanwhile, a wire summoned Gubby back to London and a rather different atmosphere. His warning had proved timely. Vivian-Smith (later to become Lord Bicester) and Richmond duly 'got out' and were properly grateful. But the great depression was under way. Jobs were hard to find, and in the circumstances Gubby was happy enough to accept one from Richmond at Debenham's stores. He was going to be allowed a certain limited time for cricket, three weeks which could be taken in days.

But we must retrace our steps briefly to the summer of 1928, for although Gubby on a short leave was able to play only twice for Middlesex the second game, in early June, was the momentous one wherein Learie Constantine put up a staggering personal performance, and in so doing gave notice that the West Indies were opponents to be reckoned with, not completely unworthy of the Test status to which they were being promoted.

Gubby, not in full practice, achieved little, but the match has a fascination which compels attention. It is one of the classics one would have most liked to see. 'Conny', a man of many qualities, of which modesty was not one, and his friend and collaborator, C. L. R. James, in his book *Cricket and I*, extract every scrap of drama from what is in any case a heroic story. The team doctor said that if Learie played with torn muscle fibres he might do himself a lot of harm. He thought, we read, of the Russian general who, when told the surgeons were going to have both his legs off, drew his pistol, saying he would shoot the first man who touched him. Needless to say, he lived to walk again. (I seem to sniff the pen of James in that bit.)

The West Indies had made no great mark thus far on the tour, and their manager, says Learie, pleaded with him to play for the sake of the 'gate'. So at the last moment he did, the doctor saying he must not bowl. On the first day Middlesex made 313 for six and he delivered twenty overs for a return of one for 77. After a Sunday of massage and hot towels, and some quick runs next morning before Middlesex declared, Learie went to the crease with the score 79 for five.

From now on it was the stuff of schoolboy fiction. He began quietly 'because of the muscle', but then set about the bowling with such elemental relish and ferocity that he made 86 (out of 107) in under an hour.

This includes 36 hit in three overs off Gubby, the most extrordinary stroke being one as to which striker and victim give slightly different versions. Constantine says: 'He sent up a widish pitched-up ball and I went at him with a horizontal bat, drive or cut as you will, but screwing the blade, and the ball fell into the seats near the scoring box.' That is to say over cover-point's head and on to the Grand Stand balcony, a prodigious blow. Gubby confirms the trajectory of the ball and its extraordinary landing-point, but reckons that Learie tried to hit straight and was late on the stroke. 'You always know where the batsman has aimed by looking at his eyes.'

Despite Constantine, Middlesex go in again 122 to the good, and at the close are 40 for two, Lee bowled by Constantine and Allen c. and b. Francis. On the last day Hearne and Hendren make the game apparently all but safe for Middlesex before the former is out and Learie brought on for a second spell, at the pavilion end. In 6.1 overs, bowling at a great pace, he took six wickets for 11, four bowled, two caught in the slips. Middlesex are shot out for 136, and the pavilion rises to applaud the hero in.

The West Indies nevertheless still need 259 to win – a tall order indeed. Learie came in at 121 for five, and at once started cracking away brilliantly. Exactly one hour later Learie is out having scored 103 out of 133 and leaving only five more runs needed for victory. For the second time in the afternoon the pavilion rises to acclaim 'the most determined match-winning cricketer in the world'.

Such was *The Times* correspondent's verdict in a lyrical report next morning. History scarcely confirms so lofty an estimate. The West Indies and Constantine himself paid for these hours of glory, for he tended now to think nothing was beyond his powers. England won all three of those 1928 Tests by an innings, and in them the future Lord Constantine's performances with both bat and ball were extremely modest. Only in the field was he, beyond argument, world-class. And in any cricket short of Test Matches he was an incomparable entertainer.

Back from France, Gubby's first public performance in 1929 was not on the cricket field, but as best man at the marriage of his first and closest Eton friend, David Bowes Lyon with Rachel Spender-Clay, on 6 February at St Margaret's, Westminster. David's sister, Elizabeth, had married the Duke of York six years earlier, and the occasion lacked nothing in sparkle and splendour. Both marriages were performed by Dr Davidson, for quarter of a century Archbishop of Canterbury, but now in 1929 aged eighty and recently retired.

Gubby tells of a little happening some years earlier during a week-end at St Paul's, Walden Bury, when the Queen Mother, as she now is, driving a vast, high Daimler, ran over a chicken. She insisted on stopping, walked back and apologized to the farmer. He remembers it as a lesson in manners. How many must there have been who have experienced over the years similar examples, both small and great, of her instinctive consideration!

Following the visit of the West Indies in 1928 the South Africans came for a Test series in 1929. It was the first time there had been Test series in successive summers – since which date no season has passed without one (except 1932 when India were granted only one match). Gubby therefore had a Test cap to aim for, and again only a limited ration of cricket with which to hold the official eye. He started operations in mid-May with the

Whitsuntide match against Sussex at Lord's, helping his side to victory (despite an injury to Jack Dunston, the beneficiary) by taking three good wickets in each innings including Duleep, twice clean bowled, for 0 and 32.

Gubby played against the South Africans for a strongish MCC side which however contained only Pat Hendren and Jack White of those who had retained the Ashes so emphatically during the winter. In the absence of a second regular opener Gubby went in first with Greville Stevens, and came off with scores of 52 and 41 not out. The first (which ended in his being bowled by the Afrikaner fast bowler with the delightfully onomatopoeic name of Ochse, pronounced Ooch!) was thought by *The Times* to be 'a delightful innings'. He shared the new ball with Bill Bowes, a studious-looking youngster on the MCC ground staff, who, aged only twenty, had at about that time taken to wearing spectacles instead of pince-nez. Spin however accounted for most of the wickets, and Gubby had to be satisfied with one, even if it was the most prestigious, that of the great Herby Taylor, for 74 runs. White gave him thirty-one overs, but in the second innings he bowled only nine, after which Plum Warner was moved to write that 'it is a pity that he is so often unable to bowl owing to minor strains and injuries'.

To this the subject would no doubt have commented that it isn't so easy for a fast bowler to keep match-fit clocking in daily at eight-thirty a.m. at Debenham's and dashing up from the office to the Lord's nets shortly before close of play. That is a fair point, as also was the contention of some that just occasionally hypochondria took over and he became over-protective of his limbs – and perhaps also of his reputation. Put another way, it was sometimes the perfectionist in him which won the argument as to whether he would bowl or not.

I wonder if Gubby had altogether dismissed his supporter Plum's words from his mind when the time came for his next appearance for Middlesex at Lord's a fortnight later. Nigel Haig, who had now succeeded Frank Mann in the captaincy, was naturally anxious for his services against Lancashire, the county champions of the preceding three seasons. Gubby's stipulation was that he could not be there in time on the Saturday since he had first to go to work at Debenham's. In fact he took the field at ten minutes to twelve, was soon put on at the pavilion end with a fair breeze behind him and at once bowled out the left-handed Hallows. No other wicket fell before lunch as Watson and Ernest Tyldesley, the utilitarian and the stylist, took the score to 90 for one.

Gubby had bowled fast before lunch, and he was faster afterwards. Out went Watson's middle and Iddon's off stump. Tyldesley and Hopwood stayed together almost until tea, adding 113 before the former, having just completed an admirable hundred, lost his leg-stump, likewise to Gubby.

At tea Lancashire were 215 for four. The end of their innings was processional. The last six wickets falling, all to Gubby for 26 more runs. Eight of his wickets were clean bowled, one was caught by Price, the wicket-keeper, who also stumped McDonald. Price, of course, stood back, but after McDonald (not Gubby's favourite cricketer) had been hit on the thigh he left his crease next ball, Price saw him coming, as did the bowler, who produced a slow, widish one, allowing Price to get to the wicket in time to make the stumping. Lancashire were all out for 241, and the last four wickets had been taken in five balls. This gave Gubby the following analysis:25·3–10–40–10.

The final surrender had been so swift that the crowd can scarcely have had time for the performance to sink in – especially as Gubby instinctively grabbed his sweater from the umpire and ran straight back into the pavilion ahead of everyone. Thus, perhaps physically and mentally exhausted, or from a sudden onrush of modesty, he cut short his immediate moment of glory, but, of course, he had added a significant feat to the records. Since Alfred Shaw in 1874 only Arthur Fielder had taken all ten at Lord's – which he did in the Gentlemen and Players of 1906. Nor has anyone done so since. The pitch was plumb, and none of the other six bowlers used looked like taking a wicket. *The Times'* tribute spoke of 'the great pace at which he made the ball leave the pitch', and of how he bowled at the stumps and kept up his speed and accuracy over long spells. 'It was in fact a truly exhilarating exhibition of fast bowling – real fast bowling at its best.'

The secret of fast bowling is rhythm, and all who achieve high speed know of those magical days when everything clicks that much more smoothly. 15 June 1929 was indeed one such for Gubby.

However the fact was that with nine Tests behind him Larwood was now the resident England fast bowler, sharing the new ball with Tate, and with Hammond and/or Geary to back them up with quicker stuff if needed. So it was that although Gubby at once followed his 'all ten' by taking five wickets, all at the head of the order, against Somerset and making the top score of 50, the selectors (who were H. D. G. Leveson Gower, Haig and White) passed him by.

However in the Third Test Larwood pulled a tendon, and for the Gentlemen at Lord's in the same week Gubby by all account bowled very well against the best professional batting to take three for 40 in nineteen overs. Had the moment come? The critics seemed inclined to think so, but for the Fourth Test against South Africa the selectors turned instead to Larwood's thirty-five-year-old new-ball partner for Notts, Fred Barratt, a fine yeoman fast-medium bowler who thus played in his first and only home Test. It must have been a close decision, and retrospec-

MIDDLESEX v LANCASHIRE

At Lord's, 15–18 June 1929

LANCASHIRE

C. Hallows b Allen	12	– b Robins	22
F. Watson b Allen	47	– b Haig	6
E. Tyldesley b Allen	102	– c Durston b Robins	31
J. Iddon b Allen	0	– c Lee b Robins	43
C. Hopwood c Price b Allen	48	– not out	106
T. M. Halliday b Allen	0	– lbw b Allen	11
W. Farrimond b Allen	6	– c Robin b Haig	0
Mr P. T. Eckersley not out	8	– b Haig	0
R. Tyldesley b Allen	0	– b Durston	53
E. A. McDonald st Price b Allen	1	– c Hearne b Durston	8
G. Hodgson b Allen	0		
B 11, l-b 5, n-b 1	17	B 23, l-b 6, n-b 1	30
	241	**(9 wkts., dec.)**	**310**

Bowling: *First Innings* – Haig 29–8–48–0; Durston 10–3–17–0; Allen 25.3–10–40–10; Robins 22–1–54–0; Peebles 12–2–26–0; Hearne 8–1–28–0; Guise 5–1–11–0. *Second Innings* – Haig 28–6–70–3; Durston 10–2–16–2; Allen 28–10–65–1; Robins 31–1–93–3; Peebles 10–2–22–0; Hearne 5–0–14–0.

MIDDLESEX

H. W. Lee b Hodgson	124	– not out	105
Mr J. L. Guise b McDonald	3	– c Farrimond b Watson	19
J. W. Hearne lbw b R. Tyldesley	10	– lbw b Watson	1
W. F. Price b R. Tyldesley	3		
Mr G. O. Allen b R. Tyldesley	5	– c Halliday b Watson	29
Lord Aberdare c Farrimond b R. Tyldesley	0	– b Watson	0
Mr R. W. V. Robins b McDonald	1	– not out	12
Mr N. Haig b McDonald	40	– lbw b R. Tyldesley	1
J. Hulme hit wkt b R. Tyldesley	20		
T. J. Durston c and b McDonald	20		
Mr I. A. R. Peebles not out	0		
L-b 1, w 1	2	B 2, l-b 1	3
	228	**(5 wkts.)**	**170**

Bowling: *First Innings* – McDonald 26.2–1–108–4; Hodgson 15–0–53–1; R. Tyldesley 21–6–40–5; Hopwood 11–3–17–0; Watson 7–6–8–0. *Second Innings* – McDonald 14–1–42–0; Hodgson 3–0–22–0; R. Tyldesley 13–5–13–1; Hopwood 3–0–16–0; Watson 15–4–37–4; Iddon 10–1–37–0.

Umpires: J. Stone and L. Benwell.

Match drawn.

tively at least it was a bad one. Gubby was extremely disappointed.

The week-end when the Fifth Test side was picked was that of the Surrey-Middlesex match at the Oval wherein Gubby made his sixth and last appearance of the summer for his county. The selectors were still looking for a substitute for Larwood. Maybe if Middlesex had fielded first on a pitch with some early freshness in it and Gubby had got among the wickets his choice for England would have followed. As it was, he took the chance to play one of the best innings of his life. He went in in mid-afternoon at 106 for one, the runs having been scored rather slowly against a keen attack. Harry Lee and Gubby were together at tea with the score now 200 for one. The crowd – or at least the Surrey portion thereof – were not satisfied at the rate of progress, and there were a few Cockney witticisms flying around – which may have prompted Surrey's great captain to make a derogatory remark over tea about the slowness of the play.

Alas, for P. G. H.! Gubby was provoked to reply (sweetly no doubt) that it was the score at close of play that really mattered, not the score at tea. Whereupon he and Lee went out on a pitch now beautifully easy and took the Surrey bowling apart. In five minutes under two hours they added another 225, Gubby being caught in the covers for 155 – of which the last 40 had come in twenty minutes. Warner's pen flowed freely in praise of both batsmen. Gubby had made upwards of 100 off his own bat since tea, while Lee, whose inelegant crouching style blossomed finally into a splendid freedom, took out his bat having been in all day for 211. For Gubby the verbal exchange at tea gives this item of his repertoire of stories a special relish!

Next day the selectors nominated a first England cap for 'Nobby' Clark of Northants as opening bowler. Gubby rounded off his summer at Scarborough by making a match-saving 75 for Lord Hawke's XI against A. P. F. Chapman's MCC Australian team. He finished thirteenth in the national batting averages, but his bowling, apart from that golden day at Lord's, suffered, it seems fair to say, from lack of consistent opportunity. Haig, Walter Robins and Ian Peebles had played all summer for Middlesex and had taken a hundred wickets apiece – for three amateurs to have done so was and remains a unique achievement. If Gubby had been likewise regularly available the likelihood is that, although that particular trio would not all have reached the target, Gubby would have been chosen for England when Larwood went out of action. However, the period of apprenticeship was nearly over.

7
For England

Every follower of the game of riper years will readily remember the summer of 1930. It was anticipated with a good deal more than the usual relish since the Australians were due to be with us for only their third post-war visit. Moreover they came to get the Ashes back after Percy Chapman's team had retained them so splendidly on their own pitches two winters earlier – a state of affairs that had occurred only twice in England since the 1890s: each time Australia had gone home empty-handed. This time things were to be different – thanks to Don Bradman.

For Gubby it was to see the realization of his ambition to play for England, which had been kindled when he was narrowly and unluckily passed over the previous summer. Moreover, his debut came at Lord's in one of the most memorable of all Test Matches. He played because Harold Larwood was ruled unfit, and, when the latter recovered, the chance did not immediately recur.

His fulfilment as a Test cricketer came in the years immediately following. Nevertheless 1930 was, of course, a definite landmark, the first stage in his ascent to the England captaincy six years later. His arrangement with Debenham's was as before, his annual three-week holiday taken in days. In fact by my reckoning he took twenty working days off, spread over ten matches, excluding the Test. Gubby's first-class season began with MCC's traditional match against the Australians in mid-May, Bradman arriving at Lord's, as a result of five visits to the wicket, with an average of 185. He was already 'the Don', so named first by Charles Fry in the *Evening Standard*: 'the Don is at his Donniest to-day'! Bradman sparkled – and so did Fry.

The two opening bowlers in the running for a Test place confronted them, Gubby and Maurice Allom – who during the winter had taken four wickets in five balls including the hat-trick in the first-ever Test against New Zealand. Allom with his height, swing and life off the pitch at fast-medium pace, now playing regularly for Surrey, was a real rival to Gubby at this point, the more so after he had taken five wickets in the first innings including that of Bradman, who played an in-swinger into his stumps for a mere 66. Also a contestant in all-round terms was Stevens, who made 48 and had Bradman lbw to his googly for 4 in the second innings. Gubby, after bowling well but without success in the first innings and making only 3, was grateful that there was enough cricket on the last day of a drawn match to enable him to take four for 28.

The Australians made 285 and 213, MCC 258, and Warner was optimistic of England's chances though 'it would be folly to under-rate them'. The fact is, looking back, that English resources were probably stronger in 1930 than at any period between the wars. For the only time in history England had had two sides playing Tests simultaneously, and with much credit, in the West Indies and New Zealand the previous winter, using twenty-nine players. Yet of the twenty-one men due to be called upon against Australia only three had toured in the winter. Some of the MCC winter tourists were not Test class, certainly, but there must have been something like forty men who in 1930 were not out of place wearing the England cap. Has that been the case since, say in the mid-1950s? I would say not.

But, to return to the immediate subject, Gubby, after a rain-ruined match against Lancashire, next appeared for Middlesex against the Australians in early June, a week before the First Test, and in the first innings, in 37.1 overs, took six for 77. Down-wind he bowled pretty fast. Warner thought he was very fit, and was 'capable of sending down a ball which might bowl anyone — what George Giffen used to call a "sneezer"'. Warner recorded that Stevens missed Grimmett twice in the gully off Allen, but failed to notice that in the second innings he also dropped Bradman in the slips off Allen. Stevens's 'apology' at the end of the over was well in character: 'Why not bowl at the bloody wicket?' Whereupon Stevens induced the Don to hit over a slow yorker, and said, 'You see what I mean?' There are other versions of this encounter, and Gubby's own recollection is not precise. The badinage of the Middlesex amateurs was perhaps something of an acquired taste. In his account of the incident Ian Peebles refers to Stevens aptly enough as 'a man of matchless effrontery'. Pat Hendren made 138 in the second innings, Middlesex going down to honourable defeat by five wickets.

Came the Whitsun Bank Holiday meeting at Lord's, made notable for the scoring of two hundreds in the match by a man on each side, Tom Enthoven for Middlesex, Duleep for Sussex. Gubby could still make no runs but had five wickets, all told. England won a thrilling victory over Australia at Trent Bridge the following week-end despite the fact that, as recorded by *Wisden*, Larwood on the last day 'owing to an attack of gastritis, had to keep to his bed.' It was perhaps the doubt as to Larwood's fitness that decided Gubby to play against Northants the week-end that the team for the Second Test was chosen. He was in luck, for Middlesex fielded first, and in 25 overs he took six for 77.

The selectors duly announced thirteen players for Lord's — including both Larwood and Allen. Fender in the *Star* was not pleased, saying in effect that Allen was only effective when things were going well for him, that he had had little first-class practice, and that both Allom and Maurice Nichols, of Essex, would have been better alternatives to Larwood. Fender assumed that Larwood and Sandham would play, the latter going in with Hobbs instead of Sutcliffe, who was unfit. Those left out on the day would be Allen and Woolley. He was wrong on both counts. Woolley (who in his later years always liked going in first, though this was the only time he did so for England) partnered Hobbs while Gubby took the place of Larwood, who had not played since gastritis had laid him low ten days before and did not do so for another week. In five matches up to now Gubby had taken 22 wickets, ten of them against the Australians.

The picture of the Lord's Test of 1930, in all its excitement and splendour, remains marvellously clear in my mind at this range of time for many reasons, of which the fact that it was the first Test I was allowed to write about is only one. There was some wonderful batmanship by some of the greatest players in the history of the game. The crowd was then the largest ever to see a match in England. The sun shone hotly throughout, and although England had their backs to the wall from the beginning of the third day it was only on the fourth and last evening that Australia won their first victory in England in the last nine attempts. Never before – and only once since, at Headingley in 1948 – had either England or Australia made 800 runs in its two innings and been beaten.

For such a feast of runs the conditions had, of course, to be ideal, and so they were. The pitch was of a wonderfully benign pace, only helping the spinners as it grew brittle on the last day. The outfield was very fast, and the crowds could only be accommodated by bringing the boundary boards forward.

As I wrote in a *Daily Telegraph* sporting anthology:

The England XI, led by Percy Chapman, contained Jack Hobbs, greatest of all professional batsmen, at the age of forty-seven playing in his tenth and final series against Australia. It contained in Maurice Tate probably the finest bowler of his type ever seen. It contained two of the greatest all-round cricketers of any country or generation, Frank Woolley and Walter Hammond. It contained Duleep, whose illness at the height of his powers was soon to deprive the game of a genius. It contained two of cricket's immortal characters, 'Patsy' Hendren and George Duckworth. Not least it contained as many as five past, present or future captains of England – Percy Chapman, Jack White, 'Gubby' Allen, Walter Robins and Walter Hammond.

It was a side brimful of personality and all the virtues. Opposing it there stood a batting order that ran: Woodfull, Ponsford, Bradman, Kippax, McCabe, Richardson and including two legendary figures in Oldfield, the perfect wicket-keeper, and Grimmett, who took more wickets against England (106) than any wrist-spinner has ever done. Above all, as this match and the next were to make manifest, Australia had a genius of a new order in Bradman.

But the pen runs on whenever these heroes of my early manhood enter the stage. I must confine myself to seeing this game chiefly through the eyes of the subject of this book. Here he was, just short of his twenty-eighth birthday, playing against the land of his birth, nine years after, as a member of the Eton XI perched on top of the Tavern Clock Tower, he had first seen Warwick Armstrong's all-conquering Australians of 1921. And here was the English hero of that match, Frank Woolley, going out with Jack to open the innings. To judge by Frank's batting – 41 in the first forty minutes before he was astonishingly caught, down by his boots, by Tim Wall, who had started in the gully but was now nearer third man – there was no early juice in the pitch, nothing to suggest to Gubby he might have got something out of it if England had lost the toss. He joined Duleep in mid-afternoon at a critical moment with the board showing 236 for five, and he was soon bowled by Alan Fairfax, hitting over a yorker. However, first Maurice Tate and then, more briefly, Jack White played valuable parts in supporting Duleep, who soon after six o'clock, forcing the game on his captain's orders, was caught at very deep mid-off by Bradman off Grimmett for a superb 173: 387 for nine.

England went on next morning to take the score to 425, before Gubby bowled the first ball of the Australian innings to Woodfull. Was he nervous? 'I was so nervous I didn't know where my legs were going,' is his answer to the question. The fact is that, however well they disguise the fact, most cricketers are nervous both before and when they are first called upon in a big match. Gubby quotes his hero, Hobbs, as saying before a Test Match, four years earlier, 'I'm already nervous – and I wouldn't have anyone who didn't feel a bit edgy.'

Nor on this occasion can Gubby have been unaffected by a quite despicable article that morning by the ace sensation-monger of the day, Trevor Wignall of the *Daily Express*. Wignall, who was a sports columnist rather than a cricket reporter, had a mesmeric effect on people at this time. They were drawn by curiosity as to what outrageous story he would come up with next. He dealt in superlatives, either of praise or censure. Thus he began his offering with a chunk of sentimental adulation of Duleep. The tumultous reception after his innings was such that 'staid elderly men in the exclusive pavilion were behaving like

ENGLAND v AUSTRALIA
(Second Test)

At Lord's, 27 June–1 July 1930

ENGLAND

J. B. Hobbs c Oldfield b Fairfax	1	– b Grimmett ... 19
F. E. Woolley c Wall b Fairfax	41	– hit wkt b Grimmett ... 28
W. R. Hammond b Grimmett	38	– c Fairfax b Grimmett ... 32
K. S. Duleepsinhji c Bradman b Grimmett	173	– c Oldfield b Hornibrook ... 48
E. H. Hendren c McCabe b Fairfax	48	– c Richardson b Grimmett ... 9
*A. P. F. Chapman c Oldfield b Wall	11	– c Oldfield b Fairfax ... 121
G. O. B. Allen b Fairfax	3	– lbw b Grimmett ... 57
M. W. Tate c McCabe b Wall	54	– c Ponsford b Grimmett ... 10
R. W. V. Robins c Oldfield b Hornibrook	5	– not out ... 11
J. C. White not out	23	– run out ... 10
†G. Duckworth c Oldfield b Wall	18	– lbw b Fairfax ... 0
B 2, l-b 7, n-b 1	10	B 16, l-b 13, w 1 ... 30

1/13 2/53 3/105 4/209 5/236   425   1/45 2/58 3/129 4/141 5/147   375
6/239 7/337 8/363 9/387 10/425   6/272 7/329 8/354 9/372 10/375

Bowling: *First Innings* – Wall 29.4–2–118–3; Fairfax 31–6–101–4; Grimmett 33–4–105–2; Hornibrook 26–6–62–1; McCabe 9–1–29–0. *Second Innings* – Wall 25–2–80–0; Fairfax 12.4–2–37–2; Grimmett 53–13–167–6; Hornibrook 22–6–49–1; McCabe 3–1–11–0; Bradman 1–0–1–0.

AUSTRALIA

*W. M. Woodfull st Duckworth b Robins	155	– not out ... 26
W. H. Ponsford c Hammond b White	81	– b Robins ... 14
D. G. Bradman c Chapman b White	254	– c Chapman b Tate ... 1
A. F. Kippax b White	83	– c Duckworth b Robins ... 3
S. J. McCabe c Woolley b Hammond	44	– not out ... 25
V. Y. Richardson c Hobbs b Tate	30		
†W. A. S. Oldfield not out	43		
A. G. Fairfax not out	20		
B 6, l-b 8, w 5	19	B 1, l-b 2 ... 3

1/162 2/393 3/585   (6 wkts., dec.) 729   1/16 2/17 3/22   (3 wkts.) 72
4/588 5/643 6/672

C. V. Grimmett, P. M. Hornibrook and T. W. Wall did not bat.

Bowling: *First Innings* – Allen 34–7–115–0; Tate 64–16–148–1; White 51–7–158–3; Robins 42–1–172–1; Hammond 35–8–82–1; Woolley 6–0–35–0. *Second Innings* – Tate 13–6–21–1; White 2–0–8–0; Robins 9–1–34–2; Hammond 4.2–1–6–0.

Umpires: F. Chester and T. W. Oates.

Australia won by 7 wickets.

schoolboys', while Duleep, unsettled at first by the thunder of the ovation, finally 'ran like a hare for the pavilion': not too fast however for Wignall to notice from the press-box that 'he was trembling violently as he reached the pavilion steps, and his dark face had taken on a peculiar hue.'

The hue, however peculiar, cannot have been more so than the changing colour of Wignall's reporting for in the next paragraph after Duleep had been praised to the skies his readers were asked to believe that 'For thousands on the ground, Australians and British alike, the pleasure of the play was affected by what was described as the extraordinary action of the selection committee in including in the England team the amateur G. O. Allen, who was born in Sydney, Australia.' It was thought, he went on, that the selectors would omit him when they became aware of public feeling, and then betrayed complete ignorance by adding 'it was rumoured they were unaware that Allen was Australian-born' — something which had been universally known in the cricket world since the start of his career. 'It is a fact that if England wins with the aid of Allen a considerable amount of the gilt will be taken off the gingerbread.' I flatter the late, departed Wignall by quoting such nonsense, but his following was considerable and the article in question would not have been pasted in Gubby's cuttings-book if he had not read it.

Woodfull and Ponsford opened soberly, scoring 38 in the first hour. Gubby thought he might once have had Ponsford lbw — 'He would certainly have been out under the new law,' still then five years into the future. Gradually Australia's opening pair accelerated, and neither Gubby nor Tate, nor White, nor Robins, nor Hammond could discomfit them. They had laid the perfect foundation when King George V made his inspection of the troops in front of the pavilion. The time was three-thirty. From the first ball after this interlude Ponsford was caught at slip by Hammond off White. Enter Bradman with the board showing 162–1–81.

As is history, in the two hours, forty minutes remaining he made 155 undefeated, out of the 242 added, and that without a glimmer of a mistake, and, further, it seemed without taking the slightest risk. It was this piece of batting in the afternoon sunshine which proclaimed to all who saw it that a star of the first magnitude had arisen. Warner thought that neigher Macartney nor Hobbs could have been more nimble. 'Indeed he is the quickest batsman on his feet I have ever seen.' Plum had already watched enough to give this verdict:

> Bradman is the most wonderful batsman the cricket world has seen for many a long day, and he stands on the threshold of what, given good health, must surely be a career which will equal and probably surpass that of any other batsman.

Gubby, of course, came in for punishment, as all the England bowlers did, and continued to do after the week-end. So well, however, did Allen and Tate bowl in the first half-hour of Monday morning that Bradman and Kippax were confined to 15 runs, and in two and a half hours up to lunch only 140 runs were added, with Bradman and Kippax still together.

Afterwards they accelerated, taking their stand to 192 when Bradman, the first time he had lifted the ball in what he has always rated his finest innings, was brilliantly caught low, right-handed by Chapman at short extra-cover for 254. Kippax was a gifted, graceful batsman who was certainly not outclassed. The other four Australians who got an innings after these two went all, naturally, chased quick runs. We saw that grotesque figure '7' in the hundreds space on the score-board before Woodfull (whose 155 had been a model innings of its kind) declared at 729 for six. He left himself upwards of eight hours to win the match on a pitch that would progressively give help to spin.

The punishment suffered by the England bowlers was more than some of the popular press could take, and for the first time a degree of inverted snobbery came to the surface. With Larwood and also George Geary (with rheumatism) out of action much of the bowling in support of Tate and Hammond was in the amateur hands of White, England's leading wicket-taker in Australia the year before, Robins, whose seven wickets and 50 not out had contributed so much to England's victory in the First Test at Trent Bridge, and Allen. A certain John Marchant, 'The Great Cricket Authority' as he was described by his newspaper, the *Sunday Express*, derided this 'pitiful' attack, and sighed for the men of Lancashire, Yorkshire and Notts. After the match the Great Authority (a writer with several aliases whose real name was Harold Lake) pitched good and strong into the Selection Committee of 'Shrimp' Leveson Gower, Mann and White, suggesting that the first two scarcely saw a ball bowled away from Lord's and not even very many there. England's six victories in their last seven Tests against Australia suddenly counted for little.

It did not need the likes of Marchant, however, to steel Gubby's resolution when he went to the wicket to join his captain on the fourth and last mornign with just over an hour and a half to go before lunch, England still 167 behind and the board showing 147 for five. The formidable batting at the top of the order was all disposed of, four of the five by Grimmett, and as the last of them, Hendren, passed Gubby in the Long Room, he remarked not very helpfully that the ball was 'turning like hell'.

England's No 7 sallied forth then into the sunny arena conscious of the criticism which had greeted his selection, of an analysis of nought for 115 and of a first innings batting failure. In fact he had an unprecedented (and unrepeated) procession of low scores behind him, 49 runs, to be precise, in eight innings. As soon as he arrived Percy Chapman, before he had scored, hit Grimmett into the air on the off-side. Woodfull, Ponsford and Richardson all started for the catch and all stopped, leaving it to someone else. (This must be a classic case of the captain failing to call out the name of his choice.) In the end no one put a finger to the ball. At the end of the over Gubby said, 'That was a bit lucky.' 'Not at all,' replied Percy, 'The bat went round in my hand.' The former's explanation is the more likely

— that Chapman had not spotted the googly, which to the left-hander was, of course, the leg-break. Grimmett squeaked out, 'Never mind, get him out next over' — a prophecy that proved a long way wide of the mark.

After this marvellous piece of luck the partnership at once began to prosper with both batsmen going for their strokes, especially against Grimmett, who spun tirelessly away from the Nursery end, using the bowlers' follow-through marks and generally displaying all the tricks of the trade on a surface which after all the wear and tear had inevitably grown a little dusty. Chapman chanced his arm and trusted his eye to punish Grimmett on the leg-side while Gubby, in his more orthodox way, batted according to *Wisden* 'with marked skill and agression'. He reached his fifty just before Chapman, and they came in to lunch at 262 for five, having scored at more than a run a minute to reduce the arrears to 42. A game which had seemed almost all over was very much alive again.

The great partnership lasted only briefly after lunch before Gubby was lbw playing forward to Grimmett. LBW! The decision was made by Frank Chester, the leading umpire, and is nevertheless privately disputed by the victim who says that at the appeal Oldfield, behind the wicket, at once said, 'No, no, no.' He went on saying no, it seems, ever afterwards when they met. Anyway, there it was. Chapman continued to bat freely, hitting Grimmett for several sixes 'with the tide' into the Mound Stand until at last he was caught behind off Fairfax for 121. It was by any reckoning a heroic effort.

When Australia went in half an hour before tea to make 72 to win Hammond was used for two de-shining overs rather than Allen, along with Tate before Robins was brought on at Grimmett's end. There came the fall of three wickets for six runs, Ponsford and Kippax to Robins, Bradman beautifully caught low down in the gully by Chapman off Tate for 1. It was 22 for three, and if Duckworth had then caught Woodfull off Robins, who knows? As it was young McCabe stayed with his captain, Robins's length faltered and by five o'clock Australia had coasted to victory.

The press made some amends to Gubby on the strength of his innings. Fender thought that no 'praise could be too high for these two for their wonderful effort', while Wignall announced regarding 'the most dis-cussed and probably the most abused person in the country since last Friday' that 'it is therefore a real pleasure to me now to state that my hat was off to him for a long time yesterday afternoon.' By the end Gubby had no doubt learned quite a bit about the value or otherwise of press criticism. He could also have learned, if he had needed to, the way to accept defeat in Test cricket. For after the match Chapman said, 'It has been a great match, and I think that the people who came each day to see it must have been well rewarded by the fine struggle they saw. Australia fully deserved their victory, for they played splendid cricket at every point.' Woodfull's comment was equally congratulatory and generous. Those were courteous days.

So much for the Test except for what might be described as a dressing-room joke that went slightly wrong. During the match Haig wired Robins telling him to 'pinch caps' for X, Y, and Z – being Middlesex and England cricketers whose caps had presumably grown old – for instance that of Haig, whose one home Test had been nine years earlier. There were, as usual, a box of new caps available in the dressing-room, and Robins did his county captain's bidding and slipped two or three into his bag. But Hobbs, renowned as a practical joker, observed what was afoot, and promptly put every new cap on sight into Walter's bag. He then alerted Frank Woolley to ask Leveson Gower for one. Seeing they had all disappeared, Leveson Gower, not pleased, made enquiries from which it was let slip that young Robins might know something about it. 'Shrimp' demanded that he open his bag, which he at first refused to do. When at length he was obliged to, there were the lot. The chairman of selectors was furious, and, though England's greatest batsman subsequently 'owned up', the damage had been done. Thus do those taking part in great matches sometimes relax!

It is a moot point whether these pleasantries took place before or after the matter of Robins's running-out of White when time meant everything towards the end of the England second innings. Robins hit the ball straight to mid-off where Bradman's swift throw beat White easily to the striker's end. Unwisely Leveson Gower remarked when Robins returned at the end of the innings that that hadn't been a very clever thing to do. This was too much for the red-haired, quick-tempered Robins to take, and he replied, as they say, in the vernacular. No one in the side was surprised that he was not chosen for the next Test at Headingley: nor, quite incidentally, was Leveson Gower again named as a selector.

In the post-mortems following this extraordinary Test Match some critics felt that if the remaining English batsmen after Gubby's dismissal – including Chapman himself – had shown a shade more restraint, and kept their eyes more steadfastly on the clock, they might have salvaged a draw. However that might be, once Australia had levelled the rubber they were always the likelier winners, if only because Bradman found the English pitches so greatly to his liking, and the supporting Australian batting was only ever less than fully adequate to the situation once, when the ball was turning on the first day of the Fourth Test at Old Trafford.

Without at all wishing to make excuses for his own failure with the ball at Lord's, Gubby certainly makes a valid point when he says:

1930 was the first year of four-day Tests in England, and the groundsmen, fearing their pitches might not last, over-prepared them with the result that they were all very easy-paced and gave no help whatever to the fast and seam bowlers. As to the Lord's pitch, it was the easiest-paced I encountered at Lord's in that era. Support for this belief is the complete dominance of the bat in that match, and the lack of success of the fast bowlers in the series.

The fact is that Tim Wall, of Australia, took thirteen Test wickets at 45 a time while Larwood in his three Tests had four for 292 – an average of 73 runs each.

Gubby played in the Lord's Gentlemen and Players which directly followed the drawn Third Test – the one wherein the insatiable Bradman made 309 in the day and England were ultimately saved by rain. The faster bowlers who played at Lord's, five of them, took two wickets in all, the four wrist-spinners by contrast twenty-two. This was Peebles's great year – he had eight of the Players to fall. Despite his year as an undergraduate the team photograph shows him very much the unsophisticated young Scot from the manse. Larwood took no wickets and neither did Gubby who, however, sent in first, helped Wyatt put on 55 in the first innings, and, going in lower in the second, made 40 not out, helping Duleep to reach his second hundred in a match much interfered with by the weather. The brothers Lyon, M. D. and B. H., were the only men in two powerful sides who had not played Test cricket.

Gubby used up the remainder of his ration of days playing three times for Middlesex, bowling fast and successfully – eighteen wickets in four innings – but making no runs. The matches against Surrey and Kent at Lord's were lost by an innings – at the end of the season Middlesex found themselves last but one in the Championship, something that had never happened before and was due to happen only once again. However there was some extraordinary cricket at Hove on a difficult pitch, Gubby bowling very fast, helped by a strong wind off the sea, to the drier end while Peebles used the other, sticky end to wreak equal havoc. The result was that Sussex were bowled out in an hour and twenty minutes for 72 and poor Maurice Tate's Benefit was over in two days. Subscriptions and takings at the gate formed the larger part of the Benefit in those days. One can therefore imagine a philosophical Tate aside or two, confidentially delivered with his hand to his mouth, but the grin which, along with outsize boots, was his trade-mark would not have been subdued for long.

Lastly Gubby went up to his favourite Scarborough and at last got top score of 77 for Lord Hawke's XI against the MCC side due shortly to sail for South Africa. He, by the way, was not considered for this tour though he had had to say no when asked about his availability for MCC's visit to South Africa three years earlier. In those happy days of Union under the Crown, when all races lived at peace, Gubby would assuredly have enjoyed South Africa, though whether he would have fared any better than other fast bowlers on the matting pitches on which all cricket was then played is open to question.

After Scarborough Gubby had another 'best man' duty to perform, this time at the marriage of his soldier brother Geoffrey, now promoted captain. It was a military wedding, the bride, Ruth Elaine Felicity Freeth, being the daughter of Major-General G. H. B. Freeth, the deputy adjutant-general at GHQ India. Geoff Allen, resplendent in the full dress uniform of the Royal Fusiliers, in the wedding photographs bears a strong resemblance to Gubby. After his honeymoon he returned with his bride to service in India. It was a continuing regret to the Allens that there elder son and brother was out of reach for years at a time.

In the winter Gubby became increasingly caught up in the then newish vogue of squash racquets. The West End clubs had been putting up courts in the 1920s, the rich built them at their country houses, and they were becoming popular in the schools and universities. Oxford and Cambridge had begun playing one another in 1925, and soon decided that participation was worth a half-blue. Even ocean liners had them. Squash appealed as a singularly quick means of keeping fit and also for the likes of Gubby helped to fulfil the competitive urge of the players of other games, especially cricket.

In 1930–31 Gubby entered for the Amateur Squash Championship held at the Bath Club under the auspices of the newly-formed Squash Racquets Association. The holder was the well-known parliamentarian, Victor Cazalet, who was to die a mysterious death in the war in the aeroplane that went down with the great Polish leader, General Sikorski. The entry was stiff with cricketers, but there was an Egyptian who was highly regarded by Gerry Weigall, of Cambridge and Kent, the well-known pundit who wrote on the game for the *Evening Standard*. Among those who had not entered previously was G. O. Allen who 'sets a good pace and is very fast about the court', etc.

Gubby won 'the most exciting match of the morning' in the first round after being two sets down and within a point of losing at 8–5 to P. D. Lindsay. In the second round he beat B. Stone, of the Eton Manor Club in the East End, and lost honourably in the third to a well-known player, P. Q. Reiss. Now here is an oddity: Stone is mentioned as one of two entrants from Eton Manor in whom D. R. Jardine had taken a great interest. That Douglas Jardine was concerned with an East End boys' club is less strange than that he should be identified with an Eton institution. The *Morning Post* correspondent notes that these young men from another world 'impressed by the spirit in which they played'. What impressed everyone even more was the genius of the Egyptian, F. D. Amr Bey, who was serving in his country's embassy in London. Amr Bey won this championship, and then the Open four times before in 1938 he retired, never having been beaten. His artistry transformed the game.

Gubby represented the Conservative Club in the Bath Club Cup and became a hard man to beat. In the second and last Championship in which he played, in the winter of 1931–32, he was beaten by W. D. Macpherson, one of the leading lights, who duly lost in the final to Amr Bey.

In the winter Gubby turned his hand to whatever came his way. He had already played cricket for Cavendish, alias Debenham's. Now, representing Cavendish in the winter lawn tennis tournament of the London Business Houses he and R. W. Ware won the doubles against a pair who were the pride of a club known as Gas Light West. His name appeared also, with that of his sister, Pat, in the more socially exalted pages of *The Tatler*.

Gubby's cricket in 1931 was due again to be rationed by business and to follow a similar pattern to that of 1930 – and indeed did so except that he took part not in one Test but in all the three played against New Zealand. Likewise also he owed his place for England in the first instance to the unfitness of Harold Larwood. He began with Hendren's Benefit at Whitsuntide and the Middlesex match against the New Zealanders, and had a large part in two notable victories. His five wickets against Sussex including getting Duleep for nought and seven, following the latter's two and eight against him at Hove the previous summer. All four dismissals were by slip catches. Duleep, of course, made big scores against Gubby at other times, but the latter always regarded him as slightly fallible at first against speed. Gubby helped turn the game by making 75 not out in the Middlesex first innings and staying while the uniquely popular beneficiary signalized the occasion by making a hundred.

The New Zealand match was hard-fought and won for Middlesex by Allen and Peebles, who had the following figures: Allen 52–22–106–7, Peebles 51.2–8–128–8. Gubby's 58 in the first innings was also (according to Warner) 'the innings of the day'. Against Lancashire and Yorkshire his performances were respectable but not spectacular, and up in the north Larwood was in great shape. Kent, faced by his 'tremendously fast bowling', crumpled for 119 and 106 (Larwood nine for 41 and two for 28). Duly chosen for England during that match, Larwood next, at Worcester, took nine more wickets but on the Thursday evening strained his left ankle and cried off the Test Match at Lord's starting two days later.

Gubby had thought he had a chance of being chosen as an all-rounder and to share the new ball with Larwood, and when the latter's young bowling partner, Bill Voce, was named instead he assuaged his disappointment by 'hitting it up a bit'. At the height of the London season it was a deb dance or two and consequent late nights. Suddenly on the Thursday evening came a telephone call from the selectors and he was in! In a hurry he did what training he could, and at half-past eleven on the Saturday was taking the field behind England's new captain – a certain Douglas Jardine. Neither Allen nor Voce made much initial impact on the batsmen, and when at lunch England came in with the score 132 for two Ian Peebles was asking Gubby how on earth the selectors had come to pick this chap, Ames. Les had had something of a nightmare morning and although he recovered later he always claimed that Lord's was one of the most difficult grounds to keep wicket on. The spinners, Peebles and Robins, took fourteen of the wickets between them in the two innings; Voce took nought for 100 and Gubby three – all top batsmen and all clean bowled, for 92 in 40 overs.

But he had a more momentous performance in store in England's first innings. Hobbs having retired from Test cricket after the Australian series of 1930, and Sutcliffe's fitness being in doubt, the selectors named an experimental opening pair in Arnold of Hampshire and Bakewell of Northants, aged respectably twenty-three and twenty-two. Hammond and Duleep were due at Nos 3 and 4, after which the captain announced: 'Woolley, you will bat No 5 and I at No 6. If however there is a crisis I shall go in at 5, and you will follow me.' I tell this bit of dresssing-room gossip because it is well-substantiated – I have heard it from at least three of the England team in addition to Frank himself – and because it exemplifies Jardine's lofty dealing with the professionals, even those of the stature and experience of Woolley. At various times in the match he called Arnold Bakewell and vice-versa but no one cared to correct him.

Jardine had a sardonic wit, but he was unlikely to choose Test cricket as a vehicle for it. There *was* a crisis, thanks to some admirable fast bowling by Ian Cromb, and he accordingly stalked in at No 5, Woolley shortly following. The captain contributed 38, while Woolley, going in where he used to bat in his all-round days on either side of the First World War, batted eighty minutes for 80! However a few minutes before the close Woolley became the sixth man out for 188 in response to New Zealand's 224, and Peebles was selected for the night-watchman's job, Allen being saved for the second day. Ian was successful in preventing Gubby from going in, but raised the mirth of the rest of the team and the irritation of Jardine by promptly getting himself stumped, bang on six thirty.

The New Zealanders had emerged from their first Test day in England with much credit, and the scoring of 414 runs for the fall of seventeen

ENGLAND v NEW ZEALAND
(First Test)

At Lord's, 27–30 June 1931

NEW ZEALAND

C. S. Dempster lbw b Peebles	53	– b Hammond	120
J. E. Mills b Peebles	34	– b Allen	0
G. L. Weir lbw b Peebles	37	– b Allen	40
J. L. Kerr st Ames b Robins	2	– (6) lbw b Peebles	0
R. C. Blunt c Hammond b Robins	7	– b Robins	96
M. L. Page b Allen	23	– (4) c and b Peebles	104
*T. C. Lowry c Hammond b Robins	1	– (9) b Peebles	34
I. B. Cromb c Ames b Peebles	20	– (7) c Voce b Robins	14
C. F. W. Allcott c Hammond b Peebles	13	– (10) not out	20
W. E. Merritt c Jardine b Hammond	17	– (8) b Peebles	5
†K. C. James not out	1		
B 2, l-b 12, w 1, n-b 1	16	B 23, l-b 10, w 1, n-b 1	36

1/58 2/130 3/136 4/140 5/153   224   1/1 2/100 3/218   (9 wkts., dec.) 469
6/161 7/190 8/191 9/209 10/224   4/360 5/360 6/389 7/404 8/406 9/469

Bowling: *First Innings* – Voce 10–1–40–0; Allen 15–2–45–1; Hammond 10.1–5–8–1; Peebles 26–3–77–5; Robins 13–3–38–3. *Second Innings* – Voce 32–11–60–0; Allen 25–8–47–2; Hammond 21–2–50–1; Peebles 42.4–6–150–4; Robins 37–5–126–2.

ENGLAND

J. Arnold c Page b Cromb	0	– c and b Blunt	34
A. H. Bakewell lbw b Cromb	9	– c Blunt b Cromb	27
W. R. Hammond b Cromb	7	– run out	46
K. S. Duleepsinhji c Kerr b Merritt	25	– c James b Allcott	11
*D. R. Jardine c Blunt b Merritt	38	– (7) not out	0
F. E. Woolley lbw b Merritt	80	– (5) b Cromb	9
†L. E. G. Ames c James b Weir	137	– (6) not out	17
I. A. R. Peebles st James b Merritt	0		
G. O. B. Allen c Lowry b Weir	122		
R. W. V. Robins c Lowry b Weir	12		
W. Voce not out	1		
B 15, l-b 8	23	L-b 2	2

1/5 2/14 3/31 4/62 5/129   454   1/62 2/62   (5 wkts.) 146
6/188 7/190 8/436 9/447 10/454   3/94 4/105 5/144

Bowling: *First Innings* – Cromb 37–7–113–3; Weir 8–1–38–3; Blunt 46–9–124–0; Allcott 17–3–34–0; Merritt 23–2–104–4; Page 3–0–18–0. *Second Innings* – Cromb 25–5–44–2; Weir 5–1–18–0; Blunt 14–5–54–1; Allcott 10–2–26–1; Merritt 1–0–2–0.

Umpires: F. Chester and J. Hardstaff, sr.

Match drawn.

wickets had given excellent value to a crowd of 25,000. On the Monday came as big a crowd and also the King, to whom the teams were presented in front of the pavilion. In those days this was still an agreeable novelty. Gubby went out to bat at eleven o'clock in company with Les Ames (15 not out) who asked him en route, 'What do you know about Merritt?' (The New Zealanders' wrist-spinner had already taken three good wickets, as well as that of Peebles.) Gubby's reply was, 'Well, I hear he doesn't like the tap.' Les duly took note.

Few batsmen were as quick on their feet as Ames, and his partner was

never averse from leaving his ground. Between them they chased New
Zealand's leading wicket-taker, and generally bustled their attack. In the
two and a half hours of the morning they added 195, Gubby being only
two short of a hundred before lunch, Ames 106. The latter had given two
chances. In the end the eighth wicket stand was worth 246, Ames 137,
Allen 122 – which is a record still for the eighth wicket in Test cricket.
England's lead, after all, was 230. By the close Gubby had taken the only
two wickets to fall, and in the evening celebrated appropriately by seeing
La Bohème with a party given by David Brand's mother, Lady Hampden,
who, being a Lady-in-Waiting, was able to entertain her guests in the
Royal Box: with two of the greatest artists, Elizabeth Schumann and
Gigli, in the lead parts it was altogether quite a day. Gubby was
appreciative of opera and good music.

New Zealand's premier batsman, C. S. Dempster, was however in the
first stages of a match-saving hundred. They declared their second
innings at 469 for nine, and a high-scoring game was comfortably drawn.
As a consequence of their good showing New Zealand, who had been
accorded only this one Test Match, were promptly rewarded with two
more.

The match produced a *Times* leader which referred to the Ames–Allen
stand as 'a masterly display of fearless and aggressive batting', and
bestowed equal praise on Dempster and M. L. Page, both of whom made
hundreds, and Roger Blunt, who fell for 96.

Those who think that modern first-class cricketers are worked to death
may be interested to know that in four and a half months the New
Zealanders had only two three-day periods of rest, that they travelled
only fourteen strong, Tom Lowry doubling up as captain-manager (until
relieved of managerial duties near the end by the president of the N.Z.
Cricket Council) and a bowler, C. F. W. Allcott, acting as the treasurer.

Walter Robins was the central figure, as at Lord's the year before, of a
dressing-room item which might be taken as an indication of how the
wind was blowing: during the lengthy eighth wicket stand Robins
amused himself with what his captain would certainly have considered
fourth-form humour by making remarks on the identity of the last man
out and the 0 under his name on the board. Who was he? How did he get
out? After putting up with a bit of this, Jardine said he wnated a word
with Robins on the balcony, whereupon they went outside and Jardine
delivered a homily on the folly of undermining a young cricketer's
confidence. 'Supposing I want him to go in overnight in a Test in
Australia this sort of thing won't do his morale any good.' Unfortunately
Jardine stood on the balcony with his back to the room while Robins,
facing him, was looking inwards, and so could not avoid the facetious
gestures made towards him by some of the team inside. Walter, trying

hard to keep a straight face, went on to the offensive and said how did he know he was going to be captain in Australia anyway. A ridiculous scene altogether!

But next in the story is a much more disagreeable encounter. The Notts captain, Arthur Carr, was, naturally enough, a fierce advocate of the fast bowler whom he had encouraged and looked after in his own robust fashion since in his teens he had come to Trent Bridge from the colliery village of Nuncargate. In the evenings after play Carr was inclined to introduce to the pleasures of the town both Larwood and his younger bowling partner, also from a mining background, Bill Voce.

After the First Test Carr in a newspaper article attacked the selectors (of whom he had been one only a year or two earlier) for choosing Gubby as a fast bowler both against Australia in 1930 and now against New Zealand. 'It was ludicrous. Why, Allen is not a fast bowler: in fact he is not a good bowler at all.' Acknowledging his success with the bat, Carr maintained that that was not the point since he had been picked as a bowler. Carr said that the selectors would have to be changed if England were to recover the Ashes in Australia. Soon after this provocative article appeared Larwood, in company with Sam Staples and George Gunn's son, G. V., were all so injured in a motor accident that they were unfit to take their places in the Notts team.

Gubby had not played a first-class match for three weeks after the First Test, but with Larwood out of action and he therefore an obvious all-round candidate for the Second Test he went up with Middlesex to Worcester a week before the Test to help get himself into shape. Out of the Middlesex first innings of 391 he made 38, and when Worcestershire answered with 236 he in 18 overs took six for 38, bowling, according to the agency report, 'at a great pace'. A spoof wire addressed to Gubby and generally credited to George Newman, a Middlesex player not engaged in the match, went the round of the dressing-room and caused some mirth: 'Regret six for 38 not good enough — Warner'. (Plum was chairman of selectors.)

Carr, however, engaged simultaneously in an extraordinary game at Edgbaston which consisted of Warwickshire declaring at 511 for three (Carr with the new ball, in the absence of Larwood, taking nought for 71) and Notts replying with 521 for seven, was not in mirthful mood, the less so after learning the news from Worcester. On the third day he left his sterile match, motored the few miles to Worcester and arrived in the Middlesex dressing-room on the afternoon having 'had a few' and plainly looking for trouble. The thought that Gubby had by now been picked again for England was too much for him. 'Suppose you think you're better than Larwood,' and similar pleasantries filled the air. The Notts fast bowlers had already in 1931 been bowling fast and short on

occasions, at the instigation of their captain, which was why Gubby was
goaded into replying to the effect that if he encouraged his bowlers to go
on bowling in that way Carr would do the game a great disservice. He
naturally recalls the remark in the light of history.

Gubby's choice for England was questioned by some more moderate
pens than that of Carr. However, as usual, he had the last laugh. He had
not been required to bat in the Second Test at the Oval when England
declared at 416 for four, whereupon Jardine opened his attack, on a pitch
hard on top but soft underneath with Tate and Freddy Brown, a twenty-
year-old playing in his first Test. Verity and Peebles had also been given a
bowl before, at 41 for no wicket, Allen was called upon. He soon bowled
out both opening batsmen, had three others caught by the wicket-keeper
and in a total of 193 came out with the following conclusive figures: 13–
7–14–5. Tom Lowry batted gallantly, but his side were required to
follow on, and were beaten by an innings. Carr's comments are
unrecorded, but for *The Times* correspondent (following the sudden
death of A. C. M. Croome in August 1930 this now – though, of course,
his work remained unsigned – was R. B. Vincent), Allen was 'the
undisputed hero of the day'. Gubby as usual answered criticism with
performance – and, also as usual, in an unexpected way.

For the last Test, at Old Trafford, Larwood, having recovered, was due
to open the bowling with Gubby. The comparison would have been of
obvious interest, but as it happened neither got on to the field. The
Manchester weather had been at its worst for days, and it was a great
surprise, especially to the New Zealanders, when just after three o'clock
on the last day the umpires decided that the game should start. Lowry
and his team had been drowning their sorrows, confident they would not
be called upon. When therefore Lowry won the toss he invited England
to bat, and asked Jardine not to declare as he doubted his batsmen's
ability to do themselves justice. The pointless exercise ended with the
board showing England 224 for three, Sutcliffe 109 not out. Poor Jardine
was barracked for not giving New Zealand a token innings.

Gubby remembers his fourth Test best for the fact of his meeting
the great jazz singer, Sophie Tucker, through R. H. Gillespie, the
impresario who controlled the theatre chain known as Moss Empires.
'R. H.' was a cricketer and a great friend of cricketers and he had
dined well before telling Gubby and Tom Webster, the cartoonist, that
they must come round to the Hippodrome and hear and meet her.
Installed in a box, 'R. H.' had a hard job keeping awake and at times
dropped into a noisy slumber. Round they went at the end to the
star's dressing-room, the impresario, now fully awake, going through
the conventional routine:

'Soph darling, you were simply marvellous.'

ENGLAND v NEW ZEALAND
(Second Test)

At the Oval, 29–31 July 1931

ENGLAND

H. Sutcliffe st James b Vivian..............117
A. H. Bakewell run out..................... 40
K. S. Duleepsinhji c Weir b Allcot.........109
W. R. Hammond not out...................100
†L. E. G. Ames c James b Vivian.......... 41
*D. R. Jardine not out..................... 7
    B 1, l-b 1 2

1/84 2/262   (4 wkts., dec.) 416
3/271 4/401

F. R. Brown, G. O. B. Allen, M. W. Tate, I. A. R. Peebles and H. Verity did not bat.

Bowling: Cromb 30–5–97–0; Allcott 44–7–108–1; Vivian 34.3–8–96–2; Weir 10–1–36–0; Merritt 12–0–75–0; Blunt 1–0–2–0.

NEW ZEALAND

J. E. Mills b Allen	27 – b Brown...........................	30
G. L. Weir b Allen	13 – b Peebles.......................	6
R. C. Blunt c Ames b Allen	2 – (4) b Peebles......................	43
M. L. Page c Peebles b Tate................	12 – (3) b Tate...........................	3
H. G. Vivian c Ames b Allen..............	3 – c Brown b Peebles...........	51
*T. C. Lowry c Jardine b Brown	62 – c Duleepsinhji b Peebles.........	0
J. L. Kerr c Ames b Allen	34 – b Tate...............................	28
†K. C. James lbw b Brown.................	4 – c Peebles b Verity................	10
I. B. Cromb c Hammond b Verity........	8 – not out	3
W. E. Merritt c Hammond b Verity.......	8 – lbw b Tate........................	4
C. F. W. Allcott not out.....................	5 – c Allen b Verity	1
B 2, l-b 9, n-b 4 15	B 6, l-b 10, n-b 2	18

1/42 2/44 3/45 4/53 5/92   193 1/19 2/38 3/51 4/139 5/143   197
6/157 7/167 8/168 9/188 10/193   6/162 7/189 8/189 9/196 10/197

Bowling: *First Innings* – Tate 18–9–15–1; Brown 29–12–52–2; Verity 22.1–8–52–2; Peebles 12–3–35–0; Allen 13–7–14–5; Hammond 1–0–10–0. *Second Innings* – Tate 21–6–22–3; Brown 16–6–38–1; Verity 12.3–4–33–2; Peebles 22–4–63–4; Allen 13–4–23–0.

Umpires: F. Chester and J. Hardstaff, sr.

England won by an innings and 26 runs.

'You great big bum,' was the lady's reply, 'I heard you snoring up there.' The damp 1931 summer ended for Gubby at Scarborough with a Gentlemen and Players ruined by rain and the last game of the New Zealanders' arduous tour against H. D. G. Leveson-Gower's XI. The latter was of almost Test strength, and Lowry's side did well to come out with a draw after being 200 behind on first innings. Larwood, who despite his mishaps headed the English averages with 129 wickets in twenty-five matches at twelve apiece, broke down after four overs. Gubby bowled forty-three in the two innings, and took five for 105. Over the season he took forty wickets in twelve matches at 18 runs each.

Until I began to research into the years on either side of 1930 for the

purpose of this book I had forgotten what in the eyes of the press was the
continuing comparison between these two. It could never be claimed for
Gubby that he was Harold's equal as a bowler – whether he might have
been if he had played regularly the summer through can only be
conjectured. Each had a perfect acion. At their respective peaks Larwood
was the faster, but not by very much. He was certainly the more accurate.
When the conditions were right for swing Gubby moved the ball more
consistently, mostly away from the bat. Harold had the deadlier break-
back. Between the wars Larwood was undoubtedly the best fast bowler
in county cricket. The legend that he was a great bowler in Test cricket
does not however stand up to analysis, apart from his outstanding
success in the Bodyline series, which we will examine in due course. At
this moment, at the conclusion of the 1931 season, he had taken 45
wickets in sixteen Tests at 35 runs each. The most he took in a home Test
rubber was nine. When Gubby's greater worth as a batsman is noted, and
also that he was at least as good in the field, there was not much in it in
terms of all-round value.

Scarborough over, Gubby returned for a winter as before: Debenham's
five and a half days a week; the social life, in London during the week
and often in the country at week-ends; squash and a little golf. In the
New Year of 1932 the headline 'Gallant Airman Engaged' told of the
betrothal of Gubby's sister, Pat, to Squadron-Leader William Forster
Dickson, DSO, AFC. At the end of the war 'Dickie' Dickson had won his
DSO before his twentieth birthday, according to the citation for 'great
skill and gallantry on the occasion of a long-distance bombing raid. He
succeeded in dropping bombs on an airship station from a low altitude
with destructive effect, and although subjected to severe fire from the
enemy obtained valuable information.' They were married in the
autumn, and, as has been mentioned, the bridegroom rose to the topmost
peak of his profession.

Of rather more interest and value was an agency message from
Melbourne entitled 'G. O. Allen's Pace' followed by a second heading,
'Bradman thinks he is faster than any Australian Bowler'. The Don
considered that Larwood should be the first bowler picked, that he could
not imagine an English side without Tate, whose nearest rival was Allom.
While Freeman was a wonderful bowler in England he thought he would
find it very difficult to get into the side for Australia that was due in the
autumn.

It scarcely needs saying that at least from the moment of his being
chosen for England in 1930 Gubby's overriding ambition was to visit the
land of his birth with an MCC team, and in 1932 he achieved what he
intended despite playing less first-class cricket than in any season
hitherto, except when he was in France in 1928. Apart from the

Whitsuntide match for Jack Hearne's benefit in which only one day's play was possible he did not play the second of only four matches for Middlesex until early June when he helped in a substantial victory over Lancashire by taking seven for 78. The last of these wickets did not take much getting since Gubby recalls just the sort of remark that might well stick in the memory: George Duckworth bustled in, saying, 'Bowl me a straight one – we want to catch the six o'clock.'

Since India on their first official visit were only accorded one Test Match, two Test Trials were played, the first at Old Trafford. The South, led by Jardine, required the North to follow on, and had much the better of the draw, but Gubby did not greatly distinguish himself though his three wickets were three more than Larwood took for the North. The game began, as I well remember, with an almost casual assault by Frank Woolley on Larwood and Voce. Woolley's choice, at the age of forty-five, as opening bat was perhaps just about as strange as that Jardine should have sent Gubby in with him. After all, Frank had been left out of Chapman's 1928–29 side to Australia four years earlier despite having in 1928 scored a matter of 3,352 runs, a total then ever exceeded only by Tom Hayward in 1906. Gubby soon fell to Voce, but it must have tickled Frank's whimsical humour to make 50 out of 73 in less than an hour before hitting a slow full-pitch into the hands of Larwood, now running about at long-on. In Australia later Jardine told Allen that it had been under consideration to try him at No 1, presumably then using him as a change bowler.

For the Test against India the selectors ignored both Larwood and Allen, giving a first cap to Bowes in harness with Voce. The two Bills took eleven of the wickets between them, and in so doing no doubt greatly helped their cause. While the Test was in progress at Lord's Gubby was opening the Middlesex innings, no doubt at the instigation of chairman of selectors Warner, at Sheffield. He made a steady 57 and 15, took three wickets in Yorkshire's only innings, and got a good press.

Gubby points to three matches which, above all others, stabilized his reputation as a cricketer. The first was the 1931 Test at Lord's; next came Gentlemen v Players 1932; and lastly the Melbourne Test of 1932–33. We come now to the second of these. There was a special significance to the occasion since the team for Australia was due shortly to be picked. Hence the presence of Hobbs who, though he had retired from Test cricket, still provided for all types of bowler the crucial examination. The bald story is of the Players being bowled out for 301, to which the Gentlemen replied with 430 for eight declared. Hobbs then saved the game for his side by carrying his bat for 161 out of 320. Gubby had five for 71 in the first innings, three for 97 in the second. His eight wickets were those of Hobbs, Woolley, Hammond (twice), Hendren, Paynter,

Larwood and Duckworth. He bowled sixty-three overs, more than anyone else, and for speed, accuracy and stamina earned fulsome encomia from all. He got Larwood for a duck, and Larwood returned the compliment. Larwood's four wickets for 54 were taken with the third new ball when there were already 400-odd runs on the board.

This was the match wherein both the Indians, Duleep and the Nawab

GENTLEMEN v PLAYERS

At Lord's, 13–15 July 1932

THE PLAYERS

*J. B. Hobbs b Allen	24	– not out	161
H. Sutcliffe c Allen b Wyatt	16	– lbw b Brown	22
F. E. Woolley c Hazlerigg b Peebles	18	– lbw b Allen	31
W. R. Hammond c Peebles b Allen	110	– b Allen	5
E. Hendren b Allom	10	– c Levett b Allen	14
E. Paynter b Allen	45	– b Wyatt	13
H. Larwood c Levett b Allen	0	– run out	9
M. W. Tate b Allom	3	– run out	0
W. Voce not out	26	– c Wyatt b Peebles	27
†G. Duckworth c Allom b Allen	4	– st Levett b Hazlerigg	16
A. P Freeman b Wyatt	31	– lbw b Hazlerigg	0
B 2, l-b 8, w 1, n-b 3	14	B 10, l-b 11, n-b 1	22
	301		320

Bowling: *First Innings* – Allen 31–9–71–5; Allom 31–5–93–2; Brown 17–3–57–0; Peebles 10–1–47–1; Wyatt 7.3–1–19–2. *Second Innings* – Allen 32–4–97–3; Allom 22–7–40–0; Brown 18–2–56–1; Peebles 13–1–63–1; Wyatt 12–4–25–1; Hazlerigg 3.5–0–17–2.

THE GENTLEMEN

A. G. Hazlerigg c Larwood b Freeman	29
R. E. S. Wyatt c Hammond b Tate	5
K. S. Duleepsinhji c Tate b Voce	132
Nawab of Pataudi c and b Woolley	165
*D. R. Jardine c Hammond b Larwood	64
A. P. F. Chapman b Larwood	11
G. O. Allen b Larwood	0
F. R. Brown b Larwood	5
M. J. C. Allom not out	1
†W. H. V. Levett not out	1
B 7, l-b 8, n-b 2	17
(8 wkts., dec.)	430

I. A. R. Peebles did not bat.

Bowling: Larwood 25–6–54–4; Tate 30–9–72–1; Voce 31–4–84–1; Freeman 25–1–111–1; Hammond 11–2–34–0; Paynter 4–1–10–0; Woolley 6–0–48–1.

Umpires: A. Morton and J. Hardstaff, sr.

Match drawn.

of Pataudi, made 132 and 164 respectively, putting on 161 together, after which 'the Noob' and Jardine added 160. Somehow it did not seem, in 1932, more than a mild talking-point that Duleep and Pataudi should be identified with English cricket while their fellow-countrymen were striving to establish themselves on the Test scene. Certainly Duleep asked not to be considered for the England XI in the Test Match. Both however accepted MCC's invitation to go to Australia, although Duleep was obliged to withdraw when his health broke down in August.

The Players were full of quality, and in their first innings a hundred by Hammond was as masterly as that of Hobbs in the second. Nevertheless Plum Warner thought this Gentlemen's side (of whom only Arthur (now Lord) Hazlerigg, the current Cambridge captain, was not a Test crick-eter) was good enough to win what would have been their first victory since 1914. They were thwarted by a superb second innings by Hobbs, but Warner and Howard Marshall (writing about cricket as well as rugby football in those days for the *Daily Telegraph*) mentioned that the Players would surely have been beaten if the Master had not been missed in the slips off Allen when the Players were only 34 runs ahead and none but the bowlers remained to be got out. The *Times* correspondent shed a tear for Percy Chapman, who had adorned the match since his freshman year at Cambridge twelve years before, and was now doing so for the last time. Alas, his magic was failing fast.

After this performance Gubby was presumably in clover with the selectors. However he had only seven Debenham holiday days left and a fortnight later a second Trial Match was due to be played in Cardiff, after which most of the party for Australia would be picked. He was chosen for the England side to open the bowling with Voce, Larwood being named for the Rest along with Ken Farnes. Gubby was not wholly sure a suspect muscle would stand the strain but was naturally loath at this stage to withdraw. The weather forecast was gloomy, for once in his life he took a chance on his fitness and accepted the invitation. As I well recall, there was only half a day's play in all and Gubby was not even called upon to step on to the field. The day after the match he was one of the seven announced in addition to the six already named, Jardine (captain), Ames, Duckworth, Duleep, Hammond and Sutcliffe. The seven were Allen, Brown, Larwood, Pataudi, Robins, Voce and Wyatt.

The letters and messages came in thick and fast, Gubby's friends noticing it as a good augury that the news came through on 31 July, his thirtieth birthday. Jack Hulbert, a Cambridge contemporary, and Cicely Courtneidge wired from Berlin where they were filming. Cables came from uncles and cousins in Australia, including the old Test cricketer, Reggie Allen, now both breeding and racing horses from his stud at South Wambo on the Hunter River.

From the thirteen above two splendid cricketers had to withdraw, Duleep because he had broken down with a recurrence of the tuberculo-sis which in fact prevented his ever playing again, and Walter Robins for 'personal reasons' which really meant business necessity. The team was completed, as it was thought, by the addition of Leyland, Mitchell (of Derbyshire), Paynter, Verity and Tate, but was finally brought to an unwieldy seventeen by the late choice of Bowes.

Gubby played no first-class cricket in August, feeling a prior duty to his employers. His absence fuelled the criticism which in some quarters had greeted his selection. However he was not without supporters in the press, and the following extract from the *Evening Standard* (written by me) is to be found among his cuttings:

At the beginning of the season few people would have rated very highly the chances of G. O. Allen. At Lord's in 1930 he seemed to have neither the pace, accuracy or stamina for an International fast bowler, and his selection was not even completely redeemed by his epic stand in the second innings with Chapman. This year, however, has seen a big change. At Manchester in the Trial Allen bowled as fast as Larwood and with great persistence. For the Gentlemen at Lord's he showed real stamina, keeping up his pace for nearly three hours between the start and the tea interval on the third day. With Larwood's complete soundness always open to question, it was essential to send another fast bowler, and Allen's all-round qualifications were undeniable.

8

The Bodyline Tour

The regular reader of cricket books may well be wondering at this point whether there is really much more still to be written on this most dramatic and over-publicized of subjects. To them I would say that this chapter contains hitherto unpublished material in the shape of extracts from the regular weekly letters that Gubby Allen wrote to his parents at the time. There is also a novel postscript to the well-known story in the shape of his considered recollection of how Bodyline evolved.

A fairly detailed account of Gubby's part in the Bodyline tour was necessary, of course, since it is the central point of his cricket career. One's hope is that it may also serve a good purpose in disabusing anyone who supposed that some modern fast bowling in Test Matches is much the same sort of thing. The essential, and crucial, difference is that by law only two fieldsmen may now be stationed behind the wicket on the leg-side. For Larwood and Voce, when they bowled Bodyline, their captain would use as many as five behind on the leg, three close for the catch, two on the boundary to save runs or make catches from the hook. If such a field and Bodyline methods were acceptable today, just imagine how it might be utilized by an attack of, say, Marshall, Holding, Roberts and Garner.

The accounts of the enthusiastic send-off given to the seventh MCC touring team to Australia make nostalgic reading to one whose good fortune it was to accompany later MCC sides by ship. Trains and ocean liners lend themselves more to romance than the fraught atmosphere of air terminals. Besides, the 1930s were less sophisticated days than the present when Test teams fly all over the globe each winter. The tour to Australia every four years was the supreme cricket adventure, the only occasion when the full flower of English cricket was gathered to travel overseas, following in the footsteps of those hardy pioneers, professionals mostly, whose missionary visits from 1859 onwards paved the way for the institution of representative matches between the two countries at the end of the 1870s.

At St Pancras Station on the morning of 17 September 1932 Gubby and the rest of the team, wearing sprigs of white heather, were hard pressed to find a way through a cheering throng, gathered to see them off to Tilbury on the first stage of their journey. Ahead lay 30,000 miles of travel round the world by ship and train, spread over seven and a half months. 'Not merely in the chance of regaining the coveted "Ashes" does the interest of the country lie,' one editorial writer declared, 'but in the knowledge that every time England and Australia meet in friendly rivalry a valuable contribution is made to the all-vital Imperial spirit.' In front of a mass of reporters and camera-men on board the Orient liner, *Orontes*, Douglas Jardine, immaculate in black homburg hat and I Zingari tie, contented himself with promising that 'We shall do our utmost to bring those Ashes back.'

They did their utmost, of course, and their quest was highly successful, apart from any sentimental concessions to the all-vital Imperial spirit. Indeed the captain was propounding to his team a very different philosophy in individual talks, pacing the decks, almost before they were out of the Bay of Biscay. The only way to beat them, he said, was to adopt a policy of 'hate'. When Jardine raised the subject with Gubby he declined to fall in with any such idea – to which his captain's reply was that in his case it didn't matter because he wouldn't be playing in the Tests anyway. Jardine was mildly annoyed by Gubby's attitude, though he should surely have known his man better than to think he would react otherwise. Such an early brush did not perhaps bode well for their relationship in the months ahead. However, it proved to be the first of only two differences on the tour, the other being the occasion, well publicized after the tour but known at the time only to Warner, the manager, and Wyatt, the vice-captain, in the dressing-room immediately before the Second Test. Jardine told Gubby he must conform with the policy and bowl Bodyline, and was met with a point-blank refusal. Otherwise a complete harmony persisted between the two throughout the trip. To Jardine's credit bowling tactics were not again referred to.

Jardine was thirty-one when the tour began, as also was Bob Wyatt. Gubby was thirty. The other two amateurs, the Nawab of Pataudi and Freddie Brown, were only down a year from Oxford and Cambridge. It was now that Gubby formed several warm and lasting friendships – with Wyatt particularly, and with others such as Les Ames, Freddie Brown, Walter Hammond and Maurice Leyland. As for Gubby and his captain, they had been friends ever since their schooldays. As the tour progressed Gubby's bond with Wyatt grew stronger. Both were instinctively opposed to Bodyline. Equally both realized the paramount need to say nothing whatever on the subject, either among Australian friends or, of course, within the touring party.

I have here used the word Bodyline in advance of its discovery and although many found it distasteful at the time and some may do so still, I use it because the phrase generally attributed to the old Australian Test cricketer-turned-journalist, Jack Worrall, describes more exactly than any other the type of attack that was in dispute.

Whether or not fast bowling plans were discussed on the *Orontes* it is beyond doubt that during the Surrey-Notts match at the Oval over the August bank holiday week-end Surrey's captain, Jardine, took Carr, his opposite number, Larwood and Voce to dine at the Piccadilly Hotel, and that fast bowling tactics were discussed there. Both Larwood and Voce on occasion in this and the preceding summer had been letting the ball fly from short of a length in county cricket and the latter, being a left-armer, was apt to lift towards the ribs whether bowling over the wicket or (as was more usual) round. It seems that some sort of agreement may have emerged from this dinner-party that the best way to contain Bradman might be to attack him at speed around the leg-stump, and to give him a good ration of the short stuff. As Gubby tells in his postscript to this chapter, if this was so the precise fielding pattern which was the logical extension of this theory emerged only as it came to be tested out on Australian pitches.

The third exponent of Bodyline in Australia was Bill Bowes, who was not a member of the touring team when, a week before it was due to sail, he took the field at the Oval for Yorkshire against the Rest of England. Bowes and Verity had bowled Yorkshire to their sixteenth Championship, and the former during a highly successful last month of the season had shown a relish for the fast bumper which was far from being reciprocated by his victims. Jack Hobbs's pointed displeasure at Bowes's tactics during a masterly innings of 90 at the Oval was observed at close range by his captain, batting at the other end, as well as by Plum Warner in his several capacities – how strange this seems today! – of chairman of selectors, *Morning Post* cricket writer and editor of *The Cricketer*. Now on the Monday of this Champion County match Bowes took seven of the eight Rest wickets which had fallen by close of play in fourteen formidable overs. There was a hurried selection meeting with Jardine, it can safely be assumed, opposing Warner and pressing hard for Bowes to be added to the party. Only a week or two before, Warner in the *Morning Post* had written, 'Yorkshire will find themselves a very unpopular side if there is a repetition of Saturday's play.' 'Moreover these things lead to reprisals, and when they begin goodness knows where they will end,' he had gone on, prophetically. Of Bowes's tactics he had written in *The Cricketer*, 'That is not bowling. Indeed it is not cricket.'

Strong words! And also at the meeting – indeed presiding by virtue of his chairmanship of the MCC Cricket Committee – there was the king-pin and personification of Yorkshire, Lord Hawke. He and Plum were, of course, friends of very old standing, but such a public slur on Yorkshire's name was not to be glossed over. Whatever was said at what can only have been a tense meeting, Jardine won the day, as he was to do without exception where his manager was concerned in the days ahead.

So Bowes was in, a fourth fast bowler and one who had shown no scruples about pitching the ball short. In fact Gubby, despite Jardine's dampening comment, was due to gain the preference over Bowes, who was selected for only one Test, to the exclusion of Verity, and he had just one memorable moment when Bradman at Melbourne dragged his first ball, a long-hop, into his stumps. Nevertheless the captain now had a potentially useful reserve if any ill befell Larwood and Voce. Indeed, once the pattern of Bodyline had emerged and Gubby had dissociated himself from it, the presence of Bowes in the party was essential in case either of the Notts pair broke down.

Just one further set-back to the selectors' original intentions must be noted. In the five days between the last-minute inclusion of Bowes and the team's departure Maurice Tate suffered some sort of nervous collapse. Nothing could have been less characteristic, nor did it last long. But it prevented his sailing with the others. Hence more early opportunities were possible for Gubby who had staked a strong claim to the Test side before Maurice played his first match, at Sydney, his old stamping-ground, a week before the First Test was due there.

A word to complete the picture about the managership arrangements: Frederick Toone, the secretary of Yorkshire, who had managed with much acclaim the three MCC sides to Australia of the 1920s, and been knighted for his services, died in 1930, and early in the summer Lord Hawke had approached Plum about taking on the job. No name stood higher in Australia than that of Warner, who had captained the first and third MCC sides there in 1903–04 and 1911–12 and returned each time with the Ashes. Who better to sound the traditional notes of Imperial cordiality, while R. C. N. Palairet, secretary of Surrey, acting as joint manager, occupied himself with the less glamorous details of administration?

Who indeed – unless he were to be obliged to work in harness with a captain of iron resolve and implacable singleness of purpose with a wholly different philosophy of cricket such as Jardine. It should be noted here, too, that in those days the touring captain was in every way the leading figure in the party. The manager stuck to the business and social side of the tour. He never interfered in cricket affairs. Such was Warner's frustrating brief – and cricket's misfortune.

The Orient and P & O liners used to make more leisurely crossings of the world than in the latter days of ocean travel. The *Orontes* indeed called in at seven ports before making the final landfall at Fremantle on 18 October. First came Gibraltar, at which Bruce Harris thought he saw

Jardine taking inspiration from the impregnability of the Rock, then Toulon, followed by Naples, where Gubby with Bob Wyatt, George Duckworth and others took the opportunity to see the ruins of Pompeii. There were brief pauses to go ashore at Port Said, Suez and Aden, then a chance to recover from the stifling heat of the Red Sea in the fresher airs of the Indian Ocean before stopping off for the traditional day and the traditional match at Colombo. In those days no Englishman would go out in the midday sun without his topee, and thus they were all arrayed. However MCC were soon in the shade again, for All-Ceylon declared early in confident expectation of rain, which did not materialize, so enabling Pataudi to spend three hours over an innings of 62 while others, including Gubby, with the game won, stretched their land-legs by making a few.

And so to the last stages of Gubby's return to his native land, which he had last seen at the age of six. Here then was Australia with so much of its cultivation still clinging close to the seaboard, its population concentrated in the five state capitals, starting with Perth and continuing with Adelaide, Melbourne and Sydney, up to Brisbane. In 1932 the vast interior was largely undeveloped, much scarcely explored, still the undisputed preserve of its strange indigenous creatures, the kangaroo, the koala bear, the flying opossum, the wombat, the wallaby – and, of course, the Aboriginals.

Neither Western Australia, nor indeed any of the other states outside New South Wales, had been settled when Gubby's great grandfather and great-great grandmother sailed into the original outpost of Sydney thousands of miles to the east little more than a century earlier. In 1932, though the economy of the state was quickening (and was to provide Gubby in due course with the wherewithal for an extremely comfortable middle and old age) Western Australia was still some years from beginning to realize its vast potential, and Perth was little more than a good-sized country town.

Docking at Fremantle to the warmest of welcomes, the team made the journey by car to Perth where they were due for six days' cricket and five days' practice. Thanks to the weather they got less cricket than most visiting sides but the rain helped them gain an important psychological success against Bradman, and in this Gubby had some part. Bradman had been greeted like a conqueror when he arrived in Perth and it was his presence on the Combined Team that brought to the ground a record crowd of 20,000. However MCC first made 583 for seven declared, and then caught their opponents on a pitch made treacherous by rain. (There was then no covering, except for the creases, during MCC's matches in Australia.) Verity was unplayable in the first innings, and at the start of the follow-on, the run-up having partially dried, Gubby with the benefit of a strong wind off the Swan River 'bowled remarkably fast and may be the surprise packet of the tour', thought Arthur Mailey. Having bowled Vic Richardson for a duck, he 'obviously rattled Bradman ... by sheer pace', getting him caught at short-leg for 10. Freddie Brown quotes Larwood, who was not playing, as saying, in the dressing-room, 'If that little bugger can do that to him, what might I do!' I doubt if Don had the faintest consolation from getting Jardine caught at mid-on two short of his hundred and Allen lbw off a full-pitch for 16. (D. G. B. with his leg-spinners took two wickets for 106.)

On the endless train journey from Perth across the Nullabor – literally 'no trees' – to Adelaide Gubby in his weekly letter home reported with his inimitable attention to detail:

> I had the longest session of bridge of my life-time on the train. We started at 7.45 in the morning of the last leg and played up to 5.45 in the evening with only intervals amounting to 50 minutes. Jardine and I won the first 13 rubbers v Hammond and Sutcliffe, lost the next 2 and won the last 4, 19 in all and 5400 points profit at 6d Auction.

Walter, it seems, was a good player of the cards but a poor caller, Herbert vice-versa. So after nine hours and ten minutes the Gents took £1.14s.0d. off the Players! But for Gubby the effort was hardly worth while for he developed a stiff neck on the train and although the captain wanted him to play against South Australia in the next match 'I could not possibly have done my best.' So he writes as on the Adelaide Oval he watches Sutcliffe and Leyland put on 223 for the first wicket:

> Leyland looks like being Sutcliffe's partner but I am sure it is wrong: he should not be risked at the start as he will be wanted to deal with the leg-tweakers and left-handers.

A good judgement! Though no ideal partner was to be found either for Sutcliffe in 1932–33 or for Charlie Barnett in 1936–37, Leyland, except for one innings, in all ten Tests batted in the middle order where he proved a regular stumbling-block to Bill O'Reilly, Australia's most formidable bowler.

MCC beat both South Australia and Victoria by an innings, Gubby having a considerable hand in the victory at Melbourne where he took Woodfull's wicket and three others of the first five in the first innings and, when Victoria were trapped on a pitch made unpleasant by rain, three in the second: seven for 66 in all. Sutcliffe being rested, Jardine as in the Old Trafford Trial Match sent Gubby in first. He made 15– but as he was now clearly in the reckoning as a fast bowler for the Tests it would obviously have demanded too much to make him also into an opening bat. This was the match wherein Hammond went in with instructions to demolish the claims of the potentially dangerous Fleetwood-Smith, and performed his mission devastatingly.

Gubby, batting at No 5, found his batting form with an innings of 48 in the next match, also played at Melbourne, against an Australian XI, which is historically notable in that the short fast bowling (of Larwood, Bowes and Voce) first called for comment. Jack Hobbs, in one of his daily cables to the London *Star*, remarked on Bradman's dislike of the 'short, bumpy stuff', saying it disconcerted him, and that he 'seemed to jib a bit'. He also reported Woodfull suffering the first wound of the campaign, 'a bad blow over the heart' from Larwood. Writing home Gubby predicted serious trouble if these bowling tactics were developed. He thought them at this stage 'unattractive rather than unfair'. In this dress rehearsal for the Tests, with Bradman due to bat on the Saturday, 53,916 turned up at Melbourne, probably — though there is no precise record of attendance outside Tests — the largest number ever to have seen a day's play in any other sort of first-class match. Before rain drew down the curtain on a dramatic contest, Larwood and Allen bowled seven very fast and eventful overs at the start of the Australian second innings. Gubby had Bradman missed at the wicket off a horrible lifter before Larwood bowled him as he aimed to cut!

It is a strange fact in the sinister Bodyline saga that at this early testing — with a strictly modified leg-side field so far as Larwood, Bowes and Voce were concerned — the MCC team were being led by Wyatt, the vice-captain, who when he came to realize its implications was as hostile to it as Gubby. Jardine was away from Melbourne, fishing!

After the Australian XI match Gubby wrote home:

> I gather I am likely to play in the First Test and in view of that fact I am staying at the Hotel Australia in Sydney and not with any of the family as I must have some quiet nights to do well. I have not felt as well as I do now for years.

And so to his birth-place:

> Well, here I am in Sydney after all this time, and wondering whether I would ever go there again. I ... was met by Dick, Uncle Arthur and Reg Bettington: they were the only ones who turned up as I wrote particularly and asked that there should be a small attendance of family.

This was a prelude to meeting and re-meeting all the numerous Allen clan in Sydney, and, though he was not himself drinking at all, attending numerous parties. Gubby had to absorb a good deal of lionizing, as may be judged:

Uncle Herbert is a darling but at parties he's a terror as he never ceases saying 'this is dear Walter's boy' and away they go.

The New South Wales match and then the First Test were due to follow one another, and in the state match 'dear Walter's boy', sharing the new ball with Voce, no doubt delighted the family by taking seven wickets, even if they were latter-end ones. This was the match wherein Maurice Tate, the hero of the last two MCC tours to Australia, made his one impact on this, his third visit to Australia by taking the first four wickets, including Bradman, Kippax and McCabe for 53 runs. Gubby thought he bowled 'beautifully', and that his own Test place was now in jeopardy. Jack Fingleton carried his bat through the NSW first innings. He suffered such bruising from Voce and, what was even worse, he was disillusioned by what he considered the hostile attitude of his opponents on the field.

It looks from this distance as though Gubby's presence in the MCC side – of special interest, naturally, to Australians – was one of the very few cordial elements in the general picture. It must have been a popular gesture, for instance, that he turned out for the NSW Cricket Association against the Combined Public Schools, and a thrill for him when he found himself batting with the great C. G. Macartney whom, in his Eton days, he had seen making short work of the England bowling at Lord's some eleven years earlier. 'The Governor-General', as he was known, at the advanced age (for Australia) of forty-six looked 'pretty damned good still'. He amused himself by cutting a yorker, and when his partner asked him whether he always cut yorkers, he said with a twinkle, 'Yes, always.'

Gubby did play in the First Test Match, but without distinction, as he wrote home:

We registered an overwhelming victory, but I am sorry to say I had very little to do with it. I bowled badly, especially in the first innings, as I have lost my run to the wicket with the result that I only bowl about half my proper pace. I am afraid I am sure to be left out of the Second Test which I shall hate as half the fun is gone then. I may be saved by the fact that I batted quite well and have done so all the trip.

There follows an assessment of some of the play and the players:

I caught two really fine catches in the Test and fielded well above form. So I may get another chance some time. Hammond played a wonderful innings of 112, but Pataudi (102) and Sutcliffe (194) were very slow and very lucky all through their innings. I believe they will play Brown and Bowes or Tate instead of Leyland and myself in the next Test. What the Australians will do I can't imagine

AUSTRALIA v ENGLAND
(First Test)

At Sydney, 2–7 December 1932

AUSTRALIA

*W. M. Woodfull c Ames b Voce	7 – b Larwood	0
W. H. Ponsford b Larwood	32 – b Voce	2
J. H. W. Fingleton c Allen b Larwood	26 – c Voce b Larwood................	40
A. F. Kippax lbw b Larwood	8 – (6) b Larwood	19
S. J. McCabe not out 187	– (4) lbw b Hammond	32
V. Y. Richardson c Hammond b Voce	49 – (5) c Voce b Hammond..........	0
†W. A. S. Oldfield c Ames b Larwood	4 – c Leyland b Larwood	1
C. V. Grimmett c Ames b Voce.............	19 – c Allen b Larwood	5
L. E. Nagel b Larwood	0 – not out	21
W. J. O'Reilly b Voce......................	4 – (11) b Voce	7
T. W. Wall c Allen b Hammond............	4 – (10) c Ames b Allen.............	20
B 12, l-b 4, n-b 4 20	B 12, l-b 2, w 1, n-b 2	17

1/22 2/65 3/82 4/87 5/216   360   1/2 2/10 3/61 4/61 5/100   164
6/231 7/299 8/300 9/305 10/360   6/104 7/105 8/113 9/151 10/
                                          164

Bowling: *First Innings* – Larwood 31–5–96–5; Voce 29–4–110–4; Allen 15–1–65–0; Hammond 14.2–0–34–1; Verity 13–4–35–0. *Second Innings* – Larwood 18–4–28–5; Voce 17.3–5–54–2; Allen 9–5–13–1; Hammond 15–6–37–2; Verity 4–1–15–0.

ENGLAND

H. Sutcliffe lbw b Wall ....194 – not out	1
R. E. S. Wyatt lbw b Grimmett............. 38 – not out	0
W. R. Hammond c Grimmett b Nagel 112	
Nawab of Pataudi, sr b Nagel 102	
M. Leyland c Oldfield b Wall............... 0	
*D. R. Jardine c Oldfield b McCabe 27	
H. Verity lbw b Wall 2	
G. O. B. Allen c and b O'Reilly............. 19	
†L. E. G. Ames c McCabe b O'Reilly 0	
H. Larwood lbw b O'Reilly 0	
W. Voce not out 0	
B 7, l-b 17, n-b 6.................... 30	

1/112 2/300 3/423 4/423 5/470   524   (0 wkts.)   1
6/479 7/519 8/522 9/522 10/524

Bowling: *First Innings* – Wall 38–4–104–3; Nagel 43.4–9–110–2; O'Reilly 67–32–117–3; Grimmett 64–22–118–1; McCabe 15–2–42–1; Kippax 2–1–3–0. *Second Innings* – McCabe 0.1–0–1–0.

Umpires: G. Borwick and G. A. Hele.

England won by 10 wickets.

as Woodfull doesn't seem to be the sticker he was and Kippax and Ponsford clearly hate the fierce bowling. Fingleton played well, but Grimmett seems to have lost his sting and Nagel was a wash-out. If they pick a side with a little more courage things will be very different.

The match is ever memorable for the first of the three innings which stamped Stan McCabe as a great player. His 187 not out – which was over half of the total of 360 with which Australia began their defence of the Ashes – was notable especially for his brave and brilliant hooking of the fast bowling. Gubby's view of McCabe is that if Bradman had never been born McCabe would have ranked near the very top of the tree. He was such a fine player of every type of bowling, especially strong off the back foot and a marvellous timer of the ball. As it was, he so often in his career – though not in this series – went in with a mountain of runs already on the board, and it was not in his nature to tot up big scores regardless of the situation. The Don, after much rumour and speculation and some conflict with the Australian Board over a newspaper contract, did not in fact play in this match. Though fears of pernicious anaemia proved unfounded, he withdrew on medical advice the day before. Nor for that matter was he in the tour to South Africa in 1935–36 when McCabe in Johannesburg played 'superbly', according to *Wisden*, for 189 not out, causing the fielding captain, H. F. Wade, to appeal against the light! Bradman was indeed playing, and already out, when at Trent Bridge in 1938 he bade his team come out on to the balcony to watch McCabe make 232 out of 300 in less than four hours – one of the epic innings of history.

A recent talk with Les Ames supplies a hitherto unrecorded footnote to this Test and indeed the series. Though he and Jardine had been fellow-members of Percy Chapman's MCC team to Australia four years earlier he didn't think they had exchanged more than a few words from start to finish of the tour. Jardine, partly maybe from shyness, was completely remote and aloof. Ames was surprised therefore when the captain approached him before this Sydney Test, and said, 'Leslie, you know as well as I do that our chance of winning this series depends on Larwood and Voce, and that they're both very fond of their beer. Well, I want you to see that they go quietly before and during the Tests.' Les promised to do his best, and did so, but confesses that he was only partially successful. 'The trouble was that what was nothing to them was too much for me.' They thrived on the stuff!

After telling of a happy week-end at Moombara, Uncle Arthur's lovely house on the Port Hacking inlet south of Sydney, when Jardine, Wyatt and Warner joined a mixed array of relations he writes of the captain:

> We all try very hard with him but I know, as time draws on, that someone will have the very hell of a row with him. It won't be me, so don't worry.

Much as Gubby was enjoying life he felt the pull of home as almost every cricketer does on every tour. Thanking his parents for writing so regularly, he says:

> My surprise and joy are equal every week when I see the envelope. I heard lots of nice things about you wherever I went in

Sydney. I am longing to go back there as it really is a lovely town.

He adds that he has met some very charming people but that he is 'completely heart-whole'. In the next letter home Gubby tells of his surprise at the engagement of his Eton cousin, Dick, to Pauline Macdonald:

> She is distinctly pretty in her own way, but very young to know what she is taking on. She is well under twenty. However, I don't think she is a fool, and I should say it ought to be a success.

More than fifty years later this looks a shrewd prediction, for the pretty brunette and my old Jap POW friend are still going strong.

Gubby's forecast as to changes for the Second Test, including his own exclusion, proved wide of the mark, the only alteration being the substitution of Bowes for Verity. Thus the attack consisted of unadulterated speed. Thinking he was sure to be dropped, Gubby on the eve of the match had accepted a dinner invitation when he ran into the captain at the hotel. Jardine normally kept the identity of the side to himself but he now gave it to Gubby who made his excuses to his friends and dined quietly in the Windsor — that gem of a hotel where so many successive MCC teams have stayed but, alas! no more. He wrote that night:

> I am playing in the Test tomorrow. I am a little surprised but even more so at the side. Four fast bowlers and not a single slow one seems mad to me. They nearly played Mitchell or Verity instead of Bowes.

Next morning in the dressing-room, but out of hearing of anyone, came the celebrated confrontation. It has been reported without much variation in several books. This is what Gubby wrote home to his father on the spot when the game was over, amplifying the story in a later letter:

> The Test here was a disaster. Our bowlers did what I consider to be a miraculous performance in getting Australia out for 228 and 191 on the easiest paced wicket ever seen in Melbourne. The wicket here up to this particular match (a curious coincidence) has always been in favour of fast bowling but on this occasion it helped spinners from the start. Even taking all that into consideration we should have made many more runs. I have said all along that if our bowlers, Voce and Larwood in particular, persisted in bowling this bouncing leg-theory stuff at the batsmen the wickets were sure to be toned down and it is just what has happened.
>
> I see from some of the paper cuttings, which I have been sent from England, that I am reported to have bowled 'bouncers' like Larwood. That is ridiculous and I have never had more than four

men on the leg side on any occasion whereas he has had eight and
often seven. I have bowled fast at times out here and made the ball
fly but never the leg-theory. I have refused to do it.

   In fact before this Test started Jardine said I ought to do it which
made me furious. I told him he could leave me out if he didn't like
the way I bowled. I then went and saw Plum and told him that if
such a thing ever occurred again I should report the whole thing to
Billy Findlay.* I don't think I shall hear anything more about it. I
really bowled very well in this match and batted much better than
the rest. Both innings I threw my wicket away as there was no one
left to stay with me. We shall probably play Verity instead of Bowes
and Paynter instead of Wyatt next time. Jardine must go in 1st as he
is so terribly nervous he is out before he goes in.

When I expressed surprise at the notion of Jardine showing any vestige
of nerves Gubby's explanation was that that was how the burden of
leadership affects captains – all the more so, no doubt, when the
atmosphere was as in this series. He himself was far more nervous when
he had not only himself to look after but the whole side to worry about.

   Gubby adds only to this letter that Jardine did start his unfortunate
effort at persuasion by saying he had been 'talking to the boys' the night
before, and they had said, 'It's because you're keen on your popularity
with the crowd that you won't bowl bouncers to a leg-side field.' It was
this that angered him so particularly, as he tells in a later letter. He adds,
'I could have bowled Bodyline, though not so well as Harold.' It is an
indication of how closely Bob Wyatt and Gubby kept their feelings to
themselves that Les, to whom Gubby was already closer than to any
other member of the side, knew nothing of the dressing-room encounter
until quite recently, though he always assumed something must have
happened between them. Not unnaturally, it made Plum Warner more
depressed than ever. He was himself scarcely on speaking terms with the
captain when, on Gubby telling him what had occurred, he murmured,
'One of the reasons we picked you was because we thought you'd get on
so well with Douglas.' On that score at any rate Plum had nothing
further to fear. But by then he was, it seems, 'a broken man'. Did Plum
ever talk of resigning the managership? Apparently not. He stuck out the
rising volume of anger at the bowling tactics as the Melbourne Test
progressed, and likewise the deplorable climax due to follow at Adelaide.

   Gubby's retrospective opinion about the unusual slowness of the pitch
is that on this occasion the groundsman may well have made a genuine
mistake. If England had had a spinner the ball would have turned on the
first day. As it was, Australia failed altogether to take advantage of again

* the MCC secretary

AUSTRALIA v ENGLAND
(Second Test)

At Melbourne, 30 December–3 January 1933

AUSTRALIA

J. H. W. Fingleton b Allen	83	– c Ames b Allen	1
*W. M. Woodfull b Allen	10	– c Allen b Larwood	26
L. P. J. O'Brien run out	10	– b Larwood	11
D. G. Bradman c Bowes b Bowes	0	– not out	103
S. J. McCabe c Jardine b Voce	32	– b Allen	0
V. Y. Richardson c Hammond b Voce	34	– lbw b Hammond	32
†W. A. S. Oldfield not out	27	– b Voce	6
C. V. Grimmett c Sutcliffe b Voce	2	– b Voce	0
T. W. Wall run out	1	– lbw b Hammond	3
W. J. O'Reilly b Larwood	15	– c Ames b Hammond	0
H. Ironmonger b Larwood	4	– run out	0
B 5, l-b 1, w 2, n-b 2	10	B 3, l-b 1, w 4, n-b 1	9

1/29 2/67 3/67 4/131 5/156   228   1/1 2/27 3/78 4/81 5/135   191
6/188 7/194 8/200 9/222 10/228   6/150 7/156 8/184 9/186 10/
                                                      191

Bowling: *First Innings* – Larwood 20.3–2–52–2; Voce 20–3–54–3; Allen 17–3–41–2; Hammond 10–3–21–0; Bowes 19–2–50–1. *Second Innings* – Larwood 15–2–50–2; Voce 15–2–47–2; Allen 12–1–44–2; Hammond 10.5–2–21–3; Bowes 4–0–20–0.

ENGLAND

H. Sutcliffe c Richardson b Wall	52	– b O'Reilly	33
R. E. S. Wyatt lbw b O'Reilly	13	– (7) lbw b O'Reilly	25
W. R. Hammond b Wall	8	– (4) c O'Brien b O'Reilly	23
Nawab of Pataudi, sr b O'Reilly	15	– (3) c Fingleton b Ironmonger	5
M. Leyland b O'Reilly	22	– (2) b Wall	19
*D. R. Jardine c Oldfield b Wall	1	– (5) c McCabe b Ironmonger	0
†L. E. G. Ames b Wall	4	– (6) c Fingleton b O'Reilly	2
G. O. B. Allen c Richardson b O'Reilly	30	– st Oldfield b Ironmonger	23
H. Larwood b O'Reilly	9	– c Wall b Ironmonger	4
W. Voce c McCabe b Grimmett	6	– c O'Brien b O'Reilly	0
W. E. Bowes not out	4	– not out	0
B 1, l-b 2, n-b 2	5	L-b 4, n-b 1	5

1/30 2/43 3/83 4/98 5/104   169   1/53 2/53 3/70 4/70 5/77   139
6/110 7/122 8/138 9/161 10/169   6/85 7/135 8/137 9/138 10/139

Bowling: *First Innings* – Wall 21–4–52–4; O'Reilly 34.3–17–63–5; Grimmett 16–4–21–1; Ironmonger 14–4–28–0. *Second Innings* – Wall 8–2–23–1; O'Reilly 24–5–66–5; Grimmett 4–0–19–0; Ironmonger 19.1–8–26–4.

Umpires: G. Borwick and G. A. Hele.

Australia won by 111 runs.

winning the toss, being bowled out for 228, with Bradman taking his famous first ball. Gubby considers this episode 'almost the most dramatic five minutes I remember'. There was the invariable very slow walk to the wicket amidst far the most deafening hullabaloo that even Bradman has ever evoked from the vast crowd round the Melbourne bowl; eventually utter quiet as Bowes came in to bowl; the swift movement of the feet well across to the off-side; Bradman, correctly anticipating a bouncer, moved into position; the attempted hook of the quick long-hop which merely dragged this first ball from the under-edge of the bat on to the leg-stump;

the shocked silence as the idol trudged back, and some nervous clapping as he disappeared into the shadows. Humiliation completed.

England's batting in answer to the first Australian innings was, however, lamentable, as Gubby has indicated, and it was on the day following when Australia batted again, with a remorseless burning sun turning the great Melbourne amphitheatre into an oven, that Gubby maintains 'the really rough stuff started'. This was when in his view the English bowling definitely went beyond the spirit of the game and became in truth Bodyline. Tempers were short, and not least Harold Larwood's. He had recurring trouble with his boots, which so nettled his captain that when Larwood returned to the field after going off Jardine asked Gubby to relay the message that he wanted him to bowl from the pavilion end. This happened again, whereat Larwood, despite the slowness of the pitch, really let the batsmen have it from one end, with Voce rattling the ribs from the other. Bowes's intentions may have been similar, but his speed and effectiveness were mild by comparison.

The heat was such that Jardine worked his bowlers in very short spells. On one occasion when Gubby was just about all in he asked him to manage just one more over, adding, 'What about giving him a bouncer fifth ball?' Gubby was never averse from bowling the occasional short one and duly did his best to oblige. The result was a not very fast long-hop which was sent whistling for four close past Jardine's nose at short-leg. 'Well bowled,' said the captain, not having flinched. 'Thank you so much.'

Wally Hammond said to Gubby as they crossed over, 'That's the worst remark I've ever heard on the cricket field, but this is a Test, so you must forget it.' He also recalls Les Ames trying to lighten the moment by asking, 'When are you going to start trying?' Les and Gubby remember the incident still because they've often laughed about it. But by now Gubby knew his man, and was fairly immune from such sardonic touches. I suppose Jardine might even have been expressing his droll amusement at having been preserved from injury. He was a queer bird if ever there was one.

This was the match wherein Gubby believes he established his position as a Test cricketer, even though he took only four wickets and made 30 and 23. The wickets were those of Fingleton (twice), Woodfull and McCabe, and his runs at least were more than anyone else got for England apart from Sutcliffe.

The Australian second innings saw the re-establishment in Australian esteem of Don Bradman who, says Gubby, batted superbly in making 103 undefeated out of a total of 191. The leg-side attack had caused him to improvise his own method of play, which he did chiefly by utilizing his unrivalled fleetness of foot, allied, of course, to his extraordinary speed at picking up the line of the ball. His object was (preferably) either to move so far inside the ball as to hit it into the unguarded places on the off, or to hop across and either hit it or let it pass by down the leg-side. The Don, says Gubby, never looked safe defying Bodyline in this way. The bowling theory completely dislocated his normal method. What could be more grotesque than to see him, from a position a foot wide of the leg stump, hitting fours through a deserted cover field? Yet, despite McCabe's great (and unrepeated) innings, at Sydney Bradman ended with an average of 56 head and shoulders above his Australian fellows and higher than any Englishman save Paynter, who played five innings and was twice not out.

Gubby's view was that England had gone most of the way to winning the Second Test Match by their bowling on the first day, had almost lost it by their batting on the second, and were in with a winning chance after the third, at the end of which they had to make a further 208 with all their wickets in hand. Then on the fourth morning they had failed so completely against the spin of O'Reilly and Ironmonger that when Gubby joined Bob Wyatt the score had fallen from 43 for no wicket overnight to 85 for six. These two put on 50 in fifty minutes before first Wyatt and then Gubby fell, the latter with Larwood, Voce and Bowes alone remaining, coming out to drive Ironmonger and being beaten by the spin and stumped.

Thus England lost by 111 runs what – if the fast bowling tactics can be put aside – was a fascinating match wherein two crowd records were broken. On the Friday of the New Year week-end a world record crowd of 63,996 saw Australia's first innings failure. On the Monday, with Australia due to bat again, 68,188 people created a new record. It was this match which made manifest Bill O'Reilly's emergence as a great bowler. Ten for 129 he took, being in harness on the last day almost exclusively with the left-armer, Bert Ironmonger, whom Gubby rates as almost the best of his type he ever saw, though he thought his action sometimes looked dubious. Ironmonger, who took four for 26, had lost the top half of both the index and second fingers of his bowling hand, and spun it strongly off the stumps.

Though both Gubby and Don Bradman disclaim knowledge of this injury to the second finger, in his encyclopaedic *Australian Cricket* Jack Pollard relates how he lost the top of the index finger in a saw-mill and the middle finger when demonstrating to the foreman how the accident occurred! There was some doubt about the age of this clumsy, ponderous fellow nicknamed 'Dainty', of whose batting the historian, A. G. Moyes, said that 'he went to the wickets mostly as a gesture to convention.' He claimed to be forty-one when first chosen for his country, but was either forty-five or forty-six. If the *Wisden* and Pollard date can be accepted he was a few months short of his fifty-first birthday at the time of this

Melbourne Test and as the oldest Test cricketer ranks second to Wilfred Rhodes.

'Dainty' was said to keep his left arm in trim as a park-keeper by spiking fallen leaves. He was also said to throw occasionally, especially when tired, that being allegedly why he was never chosen for a tour to England, where his bowling ought to have been devastating.

As had become his habit, Gubby sought distraction from the cricket when and where he could, and in Melbourne and its environs that was not difficult. He spent week-ends by the sea, down the Mornington Peninsula at Sorrento, with the Clive Baillieus, and made friends with such sportsmen as Gerald Patterson, the famous lawn tennis player, and the cricketer and golfer Keith Tolhurst. Arthur Mailey was generally about, too, when a party was in the offing. Gubby had met the delightful American tennis player Elsworth Vines and his wife in Tasmania, dined with them, and saw USA defeat Australia in the Davis Cup Challenge Round at Kooyong.

The only incident indicating any disharmony within the MCC camp came to light between the Second and Third Tests. The captain was involved but, as he had predicted, Gubby was not. Jardine and Larwood had not been on speaking terms during the Second Test, and when, up-country at Bendigo, the latter saw on the team notice-board that he was named twelfth man he either tore down the sheet of paper or crossed out his name. (The story has two versions.) Ultimately he played in the two-day match, but the Australian press seized on the morsel with relish, and when at Adelaide several days later, on the eve of the crucial Test Match, the two were still at odds, Herbert Sutcliffe in his capacity as senior professional decided over dinner that there must be a meeting to put things right. However when the rest came out of the dining-room they found the captain and his chief bowler chatting amiably together. The rift had been healed, and is only perhaps worth mentioning here as illustrating how the nerves and sensibilities of adult sportsmen can become over-tense at times of emotional stress. Of this there was due to be more serious evidence on the fair Adelaide Oval.

Before the Third Test Gubby in his weekly letter home explained what had caused Warwick Armstrong, whose Test reports were syndicated to the London *Evening News,* to have accused him at Sydney of roughing up the pitch with his spikes. He also elaborated on the conversation Jardine had had with him in the dressing-room at Melbourne:

It was very sweet of you both to be so upset because Warwick Armstrong wrote some utter rot about my running on the wicket. Actually there was no trouble about it at all. Woodfull just said, 'Be sure to keep wide of the wicket' to which I replied 'We have got to bat last so I am not likely to make a spot for Grimmett if I can help it.'

The subject never came up again or in the Second Test and no one ever pitched a ball in my mark during either match. I saw W. Armstrong today and asked what drivel he was going to work up this time: he had a good deal to say but I left him to tell the groundsman. The newspapers and general public in this country, though they have all been exceedingly nice to me, are simply dreadful and far worse than in England. They never leave Douglas Jardine alone for a minute and they publish the most unfounded statements which are certainly libelous but, of course, one can do nothing about it. D.R.J. asks for it with his manner and is then hurt when they say nasty things about him. I certainly was depressed for a short time after the First Test as I bowled badly and thought there was no chance of my playing again in a Test out here. Now it looks as though I shall play in several as I have been picked to play again tomorrow in the Third Test.

They have left out Pataudi for Paynter, which I am all against, and though Pataudi has not once impressed me the same may be said of Paynter and he has not made nearly as many runs. I have also noted that the papers talk of me bowling leg theory and bumpers. That is all nonsense. I will now tell you the story of what occurred on the morning of the Second Test to prove that to you. I didn't tell you last week as I thought you might worry but, as now the leg theory is dying and the trouble is therefore very unlikely to recur, you need have no fears.

D.R.J. came to me and said the following: 'I had a talk with the boys, Larwood and Voce, last night and they say it is quite absurd you not bowling "bouncers": they say it is only because you are keen on your popularity.' Well! I burst and said that if it had been a question only of popularity I could have bowled 'bouncers' years ago. I concluded by saying if he didn't like the way I bowled he still had time to leave me out not only in this match but until he came to his senses: it also would give me time to complete a full statement of our conversation for the benefit of the MCC Committee. He said 'Well! I am afraid you will have to.' I told him I had no intention of doing it but he had walked away by then and the matter was left. I bowled my ordinary way only I had one more man on the *off* on purpose and bowled both innings the best except possibly for Hammond. He didn't put me on in either innings against the rabbits.

To the story of the Jardine-Allen altercation, described by the latter in his two letters home, must be added the final brief exchange when he returned to the dressing-room after his talk with Warner:

'Well, am I playing?'

'Of course you are. I don't know what you're talking about.'

Gubby cannot now recall the grounds on which he predicted that leg-theory was unlikely to recur. As to the preference for Paynter over Pataudi he thinks retrospectively that it was a clever selection to bring in another left-hander with Leyland to scotch the menace of the spinners, O'Reilly and Ironmonger. At Arthur Mailey's request he made it up with Armstrong before the tour was over.

As all whose memory extends as far, or who have a knowledge of cricket history, well know the tour reached its bitter climax in the Third Test at Adelaide. England this time won the toss, and after losing four for 30 managed, thanks chiefly to Leyland, Wyatt, Paynter and Verity, to reach 341. On the Adelaide pitch Jack Hobbs rated this a poor score. However against Larwood and Allen Australia's start was scarcely better than England's had been and against the full blast of Bodyline and some excellent fast bowling by Gubby they ended 119 behind. This was the innings in which Billy Woodfull was hit over the heart by Larwood; in which Plum Warner's solicitous entry into the Australian dressing-room was rebuffed in Woodfull's never-to-be-forgotten phrase, 'Mr Warner, there are two teams out there. One is trying to play cricket and the other is not'; in which Bertie Oldfield was felled by Larwood as he aimed to hook, albeit exonerating the bowler from blame before lapsing into unconsciousness.

It was the last ball of Larwood's second over which hit Woodfull, who after some minutes was able to continue. Before Larwood bowled his third over came the fateful switching of the field from an orthodox one to Bodyline. Woodfull being at the batting end, both the crowd at Adelaide and the cricket world ever since could put on the move only one interpretation. The principal actors afterwards gave different versions in print, Jardine writing that Larwood made a sign to him indicating that he wanted a leg-side field, while Larwood stated that the initiative was the captain's. Gubby thinks of it as having been the decision of Jardine – to whom in any case fell the responsibility for an action which lost him the last vestige of Australian sympathy for his situation. According to Jardine the switch was misinterpreted, a plea which scarcely accords with his comment to Larwood, overheard by Hammond, Allen and Bradman, the non-striker, while Woodfull was recovering from the blow: 'Well bowled, Harold,' he said. At this range of time one can only add that if the change-over was not an intimidating gesture it was at least a thoroughly stupid one.

As to the remark, Gubby inclines to give Jardine the benefit of the

AUSTRALIA v ENGLAND
(Third Test)

At Adelaide, 13–19 January 1933

ENGLAND

H. Sutcliffe c Wall b O'Reilly	9	– c sub (L. P. J. O'Brien) b Wall	..	7
*D. R. Jardine b Wall	3	– lbw b Ironmonger		56
W. R. Hammond c Oldfield b Wall	2	– (5) b Bradman		85
†L. E. G. Ames b Ironmonger	3	– (7) b O'Reilly		69
M. Leyland b O'Reilly	83	– (6) c Wall b Ironmonger		42
R. E. S. Wyatt c Richardson b Grimmett ..	78	– (3) c Wall b O'Reilly		49
E. Paynter c Fingleton b Wall	77	– (10) not out		1
G. O. B. Allen lbw b Grimmett	15	– (4) lbw b Grimmett		15
H. Verity c Richardson b Wall	45	– (8) lbw b O'Reilly		40
W. Voce b Wall	8	– (11) b O'Reilly		8
H. Larwood not out	3	– (9) c Bradman b Ironmonger	...	8
B 1, l-b 7, n-b 7	15	B 17, l-b 11, n-b 4		32

1/4 2/16 3/16 4/30 5/186   341   1/7 2/91 3/123 4/154 5/245   412
6/196 7/228 8/324 9/336 10/341   6/296 7/394 8/395 9/403 10/
                                          412

Bowling: *First Innings* – Wall 34.1–10–72–5; O'Reilly 50–19–82–2; Ironmonger 20–6–50–1; Grimmett 28–6–94–2; McCabe 14–3–28–0. *Second Innings* – Wall 29–6–75–1; O'Reilly 50.3–21–79–4; Ironmonger 57–21–87–3; Grimmett 35–9–74–1; McCabe 16–0–42–0; Bradman 4–0–23–1.

AUSTRALIA

J. H. W. Fingleton c Ames b Allen	0	– b Larwood		0
*W. M. Woodfull b Allen	22	– not out		73
D. G. Bradman c Allen b Larwood	8	– (4) c and b Verity		66
S. J. McCabe c Jardine b Larwood	8	– (5) c Leyland b Allen		7
W. H. Ponsford b Voce	85	– (3) c Jardine b Larwood		3
V. Y. Richardson b Allen	28	– c Allen b Larwood		21
†W. A. S. Oldfield retired hurt	41	– absent hurt		
C. V. Grimmett c Voce b Allen	10	– (7) b Allen		6
T. W. Wall b Hammond	6	– (8) b Allen		0
W. J. O'Reilly b Larwood	0	– (9) b Larwood		5
H. Ironmonger not out	0	– (10) b Allen		0
B 2, l-b 11, n-b 1	14	B 4, l-b 2, w 1, n-b 5		12

1/1 2/18 3/34 4/51 5/131   222   1/3 2/12 3/100 4/116 5/171   193
6/194 7/212 8/222 9/222   6/183 7/183 8/192 9/193

Bowling: *First Innings* – Larwood 25–6–55–3; Allen 23–4–71–4; Hammond 17.4–4–30–1; Voce 14–5–21–1; Verity 16–7–31–0. *Second Innings* – Larwood 19–3–71–4; Allen 17.2–5–50–4; Hammond 9–3–27–0; Voce 4–1–7–0; Verity 20–12–26–1.

Umpires: G. Borwick and G. A. Hele.

England won by 338 runs.

doubt. He thinks it may have been made not because Larwood had hit Woodfull but in the midst of all the hullabaloo in order to keep up his morale.

As the crowd seethed with anger the immediate anxiety was whether, if any other batsman – and especially, of course, Bradman – were hit, the crowd would jump the picket-fence. That the authorities sensed the danger is evidenced by the presence of a considerable body of mounted police behind the stand capable of deploying on to the field at a moment's notice. Such a crowning disaster was, however, at once minimized when Bradman was c. Allen (at short-leg), b. Larwood 8. The mainstay of the Australian innings was the 85 of Ponsford, who when he had scored 3 should have been caught in the slips off Allen. Hammond, 'the best slip I ever saw', dropped a gaper, says Gubby who was amused by the form of the apology: 'Suppose you thought I was going to catch it?' If he had done so Australia would have been 50-odd for *five*.

England built solidly on their first innings advantage, and were already impregnably placed 500 runs on when Gubby began his next letter home:

> I am at present sitting in the press box with Arthur Mailey watching Ames and Verity bat in our second innings. They have put on 89 so far and this is the second time in the match that Verity has astonished everyone by batting like an opening batsman. It has been a most unpleasant match as you will have gathered from the papers. There has been nothing but rows and barracking until I am fed up with everything to do with cricket. As you will see from the enclosed paper, which is only a typical example, both the press and more especially the public are taking their set-backs very badly. Plum is worried to death and says the side may have to return at once to England, but that is rot. Premiers, Bishops and the Board of Control are all up in the air. I have not changed my mind in any way about the leg theory and all the side is aware of the fact. I just hate it and will not do it.
>
> *Later.* I need not give you the wording of the B. of Control's protest as you will have seen it in every paper. I think they have been very stupid to send it especially without having tried to come to some arrangement with Plum, Jardine, Palairet and Woodfull here first. The side, I understand, are considering sending a cable to the MCC Committee.
>
> *Later.* We polished them off fairly quickly today and 'things', meaning troubles, seem a little quieter. The cable from the team to MCC was a very reasonable one so that has passed off all right. What will happen remains to be seen. I came out with eight for 121 in the match which will give some of the gentlemen of the English press something to think over. I expect they will get their laugh later.

Gubby recalls how after the Woodfull-Warner incident Jardine locked the dressing-room door, told the team how the manager had been snubbed, and added: 'No one must say a word to the press.' Plum, convinced that the story had been leaked by the journalist Fingleton (an accusation always denied by him), offered £1 to the bowler who got him out for a duck. Larwood bowled him with what Hobbs described as an unplayable ball, pitching on the middle stump and hitting the off, and duly collected his £1. (That meant 'a pair' for Fingleton, and his exclusion from the last two Tests.)

Jardine was depressed by the news of the Australian Board's cable to MCC and thought MCC would let him down. Gubby told him that on the contrary by using the word 'unsportsmanlike' the Board had played into his hands. MCC would never stand for English sportsmanship being called into question. At this crisis in affairs Gubby planned a week-end for Douglas and him with friends by the sea at Victor Harbour. At the end of the match they walked through the crowd together across the ground amid mingled boos and cheers and were glad to jump into a taxi. The gate — at Adelaide as at Melbourne — had twice broken the ground record, on the first day with 39,301 and on the second with 50,962.

From the time of the Australian Board sending their first cable the press coverage of the tour and of the diplomatic — or undiplomatic — exchanges swelled to an unprecedented degree. The views of cricketers of every generation were sought and paraded. Nigel Haig, Gubby's county captain, is recorded, for instance, as saying he was glad he had got his wickets 'without resorting to intimidation'.

We have intimidation in Law 42 (unfair play) nowadays, and the word is, alas! in the 1980s part of the language of cricket. Haig's use of it in 1933 is an early one — but then no one until this tour had had recourse to it.

The Adelaide match, utterly deplorable though it had been in many respects, had the consolation for Gubby that it much enhanced his reputation. With Voce nursing a strain and taking only one wicket, more devolved on him, including, as in the second innings at Melbourne, the use of the new ball. The response was his eight for 121 in 40 eight-ball overs. He was lbw to Grimmett for 15 in each innings. His getting the new ball at Adelaide, incidentally, was one of those slices of luck of which cricket is compounded. Larwood during his first over decided he would prefer the other end. Gubby was therefore brought on for one over instead of Voce for the change to be made, and immediately took Fingleton's wicket. He continued to be given it in partnership with Larwood until the Fifth Test when he was not wholly fit.

While the MCC team moved on from Adelaide by way of the return match against New South Wales at Sydney and a couple of up-country games to Brisbane, the repercussions of the match that S. J. Southerton in *Wisden* was due to describe as 'probably the most unpleasant ever played' rumbled on. This was now a story of Commonwealth interest going well beyond the confines of cricket, and every newspaper in both countries was full of it. The Australian Board's cable to MCC, sent on the fifth and penultimate day of the Third Test, had said:

> Body-line bowling has assumed such proportions as to menace the best interests of the game, making protection of the body by batsmen the main consideration. This is causing intensely bitter feeling between the players as well as injury. In our opinion it is unsportsmanlike. Unless stopped at once it is likely to upset the friendly relations existing between Australia and England.

Five days later came MCC's answer the tone of which, as Gubby had assured Jardine would happen, clearly mirrored the indignation felt by the Committee at the use of the word 'unsportsmanlike'.

> We, Marylebone Cricket Club, deplore your cable. We deprecate your opinion that there has been unsportsmanlike play. We have fullest confidence in captain, team and managers and are convinced that they would do nothing to infringe either the Laws of Cricket or the spirit of the game. We have no evidence that our confidence has been misplaced. Much as we regret accidents to Woodfull and Oldfield, we understand that in neither case was the bowler to blame.
>
> If the Australian Board of Control wish to propose a new Law or Rule, it shall receive our careful consideration in due course.
>
> We hope the situation is not now as serious as your cable would seem to indicate, but if it is such as to jeopardise the good relations between English and Australian cricketers and you consider it desirable to cancel remainder of programme we would consent, but with great reluctance.

Commenting in his next letter home Gubby said:

> I thought the MCC reply was magnificent – so dignified after their common outburst. The whole thing has given Douglas a great fright and seems to have done him good ... He seems to look on the leg-theory in a more gentlemanly light.

The exchange of cables continued – there were five in all at this stage – up to the end of the Queensland match preceding the Fourth Test.

Against Queensland Gubby made 66, his highest score of the tour. He was critical of the umpires in several letters and here remarks:

> I caught Oxenham at close in short-leg, though I say so myself, brilliantly eighteen inches off the ground and he was given not out.

This was the only time Gubby saw Eddie Gilbert, the Aboriginal, who was said from a short run to bowl very fast and to have a dubious action. He was possibly somewhat nervous of letting himself go against MCC.

Anyway Gubby thought he was neither very quick nor suspect. It was almost unbearably hot and humid in Brisbane – England have never since been asked to play a Test there in February – and on a lifeless pitch the Fourth Test pursued a leisurely progress. Australia won the toss and batted, and it was here that an Australian player said something to Gubby about the bowling tactics.

Vic Richardson, promoted as Woodfull's opening partner instead of Fingleton, remarked to Gubby, fielding at short-leg, on how often he was having to duck. He said, 'I'll take guard well outside the leg-stump.' Gubby replied that he could stand where he liked, but he never discussed the English bowling tactics with anyone – but he remembers that when Richardson took guard two or three inches outside the leg-stump he was still repeatedly having to duck. In other words the attack was on the line of the body rather than on the stumps. Richardson at the cost of numerous bruises made 83 and 32. No one ever doubted his courage.

With Voce unfit, more work than usual was required of Gubby – and also of Hammond, who was a valuable relief bowler throughout the tour. Up to a point Australia looked as though they might win this match and so square the series. Against Australia's 340 England, with Paynter supposedly in hospital with tonsillitis, struggled to 198 for five when Paynter appeared in the dressing-room in his pyjamas having been brought by Bill Voce in a taxi. Gubby lasted half an hour for 13 before being caught behind off the new ball. At this point to the surprise of all Paynter appeared, walking very slowly to the wicket under a panama hat and to great applause. His appearance was instigated by Jardine, as Warner records. When the manager had reported Paynter's illness to the captain the latter said, 'What about those fellows who marched to Kandahar with fever on them?' Paynter had reached 24 not out at the close, went back to hospital for the night, and returned next day to take his score to 83 and so enable England to lead by 15 runs.

Gubby had bowled well and without luck for two wickets in the first innings. Writing of the 'frightful, killing heat' on the first day Jack Hobbs in his *Fight for the Ashes* wrote that: 'Our players were knocked right out. Allen, one of the tour's successes, looked positively ill, with sunken eyes, though he said he felt well. Actually he had bowled himself to a complete standstill. That is just one example of how each man did his utmost.' Early in the second innings Gubby badly wrenched his left side. He carried on as best he could, picking up three more wickets in 17 overs and helping to bowl out Australia for 175. Hobbs wrote 'that it was only when a tentative hand just touched the aching spot that we had any proof he was quite unfit to play. This time my medal went to Allen for pluck.'

So only 160 runs stood between England and the recovery of the Ashes. There were storms in the offing to keep Australia's hopes alive,

AUSTRALIA v ENGLAND
(Fourth Test)

AUSTRALIA

V. Y. Richardson st Ames b Hammond....	83	– c Jardine b Verity.................	32
*W. M. Woodfull b Mitchell................	67	– c Hammond b Mitchell	19
D. G. Bradman b Larwood.................	76	– c Mitchell b Larwood............	24
S. J. McCabe c Jardine b Allen.............	20	– (5) b Verity	22
W. H. Ponsford b Larwood	19	– (4) c Larwood b Allen	0
L. S. Darling c Ames b Allen................	17	– run out	39
E. H. Bromley c Verity b Larwood	26	– c Hammond b Allen.............	7
†H. S. B. Love lbw b Mitchell	5	– lbw b Larwood	3
T. W. Wall not out	6	– c Jardine b Allen.................	2
W. J. O'Reilly c Hammond b Larwood	6	– b Larwood	4
H. Ironmonger st Ames b Hammond.......	8	– not out	0
B 5, l-b 1, n-b 1	7	B 13, l-b 9, n-b 1	23

1/133 2/200 3/233 4/264 5/267	340	1/46 2/79 3/81 4/91 5/136	175
6/292 7/315 8/317 9/329 10/340		6/163 7/169 8/169 9/171 10/	
		175	

Bowling: *First Innings* – Larwood 31–7–101–4; Allen 24–4–83–2; Hammond 23–5–61–2; Mitchell 16–5–49–2; Verity 27–12–39–0. *Second Innings* – Larwood 17.3–3–49–3; Allen 17–3–44–3; Hammond 10–4–18–0; Mitchell 5–0–11–1; Verity 19–6–30–2.

ENGLAND

*D. R. Jardine c Love b O'Reilly	46	– lbw b Ironmonger	24
H. Sutcliffe lbw b O'Reilly	86	– c Darling b Wall..................	2
W. R. Hammond b McCabe	20	– (4) c Bromley b Ironmonger	14
R. E. S. Wyatt c Love b Ironmonger	12		
M. Leyland c Bradman b O'Reilly.........	12	– (3) c McCabe b O'Reilly.........	86
†L. E. G. Ames c Darling b Ironmonger ...	17	– (5) not out	14
G. O. B. Allen c Love b Wall	13		
E. Paynter c Richardson b Ironmonger.....	83	– (6) not out	14
H. Larwood b McCabe......................	23		
H. Verity not out............................	23		
T. B. Mitchell lbw b O'Reilly	0		
B 6, l-b 12, n-b 3	21	B 2, l-b 4, n-b 2	8

1/114 2/157 3/165 4/188 5/198	356	1/5 2/78	(4 wkts.) 162
6/216 7/225 8/264 9/356 10/356		3/118 4/138	

Bowling: *First Innings* – Wall 33–6–66–1; O'Reilly 67.4–27–120–4; Ironmonger 43–19–69–3; McCabe 23–7–40–2; Bromley 10–4–19–0; Bradman 7–1–17–0; Darling 2–0–4–0. *Second Innings* – Wall 7–1–17–1; O'Reilly 30–11–65–1; Ironmonger 35–13–47–2; McCabe 7.4–2–25–0.

Umpires: G. Borwick and G. A. Hele.

England won by 6 wickets.

and they were fortified by the dismissal of Sutcliffe at once. However Leyland, promoted probably to scotch the spinners, stayed with his obdurate captain until the latter left when half the runs needed had been made. Leyland dominated the last day, staying until only 24 were needed. In gathering rain Ames and Paynter knocked off the runs, to give England victory by six wickets. The Ashes – at a price – were regained.

Gubby's next letter home was written from the SS *Orungal*, 'a very nice little boat of about 6000 tons cruising slowly down to Sydney from

Brisbane', with eight of the side 'trying to recover from the heat and celebrations':

> It is a great relief to us all that the series is decided and in our favour. We had another very exciting Test up there and I thought twice we had lost it. Our batting has terrified me ever since the débâcle in the Second Test at Melbourne as none of our leading players ever play a shot and consequently the rather limited, but accurate, Australian attack has been on top of us. I strained my left side rather badly. From then on I only bowled fairly well and everything went right. I am afraid I may not be fit enough to play in the Fifth Test but I hope I shall be as Douglas is very anxious that I should play and I would like to try and show the Sydneyites that after all I can bowl a bit. I went down and stayed with the Wilsons at their house by the sea as soon as the match was over and had one complete day with them. It rained the whole time but I enjoyed it.

Sir Leslie Wilson was the Governor of Queensland, he who with Toby Watt had shown such friendliness to Gubby and his brother when they were children in Sydney. Gubby's criticism of the English batting will not perhaps surprise those who have had to endure the over-cautious methods of our batsmen abroad in more recent times. This side, in fact, was short of high-class natural stroke-makers, Hammond apart. He it was who could have given the example. However he had had a great tour in 1928–29 waiting for the runs to come, and he stuck to the method which had stood him in good stead before. Nor had he forgotten 1928–29 in 1946–47 when as captain he laid down a policy of attrition which doomed his side to failure.

Gubby was not very communicative in his correspondence about the Fifth Test at Sydney, except to say he asked not to play because his left side was still troubling him. However he was persuaded to do so by Jardine because there was some doubt about the fitness of Larwood. Gubby, though at well below his best pace, struggled through the game, and, happily, Voce was now back in harness though not bowling with his previous effect. It was Verity who, having captured only three wickets in three Tests hitherto, came good at this last opportunity, taking eight for 95. Perhaps because the batsmen had lasted the series more strongly than the bowlers runs came more freely in this Test than in any of the others. Australia, after Woodfull had won his fourth toss out of five, made 435, much their best score of the series, nearly everyone making runs and notably Oldfield – fit again after missing the Fourth Test – with 52 not out. Larwood bowled 32.2 overs to take four for 98 and O'Reilly's wicket in twenty-five overs cost Gubby 128 runs. England dropped ten catches, six off Larwood, three off Allen including a caught and bowled.

The most dramatic part in this concluding Test was indeed played by Larwood. When Sutcliffe and Hammond were engaged on a lengthy second wicket partnership late on the second afternoon Jardine, himself out for 18, told Larwood, weary after all his bowling, apparently without preamble or special explanation, to put his pads on, prepared to go in as night-watchman. Although Gubby has no recollection of this episode it is well authenticated, by Larwood himself among others. His friends calmed down Larwood who was still so angry when called upon to go in a few minutes before time that he told Ames to get ready as he was going to throw his wicket away. He tried without success, taking a suicidal run, only for Bradman's throw to miss the stumps by a hairsbreadth.

It was still with a sense of being ill-used that Larwood went in as Hammond's partner next morning – went in and proceeded to play with freedom and style. His resentment presumably melted as his score mounted and when they had added 92 it was Hammond who departed, directly after reaching his hundred. Larwood made 98 before having the singular ill-luck to be caught by clumsy old Ironmonger down by his toes at mid-on – whereupon the Sydney crowd, who had booed his bowling tactics unceasingly both in this Test and the First, stood and gave him the most remarkable sustained ovation. Such is human nature! He had batted for no more than two and a quarter hours – it had been the fastest English innings of the series.

A slump occurred after Larwood left, but Gubby sustained the tail with a thoroughly good and valuable 48 before, with England narrowly in the lead, he was once again last out having a go, this time to a marvellous catch. Bradman turning and running full tilt, just reached the ball with arms out-stretched mid-way between cover-point and the boundary. Hobbs thought that no one else could have made it. When Australia went in for their tenth and final innings of the series Larwood at once had Richardson caught by Gubby at short-leg. This was his seventh catch of the series and one of the best as he jumped and checked the ball with his right hand before recovering in time to grasp it with his left. It was Larwood's thirty-third wicket of the series and it was to be his last in Test cricket.

Woodfull and Bradman now engaged in a fruitful stand of 115 for the second wicket, Woodfull stolid as ever, Bradman as always in the rubber living dangerously, improvising a daring array of strokes and moving his feet laterally – and mostly to leg-ward – against the Bodyline. Hobbs records that 'when he had drawn away more than a yard he was struck on an arm above the elbow.' This incident tells much, both of the degree to which he forsook the orthodox and the width to which Larwood (and Voce) were prepared, if necessary, to bowl in chase of him. (This was reputed to be the only time either of the bowlers registered a hit on

AUSTRALIA v ENGLAND
(Fifth Test)

At Sydney, 23–28 February 1933

AUSTRALIA

V. Y. Richardson c Jardine b Larwood.....	0	– c Allen b Larwood	0
*W. M. Woodfull b Larwood...............	14	– b Allen	67
D. G. Bradman b Larwood.................	48	– b Verity	71
L. P. J. O'Brien c Larwood b Voce	61	– c Verity b Voce	5
S. J. McCabe c Hammond b Verity.........	73	– c Jardine b Voce.................	4
L. S. Darling b Verity.......................	85	– c Wyatt b Verity.................	7
†W. A. S. Oldfield run out	52	– c Wyatt b Verity.................	5
P. K. Lee c Jardine b Verity	42	– b Allen	15
W. J. O'Reilly b Allen	19	– b Verity	1
H. H. Alexander not out	17	– lbw, b Verity......................	0
H. Ironmonger b Larwood	1	– not out	0
B 13, l-b 9, w 1......................	23	B 4, n-b 3	7

1/0 2/59 3/64 4/163 5/244   **435** 1/0 2/115 3/135 4/139 5/148   **182**
6/328 7/385 8/414 9/430 10/435   6/161 7/177 8/178 9/178 10/
182

Bowling: *First Innings* – Larwood 32.2–10–98–4; Voce 24–4–80–1; Allen 25–1–128–1; Hammond 8–0–32–0; Verity 17–3–62–3; Wyatt 2–0–12–0. *Second Innings* – Larwood 11–0–44–1; Voce 10–0–34–2; Allen 11.4–2–54–2; Hammond 3–0–10–0; Verity 19–9–33–5.

ENGLAND

*D. R. Jardine c Oldfield b O'Reilly........	18	– c Richardson b Ironmonger......	24
H. Sutcliffe c Richardson b O'Reilly........	56		
W. R. Hammond lbw b Lee.................101		– (4) not out	75
H. Larwood c Ironmonger b Lee	98		
M. Leyland run out...........................	42	– (3) b Ironmonger	0
R. E. S. Wyatt c Ironmonger b O'Reilly....	51	– (2) not out	61
†L. E. G. Ames run out.....................	4		
E. Paynter b Lee............................	9		
G. O. B. Allen c Bradman b Lee............	48		
H. Verity c Oldfield b Alexander	4		
W. Voce not out	7		
B 7, l-b 7, n-b 2	16	B 6, l-b 1, n-b 1	8

1/31 2/153 3/245 4/310 5/330   **454** 1/43 2/43   (2 wkts.) **168**
6/349 7/374 8/418 9/434 10/454

Bowling: *First Innings* – Alexander 35–1–129–1; McCabe 12–1–27–0; O'Reilly 45–7–100–3; Ironmonger 31–13–64–0; Lee 40.2–11–111–4; Darling 7–5–3–0; Bradman 1–0–4–0. *Second Innings* – Alexander 11–2–25–0; McCabe 5–2–10–0; O'Reilly 15–5–32–0; Ironmonger 26–12–34–2; Lee 12.2–3–52–0; Darling 2–0–7–0.

Umpires: G. Borwick and G. A. Hele.

England won by 8 wickets.

Bradman throughout the tour.

Larwood had been suffering awhile from a sore left toe, a not surprising result of the pounding of that left foot over after over, match after match, on the hard unyielding pitches. Now suddenly in mid-over he pulled up in great pain. He stood and delivered the balls remaining, off which Woodfull made no attempt to score. Though now a passenger, Larwood was required by his captain to remain on the field so long as Bradman batted. When the latter was bowled by Verity for 71, Larwood was allowed to go off. Thus the two chief actors of the Test series of 1932–33 left the field together, neither, it is said, having a word for the other.

For Larwood it was the last exit. After the next interval with six Australian wickets standing, Jardine expected him to return. Gubby, however, with a good deal more sympathy for a fellow bowler and friend, made his own examination. He at once saw that the toe was swollen and inflamed and there was no possibility of Larwood bowling again. This Gubby relayed to the captain. The sad fact was that Larwood had fractured a bone in the toe. He played for Notts as a batsman during the first half of the 1933 summer, and though for a few seasons he could generate a degree of pace off a shortened run he never bowled truly fast again.

So long as Woodfull stayed against the depleted and tired attack Australia had a good chance of setting England a stiff target, but Woodfull played on to Allen who later bowled Lee, and Verity did the rest. England thus had to make only 164 to win, and this they did thanks to a long, defensive innings by Wyatt, who went in first and took out his bat for 61, and a fluent one by Hammond, who won the match with a six.

With the finish of the rubber Gubby's cricket in Australia was all but over. He played as a batsman against Victoria in an agreeable and exciting game which ended with the scores level. It was a moral victory for Victoria, who had lost only three second innings wickets. Gubby's contribution was 0 and 48. Far from being considered an anti-climax, incidentally, 36,000 paid at Melbourne to see this match. MCC even went on to Adelaide for the return South Australia match, but Gubby was rested, and so was able, before moving on to New Zealand, to return to Sydney and give a party to the Allen family and 'all the people who have been most kind to me'. His last letter from Australia sums up his feelings.

I have simply loved it all and particularly Sydney. After all, I have seen it in the very best possible manner with no work to do and not a care in the world.

Gubby's personal farewells were in pathetic contrast to that accorded the team. When they sailed from Sydney for New Zealand there was said (by Fingleton) to be not a single man prominent in the world of Australian cricket to bid them goodbye.

The most tragic figure was, of course, that of Douglas Jardine. There he was, this dedicated, surely misguided man sailing out of Sydney with scarcely a friendly wave. He had antagonized Australians of all sorts both by what he had done and the apparent disregard he showed for public opinion. Off the field one man who had gone out of his way to ease his path was Gubby, one of the few truly popular members of the touring party and the one best able to bring him into the circle of his family and friends. Far from resenting either Gubby's place in the social scene, or his refusal to fall in with his Bodyline plan, Jardine on his return home wrote this personal note to Gubby's father.

Dear Sir Walter,
    Please excuse great haste and this paper — I have taken refuge here from Press men and Publishers who made my home pretty trying for my people to live in!
    This just on the subject of Obbie — I don't think I am betraying any confidence if I give you my written report to MCC as far as he is concerned, you I know will not broadcast it.
        'G. O. Allen set a truly magnificent example to the side, knocking off smoking and drinking — an excellent tourer in every way, and one who deserved every atom of success which came his way, and was, in fact unlucky — or so it seemed to me, in not having more success with the bat — a wonderful short leg.'
    I can't say more than that for I mean every word of it — how pleased and justly proud you and Lady Allen will be to have him back. I hope you are both very well. Your family were extraordinarily good to me in Australia.
                                In haste, yours sincerely,
                                    Douglas R. Jardine

As to the personal relationship between Gubby and his captain it answers every question. Now for the picture that has ever since remained clear in his mind, and which he here records, of how Bodyline came into existence:

The story may have begun as far back as 1928–29 when some of the spectators in Australia were childishly unpleasant to Douglas Jardine, mainly because he frequently wore the colourful Harlequin cap. Douglas was a very determined man, of that there is no doubt, but he was also a rather shy, sensitive one and the behaviour of some of the crowds did not endear them to him. He did not hate all Australians, as has often been written, but he may have felt when he accepted the captaincy that he had something of an account to settle.
    In the summer of 1930, Don Bradman, with his dedication, immense ability and range of stroke established himself as the major threat to England for the foreseeable future. On the other hand some ventured the opinion that during his innings in the Fifth

Test at The Oval he had appeared 'hesitant' against the pace of Larwood. Be that as it may, he made 232, some of it on a pitch helpful to the bowlers, and Larwood's analysis was one for 132. I don't know whether Douglas saw the innings, but if not he was certainly made aware of the 'rumours'.

As soon as he was appointed captain for the coming tour, and possibly earlier, Douglas clearly set his mind not so much as to how Don could be got out, but as to how best to contain him. He unquestionably had discussions with the Notts captain, Arthur Carr, and his two fast bowlers, Harold Larwood and Bill Voce. He also questioned F. R. Foster, the great pre-war fastish left-arm bowler about his field placing.

There are many stories about what took place at those meetings. I think Douglas certainly asked Larwood if he thought he could keep Bradman quiet bowling leg-theory, NOT what became known as Bodyline. It is important to establish the difference: leg theory means a packed leg-side field with the bowler aiming at leg-stump with only an occasional 'bouncer': Bodyline means approximately the same field, plenty of 'bouncers' many of them on the line of the batsman. It is my belief that Douglas came to no definite conclusions as a result of these discussions other than that fast leg-theory would probably be the best bet. So when the selectors and captain met to choose the team, Douglas asked for plenty of pace and got what he wanted. I am convinced that there is no truth whatsoever in the theory that the selectors, all of whom I came to know well, were involved in any preconceived plot.

Harold Larwood, and I think Bill Bowes, are on record as saying 'bouncers' and leg-theory were discussed on the ship. I have checked recently with Bob Wyatt, the vice-captain, Les Ames and Freddie Brown and they all agree with me that they never once heard the subject mentioned. There was, however, some childish talk of the only way to beat the Australians was by hating them.

In the early state matches nothing unusual took place. It was not until the MCC v An Australian XI match at Melbourne in mid-November in which Don Bradman, Bill Woodfull, and several Test match candidates were playing, that a leg-side field, at times five or six strong, was set. Rather more 'bouncers' were bowled, mainly by Voce and Bowes, neither of whom had anything approaching Larwood's pace or accuracy. The Australian press made a meal of it, but were unable to pin it on Douglas as he was not playing.

Bradman did not play in the First Test match. Whilst the field placing was about the same, there was a further increase in the number of 'bouncers', but as Larwood's and Voce's line of attack was still mainly at the leg stump, it was in my opinion 'within bounds', though a poor type of cricket. Bradman returned to the Australian team for the Second Test match at Melbourne and I became suspicious about our tactics when I learned that all four fast bowlers were to play to the exclusion of a spinner. My suspicions were further aroused when just before the start of play Douglas tried unsuccessfully to persuade me to bowl more 'bouncers' to a stronger leg-side field.

In the first innings Don played-on first ball to a 'bouncer' from Bowes — and Larwood, Voce and Bowes bowled much as they had previously. It was in the second innings when he was making his famous hundred and Harold had returned to the field having had boot-trouble that, in my opinion, the dramatic change came about. Incensed by a highly vociferous crowd and not being in one of his happier frames of mind, Harold started to bowl many more 'bouncers' and to alter his line of attack away from leg stump to that of the batsman, Bill Voce following suit. As they did so, Douglas moved more fielders across to the leg-side and by the close of the innings in my opinion Bodyline was born. I appreciate the term had been coined earlier by the Australian press, but I maintain that this was the first occasion its use was justified. And bearing in mind the Melbourne pitch, normally helpful to fast bowlers, had had no pace or lift in it from the start, it was blatantly clear that it would become an extremely hostile and totally unacceptable form of attack on faster pitches with their inherent uneven bounce of the ball. I have little to add to my story other than that in subsequent Tests the field placing was carefully adjusted for selected batsmen according to whether and if so how they hooked. In other words I maintain Bodyline developed, rather than was planned in advance. Incidentally it was never bowled at tail-enders.

Finally I must make further reference to 'uneven bounce'. It is extraordinary that virtually no one writing at the time or since about Bodyline mentions it. Nowadays it is a major topic. I call it 'the new dimension of excuse'. But I am sure uneven bounce has existed since the game began. In my day it was accepted as a fact of life but, if ever there was a time when it must have played a major part it was when Bodyline was being employed. Harold would drop three on the same spot: one would come through head high, the next hip high and the next chest high. Surely that must have added many of them were hit. I think Bodyline would have succeeded regardless of the uneven bounce, but not to the extent that it did.

I have been questioned many times by authors and journalists and on television about Bodyline, but what I have said has generally been edited, and vital points sometimes omitted. I am glad to have had the chance of telling the complete story of its evolution for the first time.

9
Between Two Tours

The last stage of the old MCC Australasian tours, consisting of a few weeks and at least three matches in New Zealand, were seldom satisfactory affairs if only because successive teams could not summon the resources to do justice to the warmth of the hospitality invariably extended or the scenic delights of a beautiful country. In the case of most of Jardine's side though not of Gubby, after all that had happened there was a specially keen urge to get home. Moreover bad weather interfered with the three matches, at Wellington, Christchurch and Auckland. All were drawn, the latter two being three-day Tests wherein England made, respectively, 560 for eight declared and 548 for seven declared. The modest bowling was hammered by Hammond to the extent of 227 and 336 not out. The latter effort, virtuoso performance though it was, had a strong element of bathos seeing that New Zealand had been previously bowled out for 158. Gubby went gingerly, nervous of the muscle in the side which had troubled him since the second innings of the Brisbane Test, taking only two wickets, one of them that of Dempster, the man who mattered most. Dempster headed the first generation of New Zealand Test batsmen, and it is doubtful, with due respect to Donnelly, Sutcliffe, and Turner, whether they have ever produced a better.

Gubby enjoyed seeing Tom Lowry again, visiting the Maoris in their Rotorua reserve, and traversing the North Island by car, but with an American holiday in view he stepped thankfully on to the RMMS *Aorangi*, bound from Auckland to Vancouver, with stops at Suva and Honolulu. In Fiji there was a great welcome, but in Hawaii they were for the first time in seven months or so private citizens and could breast or capsize on the Waikiki breakers without attracting the slightest attention.

The team crossed the Rockies by the Canadian Pacific Railway and sailed from Montreal to Liverpool in the *Duchess of Atholl*, but for Gubby the chance of seeing Hollywood at the invitation of friends was too alluring to miss. He therefore arranged to take ship from Vancouver down to Los Angeles, and thence after his Hollywood interlude, by train to New York and the most convenient liner home.

He sailed from Vancouver to San Francisco on a ship of the Grace line – a name soon to mean a lot to him – called the *Santa Elena* which he and his Jap steward were convinced was top-heavy and might easily roll over, like the *Waratah*. An air trip (which in those days was surely more hazardous than any ship) in a private de Havilland Fox Moth, piloted by the son of friends met on the voyage across the Pacific, took him to their home at San Mateo. Thence the kind Heatons drove him down to Hollywood where they and Gubby, too, were to stay with the ultra-glamorous English-born star, Elissa Landi. He treasures the book she inscribed for him, written purportedly with her own fair hand, a sentimental novel of some merit called *House for Sale*. With such a start Gubby was assured of a high old time – which he duly enjoyed to the hilt. He had always been fervently attracted to the movies, and here he was where it all happened with the stars themselves. He saw the film *Morning Glory* being made at the R.K.O. Studios with Katherine Hepburn, as delightful off the set as she was a termagant on it. At Fox they were making *Berkeley Square* with Leslie Howard and Heather Angel in the lead. At Fox he met Marlene Dietrich. The 'in' place was the Brown Derby, so, of course, he went there. He dined with Joe Lasky, the famous director, with the matinée idol, Robert Montgomery, Leslie (another) and Ruth Howard, and Douglas Fairbanks junior, and moved on to stay with Nigel Bruce and his wife. He was a regular attender at Lord's whom Gubby had known for many years. Nigel Bruce had made a considerable name on the London stage and had played cricket for MCC and the actors' club, the Thespids. C. Aubrey Smith and he looked the part of the archetypal Englishmen both in front of the cameras and in the glittering life of Hollywood. Bruce arranged for his guest to see a baseball game from 'behind the plate', and Gubby watched with admiration the pitchers not only swinging the strangely stitched ball either way but, according to their grip, making it rise and dip. Finally when the moment came to board the train to the east who should be travelling but Marlene herself! At stops Gubby accompanied her as she walked the platform exercising her small dog. Changing trains at Chicago he took the chance of a preview look at the forthcoming World Fair.

New York he found only marginally less enjoyable a spot than Hollywood. An old Eton friend, Roger Chetwode, working for the bankers, J. P. Morgan, showed him round town. He saw the great sprawling city from the top of the Empire State Building. He lunched at the bank with Harry Morgan, son of the chief, dined at the Famous 21 Club, and played golf on Long Island at The Links, the club of the millionaires where no one paid for anything until at the end of the year the expenditure was totted up, and the total bill divided among the members – a simple arrangement when all is said and done – if one is rich enough.

Not least Gubby met in New York a sweet-natured girl, pretty perhaps rather than beautiful, called Norah Grace, of the family who owned the shipping line already mentioned. He was strongly attracted, as also was Chetwode.

Norah Grace came to England that summer but Gubby did not see much of her as Chetwode amongst others was in hot pursuit. It was in the following summer that romance was very much in the air, the main problem for Gubby being her abundance of money and his lack of it. Many letters were exchanged during the winter of 1934–35 and they had planned to go with a party of friends for a short holiday in a villa on Lake Como belonging to one of them. On arrival in England late in July Norah was clearly very far from well and was promptly put into a nursing home for a complete rest and tests which the specialist said would last at least a fortnight. After much discussion she persuaded Gubby to go with the others. The day before he was due to return he was cabled that she was seriously ill, and by the time he reached London she had died, swiftly, tragically of Bright's Disease. What the outcome might have been Gubby cannot say, but that this was a serious affair of the heart there was no doubt.

His immediate concern when he got back from the States was not cricket but a change of job. When in 1929 on his hasty return from Lyons Debenham's Stores had offered him employment, with the great slump on and jobs hard to come by, he accepted gratefully and buckled down well enough. The picture of a debonair young Allen parading the departments in black coat and striped trousers is an appealing one which does not however exactly fit the facts. He was at first assistant to the manager of the Works Department, where they made and altered clothes. After two years of this he became assistant to the assistant general manager, dealing with customers' correspondence, interviewing them from time to time, listening to complaints and so forth. As can be imagined, though, he was scarcely cut out for a life in 'the rag trade'. After three years at Debenham's, and before he had left in September 1932 for Australia, he had put certain feelers out in other directions but wanted to keep his options open with Debenham's. They accepted this situation though the chairman preferred to pay his salary while he was away. Now came the offer of a job with the stockbrokers, David Bevan and Co, and with the good will of Sir Frederick Richmond he accepted it. It was his third change of business scene and it was to be his last. David Bevan duly changed to Bevan, Simpson, which in turn — though after Gubby ceased to be an active partner — became de Zoete and Bevan.

Always both careful and meticulous about money, Gubby had banked his Debenham salary in a separate account. He offered now to repay it, but found Richmond reluctant to accept. He thinks probably they agreed to split the amount fifty-fifty. At all events it must have been a wholly amiable parting for the good Sir Frederick became Gubby's first Stock Exchange client. As to his finances on the trip, MCC's provision was confined to an initial £100 clothing allowance and for the seven and a half months either £25 or £50 (the memory is not clear) for out-of-pocket expenses! The assumption at Lord's apparently was still that an amateur was a moneyed man. Happily in this case Sir Walter Allen augmented the miserable pittance to the tune of £150. In his last letter from New York, incidentally, Gubby struck a characteristic note which must have amused his father: 'I have finally decided to sail in the *Berengaria* ... and I am coming Tourist Class, which I hear is excellent, as it is so much cheaper.' For all the star treatment and surrounding luxury the young man's head was still firmly on his shoulders.

Gubby's holiday in the States did not exactly suit Plum Warner, already home with the team and needing moral reinforcement at Lord's. He even cabled Gubby to that effect. Arriving at last on the *Berengaria* on 24 May it did not take Gubby long to see how the land lay. When he first came into the Long Room Billy Findlay, the secretary, was in a group of four or five members of the Committee. Time has shrouded the identity of the others, but they are incidental. The exchange was short and pointed:

Findlay: 'You must have had a terrible time in Australia.'
G.O.A.: 'What do you mean? I had a marvellous time.'
Findlay: 'But the Australians behaved disgracefully. I can't believe any of our chaps bowled at anyone.'
G.O.A.: 'I don't know what's been going on here, but the sooner you try to find out what did happen the better for cricket.'

Whereat Gubby took his leave, and he and Findlay had nothing further to say to one another either that summer of 1933 or the next.

Joining David Bevan in May 1933, Gubby accepted the fact that his new chance in the City would restrict his summer's first-class cricket to the Sussex matches over the two bank holidays, and that he therefore could not possibly compete for a Test place against the West Indies. The Whitsun fixture occurred only ten days after he had returned from the bright lights of Hollywood and New York. He had not had a game of any consequence for a couple of months. Yet he put up a remarkable performance. Taking the new ball on the first morning he demolished the Sussex batting by sheer speed on a lively pitch. He finished with seven for 41 in twenty overs, which moved Thomas Moult of the *Sunday Dispatch* to remark, 'seldom in contemporary cricket do we witness fast bowling so thrilling'. A crowd of 20,000, in recognition of his success in Australia, gave him a hero's welcome on the bank holiday, applauding him all the way from the pavilion door to the middle. He responded by making 80 brisk runs out of 120, and then taking the wickets of the first three Sussex batsmen, to give himself figures of ten for 63 in the match, which Middlesex won by an innings.

Gubby after this match made his unavailability known to all, including the selectors, the chairman of whom in 1933, Warner having declined the job, was Lord Hawke. The state of affairs was fully brought out in the press. However, with Larwood out of action as a bowler all summer and Voce, after his exertions and without his partner, showing indifferent form, he suspected that pressure might be put on him to play in the first of the three Tests against the West Indies at Lord's late in June. Accordingly when he went off to stay with friends in the country the week-end the Test team was due to be chosen, no one but his father knew where he was, and he was under strict instructions not to disclose the telephone number to anyone. Sir Walter, as it turned out, was not proof against the chairman's persuasion, as Gubby realized when the butler — there were plenty about in those days in the houses he frequented — announced that Lord Hawke was on the line.

Far from pleased with his father, Gubby protested to Hawke that he was not Test Match fit. How could he be? Yet he finally allowed himself to be persuaded — one of the few cases perhaps of his being overborne in argument. In the event he was able to justify his inclusion, and help England to victory, by getting the great George Headley in both innings and Roach, the opening bat, in the first. In his only innings he thought he had hit past mid-off for four but Jack Grant, the West Indies captain and a high-class fielder, stopped the ball by diving for it and when still on the ground threw down the bowler's wicket: so it was run out 16, the only such dismissal out of his thirty-one in Tests. (For those with a nose for such things G. O. Allen was bowled four times, caught seventeen, lbw seven and stumped twice.)

Gubby remembers that Test for a special reason. On the first morning the King came, and since it was raining the teams were presented to him in the pavilion. Douglas Jardine was first received for a private talk, after which the King asked to speak to Mr Allen and began questioning him about the happenings in Australia. He wasn't quite sure that the captain had told him everything. The picture remains of George V sitting in the Committee Room wearing brown leather black-ribbed gloves and smoking from a long holder. In the course of quite a lengthy talk wherein the King showed a knowledge of the bowling tactics that astonished him, Gubby said, 'I didn't know you took an interest in cricket, sir'; to which came the reply in that slightly guttural voice, 'I take great interest in my subjects.' Then he added, 'My secretaries mark items in the papers for my attention — sometimes I also look elsewhere.'

In this case my surmise is that in addition to what he had read he had

ENGLAND v WEST INDIES

At Lord's, 24–27 June 1933

ENGLAND

C. F. Walters c Barrow b Martindale		51
H. Sutcliffe c Grant b Martindale		21
W. R. Hammond c Headley b Griffith		29
M. Leyland c Barrow b Griffith		1
*D. R. Jardine c Da Costa b Achong		21
M. J. L. Turnbull c Barrow b Achong		28
†L. E. G. Ames not out		83
G. O. B. Allen run out		16
R. W. V. Robins b Martindale		8
H. Verity c Achong b Griffith		21
G. G. Macaulay lbw b Martindale		9
B 3, l-b 5		8

1/49 2/103 3/105 4/106 5/154   296
6/155 7/194 8/217 9/265 10/296

Bowling: Martindale 24–3–85–4; Francis 18–3–52–0; Griffith 20–7–48–3; Achong 35–9–88–2; Da Costa 4–0–15–0.

WEST INDIES

C. A. Roach b Allen	0	– c Sutcliffe b Macaulay		0
†I. Barrow c and b Verity	7	– lbw b Robins		12
G. A. Headley lbw b Allen	13	– b Allen		50
E. L. G. Hoad lbw b Robins	6	– c and b Verity		36
*G. C. Grant hit wkt b Robins	26	– lbw b Macaulay		28
O. C. Da Costa b Robins	6	– lbw b Verity		1
C. A. Merry lbw b Macaulay	9	– b Macaulay		1
E. E. Achong b Robins	15	– c Hammond b Verity		10
G. N. Francis b Robins	4	– (10) not out		11
E. A. Martindale b Robins	4	– (9) b Macaulay		4
H. C. Griffith not out	1	– b Verity		18
B 3, l-b 1, n-b 2	6	B 1		1

1/1 2/17 3/27 4/31 5/40   97   1/0 2/56 3/64 4/116 5/119   172
6/51 7/87 8/92 9/96 10/97   6/120 7/133 8/138 9/146 10/
172

Bowling: *First Innings* – Macaulay 18–7–25–1; Allen 13–6–13–2; Verity 16–8–21–1; Robins 11.5–1–32–6. *Second Innings* – Macaulay 20–6–57–4; Allen 11–2–33–1; Verity 18.1–4–45–4; Robins 12–2–36–1.

Umpires: F. Chester and A. Dolphin.

England won by an innings and 27 runs.

made enquiries elsewhere also. J. H. Thomas, the former miners' leader who was then Dominions Secretary in the National Government, always hit it off well with the King, who enjoyed his earthy talk and humour. The Governor of South Australia, Sir Alexander Hore-Ruthven (afterwards Lord Gowrie) had seen Jimmy Thomas about the threat to Anglo-Australian relations during his leave in London earlier in the year.

Gradually, from the monarch downwards, something of the true nature of Bodyline began to filter through during that 1933 summer, the situation being much helped by the Second Test at Old Trafford wherein Bodyline was bowled by Constantine and Martindale for the West Indies, and then by Clark for England, and was generally reckoned an unsavoury as well as a dangerous type of cricket. (Not having played a first-class match in the intervening month, Gubby this time was not put under duress. He was however approached by Lord Hawke, who pressed him to go with Jardine's MCC team to India, and declined with thanks.)

It was immediately before this Test that he attended the Complimentary Dinner given by MCC at the Dorchester to Jardine and his team, with the president, Lord Hailsham, in the chair. *The Times* reported the President – not inappropriately Minister for War, by the way, and so a cabinet colleague of Thomas – as being 'profuse in his congratulations of the great things which had been done in Australia'. No dirty linen, obviously, was to be washed by MCC in public, nor even the slightest hint of any little local difficulty. However the Right Hon. Stanley Bruce, subsequently Lord Bruce of Melbourne, a former Prime Minister but in 1933 the Resident Minister for Australia in London, let in a breath of fresh air and common sense when he said (in answer to Thomas's Commonwealth toast): 'Whatever has to be done to restore cricket – which does not at the moment hold the position it should hold – whatever is necessary to straighten out the trouble do it by personal contact. For God's sake, not by exchanging notes, but by coming face to face.'

Considering that at the time of the dinner six of the twelve cables altogether exchanged by the Australian Board and MCC had already passed, *The Times*' concluding comment quite failed to measure up to the scale of the problem. Those at the dinner, it said, 'wandered down Park Lane, still full of praise of Mr Jardine and the great things that he had done, and with a great admiration for Mr Bruce, who had done his utmost to stop all this nonsensical bickering.'

A week later, after Old Trafford, a great many more people realized that the cricket world had more than a bicker on its hands.

Gubby's third and last public appearance of the summer proved to be a historic occasion though he was personally almost uninvolved. At Hove on Saturday, 5 August, Ted Bowley and John Langridge put on 490 for the first wicket against Middlesex, Sussex ending the day at 512 for three. Bowley scored 283, Langridge 195, neither giving a chance. Their partnership is still the third highest ever made in county cricket. Gubby, nursing a rib strain, went down to Hove as a batsman and when Middlesex followed on made 80 out of a total of 157 all out. Middlesex, whether under Haig or Tom Enthoven, who for two summers shared office with him, were in the deepest trough in their history, with fewer truly first-class amateurs sparing the time to play much and the professional stalwarts (Hendren apart) showing their ages. Nor was Haig, great trier though he was, exactly at that stage in his career an ideal captain.

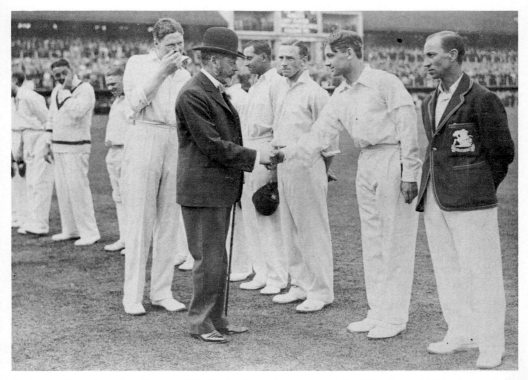

England v Australia, at Lord's 1930 – The England team being presented to King George V. The players shown are Tate, Duckworth, Chapman, 'Duleep', Robins, GOA and Sandham (12th man)

Bradman in his inning of 254 goes down the pitch to White. Note the distance he has moved and his perfect balance. Duckworth is the wicket-keeper, Frank Chester the umpire, Tate the short-leg

GOA (57) and his captain (121) scored 125 together for the 6th wicket in England's second innings

England v. New Zealand at Lord's, 1931. GOA (122) and Leslie Ames (137) put on 246 for the 8th wicket – still a Test record

MCC Australian Team 1932–33. Back row, G. Duckworth, T. B. Mitchell, Nawab of Pataudi, M. Leyland, H. Larwood, E. Paynter, W. Ferguson (Baggageman); middle row, P. F. Warner (Joint-Manager), L. Ames, H. Verity, W. Voce, W. E. Bowes, F. R. Brown, M. W. Tate, R. C. N. Palairet (Joint-Manager); sitting, H. Sutcliffe, R. E. S. Wyatt (Vice-Captain) D. R. Jardine (Captain), G. O. Allen, W. R. Hammond

Holy Trinity, Brompton, 7 September 1932. Patricia Allen was married to Squadron-Leader W. F. Dickson

Relaxed! Douglas Jardine and Herbert Sutcliffe about to push the boat out at Arthur Allen's house, Moombarra, Port Hacking

Melbourne, 1932–33. Woodfull, known as 'The Unbowlable', plays on to GOA for 10. In the gully Jardine, at second slip Voce, wicket-keeper Ames, at short-leg Larwood, at mid-on Leyland. At first slip deeper than Ames and out of the picture was Hammond

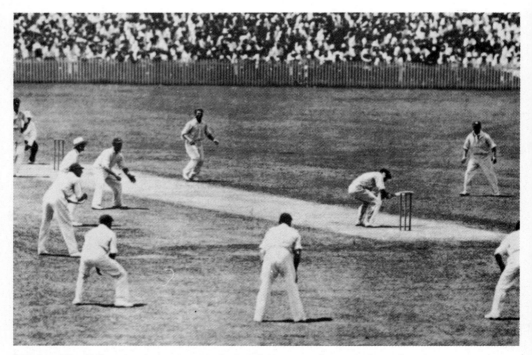

Bodyline: Woodfull getting the treatment in the Fourth Test at Brisbane. Clockwise from bottom right are Verity, Hammond, Sutcliffe, Jardine, Allen, Leyland, Larwood and Wyatt. The other two fielders, Paynter and Tommy Mitchell, will have been at long-leg and fine third-man

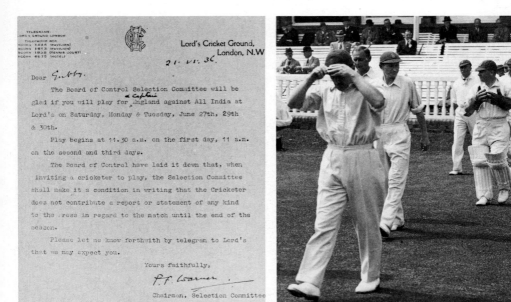

Warner's letter to Gubby, asking him to play for England v. India and – seemingly as an afterthought – to be captain for the first time

The Lord's Test v. India, 27 June 1936. GOA leads England on to the field. From left to right are Verity, Turnbull, Arthur Mitchell, Duckworth, Langridge

MCC Australian Team 1936–37. Back row, W. Ferguson (scorer), L. B. Fishlock, T. S. Worthington, A. Fagg, J. Hardstaff, Capt. R. Howard (Manager); middle row, T. H. Wade, H. Verity, C. J. Barnett, K. Farnes, W. H. Copson, J. M. Sims, W. Voce; sitting, L. E. G. Ames, W. R. Hammond, R. W. V. Robins (Vice-Captain), G. O. Allen (Captain), R. E. S. Wyatt, M. Leyland, G. Duckworth

GOA and Jack Hobbs at Melbourne, 1936–37: the great batsman (with an amanuensis) was covering the tour for the London *Star*. They were always firm friends

First Test, Brisbane, 1936 – GOA to McCabe: the classic of cricket action shots, showing not only a model fast bowling follow-through but the making of a copy-book stroke

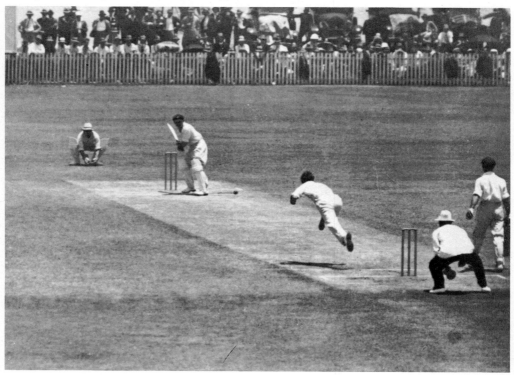

GOA drives O'Reilly straight for 6 when making top score of 68 in the second innings

Bradman, playing back on a spiteful pitch, is c. Fagg b. Allen o (not a bad double!). The slips are out of the picture. GOA and Voce bowled out Australia for 58, their second lowest Test score at home

Melbourne 'Gluepot': In the Third Test of 1936–37 England were trapped on an impossible pitch after rain. Here Leyland has left alone a ball from Sievers that struck him on the shoulder. The seven close fielders, from left to right, are Fingleton, Brown, Darling, Bradman, Fleetwood-Smith, McCabe and Rigg.

'This picture tells a tale' was the Australian press comment. The scene is the toss before the Fifth and conclusive Test at Melbourne. GOA turns away in chagrin, Bradman happily picks up the coin

Thursday, 23 November 1933 is a landmark in Gubby's life story since it was on that day more than fifty years ago that, in company with Haig, he represented Middlesex for the first time at a high-level Lord's meeting. The Advisory County Cricket Committee, at which all the county captains bar two were present, considered the replies of the individual county clubs as to whether any change in the law might be necessary in regard to Bodyline, the MCC Committee having already resolved 'That any form of bowling which is obviously a direct attack by the bowler upon the batsman would be an offence against the spirit of the game.' The decision was that no change was desirable, and that the matter could be safely left with the captains who 'would not commit or countenance bowling of such type'. Arthur Carr, it should be noted for future reference, stated (according to the editor of *Wisden* in his 1935 Notes) 'not only was he opposed to "direct attack" bowling but that neither Larwood nor Voce practised it.'

A few weeks after this meeting final cables to and fro announced that the Australians would tour England in 1934 and that the home authorities would do all in their power to make the visit enjoyable. The question was whether, after all that had passed, and although Jardine stated he had no intention of playing against them, good intentions would be enough.

In December Gubby was duly elected a member of the Stock Exchange, but almost simultaneously he was taken ill and spent Christmas in bed. Either, it seemed, he was suffering from a congenital rupture or from the delayed result of a blow from the ball in Australia, when batting or fielding. It took the doctors some time to decide on an exploratory operation. As it did not take place until March 1934 and the trouble turned out to be a rupture it automatically put his summer's cricket at risk. While in hospital the patient admits to having grown a black beard but thinks a press report that it made him look rather like W.G. was somewhat overstating it. More Gatting apparently than Grace!

The papers were much exercised as to whether he would be fit to confront the Australians once more. In March it was being said he might not be able to play until mid-July. In April 'G. O. Allen has a Seven Mile Walk' made a big headline, followed by the news that he was due to put himself in the hands of Arsenal's famous trainer of the day, Tom Whittaker. In fact he played as a batsman only for Middlesex at the end of May against the Australians in a match notable chiefly for an innings of which Gubby declares, 'I rarely saw Don play better.' This is almost tantamount to rating it as one of the most brilliant of his career. Going in well after five o'clock on the first day, and both Woodfull and Ponsford having made ducks, Bradman by close of play had reached 100 out of 135 for two in seventy minutes. A further 60 on the second morning took another fifty minutes: 160 in all, without a mistake.

Had the rigours of Bodyline left their mark? Only surely in that from 1934 onwards Don's batting was less automatic than it had been in 1930, more an answer to mood and challenge and therefore even more captivating to watch. 'Beau' Vincent in *The Times*, reporting this innings, thought he was now every bit as dear to English crowds as Trumper and Macartney.

Gubby in this match was twice lbw to the spinners, Bill O'Reilly and Clarrie Grimmett, for 4 and 0, and Australia had won the First Test at Trent Bridge before, in the middle of June, he next played in a first-class game. This was at Lord's against Glamorgan, who capitulated by an innings and plenty. On the first day there were three Middlesex hundreds in an ample 476 for six, Gubby's 112 not out being the third of them. More importantly with some 'really fast bowling' he had five for 81 in the match. However he hurt a finger attempting a slip catch, and had to cry off from the Gentlemen's team against the Australians next day at Lord's. This ruled him out for the Second Test there the following week-end – the famous one known as Verity's Match wherein the Australians were caught on a turning pitch after week-end rain and surrendered eighteen wickets and, of course, the match on the Monday: Verity fifteen for 104!

The selectors, chaired by Stanley Jackson, with P. Perrin and T. A. Higson as his assistants, wanted Gubby to play in the Third Test at Old Trafford, but the Middlesex fixtures happened not to fall kindly for his prospect of practice and when he turned out for MCC against Oxford, though he made 79 and let himself go with the ball, his three wickets in forty overs cost 131 and the university piled up a mountain of runs. He pasted two photographs in the appropriate cuttings book which 'showed clearly how my action was at fault' – a characteristic touch. For once in his life he was not sideways on at the moment of delivery. There was no time for another game, and though Gubby was named among a party of thirteen for Old Trafford, doubtful of his Test fitness, he accepted reluctantly the invitation that went out in its usual form as follows –

> Lord's Cricket Ground
> London, N.W.8
> 2nd July 1934

Dear Sir,

The Board of Control Selection Committee will be glad if you will be at Old Trafford and hold yourself in readiness to play for England against Australia on July 6, 7, 9 and 10. It will not be possible to make the final selection of the team until Friday morning next, July 6.

Play begins at 11.30 a.m. on the first day and 11 a.m. on subsequent days.

When inviting a cricketer to play, the Board of Control have laid it down that the Selection Committee shall make it a condition in writing that the cricketer does not contribute a report or statement of any kind to the Press in regard to the match until the end of the season.

Expenses are allowed up to 30/– per day, plus first class return railway fare.

Please notify me on receipt of this invitation whether or not a room is to be reserved for you at the Midland Hotel, Manchester, price 18/6 per day, excluding lunch. If you do not ask me to reserve a room, I shall conclude you are making your own Hotel arrangements.

Kindly let me know by telegram that we may expect you.

Yours faithfully,
F. Stanley Jackson
Chairman, Selection Committee

There are many happenings still sharply etched in one's mind of the Old Trafford Test of 1934. One was the overbearing heat throughout – when Manchester *is* hot it almost beats Melbourne or Madras. There was a gem of an innings on the first morning by one of England's five survivors today of that game of half a century ago, Cyril Walters. Gubby thought him 'a beautiful-looking player, especially good against fast bowling'. Opening the innings, he made 52 in the first hour, before ending the only home series he ever played in averaging 50 with a top score of 82.

Then we had Bill O'Reilly's three wickets in four balls – Walters, Wyatt, and Hammond – and then the long innings by Hendren (132) and Leyland (153) which led to England reaching their then record Test score at home. O'Reilly and Grimmett toiled tirelessly away, but the pitch was of a wondrous ease, and England naturally endeavoured to make the most of it. On the second afternoon Gubby, having been missed from an easy chance to Wall at long-leg when two, was enjoying himself in a brisk ninth wicket stand with Verity which had already added 95 in eighty minutes and hoisted the 600. At this point, with 61 to his name, looking up at the players' balcony, perhaps half-expecting some indication from his captain as to his intentions, he got from Bob Wyatt a cheerful wave of his handkerchief. Translating this as an indication that he was about to declare, Gubby promptly had a good old-fashioned fling and was bowled by McCabe. Thereupon Verity (60 not out) and Clark, the No 11 (2 not out) were allowed to bat for a further forty minutes or so and add 25

ENGLAND v AUSTRALIA
(Third Test)
At Old Trafford, 6–10 July 1934

ENGLAND

C. F. Walters c Darling b O'Reilly	52	– not out	50
H. Sutcliffe c Chipperfield b O'Reilly	63	– not out	69
*R. E. S. Wyatt b O'Reilly	0		
W. R. Hammond b O'Reilly	4		
E. H. Hendren c and b O'Reilly	132		
M. Leyland c sub (B. A. Barnett) b O'Reilly	153		
†L. E. G. Ames c Ponsford b Grimmett	72		
J. L. Hopwood b O'Reilly	2		
G. O. B. Allen b McCabe	61		
H. Verity not out	60		
E. W. Clark not out	2		
B 6, l-b 18, w 2	26	B 2, l-b 1, w 1	4
	(9 wkts., dec.) 627	(0 wkts., dec.)	123

1/68 2/68 3/72 4/149 5/340
6/482 7/492 8/510 9/605

Bowling: *First Innings* – Wall 36–3–131–0; McCabe 32–3–98–1; Grimmett 57–20–122–1; O'Reilly 59–9–189–7; Chipperfield 7–0–29–0; Darling 10–0–32–0. *Second Innings* – Wall 9–0–31–0; McCabe 13–4–35–0; Grimmett 17–5–28–0; O'Reilly 13–4–25–0.

AUSTRALIA

W. A. Brown c Walters b Clark	72	– c Hammond b Allen	0
W. H. Ponsford c Hendren b Hammond	12	– not out	30
S. J. McCabe c Verity b Hammond	137	– not out	33
*W. M. Woodfull run out	73		
L. S. Darling b Verity	37		
D. G. Bradman c Ames b Hammond	30		
†W. A. S. Oldfield c Wyatt b Verity	13		
A. G. Chipperfield c Walters b Verity	26		
C. V. Grimmett b Verity	0		
W. J. O'Reilly not out	30		
T. W. Wall run out	18		
B 20, l-b 13, w 4, n-b 6	43	B 1, l-b 2	3
	491	(1 wkt.)	66

1/34 2/230 3/242 4/320 5/378   1/1
6/409 7/411 8/419 9/454 10/491

Bowling: *First Innings* – Clark 40–9–100–1; Allen 31–3–113–0; Hammond 28.3–6–111–3; Verity 53–24–78–4; Hopwood 38–20–46–0. *Second Innings* – Clark 4–1–16–0; Allen 6–0–23–1; Hammond 2–1–2–0; Verity 5–4–2–0; Hopwood 9–5–16–0; Hendren 1–0–4–0.

Umpires: J. Hardstaff, sr and F. Walden.

Match drawn.

more runs before the declaration came.

Every cricketer knows how signals and messages can be misunderstood in the heat of the moment, and this was surely a classic case. At the rate Allen and Verity were going when the former got out, another forty minutes should have seen Gubby – perhaps his partner also – within sight of a hundred, which Wyatt would surely have allowed either to complete. The Australians in fact were not only exhausted but several, Bradman included, were suffering from what *Wisden* called 'an affection of the throat', which caused them to change their batting order. On the face of it our hero, I think, was unlucky so to miss a golden chance of a Test hundred against Australia. But now was to follow ill-luck of a much more sensational order.

No regulations existed in those days for the repair of bowlers' foot-holes during the course of a match and after many hours of toil O'Reilly's pounding left foot had left a particularly deep chasm at the Warwick Road end. There being absolutely no wind it seemed not to matter which end was allotted to which bowler, Clark and Allen being the opening pair. The Australians' marks made no difference to Nobby because with the new ball he bowled left arm over the wicket. Always a temperamental fellow, he was given the choice and to Gubby's dismay plumped solidly for the Stretford end, leaving Gubby to cope with O'Reilly's excavations as best he could. Hence the notorious, unrepeatable, first thirteen-ball over wherein Gubby bowled three wides and four no-balls. Trying to avoid the hole, and losing the rhythm of his last few strides in the process he four times overstepped the bowling crease. As to the wides, well, the ball certainly swung a lot. That Billy Brown took three fours off the over is indisputable. What the reporters presumably missed in the excitement – for no one seems to have recorded it – was the two chances, admittedly fast-travelling, which Gubby maintains were missed in the gully by Verity. He is cheerfully adamant on the point, and quotes Wally Hammond as saying: 'How could you expect us to catch anything? We were all in hysterics.' Gubby is philosophical about it, saying that of the 35,000 who have since come up to him and claimed to have seen the 13-ball over – the official attendance, by the way, was 32,000 – no one remembers any chances having been missed! He recalls, as a point of interest rather than an excuse, that he was very tired after batting so long in the heat and at Wally Hammond's suggestion drank a whisky and soda before going out into the field. He does *not* suggest the drink affected his first over. Nevertheless 'It was the only time in my cricket career that I touched alcohol before the close of play.' Not even at lunch in a club match, one asks? No, he didn't like beer. He *never* drank until evening. What Gubby chiefly remembers is the humour and good nature of the Old Trafford crowd, both at the time and afterwards. 'Take him off,' called out one chap in mock despair, 'or he'll pass our total on his own.' When Gubby went up to Manchester with Middlesex a year later they cried, 'What about another thirteen-ball over?' This time, though, the laugh was on the Lancastrians, for he took ten for 74 in the match and Middlesex, led now by Walter Robins, had a great victory by 247 runs.

But now England, despite their 627 runs and Australian indispositions, could not force a victory in this Third Test of 1934. On a still blameless pitch the attack of Clark, Allen, Hammond, Verity and Len Hopwood, of Lancashire, toiled almost as profitlessly as O'Reilly and co. had done. They were almost safe at 423 for eight at the close on the third day and completely so when their tail saved the follow-on next morning. (The follow-on for matches of three days or more was then 150, except in Australia where it was 200.)

At the end of the match Warner (now the *Daily Telegraph* correspondent) advocated groundsmen being allowed to re-turf worn bowling patches, a change also advocated by Gubby himself when he was elected to the MCC Committee the following year but not brought into effect until well after the war.

One more personal Allen memory of his visit to Old Trafford, and a vivid one, concerns George Duckworth. A few weeks earlier at Trent Bridge Notts, despite Carr's protestations at the counties' meeting at Lord's the previous winter, had subjected Lancashire to a severe dose of Bodyline. When Peter Eckersley and his team (who, incidentally, stood up magnificently to the barrage and had the reward of a totally unexpected victory in the last over) returned to Old Trafford they told their Committee that it would give them no pleasure to play at Trent Bridge in such circumstances again. Now George was one of the few members of Douglas Jardine's team in Australia who on its return had defended the tactics employed and he had taken such a battering from Voce in the Notts match that Lancashire ordered his bruised body to be photographed as evidence.

'Well, Duckie, so it's all right when we do it to the Aussies but not so good when Notts do it to you, eh?' was Gubby's salvo when they met in the pavilion. 'That was quite different,' was the gist of the reply. But it was not maintained with much conviction. It was typical of Gubby that he should pursue George (who did his best to avoid him) and hammer his point home – and of them both that they remained, as they had been and always were thereafter, warm and loyal friends. Gubby recalls an occasion at Melbourne before the first Test when he said to George at a time when the crowd were comparatively quiet:

'Thought you said, they were a bit lively round these parts.'

'Would you like to hear them?'

Thereupon George made a selection of his best appeals, yelling his head off. The effect was electric. 'Quack, quack,' they cried back, with other pleasantries, and so continued the afternoon through.

'See what I mean?' asked George with a grin.

Although Gubby told the selectors after Old Trafford that this match had convinced him he was not fit enough for a Test Match they named him among fourteen chosen for Headingley. Hearing the side on the wireless on Sunday he at once wrote to Lord's declining the invitation. The press thought this a sporting gesture and did not change their tune when simultaneously a different England attack took another pasting while Gubby was taking six for 47 down at Clacton. On this ground generally friendly to fast bowling, incidentally, H. D. Read – known as Hopper – likewise took six for Essex. In 1934 Larwood on his day was still almost the fastest man in England, and it was sad that a series of inflammatory articles under his name had put him out of court.

In *The Larwood Story*, written reflectively in 1965, Larwood gave this view of his contemporaries: 'In my era I put Bill Voce first among the English fast bowlers, followed by Gubby Allen, Bill Bowes (in England) and Ken Farnes. Allen was particularly good when he had his tail up.' 'Hopper' Read was described in *Wisden* as 'the find of the season', and for sheer speed in the early 1930s only Larwood and possibly Allen were ahead of him. Gubby thought he was 'really quick through the air, had a good action and was a delightful man'. He also met in that Clacton match a delightful girl, Kay Stammers, the tennis player – then engaged in the Frinton Tournament – with whom he began a warm and long-standing friendship.

Thanks to a providential storm England escaped at Headingley which kept cricket interest at a high pitch until the last and conclusive Test at the Oval. Gubby was naturally keen to prove himself as a bowler against Australia in England, and did his best to prepare himself, in the intervening three weeks, with three matches all in their ways notable. First was Gents and Players at Lord's wherein came the first amateur victory since 1914. It was achieved, certainly, by courtesy of Pat Hendren who set a target of 232 in the fourth innings in two hours fifty minutes. Both sides therefore had a winning chance on the last afternoon after some excellent cricket, the Gentlemen having put the Players in and narrowly led them on first innings and the latter declaring with five men out in their second. There were several distinguished performances on both sides and in particular the second innings partnership of 160 for the first wicket by Wyatt and Walters which kept their side ahead of the clock and enabled them to win by seven wickets with twenty-five minutes to spare.

Gubby's own part was important, for in the first innings he went in when six men were out for 132, and with John Human turned the game with a partnership of 96. His 63 was highly praised. Sharing the new ball with A. D. Baxter, he had the wickets of Arthur Mitchell, Ames and Nichols in the first innings and of Sutcliffe in the second. The score-card makes nostalgic reading, recalling several first-rate amateur cricketers too little remembered today: W. H. V. Levett – also known as 'Hopper' – for example, Les Ames's understudy for Kent, whom Gubby rated highly as a wicket-keeper, and Sandy Baxter, a Scot who bowled pretty fast in-swingers off the wrong foot. Here was a true amateur who, as happened in those days, could step from club to first-class cricket without looking in the least out of his class. There was Human, too, a fine natural cricketer who might have made the England XI if he had not married an Australian girl and settled in Sydney.

The Sussex match at Hove over August bank holiday illustrated as emphatically as any what Gubby's value was to Middlesex when he could get away from the City. Sussex were runners-up in the Championship three years consecutively, from 1932 and 1934, and they were leading the field when on the first day Gubby demolished them with eight for 58. In the second innings he had five for 90 – despite which Middlesex only just saved the game.

Gubby if in form and practice was an almost automatic Test selection, and his name, along with twelve others, duly appeared when the team for the Oval Test was chosen. The list for this timeless Test which would decide the destination of the Ashes was: Wyatt (captain), Walters, Allen, Peebles, Sutcliffe, Hammond, Hendren, Leyland, Ames, Bowes, Verity, Clark and Gover. P. G. H. Fender thought that with one exception the team 'will meet with not only universal approval, but also with universal support'. The exception was Ian Peebles, who had not played for Middlesex for six weeks and was completely astonished that he was being considered. In the event Peebles did not play, but the fact that he was asked suggested that Stanley Jackson and co. were distinctly rattled. Their next move was almost equally open to criticism, for when Hendren cried off with an injury they brought in Frank Woolley. As ever, Frank was in sparkling form, with ten hundreds for Kent in the book, but he was forty-seven, he was no longer mobile in the field – and he had never seen 'Tiger' O'Reilly. As things turned out, it was asking too much.

If it be wondered why neither Larwood or Voce appeared in any of the 1934 Tests, let Sydney Southerton, editor of *Wisden*, tell the story in the 1935 edition in regard to Larwood. As to Voce, he was in those days still bowling fast round the wicket to a short-leg crescent, and with this method was rated as unlikely to be dangerous to Test-class batsmen unless he started pitching short at the body – which the authorities would not countenance. Here is Southerton on Larwood's position:

No greater disservice was ever done to English cricket than when Larwood was induced to dash into print and become responsible for statements which put him beyond the pale of being selected for England. I think I am right in saying that he would have been chosen for the Test Match at Lord's – to mention only one – but for the article under his name which appeared shortly before that game. No Selection Committee worthy of the name could possibly have considered him after that and the backing which unfortunately he received in the Press from certain quarters merely added fuel to the flames of controversy about this unhappy incident.

Southerton went on to say he felt it would have been better if the tour had been postponed until the echoes of the verbal war had faded away. In Larwood's ghosted article, by the way, it was asserted in the most lurid prose that if he were to play against Australia he would bowl as he had done on the Bodyline tour.

Such was the background to what turned out to be one of the most one-sided Tests ever played. Gover and Peebles were excluded on the morning of the match when Gubby, frank as ever and talking over the prospect with Peter Perrin, offered the selector his opinion that this was one of the worst fielding sides ever to take the field. 'Some bowler who might have had two for 60 is going to get nought for 100.' Perrin's answer, laconic no doubt, is unrecorded.

The outcome was foreshadowed on the first day, which was completely dominated by Bradman and Ponsford who made 451 together for the second wicket. The former batted to perfection with complete certainty and command while Ponsford played an extraordinary innings, in part fluent and in part a grotesque parody when the fast bowlers let go a short one, the whole punctuated by a degree of luck frustrating beyond measure. On the first day he gave four distinct chances, three of them off Gubby, two in consecutive overs to Wyatt at short-leg when in his forties, and another low to Woolley in the slips soon after his hundred. In this period, too, Ponsford gave a chance to the luckless captain at mid-off, off Verity. None of these catches was easy, but, as *The Times* remarked, it was not too much to ask for one in four to be held. 'As for the bowlers,' wrote Vincent, 'they were slaving on a pitch which might have broken the heart of Tom Richardson, and no available contemporary fast bowlers could have kept up a better pace than did Allen and Clark.' After 475 for two at the close it was surprising that Australia did not tot up more than 701 considering that even more catches were dropped on the Monday than on the Saturday, two of them off Gubby. He soon knocked McCabe's middle stump out with the unplayable, and theoretically unbowlable, ball which swings away and then comes back – just as he had done at Melbourne eighteen months before. Gubby at last induced Ponsford to back away once too often and hit his own wicket. In making 266 he had given in all six chances.

There were various estimates as to exactly how many catches England put down. The fact is that only Les Ames caught anything, and when Gubby held on to a chance at the start of Australia's second innings it was reported as the tenth offered to the fielders. Gubby took four for 170 in thirty-four overs, Bowes had four for 164, Clark two for 110, Verity nought for 123.

From the England view-point the game was an unmitigated nightmare,

ENGLAND v AUSTRALIA
(Fifth Test)

At the Oval, 18–22 August 1934

AUSTRALIA

W. A. Brown b Clark	10	– c Allen b Clark	1
W. H. Ponsford hit wkt b Allen	266	– c Hammond b Clark	22
D. G. Bradman c Ames b Bowes	244	– b Bowes	77
S. J. McCabe b Allen	10	– c Walters b Clark	70
*W. M. Woodfull b Bowes	49	– b Bowes	13
A. F. Kippax lbw b Bowes	28	– c Walters b Clark	8
A. G. Chipperfield b Bowes	3	– c Woolley b Clark	16
†W. A. S. Oldfield not out	42	– c Hammond b Bowes	0
C. V. Grimmett c Ames b Allen	7	– c Hammond b Bowes	14
H. I. Ebeling b Allen	2	– c Allen b Bowes	41
W. J. O'Reilly b Clark	7	– not out	15
B 4, l-b 14, w 2, n-b 13	33	B 37, l-b 8, w 1, n-b 4	50

1/21 2/472 3/488 4/574 5/626   701   1/13 2/42 3/192 4/213 5/224   327
6/631 7/638 8/676 9/682 10/701   6/236 7/236 8/256 9/272 10/327

Bowling: *First Innings* – Bowes 38–2–164–4; Allen 34–5–170–4; Clark 37.2–4–110–2; Hammond 12–0–53–0; Verity 43–7–123–0; Wyatt 4–0–28–0; Leyland 3–0–20–0. *Second Innings* – Bowes 11.3–3–55–5; Allen 16–2–63–0; Clark 20–1–98–5; Hammond 7–1–18–0; Verity 14–3–43–0.

ENGLAND

C. F. Walters c Kippax b O'Reilly	64	– b McCabe	1
H. Sutcliffe c Oldfield b Grimmett	38	– c McCabe b Grimmett	28
F. E. Woolley c McCabe b O'Reilly	4	– b Ponsford b McCabe	0
W. R. Hammond c Oldfield b Ebeling	15	– c and b O'Reilly	43
*R. E. S. Wyatt b Grimmett	17	– (6) c Ponsford b Grimmett	22
M. Leyland b Grimmett	110	– (5) c Brown b Grimmett	17
†L. E. G. Ames retired hurt	33	– absent hurt	
G. O. B. Allen b Ebeling	19	– (7) st Oldfield b Grimmett	26
H. Verity b Ebeling	11	– (8) c McCabe b Grimmett	1
E. W. Clark not out	2	– not out	2
W. E. Bowes absent ill	–	(9) c Bradman b O'Reilly	2
B 4, l-b 3, n-b 1	8	L-b 1, n-b 2	3

1/104 2/108 3/111 4/136 5/142   321   1/1 2/3 3/67 4/89 5/109   145
6/263 7/311 8/321   6/122 7/138 8/141 9/145

Bowling: *First Innings* – Ebeling 21–4–74–3; McCabe 6–1–21–0; Grimmett 49.3–13–103–3; O'Reilly 37–10–93–3; Chipperfield 4–0–22–0. *Second Innings* – Ebeling 10–5–15–0; McCabe 5–3–5–2; Grimmett 26.3–10–64–5; O'Reilly 22–9–58–2.

Umpires: F. Chester and F. Walden.

Australia won by 562 runs.

except for the partnership of 104 with which Sutcliffe and Walters opened the England first innings and a courageous hundred later by Leyland. Following a middle-order collapse a stand between him and Ames for the sixth wicket had raised 85 in an hour when the latter suffered a violent attack of lumbago and had to be helped off the field. That was the end of his participation. Bowes was absent ill, undergoing an operation for piles. Gubby contributed 19. England's total of 321 left them 380 behind, whereupon Australia elected to bat again. Seeing this was a match to be played to a finish the decision could scarcely be criticized – after all, Percy Chapman had done the same thing at Brisbane in 1928–29 when England's lead was 399.

It made, of course, for an unrealistic situation. The great Frank Woolley kept wicket, rather well it was said though there were thirty-seven byes – a supreme example of bathos that was wholly unappreciated in Kent; Bowes limped pluckily on to the field, and at medium-pace or thereabouts took five wickets; Walters and Sutcliffe missed McCabe twice off Gubby, who took none, and England, having been set 708 to win, subsided by 562 runs.

Gubby's next impact on the cricket scene was made not on the field but in the committee room. In the last county fixture of the season at Lord's Middlesex protested at the bowling methods of Voce for Notts. Two young cricketers, Muncer and Beveridge, were hurt, and the atmosphere was thoroughly unpleasant. Accordingly at the next Middlesex Cricket Committee the umpires, Alec Skelding and Bill Bestwick, were invited to Lord's to give their account of what had occurred. In those days it was the custom for the secretary of MCC to attend Middlesex meetings and Plum Warner, knowing how well aware Findlay was of his anti-Bodyline views, suggested to Gubby that he should do the talking. It was Gubby then who interrogated these well-respected old players, both themselves, as it happened, fast bowlers. Both were quite firm that at periods during the match Voce had bowled deliberately *at* the batsmen, thus contravening the 'gentlemen's agreement' to which the county captains had subscribed at the November 1933 meeting. They had taken no action because they had been given no specific powers to do so. It was in this context that Gubby then, for the first time, unburdened his heart about the happenings in Australia. As a result the meeting decided, on the evidence they had both seen and heard, that Middlesex would attack Bodyline at the autumn meeting of the Advisory County Cricket Committee. They knew that they would at least have the support of Lancashire, and when the meeting came along, of course, the other counties were won over.

But what of the presence of the secretary of MCC with whom Gubby had had such a sharp brush on his return from Australia? Billy Findlay behind a bland and ever-courteous exterior was, in my estimation, by nature reactionary to a degree. The idea that in a moral issue of this kind between England and Australia 'our Colonial cousins' might have the balance of right on their side was, when the storm broke, beyond not only his consideration but that of most of his generation and back-ground. The reflections on English sportsmanship in the first Australian cable had been deeply — and not unnaturally — resented by the powers-that-be. Findlay, as assistant-secretary of MCC to Francis Lacey from the end of the First World War until he succeeded him in 1926, cannot have forgotten the rough, uncompromising manner of Warwick Armstrong, captain of Australia in that humiliating summer for English cricket of 1921. Had the picture of Bodyline as it had been portrayed at the Middlesex meeting caused him to change his stance?

Gubby had not long to wait. The next time he was at Lord's Findlay asked him to come to his office and at once said, 'Obbie, I owe you an apology.' The nickname, used only by the family and his closest friends, signalled the olive-branch. When Gubby asked why, the answer came: 'Until you spoke as you did at the Middlesex meeting I've never understood what went on.' The apology was, of course, accepted though Gubby was moved to add, 'Perhaps you might have made a bigger effort to find out.' Findlay replied, 'I'm afraid I must admit that too.' Thus was an old and valued friendship rekindled.

Things moved swiftly now in that autumn of 1934. When 'the Advisory' met at Lord's on 21 November Gubby, attending as Middlesex representative with Haig, led the debate on Bodyline. He painted again the picture of events in Australia as he saw them. Lancashire strongly supported the Middlesex attitude, as did other counties whose players had been intimidated by Notts and/or possibly by Yorkshire in the form of Bowes. In the eighteen months since the 1932–33 series ended the true nature of Bodyline had gradually begun to be 'understood' throughout English cricket, and Gubby's lucid analysis must have persuaded any waverers. Suddenly Notts found themselves friendless, and when Carr exclaimed that it was ridiculous to suggest that he would ever allow one of his bowlers to bowl at a batsman Gubby's final shaft, 'Now, gentlemen, you've heard everything,' drew general applause. The counties went on to approve a ruling suggested to them by the MCC Committee, who had been obliged to realize that the 'gentlemen's agreement' passed a twelvemonth earlier needed fortifying. The ruling stated:

> That the type of bowling regarded as a direct attack by the bowler upon the batsman and therefore unfair consists in persistent and systematic bowling of fast short-pitched balls at the batsman standing clear of his wicket.

This wording was embodied in the instructions to first-class umpires, who were empowered to apply the same sanctions under the unfair play law as exist today: that is to say first the umpire was to give a caution to the bowler; secondly, if that proved ineffective, he was to inform the fielding captain and other umpire; thirdly, if the offence persisted he was to call 'dead ball' and request the captain to take the bowler off. Anyone so removed would not be allowed to bowl again during the remainder of the innings. A similar form of words is now embodied in the laws. The fact is that in half a century the final sanction has never been applied – but that is another story.

MCC promulgated their new ruling later that same day. But they also simultaneously announced an experimental change in the LBW Law whereby the batsman was to be given out to the ball pitching outside the off-stump provided he was hit 'between wicket and wicket', i.e. straight. The experiment was generally approved by the leading players including Gubby, and it was ratified into law in 1936. Since then opinion has inclined to the view that the change was a grave error but of that more anon.

It was not surprising that in the winter of 1934–35 it was speculated that Gubby might be offered the England captaincy against South Africa next summer. He had obvious personal qualifications for the job even though he had had no leadership experience beyond club level since his preparatory schooldays. It was primarily to bring him on as a captain that Plum Warner arranged for him to take an amateur side to Gibraltar before the season opened. Percy Chapman was the other bright particular star in an agreeable party of friends, all bar H. P. Hunloke first-class cricketers, with several wives attendant, which played three matches, against the Garrison, a local team containing some Gibraltarians, and lastly against their combined strengths. Gubby was in sparkling all-round form, and a good time was had by all. They crossed to the mainland for some golf at Algeciras and to see a bull-fight in Seville.

Unhappily, however, coming through the Bay of Biscay on the return journey, playing deck cricket with the crew, the ship rolled and Gubby pulled the adductor muscle in the right thigh. The date was the last week of April, and after a little club cricket he tried himself out in the Whitsuntide Testimonial match for Pat Hendren on 8 June. In his third over, however, having bowled out Jim Parks, he pulled up in pain. The muscle had gone again, and with it his chance of Test cricket for, at best, most of the summer. He went to the famous Morton Smart, who stretched the muscle under anaesthetic.

But there's no keeping a good man down, and five weeks later this one was at Old Trafford, scene of some dramatics a year before, playing against the Champion County for a Middlesex side much revived by the leadership of Walter Robins. The subsequently distinguished Trinidad cricket writer and polemicist, C. L. R. James, reporting for the *Manchester Guardian*, thought a good deal of an innings-saving partnership between Gubby and his captain on the first day. 'Cricketers of such skill and vigour and fighting spirit are rare in county cricket,' wrote James, who never where amateurs were concerned allowed his Communist convictions to obscure his judgement.

Gubby had bowled twenty-four fastish overs in Lancashire's first innings with figures of three for 32 before retiring from the field with a strain, and at once crying off from the Gentlemen's team for the match at Lord's immediately following.

That surely was that — but read on. 'Injured Bowler Riddles Lancs — Amazing Allen' was the next day's headline, above a report which said that in taking seven wickets for 42 he 'put all his energy behind every delivery'. Gubby, recalling the game clearly, is sure he was not bowling at his full pace, and he was no doubt helped by rain on the pitch overnight. At all events there were the facts: ten wickets for 74 in the match, and Lancashire beaten by 247 runs.

What next, one may ask. The answer is anti-climax. The trouble would not go away, and on Morton Smart's advice Gubby played no more first-class cricket that summer. He was thus unable to play, as he would assuredly have wished, in J. W. Hearne's last match at Lord's, an occasion made especially sentimental since his retirement severed what until then was the most celebrated of all Middlesex partnerships, that between himself and Hendren. Gubby says, 'J.W. was always my pin-up. He was a delightful chap who used to go out of his way to help a young cricketer. He certainly helped me more than any other Middlesex professional. As a batsman he was essentially a back-foot player — a fact which does not support the theory that at Lord's one should always play forward. As a bowler he spun the leg-break more than anyone I ever played with except Arthur Mailey. Latterly when we had several fine wrist-spinners to choose from he turned himself into a useful bowler of off-breaks.'

The County Cricketers' Golfing Society was founded in 1935 by the Hon F. S. G. Calthorpe, until recently captain of Warwickshire and captain also of two MCC teams to the West Indies, and Captain E. I. M. Barrett of Hampshire. The idea clicked from the start, giving cricketers of all ages the chance of getting together in matches and meetings out of season. Gubby was an enthusiastic member from the first Autumn Meeting at Worplesdon, then as now the Society's spiritual home, and for the scratch prize he finished third to Cyril Gray and Bryan Valentine with an 82. His handicap of seven gave him a nett 75 and made him runner-up for the Captain's Prize. There were forty competitors that October day amidst the heather and gorse of Worplesdon from veterans such as Stanley Jackson, the Society's first President, the legendary General R. M. Poore of Hampshire (in 1899 1551 runs, average 91!) and R. H. de Montmorency, down to youngsters in their twenties, Freddy Brown and Ian Akers-Douglas.

I have written elsewhere of my wife's father whom I never knew, Reymond de Montmorency, known universally as Monty. With Leonard Crawley he was about the best golfer the Society ever had. I am reminded of the story Gubby tells of how when at Eton he was taken out by Monty, who was a house-master, to play at Stoke Poges. At one hole young Allen played a second shot he was rather pleased with, dead on the flag. To his surprise Monty said 'Bad luck,' and on enquiry, added, pointing, 'That's the green we're playing to. You're on the wrong one.' 'Oh,' said Gubby, who was unfamiliar with the course, 'can I have it again then?' 'No, I'm afraid not,' came the answer. Like Charles Lamb's Mrs Battle at the whist table, Monty was all for the rigour of the game. After the best part of seventy years the cautionary tale still sticks!

In those more spacious days when the amateur side of games was rated as of some public interest, the budding CCGS had good coverage in the 'quality press' as well as pages of photographs and cartoons in the glossy magazines. With regular squash, week-end golf, and April runs in the Park Gubby did all he could to approach the 1936 cricket season in the best possible trim. India's second tour of England was coming up, with three Tests this time instead of one, and MCC were due to tour Australia in the winter. If he were to captain England it was almost certainly now or never.

The prophets were early in the field, with odds offered and taken – I discover with surprise that I gave in *The Cricketer* the chances as quoted in the *Times of India*. Apparently it was Allen 5 to 4, C. T. Ashton 4 to 1, Brian Sellers 9 to 2, Robins 5 to 1 and Bob Wyatt 33 to 1. The proper odds against poor Wyatt in reality, of course, cannot have been anything like so high. There was no doubt, though, that Gubby was the front runner. Incidentally Errol Holmes, on his way home after leading with much acclaim an MCC team to New Zealand and Australia (for matches against the states), must have been a better bet than, say, Claude Ashton.

As usual Gubby was obliged to some extent to ration his cricket, but he was due to play in sixteen first-class matches including the three Tests, which was more than in any season since his Cambridge days. He was also to take more wickets, eighty-one, in more overs, 500, than in any other season.

In contrast with 1935 and some earlier years things went well from the start. In early county matches at Lord's he got both runs and wickets – including 137 and seven wickets against Worcestershire. He was also chosen to lead MCC against All India (as they were then called), and brought off an innings win, making 54 at No 8, and taking two of the foremost wickets on a pitch best suited to the spin of Jim Sims.

Here is a glimpse for modern digestion of pre-war attitudes. When John Human had made 97 the Maharaj Kumar of Vizianagram put himself on and first ball offered a slow pitch which was duly hit for six, the bowler leading the applause. Noblesse oblige! 'Vizzy' – subsequently well known as a broadcaster – finished the over properly according to William Pollock, of the *Daily Express*.

The Sussex match at Whitsun is memorable for all present and still alive because it marked Denis Compton's first appearance for Middlesex. His performance and Gubby's were both notable and related. The latter began the game by bowling fast and taking three of the first four wickets. He then suffered a dislocation of the little finger of the left hand taking a throw-in, and, returning with the last two fingers strapped together, could not recover his form. Explanation: 'Pace has always come from throwing up the left arm before delivery. I just couldn't get my rhythm back.' Hence no doubt his fielding well away from the wicket at deep mid-on when Denis (slow left-arm) was given a bowl. Harry Parks aimed to hit the young man out of sight, but, said *The Times*, 'Allen made as fine a catch as will be seen this year at Lord's, or anywhere else for that matter,' running back full tilt and taking the ball over his shoulder with arms out-stretched. The catch made headlines – there was no keeping him out of the news!

It was because of his injury that Gubby was put down at No 9 in the order with the new recruit and Jim Smith following at Nos 10 and 11. However Maurice Tate, stimulated maybe by a big crowd and some life in the pitch, bowled dangerously well on the bank holiday as in 1936 he still could on his day. After eleven overs he had taken five for 17. Robins in a crisis would sometimes send in 'Big Jim' to lay about him in his own unique, richly entertaining way. On the days when he connected and the gods were kind Jim was guaranteed to reduce any fielding side to a state of confusion and the crowd to applause and laughter bordering on hysteria. This happened now, Smith coming in in front of Gubby and, with strokes issuing forth from every part of the blade, scoring a rapid and invaluable 28. It was therefore in a well-charged atmosphere that the eighteen-year-old Compton joined Gubby at No 11 with Middlesex, at 152 for nine, needing 34 for first innings lead. The well-known story can well bear re-telling. As Compton came in to face Tate, bowling at the pavilion end, Gubby went a little way to meet him to wish him good luck and say, 'Whatever you do, play forward to Tate.' To the first ball Compton went back, and it passed an inch or two above the stumps. Much the same happened next ball. At the end of the over no doubt it was, 'You silly little boy – what did I tell you?' After this escape Denis played with coolness and skill. They were together at lunch, reached the target afterwards, and had put on 41 when Denis was given out, lbw b. Parks 14. Gubby, who was not out 18, remonstrated more in sorrow than in anger with the umpire in question, Bill Bestwick, the old Derbyshire fast

MIDDLESEX v SUSSEX

At Lord's, 30 May–2 June 1936

SUSSEX

J. H. Parks c Compton b Smith	27	– b Smith	26
John Langridge c Price b Allen	3	– not out	83
Mr A. Melville b Allen	22	– c Price b Compton	42
G. Cox b Allen	6	– lbw b Robins	22
Jas. Langridge run out	53		
H. W. Parks c Allen b Compton	50		
T. Cook b Smith	13		
M. W. Tate c Price b Smith	0		
A. F. Wensley c Benka b Hulme	0		
W. Cornford c Robins b Smith	4	– not out	2
J. Cornford not out	1		
B 2, l-b 2, n-b 2	6	B 6, l-b 1, w 1, n-b 6	14
	185	**(3 wkts.)**	**189**

Bowling: *First Innings* – Allen 15.2–1–61–3; Smith 20.1–4–49–4; Robins 10–3–28–0; Sims 6–1–15–0; Compton 4–1–10–1; Hulme 6–0–16–1. *Second Innings* – Allen 13–4–39–0; Smith 21–5–50–1; Robins 9–2–30–1; Sims 11–3–31–0; Compton 10–3–25–1.

MIDDLESEX

G. E. Hart b Tate	25
W. F. Price b Tate	9
C. Fairservice b J. Cornford	3
E. Hendren c W. Cornford b Tate	1
J. Hulme b Tate	0
Mr R. W. V. Robins c Cook b J. Parks	21
Mr H. F. Benka b Wensley	22
J. Sims c J. Parks b Tate	34
J. Smith c Melville b Tate	28
Mr G. O. Allen not out	18
D. Compton lbw b J. Parks	14
B 16, l-b 7	23
	198

Bowling: Tate 30–10–48–6; J. Cornford 24–7–58–1; J. H. Parks 8.3–3–22–2; Jas. Langridge 4–1–15–0; Wensley 4–0–32–1.

Umpires: E. Cooke and W. Bestwick.

Match drawn.

bowler, when Middlesex went out to field:

'Bill, that wan't a very good lbw decision, was it?'

'Very sorry, Mr Allen, I had to pump ship. Pity, he'll be a good player.'

'He'll be much better than that, Bill'.

Bestwick continued on the first-class list, his water-works presumably under control, until the end of the following season, by which time he was getting on for sixty-two.

Before the more crucial cricket came along Gubby had a very satisfactory match at Lord's against Yorkshire, taking six for 91 in the two innings and, in making 42 not out in the Middlesex second innings out of 77 for six, saving them from defeat. There is a significant photograph among his cuttings showing a convincing stroke and captioned 'Self hooking a "bouncer" from Bowes.' It was one of several, the bowler's comment being still remembered in answer to Gubby's enquiry.

'What's going on?'

'They told me you couldn't hook.'

In view of the MCC Australian tour a Trial Match between North and South was held at Lord's in advance of the Test. There was apt to be a somewhat artificial atmosphere about trials and in this case it did not help that rain prevented any cricket on the first day and left the pitch still affected thereafter. Robins, Hardstaff, Wyatt, Verity, and Fishlock of those who eventually went to Australia, and Turnbull, Gover and Arthur Mitchell, who did not, all left their mark on the game. Gover, sharing the new ball with Gubby, took five more wickets than his captain, who had none.

His leadership however must have been approved by the trinity of Warner, Perrin and Higson for he was promptly named as captain for the First Test. The appointment was generally well received since, without any aspersions on Bob Wyatt, it seemed time for England to be put under fresh direction. After the surrender of the Ashes to Australia in 1934 Wyatt's MCC side had lost a four-Test rubber in West Indies. Then in 1935 England, also under him, had been beaten at home by South Africa. With Hammond temporarily in the wings after a tonsils operation, only Leyland and Duckworth (brought back in Ames's absence) of England's victorious side of 1928–29 took the field with Gubby against All India at Lord's. His side in batting order was: Mitchell, Gimblett, Turnbull, Leyland, Wyatt, Hardstaff, Langridge (James), Allen, Robins, Duckworth and Verity. Compared with the great names of yore – Hobbs, Sutcliffe, Woolley, Hendren, Duleepsinhji, Tate, Larwood and others – it wore a modest look albeit it proved more than strong enough for the immediate job on hand.

The only responsible writer who was unhappy about the captaincy seems to have been Vincent of *The Times*. He wrote:

With all due respect I have the very highest opinion of Allen as a cricketer. No one who has a memory which can retain facts for more than a year can ever forget how magnificently he did in Australia under Jardine. I believe, too, that he has many of the qualities – keenness, energy, and spirit – which make for a good captain, but I believe that the mere fact that he is a fast bowler at once disqualifies him. He is the type of man who would work until the soles of his boots wore out for his captain, but I do not consider it fair for Allen himself to have to decide when and how much he is to bowl.

India cannot have faced the First Test with anything but misgiving, for they came to Lord's with seven defeats behind them and only a single win over Minor Counties. There were early signs of disharmony, culminating in the sending home for 'disciplinary reasons' just before the First Test of L. Amar Nath, the best all-rounder in the side. Another splendid cricketer, as we had seen in 1932, Amar Singh, was only able to play occasionally, being professional to Colne in the Lancashire League. Jahangir Khan joined the team only after the Cambridge season. 'Vizzy' presided as genially as he could over a collection of whom twenty-two took some part in the tour.

As the Test started on a wet pitch Gubby omitted Gover from his twelve, which left only Wyatt's gentle swing to share the new ball with him. He won the toss and, after taking Verity out to look at the pitch, and having been told by the chairman, 'It's your decision,' put India in, confident in the ability of Jim Langridge as well as Verity to worry the opposition with orthodox left-arm spin. Robins's leg-breaks and googlies were also available. At any stage of cricket history it would seem on paper a thin attack, as perhaps Gubby was thinking when, after he and Wyatt had quickly given way to the spinners, Merchant and Hindlekar had put on 62 for the first wicket. Nevertheless he came on again only for a single over at the Nursery end so that the spinners could change ends. In this over he first bowled Merchant with a fast full pitch that yorked the stumps and also had the dangerous Mushtaq Ali caught at backward square-leg glancing. When he soon had C. K. Nayudu lbw (N) – the N signifying the experimental law – and Robins before lunch also bowled the patient little Hindlekar, India's resistance declined steeply. Gubby had four of the first five wickets and, in all, five for 35 in seventeen overs. India made only 147.

But what Gubby achieved was at least equalled by Amar Singh when England batted. With his swing and lift off the pitch England were soon half out for 41, Amar Singh after nine overs having taken four for 13. Two left-handers, Leyland and Langridge, steadied the ship in a stand of 55, Leyland making 60. Gubby got 13, so mistiming a stroke on the leg side that he was caught off the back of the bat by slip running back. Next day England, after more rain, finished 13 runs behind. Gubby rated Amar Singh 'in the highest class. He did so much with the ball,' this at a pace distinctly over medium from a superb, lissom action. The rather fat, bounding Nissar was distinctly quick and no push-over. Both had shown their quality, of course, in 1932.

The game continued on a damp pitch of varying heights and paces when India again found Gubby altogether too much for them. Duckworth made a great catch off him before there was a run on the board to dispose of Merchant who, with some decline in Nayudu's powers, was

ENGLAND v INDIA
(First Test)

At Lord's, 27–30 June 1936

INDIA

V. M. Merchant b Allen	35	– c Duckworth b Allen	0
†D. D. Hindlekar b Robins	26	– lbw b Robins	17
Mushtaq Ali c Langridge b Allen	0	– lbw b Allen	8
C. K. Nayudu lbw b Allen	1	– c Robins b Allen	3
S. Wazir Ali b Allen	11	– c Verity b Allen	4
L. Amar Singh c Langridge b Robins	12	– lbw b Verity	7
P. E. Palia c Mitchell b Verity	11	– c Leyland b Verity	16
M. Jahangir Khan b Allen	13	– c Duckworth b Verity	13
*Maharaj Vizianagram not out	19	– c Mitchell b Verity	6
C. S. Nayudu c Wyatt b Robins	6	– c Hardstaff b Allen	9
Mahomed Nissar st Duckworth b Verity	9	– not out	2
B 4	4	B 4, l-b 3, n-b 1	8

1/62 2/62 3/64 4/66 5/85   147   1/0 2/18 3/22 4/28 5/39   93
6/97 7/107 8/119 9/137 10/147   6/45 7/64 8/80 9/90 10/93

Bowling: *First Innings* – Allen 17–7–35–5; Wyatt 3–2–7–0; Verity 18.1–5–42–2; Langridge 4–1–9–0; Robins 13–4–50–3. *Second Innings* – Allen 18–1–43–5; Wyatt 7–4–8–0; Verity 16–8–17–4; Robins 5–1–17–1.

ENGLAND

A. Mitchell b Amar Singh	14	– c Merchant b Nissar	0
H. Gimblett c Mushtaq Ali b Amar Singh	11	– not out	67
M. J. L. Turnbull b Amar Singh	0	– not out	37
M. Leyland lbw b Amar Singh	60		
R. E. S. Wyatt c Jahangir Khan b Amar Singh	0		
J. Hardstaff, jr b Nissar	2		
James Langridge c Jahangir Khan b C. K. Nayudu	19		
*G. O. B. Allen c Jahangir Khan b Amar Singh	13		
†G. Duckworth c Vizianagram b Nissar	2		
R. W. V. Robins c C. K. Nayudu b Nissar	0		
H. Verity not out	2		
B 4, l-b 4, n-b 3	11	B 4	4

1/16 2/16 3/30 4/34 5/41   134 1/0   (1 wkt.) 108
6/96 7/129 8/132 9/132 10/134

Bowling: *First Innings* – Nissar 17–5–36–3; Amar Singh 25.1–11–35–6; Jahangir Khan 9–0–27–0; C. K. Nayudu 7–2–17–1; C. S. Nayudu 3–0–8–0. *Second Innings* – Nissar 6–3–26–1; Amar Singh 16.3–6–36–0; Jahangir Khan 10–3–20–0; C. K. Nayudu 7–2–22–0.

Umpires: A. Dolphin and F. Walden.

England won by 9 wickets.

now far the most consistent and well-equipped of India's batsmen. This time Gubby had five for 43 – ten for 78 in the match, Verity mopping up the lower order. *Wisden* thought Verity 'disappointing in length' in this match, an unlikely criticism so far as he was concerned.

Though the pitch had eased somewhat when England went in to make 107 to win, they lost Mitchell for a duck, and both Gimblett and Turnbull gave chances before the young man from Somerset, who had burst on to the scene so dramatically the previous year and was now playing in his first Test, unleashed some refreshing strokes and hurried his side to victory by nine wickets.

Gubby went to Trent Bridge for Middlesex after this Test against a Notts now under the leadership of a marvellous type of yeoman farmer, George Heane. The latter had the better of a drawn game wherein Gubby's six for 58 after Notts won the toss was matched by Larwood's five for 50 when Middlesex batted. Rain interfered a good deal, Gubby having the unusual experience of batting on all three days for a score of 6 not out.

Then, just before the Second Test, came Gents and Players, wherein there was much spectacular cricket and – despite the loss of the first day – an exciting climax. The great performance was that of J. W. A. Stephenson, a subaltern in the Middlesex Regiment who when he could get leave played with effect and uninhibited enthusiasm for Essex. After Gubby, leading the Gentlemen for the one and only time, had got Barnett's wicket Stephenson gobbled up the other nine, finishing with nine for 46, the best analysis ever recorded by an amateur in the long history of the match. When he had Barnett's wicket in the second innings he had taken ten in a row. His pace was fast-medium from a short run-up, and on his day with his swing and lift off the ground he tested the best. These were the early days of the reputed Lord's 'ridge' on the pitch at the Nursery end whereby, it was alleged, whereas one ball might lift unduly high, the next would keep correspondingly low. There was certainly at times an unusual variety of bounce, but perhaps psychology meant more than physical idiosyncrasy.

A staunch 85 in the Gentlemen's second innings by Tom Pearce of Essex enabled Gubby to leave the Players 132 to get in 1¼ hours – a quixotic gesture which produced more sensational cricket wherein Ken Farnes this time played the leading part. He bowled, said *Wisden*, 'at a pace unequalled at Headquarters since the days of C. J. Kortright. When Farnes bowled Gimblett, Hammond and Hardstaff he each time sent a stump catapulting head high to drop at the feet of Levett, who stood back more than a dozen yards.' The Players, after Farnes's onslaught, were happy enough to settle for 63 for five at the finish.

Within a few days of the classic fixture MCC announced that Gubby had accepted their invitation to captain the side in Australia. At the same time they named the manager as Captain Rupert Howard, the secretary of Lancashire, with six further invitations, as follows: Robins, Hammond, Leyland, Verity, Hardstaff and Fishlock.

The custom in selecting MCC teams abroad was followed, in that the club provided the chairman, Sir Stanley Jackson, who presided over a committee also including the three Test selectors, another from MCC, in

GENTLEMEN v PLAYERS

At Lord's, 15–17 July 1936

THE GENTLEMEN

R. E. S. Wyatt, b Gover	0 – c Hammond, b Sinfield	4
N. S. Mitchell-Innes, lbw b Gover	3 – c Copson b Sinfield	19
A. Melville, c Verity b Copson	1 – b Verity	13
M. J. Turnbull, c Gimblett b Gover	4 – lbw b Verity	1
T. N. Pearce b Gover	1 – st McCorkell b Verity	85
E. R. T. Holmes b Gover	30 – c Fishlock b Hammond	37
*G. O. Allen lbw b Copson	3 – c Copson b Hammond	13
F. R. Brown c Copson b Gover	55 – c Hammond b Sinfield	4
†W. H. V. Levett not out	9 – not out	15
J. W. A. Stephenson b Copson	9	
K. Farnes b Copson	5	
B 4, l-b 6	10　　　L-b 3, n-b 1	4
	130　　　(8 wkts., dec.)	195

Bowling: *First Innings* – Gover 15–3–41–6; Copson 17.1–6–29–4; Verity 15–5–35–0; Sinfield 6–3–15–0. *Second Innings* – Gover 12–2–46–0; Copson 13–1–25–0; Verity 26.3–13–33–3; Sinfield 23–7–39–3; Hammond 8–2–32–2; Leyland 4–1–16–0.

THE PLAYERS

H. Gimblett c and b Stephenson	3 – b Farnes	1
C. J. Barnett c Levett b Allen	0 – lbw b Stephenson	2
*W. R. Hammond b Stephenson	72 – b Farnes	7
M. Leyland b Stephenson	0 – b Allen	11
J. Hardstaff c Pearce b Stephenson	69 – b Farnes	4
L. B. Fishlock, not out	21 – not out	26
R. A. Sinfield lbw b Stephenson	0 – not out	12
†N. McCorkell b Stephenson	0	
A. R. Gover c Levett b Stephenson	3	
W. Copson b Stephenson	8	
B 14, l-b 2	16	
	194　　　(5 wkts.)	63

Bowling: *First Innings* – Allen 14–3–46–1; Farnes 16–3–43–0; Stephenson 16.5–6–46–9; Brown 7–0–37–0; Wyatt 1–0–6–0. *Second Innings* – Allen 2–0–16–1; Farnes 9–3–22–3; Stephenson 9–3–20–1; Brown 2–0–5–0.

Umpires: J. Hardstaff and J. Newman.

Match Drawn.

this case the president, Lord Somers, and also, of course, the captain. This captain did not at all agree with the side being chosen piecemeal, but he had to go along with the system. The lucky man of these six must have been the twenty-nine-year-old Fishlock in that while he was having a very good season for Surrey he was yet to be blooded in a Test Match.

The Second Test at Old Trafford was played on what *Wisden* called an easy-paced pitch that 'left the fast bowlers powerless', the result being a mountain of runs by England and, compared with their modest first innings, a vigorous and heartening batting performance by India to save the game. Robins and Verity took five wickets apiece in the two innings, but Gover, playing in his first Test (and seeing two early chances go down) had nought for 100, while Gubby after taking two wickets in the first innings was punished severely in a record first-wicket partnership for India of 203 between Merchant and the elegant, wristy Mushtaq Ali. He, Gimblett and Fishlock were the only three who contributed little to England's 571 for eight declared. Hammond, now fit again, played one of his most commanding innings (167 in three hours) and in his wake the hopefuls, Fagg, Worthington, and Hardstaff all made scores, as also did Robins and Verity.

Directly after this Second Test Gubby was called to a Selection Committee at Lord's. Arriving from the City a little late he was greeted by Jackson with the surprising news that they had decided to pick Voce for Australia. 'But we agreed we wouldn't consider him,' was Gubby's immediate reaction, to which the answer came that 'Our bowling at Old Trafford was so weak. We simply must try and strengthen it.' On the face of it, and in the light of all the circumstances, it seems surprising that the other selectors – and Warner especially – apparently thought that they would get Gubby's compliance with so crucial a change of policy, decided in his absence. As the discussion ensued Gubby went so far as to say that he must now reconsider his own acceptance. 'Perhaps I should stick to business and not have said "yes" in the first place.' This must have put the rest of the Committee into a rare confusion. If the captain had at this late hour changed his mind, their plans would have collapsed – especially as the naming of Voce would make his reason obvious. As for Gubby, he could see the prospect of his tour's success threatened before it started if Australia were to be asked to welcome one of the chief aggressors of the Bodyline tour as though nothing had happened.

It was Gubby who at this point broke the stalemate with a suggestion. He said that he for one was willing to talk to Voce. He would cry off the bank holiday match at Hove the following week-end on the pretext of injury and go instead to the Oval where Notts were due for the traditional match against Surrey. Thus it was arranged, and Gubby, with Jackson and Somers, duly met Voce at the Oval. Difficult at first, as was only natural, the atmosphere thawed to the extent that Voce asked for time to make up his mind. He had been left in no doubt that he must express regret for his part in what had occurred and give assurances for the future.

The outcome was a happy one. Bill Voce – a good man led astray if ever there was one – proved willing to withdraw for his part the statement that both he and Larwood had made the previous year upon enquiry by MCC, saying that they had no desire to play in first-class cricket other than for Notts. He also signed a statement saying that he deeply regretted any trouble there had been in the past.

ENGLAND v INDIA
(Second Test)

At Old Trafford, 25–28 July 1936

INDIA

V. M. Merchant c Hammond b Verity	33	– lbw b Hammond	114
Mushtaq Ali run out	13	– c and b Robins	112
L. Amar Singh c Duckworth b Worth-ington	27	– (6) not out	48
C. K. Nayudu lbw b Allen	16	– st Duckworth b Verity	34
S. Wazir Ali c Worthington b Verity	42	– b Robins	4
C. Ramaswami b Verity	40	– (3) b Robins	60
M. Jahangir Khan c Duckworth b Allen	2		
C. S. Nayudu b Verity	10		
*Maharaj Vizianagram b Robins	6	– (7) not out	0
†K. R. Meherhomji not out	0		
Mahomed Nissar c Hardstaff b Robins	13		
B 1	1	B 9, l-b 7, n-b 2	18

1/18 2/67 3/73 4/100 5/161   203   (5 wkts.) 390
6/164 7/181 8/188 9/190 10/203   1/203 2/279 3/313 4/317 5/390

Bowling: *First Innings* – Allen 14–3–39–2; Gover 15–2–39–0; Hammond 9–1–34–0; Robins 9.1–1–34–2; Verity 17–5–51–4; Worthington 4–0–15–1. *Second Innings* – Allen 19–2–96–0; Gover 20–2–61–0; Hammond 12–2–19–1; Robins 29–2–103–3; Verity 22–8–66–1; Worthington 13–4–27–0.

ENGLAND

H. Gimblett b Nissar	9
A. E. Fagg lbw b Mushtaq Ali	39
W. R. Hammond b C. K. Nayudu	167
T. S. Worthington c C. K. Nayudu b C. S. Nayudu	87
L. B. Fishlock b C. K. Nayudu	6
J. Hardstaff, jr c and b Amar Singh	94
*G. O. B. Allen c Meherhomji b Amar Singh	1
R. W. V. Robins c Merchant b Nissar	76
H. Verity not out	66
†G. Duckworth not out	10
B 5, l-b 9, w 1, n-b 1	16

(8 wkts., dec.) 571

1/12 2/146 3/273 4/289 5/375
6/376 7/409 8/547

A. R. Glover did not bat.

Bowling: Nissar 28–5–125–2; Amar Singh 41–8–121–2; C. S. Nayudu 17–1–87–1; C. K. Nayudu 22–1–84–2; Jahangir Khan 18–5–57–0; Mushtaq Ali 13–1–64–1; Merchant 3–0–17–0.

Umpires: F. Chester and F. Walden.

Match drawn.

Once the bargain was struck it was stuck to implicitly, and Gubby recalls the remark of the man whose career had thus been rescued by a generosity of spirit on both sides: 'Anyone can lead me, but no bugger can drive me.'

When MCC announced the batch of selections which included Voce they said they had treated the exchanges between the club and Larwood and Voce in 1935 'as confidential in the hope that the players might alter their attitude', and added that 'the MCC has now received an entirely satisfactory statement from Voce, who has placed himself unreservedly at the disposal of the Board of Control and MCC Selection Committees whenever his services may be required'. It would have meant a complete burial of the hatchet if Larwood's name could have been included in MCC's statement, but though he headed the English bowling averages with 119 wickets at the exceptionally low cost of 12.97 each he had had to be carefully nursed by Heane and was happier when the ground was soft. Could that left foot have again survived a season's work on Australian pitches? According to Gubby for these reasons the possibility of Larwood's selection never came into the reckoning.

In early August MCC had given out four more names for the party: Duckworth, Copson, Worthington and Fagg. Then, once the Voce affair was satisfactorily settled, came these five: E. R. T. Holmes, Barnett, Farnes, Sims and Voce. When Holmes had to decline Wyatt was picked as his replacement. This made sixteen, a place being left for another wicket-keeper – which was clearly going to be Les Ames if fit. He had not played all season owing to back trouble but took the field in the nick of time in mid-August, then at once found form and became the seventeenth and final selection.

Gubby, though of the view that it is better and fairer to pick a touring side as a whole – as happens nowadays – and not in sections, does not think, retrospectively, that the selectors could have done much, if any better. The truth was that as the state of the market was in 1936 the choice of several men untried in Test cricket was inevitable. It was not necessarily the selectors' fault that as many as seven failed to make much, if any, subsequent mark in Test cricket. Out of the seventeen only seven played for England at home the following summer. Denis Compton was certainly considered despite less than a full first-class season, but Gubby and his fellow-selectors felt, he says, that there might be too much of a risk in bringing him on too quickly. The tour was just a year too soon both for him and Len Hutton. Sutcliffe was forty-one and not quite the batsman he had been, apart from slowness in the field. The one culpable omission among the batsmen, looking retrospectively, is generally thought to have been Eddie Paynter. Copson, whose movement was off the pitch rather than in the air, had the captain's support in preference to Gover whose out-swing would not have outlived the shine on the ball which then in Australia lasted only an over or two. (He took 200 wickets in 1936.) The author's view, with due respect, since the captain does not share it, strongly favoured Stephenson, who I think might almost have been in the Maurice Tate mould, and whose infectious enthusiasm the crowd would have loved.

It was important for morale generally and the captain's self-esteem

ENGLAND v INDIA
(Third Test)

At the Oval, 15–18 August 1936

ENGLAND

C. J. Barnett lbw b Nayudu	43	– not out	32
A. E. Fagg c Hussain b Amar Singh	8	– c Amar Singh b Nissar	22
W. R. Hammond b Nissar	217	– not out	5
M. Leyland b Nissar	26		
T. S. Worthington b Nissar	128		
L. B. Fishlock not out	19		
*G. O. B. Allen c Hussain b Nissar	13		
H. Verity c Hussain b Nissar	4		
J. M. Sims lbw b Amar Singh	1		
W. Voce not out	1		
L-b 10, n-b 1	11	B 4, n-b 1	5

1/19 2/93 3/156 4/422   (8 wkts., dec.) 471 1/48   (1 wkt.) 64
5/437 6/455 7/463 8/468

†G. Duckworth did not bat.

Bowling: *First Innings* – Nissar 26–1–120–5; Amar Singh 39–8–102–2; Baqa Jilani 15–4–55–0; Nayudu 24–1–82–1; Jahangir Khan 17–1–65–0; Mushtaq Ali 2–0–13–0; Merchant 6–0–23–0. *Second Innings* – Nissar 7–0–36–1; Amar Singh 6–0–23–0.

INDIA

V. M. Merchant b Allen	52	– c Worthington b Allen	48
Mushtaq Ali st Duckworth b Verity	52	– c Hammond b Allen	17
†Dilawar Hussain st Duckworth b Verity	35	– lbw b Sims	54
C. K. Nayudu c Allen b Voce	5	– (6) b Allen	81
C. Ramaswami b Sims	29	– (8) not out	41
S. Wazir Ali lbw b Sims	2	– (7) c Duckworth b Allen	1
L. Amar Singh b Verity	5	– (4) c Sims b Verity	44
M. Jahangir Khan c Fagg b Sims	9	– (10) c Voce b Allen	1
*Maharaj Vizianagram b Sims	1	– b Allen	1
M. Baqa Jilani not out	4	– (5) c Fagg b Allen	12
Mahomed Nissar c Worthington b Sims	14	– c Voce b Sims	0
B 8, l-b 6	14	B 3, l-b 7, n-b 2	12

1/81 2/125 3/130 4/185 5/187   222 1/64 2/71 3/122 4/159 5/212   312
6/192 7/195 8/203 9/206 10/222   6/222 7/295 8/307 9/309 10/
                                          312

Bowling: *First Innings* – Voce–20–5–46–1; Allen 12–3–37–1; Hammond 8–2–17–0; Verity 25–12–30–3; Sims 18.5–1–73–5; Leyland 2–0–5–0. *Second Innings* – Voce 20–5–40–0; Allen 20–3–80–7; Hammond 7–0–24–0; Verity 16–6–32–1; Sims 25–1–95–2; Leyland 3–0–19–0; Worthington 2–0–10–0.

Umpires: F. Chester and F. Walden.

England won by 9 wickets.

that he should end the English season on a successful note, and this he certainly did. Immediately before the Third Test, with Middlesex fighting hard for the Championship, he had a fruitful part in a thorough victory over Hampshire, making 54 and 28, and taking nine wickets for 129 in thirty eight overs. To have bowled for so long on the eve of a Test Match suggests that he was at this time just about at his peak as a cricketer.

At the Oval England clinched the rubber with an easy win by nine wickets after India had followed on. Hammond this time made a double hundred after Gubby had won the toss, he and Stan Worthington making 266 together for the fourth in little more than three hours. Worthington was a tall, commanding player, and in this sort of mood showed glimpses of Hammond himself. But the solidity was lacking, and this innings proved a flash in the pan. In India's second innings the captain took seven for 80, but he would gladly have seen some of them go to Bill Voce who, playing in his first Test for more than three years, bowled beautifully but with no tangible reward. 'That sort of luck can't last.' Gubby told him and of course, when the crunch came Bill amply repaid his captain's confidence and trust.

Middlesex had to concede this 1936 Championship to Derbyshire, they being runners-up and Yorkshire third. Before August was out Gubby at Lord's took six for 36 against Kent, who were bowled out for 85, and well beaten. So were Surrey, against whom Gubby had five. Topping the batting with 456 runs and an average of 50 and being second in the bowling with fifty-four wickets at sixteen each, he had had probably his best season for Middlesex as a preparation for the climax of his career in Australia.

10

1936–37 – Promise

G. O. Allen's MCC team to Australia and New Zealand sailed from Southampton on the Orient Line's Royal Mail Ship *Orion* amid the usual scenes of sentimental enthusiasm on 12 September 1936. They were due to be away for seven and a half months, in the captain's case a full fortnight longer. As with the previous tour it was to be a round-the-world journey, the route after the three-week visit to New Zealand taking them via the Pacific to Los Angeles, thence by train across America and from New York home to Southampton on the *Queen Mary*.

The captain had with him seven others who had made the same tour four years earlier with Douglas Jardine – Ames, Duckworth, Hammond, Leyland, Verity, Voce and Wyatt. Barnett had been meanwhile with MCC to India, Farnes to the West Indies, Hardstaff to Australia and New Zealand the previous winter with Errol Holmes. The remaining six were making their first tour – Robins, the vice-captain, Copson, Fagg, Fishlock, Sims and Worthington. Between them these men, Robins apart, played a negligible part in Test cricket thereafter, and only Fishlock was ever asked to tour again. The team were mostly at an age when they might have been rated as in their prime. At thirty-seven Maurice Leyland was the oldest. Arthur Fagg, who had had to cut short his honeymoon, at twenty-one was much the youngest, indeed the only man in the side under twenty-five. The average age was twenty-nine, a year older than Jardine's, three years younger than Percy Chapman's in 1928–29.

The fact that neither his vice-captain nor, more importantly, Rupert Howard, his manager, had toured before meant that Gubby had his hands full from the start. Wherever they went, whatever they were due to do, he knew the ropes. Temperamentally this suited Gubby well. It was his tour, and he wanted it to run his way. As we shall see, though, too much fell on his shoulders, and this was ultimately to the detriment of his cricket.

His first job now was to blend a happy side, and the foundations, of course, had to be laid on board. Gubby's friendliness has always come as second nature, and in William Pollock's first press cable from the ship he was able to assure *Daily Express* readers that the team had 'a most matey captain'. The old hands of 1932–33 were duly struck with the more relaxed atmosphere.

Les Ames is particularly interesting on the differences of attitude during his touring days between amateurs and professionals. Although as a raw youngster he enjoyed his first tour with Percy Chapman's side, and under the 'magnificent', if strict, managership of F. C. Toone probably most of all, the social divisions were rigid. The custom was for amateurs and professionals to go their own ways off the field. He had had no chance, for instance, of forming a personal impression of Jardine in 1928–29 since they hardly exchanged half a dozen words on the trip. On his own tour Jardine was aloof, unable to 'get through', and the atmosphere suffered accordingly. On Gubby's tour things were different from the start. 'For one thing,' says Ames, 'apart from the captain, who was "skipper", everyone called one another by their christian names.'

There was another factor which was novel to this tour though it had to be taken into account for ever thereafter, and that was the presence of a sizeable handful of cricket-writers. Whereas the 1932–33 team were accompanied by only two English journalists, Bruce Harris and Jack Hobbs's amanuensis, Jack Ingham, there were now not only Harris and Pollock on board but H. A. H. Carson of the London *Evening News*, the inimitable Arthur Mailey, and a pair also distinguished in fields other than cricket, C. B. Fry and Neville Cardus. All have long since passed on, but there is not the slightest reason to doubt Gubby's comment: 'I always had a happy relationship with the press.' From subsequent experience in the West Indies I am sure he applied instinctively the golden rule that so many – to their cost – never learn. He was friendly and cooperative, and the sporting press accordingly respected his confidence. Apart from two or three columnists whose job was to peddle in gossip and controversy, Gubby all through his cricket life has had a good press – and deservedly so. On *Orion* the team and press got to know one another, with no intervening barrier.

The great liners in those days used to make leisurely progress down the Mediterranean. First stop was Gibraltar within sound, it was claimed, if not sight of the Spanish Civil War. At Toulon Gubby posted his first family letter, recording therein, after five days' sailing, with the usual incontrovertible detail that 'this will be my 106th letter or postcard, and my bill for stamps at mid-day today was 11/8.' Having reported that 'a red destroyer all of whose officers had been murdered came nosing around us', he makes a judgement which he had no subsequent reason to qualify: 'The more I see of all the side the more I like them. They are all absolutely charming and I am sure will be no trouble at all.'

In his next letter Gubby writes of the first tour casualty, and this only just out of Naples. Maurice Leyland had contracted an illness described as 'kidney trouble'. 'I tried to make it sound only fairly bad but I am afraid between you and me and the door-post he will not be fit to play for the first four or five weeks. In other words we have had a reverse, and it would happen to one of the left-handers after I had turned down a third.' This was the first item, as things turned out, in a long catalogue of misfortune. The third left-hander, incidentally, was Paynter who, thought Ames for one, should have been chosen.

At Port Said travellers from passenger ships have been fleeced from time immemorial. Nevertheless it was amusing that it was sharp little Robbie who bought a pair of binoculars from which, just before sailing, the lenses had been removed, and also a suit of clothes which, not having been stitched, fell about him when, later on board, he tried to put it on. At the fancy-dress ball 'Leslie Ames dressed up as Hitler and was absolutely magnificent.' They had the usual one-day game at Colombo, the team decked out to a man in the solar topees then reckoned obligatory for white men in the tropics.

From the moment the ship docked at Fremantle the captain was plunged into speech-making and functions of welcome. 'I made five speeches in my first forty-eight hours in the country,' he wrote home, 'and though I say so who perhaps shouldn't, they seem to have gone very well indeed. Charles Fry said they reminded him of someone stroking a cat.' The most important of these efforts (about which Gubby was highly nervous) did not however go according to plan. This was an intended Australian Broadcasting Commission nation-wide hook-up, which in the Eastern States had to give place to an even more momentous event than a speech by the MCC captain. At precisely the wrong moment the woman aviator, Jean Batten, arrived on a solo flight in world record time, and this news was accorded preference. So MCC's nervous captain had to put his speech across again.

Fry, let me say, was one of four writers giving 'blanket coverage' of the tour for the *Evening Standard*. There was Harris for news and facts, Cardus for a more colourful picture, Jardine for comment from home, and — well, 'C. B. Fry says.' What did he not say in that crisp, light-hearted column under a picture of the handsome head, complete with monocle? His opening piece started thus:

> They told me in the *Orion*, the Easterners, that the Continent opens flat at Perth. Not at all; for Perth is the Athens of Australia and Fremantle its Piraeus.
>
> The Perth ground is oval, with its major axis at right angles to the pitch. The outfield smooth couch grass. The wicket Callender Creek soil, the colour of oyster shell. Smooth as vulcanite.
>
> A soft, grey light at the start. A sky with white cumulus. Perfect

for batting, and Kenneth Farnes flings down his first over to Bryant, of Western Australia.

Then our smiling, resolute captain lets loose his swifts.

And Allen's swifter one drew first blood. Bryant at 17 flung a cross bat at the off ball and, like others of us, pulled the ball into his wicket.

... Allen has bowled quite impressively this morning.

Full of life, vigour and cheerful élan. I like his prospects.

He has said he will make more speeches than he will get wickets. His tongue was in cheek, believe me. 'Gubby' is full of velvety, Etonian confidence.

That 'confidence' was due for a swift testing. MCC won their first match, against Western Australia, by an innings and plenty, but during it Duckworth dislocated a finger and afterwards Robins, at fielding practice of all unlucky things, fractured and split the middle finger of his right hand. Duckworth's hurt was transient but more than tiresome since Ames was afflicted with a recurrence of his back trouble, while Robins was evidently out of action for a month or more. This, of course, was his chief spinning finger, and events proved the effect of the injury to be permanent. When practising MCC had lost their most brilliant all-round fielder.

In between the first match and that at Perth against a Combined XI Gubby motored all but 400 miles on 'terrible' roads to the Kalgoorlie Gold Mines. He was shown over four, going down 5,000 feet, which, he tells his father, 'taught me more about the subject than I could learn in six months.' However a telephone call from Howard brought him to earth, so to speak, with a horrid jerk. Ames's back, said the manager, was worse and he was determined to return home. Thereat Gubby in his hurry to get back to Perth attempted to do so by air. This part of his journey proved even more uncomfortable than the rest for the aircraft, bumping about in a strong head-wind, made little headway. When Gubby had filled a paper-bag or two, noticing that cars were travelling faster than he was, he urgently requested to be put down alongside the road, and humped a lift the rest of the way.

He found poor Ames in much pain and the depths of despair, convinced his tour was over before it was begun. Privately his captain thought so too, but with rare presence of mind, and fearing the further ill-effects of the endless train journey across the Nullabor Plain that was looming up, he arranged for Robins to take Ames round by sea to Melbourne where the best doctors and surgeons were to be found. The captain's deal with his number one wicket-keeper was that if the Melbourne report was bad Les would return forthwith. The medics would decide. If the worst came to the worst Wade, of Essex, who was in Australia, would have been recruited as Duckworth's understudy.

Fagg, who had had some experience with the gloves, despite a bruised thumb kept wicket in the drawn match against the Combined XI wherein many runs were scored including a 65 by Gubby that he was very pleased with. There followed the gruelling train ride east to Port Augusta with its 360 miles dead straight — the longest such stretch in the world — without sight of a tree. Bruce Harris thus described the experience to his readers:

> The MCC cricketers and the rest of our party are living strenuously. Behind us lie three nights in a transcontinental train, equivalent to the journey from London to Constantinople, and then, after a six a.m. reveille, we have had 125 miles of dusty, bumpety-bump motoring, until now we are at Clare Country race meeting.
>
> Ahead of us is a dance to which the countryside has been invited. To-morrow comes the one-day cricket match against the Clare Country team, and then an eighty-mile night drive to Adelaide.
>
> At the moment G. O. Allen is making his tenth speech of the day. Our way from Port Augusta, where we left the train, has been like a Royal progress. Every few miles Allen has been invited to halt and address cheering, waving children. Every time he has complied.

(Can a greater contrast in strain be imagined, between this scenario of the 1930s and the present rushing about by air from one capital city to the next, with extremely little cricket outside Tests and one-day Internationals?)

Not surprisingly Gubby, writing home from Adelaide, decided he was going to do all his speechifying before the Tests, adding:

> I am sure the reason why every English captain out here has failed at cricket since the war is because he has been worked too hard, and I am going to refuse not being allowed a chance of doing my best.

When the composition of the team's selection committee had been discussed before sailing Jackson wanted it restricted to the captain, Robins and Wyatt, with no professionals. Gubby wished to add Leyland and Hammond. When Jackson declined to budge, Gubby's response was to say he would do without an official selection committee. He knew that once the tour was under way he could make his own arrangements, and soon after the team's arrival in Perth named the men he wanted. Robins, Wyatt, Leyland, Hammond and he accordingly functioned as selectors and none of the four knew that their appointment was unofficial. Jackson's intransigence in the matter surely did him little credit. He had been a magnificent cricketer and captain, who could have

gone to Australia four or five times around the turn of the century if he
had wished. As it was, apart from one minor visit he had never toured
abroad. If he had had any idea of the tactics, selection and otherwise,
involved in the running of a major tour he would not have quibbled
about giving the captain the men he wanted to help him.

However when the selectors sat down to name the side for the South
Australian match no question of choice arose. For they had to face
another serious casualty – Bob Wyatt at Clare had broken a bone just
above the left wrist, and was reckoned to be out of action for five or six
weeks. (It proved, in fact, to be nine.) Minor injuries to Fagg and Copson
brought the casualties to seven, so that MCC could not have turned out a
full team if they had not luckily picked up the young Essex wicket-
keeper, T. H. Wade, who had worked his way out as a ship's steward.
Tommy Wade kept well in the next two matches, was extremely popular,
and was rewarded by an MCC touring cap.

MCC beat South Australia by 105 runs thanks chiefly to Hammond
and Gubby. The captain, easing himself gradually into form, had nine
wickets for 85 in the match, while the former, having scored a hundred in
each innings at Perth now made it four in a row by getting one in each
innings at Adelaide. In his weekly letter the captain wrote that 'Wally
Hammond is a wonderful head professional, as they all admire him so
much, and listen to all he has to say.' He also reported the welcome offer
of a Hillman Minx in each state for town work and a Humber Snipe for
long trips.

The side's form at Melbourne and Sydney gave Gubby little joy, apart
from three auspicious innings in a row by Barnett, and the highly
successful appearance at last of Leyland. In public he continued to show
a confident front, but it did his self-esteem no good that against NSW in
his 'home town' – which had not seen the best of him on the last tour – he
made what up till then was the only 'pair' of his life.

In a letter to Plum Warner from Sydney on this first visit there he
laments how he has been 'really grossly over-worked', partly at least
because the absence of Robins and Wyatt meant he had to play in every
match, and also because the manager comes to him for all the decisions.
'The result is I have to decide on all the tips, arrange the rooms, the
sleeping compartments on the train, and interview all the press and the
doctors ... I have felt so tired and worried at times. I don't think any
captain has ever had quite what I have had to put up with as I really have
had no one to help me off the field.' The whole team had been delightful,
and 'Voce has been charm itself ever since we sailed and will do anything
I ask him.' However, most of them have been terribly slow to adapt to
Australian pitches and conditions, and 'I wish you had been here this
time as it is a cricket brain which is badly needed at this moment:

someone who could help Hardstaff, Fishlock, Farnes, Fagg, Sims and Copson: in fact all the newcomers.' He went on to forecast what the side for the First Test looked like being — and in fact was — and added 'we were unquestionably cheated out of the match v N. S. Wales ... Barnett, Fagg, Allen and Hardstaff all suffering in the last innings'.

Hardstaff's dismissal lbw to O'Reilly 'when only two balls remained was just a joke', wrote Gubby later to his father, and then added:

> I have never seen a whole team more infuriated and after hearing one injudicious comment in the bar I called them all into the dressing room and told them that they could say what they liked in the dressing room but never to mention the subject outside as I was going to lodge an official complaint. This I did sparing nothing and no one, and when we turned up in the next match two days later we found a new umpire and many apologies ... We still look a badish side but the fielding has improved and when we turn out the best XI which we have never done yet it may be better than anyone expects.

Bad umpiring aside, Plum's hopes for the forthcoming series can hardly have been fortified by the letter, but there is little doubt it was a realistic assessment. Reporting the Queensland match immediately before the First Test — Gubby rested from it, handing over to Robins — even Hobbs was constrained to say that 'the tail-enders shaped like Clapham Common cricketers against slow bowling'. Gubby in his letters had been bemoaning English batting against leg-spin because so few were prepared to use their feet.

However, MCC's first innings failure at Brisbane was the darkness that heralded a brighter dawn. When they batted again Charlie Barnett (259!) and Arthur Fagg (112) put on 295 for the first wicket, the former earning all the superlatives in the book, while the latter's batting confirmed the captain's notably high opinion of him. Fagg thus clinched his place in the Test side, and with Robins having done at least enough to be preferred to Sims the selectors' most serious problem was whether Farnes or Voce should share the new ball with the captain. To his parents Gubby wrote:

> Choosing the team was not easy but after much argument I got the side I wanted. Robbie was splendid and backed me up all the way. The other three wanted Fishlock instead of Hardstaff and Farnes instead of Voce. I must say Farnes has out-bowled Voce in every match and he is very unlucky not to be playing but with Robbie practically a non-bowler and with the certainty of an easy paced wicket I thought Voce would stand up to it best. So far both my gambles have come off ...

Few sides, I suppose, in the history of England-Australia Tests have taken the field with slimmer prospects than those of England at Brisbane in December 1936, and when McCormick shot out the first three for 20 on a fresh first morning pitch, including Hammond first ball, much of the advantage Gubby had won with the toss had been surrendered. However from this point first Barnett and Leyland (126) and then Leyland with Ames and Hardstaff fought back admirably, and the rearguard was continued next day right down the order. Gubby, coming in at No 9, contributed an invaluable 35 in an hour and a quarter including a six into the grandstand off O'Reilly, and was last out, having a fling, to a brilliant catch at mid-on by McCabe. England's 358 was at least a fighting score, though Australia deserved sympathy in losing McCormick with an attack of lumbago after he had bowled eight overs and taken three wickets.

Australia's forceful reply at the close on the second day was 151 for two, the foundation of a strong answer even if Bradman had been caught in the gully off Voce for what was, for him, an unconvincing 38. After the week-end however everything went England's way. Voce's luck changed with a vengeance, and there was high praise for Gubby's handling of his attack. It was 'G. O. Allen's clever tactics, and Voce was Truly Marvellous', says Jack Hobbs in a headline over six columns. Fingleton's hundred was his fourth in successive Test innings – a sequence only Alan Melville subsequently equalled and Everton Weekes bettered by one.

When England went in again 124 to the good their batting once more was a struggle, especially against O'Reilly, though he did not get a wicket, and Ward, another leg-spinner, who with a flattish trajectory and considerable power of spin took six. Gubby promoted himself from No 9 to 7, and arrived at the parlous pass of 122 for five. He soon lost Leyland to a magnificent running catch by Bradman, and from this point first Hardstaff and later Verity played minor parts while Gubby rescued the situation with the utmost determination and skill.

He made 68 out of 134 in three and a quarter hours before being last out to a catch behind the bowler. Gubby has always rated this his best innings, for apart from the heavy responsibility on his shoulders the ball was definitely turning, and he was up against one of the best-ever in O'Reilly. He got out in the end because Bradman seemed to have decided he did not want Australia to go in that evening. Gubby accordingly thought he would go flat out – either 100 or a bowl at them before the close. As it happened, he holed out at once. Well could Jack Hobbs write 'Allen has had a great triumph!' Now on a pitch readily taking spin Australia needed 381 to win, a proposition too difficult to need underlining. In a dull light Fingleton was then bowled by Voce with the first ball of the innings. After the fifth appeal in less than two overs the umpires ended play.

When rain fell in the night Australia's slim vestige of a chance

AUSTRALIA v ENGLAND
(First Test)

At Brisbane, 4–9 December 1936

ENGLAND

T. S. Worthington c Oldfield b McCormick	0	– st Oldfield b McCabe	8
C. J. Barnett c Oldfield b O'Reilly	69	– c Badcock b Ward	26
A. E. Fagg c Oldfield b McCormick	4	– st Oldfield b Ward	27
W. R. Hammond c Robinson b McCormick	0	– hit wkt b Ward	25
M. Leyland b Ward	126	– c Bradman b Ward	33
†L. E. G. Ames c Chipperfield b Ward	24	– b Sievers	9
J. Hardstaff, jr c McCabe b O'Reilly	43	– (8) st Oldfield b Ward	20
R. W. V. Robins c sub (W. A. Brown) b O'Reilly	38	– (9) c Chipperfield b Ward	0
*G. O. B. Allen c McCabe b O'Reilly	35	– (7) c Fingleton b Sievers	68
H. Verity c Sievers b O'Reilly	7	– lbw b Sievers	19
W. Voce not out	4	– not out	2
B 1, l-b 3, n-b 4	8	B 14, l-b 4, n-b 1	19

1/0 2/20 3/20 4/119 5/162   **358** 1/17 2/50 3/82 4/105 5/122 **256**
6/252 7/311 8/311 9/343 10/358   6/144 7/205 8/205 9/247 10/256

Bowling: *First Innings* – McCormick 8–1–26–3; Sievers 16–5–42–0; O'Reilly 40.6–13–102–5; Ward 36–3–138–2; Chipperfield 11–3–32–0; McCabe 2–0–10–0. *Second Innings* – Sievers 19.6–9–29–3; O'Reilly 35–15–59–0; Ward 46–16–102–6; Chipperfield 10–2–33–0; McCabe 6–1–14–1.

AUSTRALIA

J. H. W. Fingleton b Verity	100	– b Voce	0
C. L. Badcock b Allen	8	– c Fagg b Allen	0
*D. G. Bradman c Worthington b Voce	38	– (5) c Fagg b Allen	0
S. J. McCabe c Barnett b Voce	51	– (6) c Leyland b Allen	7
R. H. Robinson c Hammond b Voce	2	– (7) c Hammond b Voce	3
A. G. Chipperfield c Ames b Voce	7	– (8) not out	26
M. W. Sievers b Allen	8	– (3) c Voce b Allen	5
†W. A. S. Oldfield c Ames b Voce	6	– (4) b Voce	10
W. J. O'Reilly c Leyland b Voce	3	– b Allen	0
F. A. Ward c Hardstaff b Allen	0	– b Voce	1
E. L. McCormick not out	1	– absent ill	
B 4, l-b 1, n-b 5	10	N-b 6	6

1/13 2/89 3/166 4/176 5/202   **234** 1/0 2/3 3/7 4/7 5/16   **58**
6/220 7/229 8/231 9/231 10/234   6/20 7/35 8/41 9/58

Bowling: *First Innings* – Allen 16–2–71–3; Voce 20.6–5–41–6; Hammond 4–0–12–0; Verity 28–11–52–1; Robins 17–0–48–0. *Second Innings* – Allen 6–0–36–5; Voce 6.3–0–16–4.

Umpires: G. Borwick and J. D. Scott.

England won by 322 runs.

dissolved completely. Gubby within the first quarter of an hour had Badcock, Sievers, and then (second ball) Bradman himself for a duck, this off a good length ball that lifted viciously: Australia 7 for four. Thereafter the cricket was a formality. Gubby had five for 36, Voce four for 16, and in little more than an hour the innings was over for 58, the second lowest total ever made by Australia in their own country.

'We had all the luck,' said the England captain in his hour of triumph, adding, since he and his side had enjoyed none of it hitherto, 'The age of miracles is not past.' The Australian Prime Minister wired:

> Heartiest Congratulations to your team on magnificent win and to
> you personally for part you played in achieving result stop feel sure
> all Australians will accept defeat in the true spirit of cricket.
>
> J. A. Lyons

A warm friend from 1932–33 and a future Prime Minister sent:

> Congratulations your fine win also your splendid part in it.
>
> R. G. Menzies

In English and Australian press alike superlatives were sprinkled
everywhere. Gubby's father procured a newspaper bill-board ALLEN'S
GREAT DAY IN THE CRISIS. But the words held a dual meaning, for
the Test ended on 9 December, and the Act of Abdication was passed on
the 10th. Edward VIII's farewell message and departure came on the
11th. Gubby's wry comment is that he had been upstaged! He must have
the last word on the Brisbane Test of 1936:

> It was a wonderful match, full of up's and down's, but we gradually
> pushed ahead and would, I am sure, have won whether it had
> rained or not. The wicket was turning a lot on the Tuesday
> afternoon when I was batting and Verity must have got them out by
> degrees on the last day. Though I say so who shouldn't, I suppose,
> my 68 was far and away the best and most timely innings of my life
> and I enjoyed every second of it. If I had got out for say 10 it would
> have meant that they would have had approx: $2\frac{3}{4}$ hours batting
> before the rain came and only about 275 to make to win.

Exactly! In fact it was Allen's match.

After it the captain awarded himself a rest, and, avoiding an up-
country game, in the enviable way possible in those days stepped aboard
the *Otranto* just leaving Brisbane and sailed the thirty-six hours to
Sydney. On the promenade deck he heard a twangy voice over the ship's
radio. 'For Heaven's sake turn off that noise,' he asked a steward. 'But
it's the King abdicating, sir,' was the answer.

In a letter home written during the Test Gubby, a devoted Royalist if
ever there was one, commented:

> I am so far away and don't really know the facts, but it does seem to
> me he has behaved disgracefully. I believe he thought he was so
> popular with British people all over the world that he could get
> away with anything. If she had any decency she should have walked
> out when she saw what was going to happen.

His scrap-books cover all the historic occasions as they occurred. None of the entries are more moving than the *Sydney Morning Herald* pages that tell the story from London of the final scenes and the accession of the new King, and of the almost unanimous reaction of support for Stanley Baldwin and his government by the Federal Parliament of Australia.

The Second Test, following closely on the First, was at Sydney, which Gubby rated as his unlucky ground. Not so this time. He began by winning the toss and seeing England end the first day at 279 for three with Hammond not out 147. On the Saturday, with Hammond again quietly in the ascendant, they took the score to 426 for six before rain made a second intrusion and ended play for the day. Gubby, batting at No 6, was lbw for 9, but Ames and Hardstaff helped Hammond take his score to 231 – and he was still there at the end. (Hammond and Sydney were synonymous between the wars. He is the only man to make four Test hundreds there, let alone, on what was then surely the perfect Test ground, to average, in all, 160.)

Then on the Sunday night came to English ears the sweet music of more rain – three-quarters of an inch of it. Gubby took Robins and Verity with him to look at the pitch next morning, and, not without some misgiving, announced his declaration. England then bowled out Australia for 80. It was the Brisbane story over again except that the pitch to English eyes was not quite so difficult. The fact was that Australia had little experience of batting when the ball was inclined to 'stop' and lift because in the Sheffield Shield and senior club cricket pitches were always covered. The Australians had a holy dread of English bowlers in such conditions and Voce justified their fears by bowling admirably over the wicket to a cordon of slips.

Now, of course, another decision for Gubby: should he order the follow-on or bat again? He opted for the follow-on, and when at close of play Australia's second innings score stood at 145 for one heads were wagged solemnly. Had Allen erred? The pitch had rolled out plumb and Bradman was not out 57. Hobbs was 'inclined to think' he had. Charlie Macartney in the *Daily Telegraph* was more definite and so, in England, was Chapman. However, the captain had the last laugh. By the fourth evening Australia had been bowled out for 324, and England had gone two up in the series by the margin of an innings and 22 runs.

Fortunately, as usual, Gubby in a letter to his father a few days after the match explained his thinking and also summed up Don Bradman's difficulties as he saw them at the moment:

> The rain came down pretty heavily on Sunday night but the wicket was never as bad as the Australians thought. I was very nervous about declaring but had no fears of making them follow on though I seem to have been criticised in the English papers for doing so. I

AUSTRALIA v ENGLAND
(Second Test)

At Sydney, 18–22 December 1936

ENGLAND

A. E. Fagg c Sievers b McCormick	11
C. J. Barnett b Ward.........................	57
W. R. Hammond not out....................	231
M. Leyland lbw b McCabe..................	42
†L. E. G. Ames c sub (R. H. Robinson) b Ward....................................	29
*G. O. B. Allen lbw b O'Reilly	9
J. Hardstaff, jr b McCormick	26
H. Verity not out...........................	0
B 8, l-b 8, w 1, n-b 4	21

1/27 2/118   (6 wkts., dec.) 426
3/247 4/351 5/368 6/424

J. M. Sims, R. W. V. Robins and W. Voce did not bat.

Bowling: McCormick 20–1–79–2; Sievers 16.2–4–30–2; Ward 42–8–132–2; O'Reilly 41–17–86–1; Chipperfield 13–2–47–0; McCabe 9–1–31–1.

AUSTRALIA

J. H. W. Fingleton c Verity b Voce	12	– b Sims	73
L. P. J. O'Reilly c Sims b Voce..............	0	– c Allen b Hammond..............	17
*D. G. Bradman c Allen b Voce	0	– b Verity	82
S. J. McCabe c Sims b Voce	0	– lbw b Voce........................	93
A. G. Chipperfield c Sims b Allen..........	13	– b Voce............................	21
M. W. Sievers c Voce b Verity	4	(7) run out........................	24
†W. A. S. Oldfield b Verity	1	(8) c Ames b Voce	1
W. J. O'Reilly not out	37	(9) b Hammond	3
E. L. McCormick b Allen....................	10	(10) lbw b Hammond............	0
F. A. Ward b Allen...........................	0	(11) not out.......................	1
C. L. Badcock absent ill		(6) lbw b Allen	2
B 1, l-b 1, n-b 1	3	L-b 3, n-b 4	7

1/1 2/1 3/1 4/16 5/28   80   1/38 2/162 3/186 4/220 5/226   324
6/30 7/37 8/80 9/80   6/318 7/319 8/323 9/323 10/
                                    324

Bowling: *First Innings* – Voce 8–1–10–4; Allen 5.7–1–19–3; Verity 3–0–17–2; Hammond 4–0–6–0; Sims 2–0–20–0; Robins 1–0–5–0. *Second Innings* – Voce 19–4–66–4; Allen 19–4–61–1; Verity 19–7–55–1; Hammond 15.7–3–29–3; Sims 17–0–80–1; Robins 7–0–26–0.

Umpires: G. Borwick and J. D. Scott.

England won by an innings and 22 runs.

knew the wicket would roll out easy the second time but we had them well and truly depressed and I wanted to keep them like that. If Robbie had caught Bradman off me when he had made 24, as he most certainly ought to have done, the question could never have been raised. My real reason for making them bat again has never been mentioned in any paper as far as I know and is this. We have got on top of O'Reilly for the time being and he knows it and I don't want to give him any chance of bowling on a wicket which will help him. He has undoubtedly lost his leg break and will not be dangerous again until he gets it back. It is the case of Peebles all over again. Bradman is still very nervy and never batted well during his 82. I am very sorry for him as I like him enormously and I don't think he is getting full support. We surely ought now to win the rubber but I am frightened of our side as there are too many passengers in it and Fleetwood-Smith may easily be awkward under the new lbw rule.

That Bradman, in his arduous dual role as world's best batsman and untried captain, held the key to the series comes through in all that was written about it. He had looked in poor form, by his own standards, at Brisbane, had made his second successive duck at Sydney in the first innings. Gubby's anguish at poor Walter Robins's missed catch after the Don had made a scratchy 24 can well be imagined. When Robins apologized, the picture of remorse, Gubby made his often quoted remark: 'Oh, forget it, old boy, it's probably cost us the rubber, but what the hell!' Gubby, recalling the fateful moment today, says that what made it worse was that he had moved Walter from square-leg to short mid-wicket some thirty yards from the bat because Bradman normally hooked in front of square. The trap was laid and baited, and the man who scarcely ever dropped a catch floored one which was going hard but straight at his throat. Explaining his comment, Gubby says 'Robbie was such a temperamental chap I thought the best thing was to try and make him laugh.' And — in later years at least — the culprit did laugh about it, long and often.

Bradman added 25 more to his overnight score on the last morning, still struggling to regain his habitual mastery, before, with minutes to go to lunch, Gubby brought on Verity. Thereupon he aimed to hook something near a long-hop, missed it, and was bowled off his pads. It was a strange dismissal for anyone, let alone Bradman, who had 82 runs to his name on a now perfectly good pitch. That was 186 for three, and though McCabe played beautifully, being lbw for 93, he found little support, and soon after tea the game was over. (Gubby remembered how as McCabe passed him, 'I said, "Surely you hit that one?" Being the man he was he only smiled. It was an appalling decision.')

England's captain said in the moment of victory: 'I am terribly glad we have won. It will help us to digest our Christmas dinner. We had all the luck again.' His opposite number said, 'I immediately went to Gubby Allen at the finish and warmly congratulated him on his team's success, but I promised him a much harder game at Melbourne.' The Australian press, while critical of their own side, did not stint their praise of the winners, while the English press was euphoric to a degree. The *Evening News* gave their correspondent's verdict on the result in a seven-column banner headline:

WE ARE PRACTICALLY CERTAIN TO WIN BACK THE
ASHES, SAYS H. A. H. CARSON.

There is a letter extant from Walter Robins to Sir Walter Allen, written
on Christmas Eve, which in his usual direct way put the current position
in fair perspective:

> It's been marvellous – of course we've been lucky, but goodness
> they've been gutless! We may lose the next three Tests but we've
> blended ourselves into a team and Gubby has been magnificent.
> Although I haven't done a thing he really makes me believe that I've
> actually done wonders ... Personally I don't think I really mind
> what happens now – of course to win the Rubber would be
> marvellous – but we are two up (nearly dormy) and that's two more
> than 75% of the Australian cricketing public thought we would ...
> Gubby is in great form and as fit as a fiddle.

He was fit enough indeed at this point to give the Don seven points and
beat him on the squash court, the significance being, of course, that they
played, and lunched together afterwards. The English party had little
more than a week to rest on their laurels, and this period included a two-
day game directly after Christmas at Newcastle. For the Third Test,
starting at Melbourne on New Year's Day, they made one change in their
side, Worthington as Barnett's partner instead of Fagg. More importantly, Australia picked Fleetwood-Smith who had been out of consideration hitherto because of a finger injury, and when McCormick, the fast
bowler, dropped out of their chosen twelve they replaced him with an all-
rounder in Sievers, who had been omitted. So nervous were Australia of
their batting that they went into the match with McCabe and Sievers to
share the new ball, plus two right-arm wrist-spinners, O'Reilly and
Ward, and the left-arm back-of-the-hand spinner, Fleetwood-Smith. It
was an attack which could have left Bradman horribly vulnerable if the
England batting had prospered on a good pitch.

11

1936–37 – and Reality

The Third Test at the New Year on the world's largest cricket amphitheatre is so placed as to form the major focal point of almost every tour of Australia. Now the challenge to Bradman and his team brought crowds that even Melbourne had never seen before. Gubby had won the two previous tosses by calling 'Heads'. For this and the remaining Tests he changed to 'Tails' and lost all three. The shift in the luck was symbolic – for Providence had changed sides completely. This was not at first apparent for recent rain had interfered with the preparation of the pitch which was, according to Hobbs, slow and easy-paced. 'Allen lost the toss,' wrote Hobbs, 'after confiding to me that he would be quite content to do so.'

At the end of the first day all the advantage was with England who, according to Victor Richardson – one of the strong contingent of old Test cricketers in the press-box – 'played like a victorious team from the start.' The crowd, as the game unfolded, were full of gloom – 78,630 of them, the largest by 16,000 ever to see a day's cricket. Bradman failed again. He was missed by Worthington in the gully off Gubby before being out in a way he probably never otherwise experienced. Gubby at 33 for one, with Bradman 13, brought on Verity. His first ball was a faster one which was played deliberately just behind square on the leg-side, straight into Robins's hands. For once the Don had not given his usual close attention to the field-placing. In five innings now he had made only 133 runs – an extraordinary fact and an ominous one. Oldfield joined McCabe at 130 for six, Gubby's part having been to take Rigg's wicket, thanks to a brilliant catch by Verity in much the same position in which Bradman was caught, and to make an awkward catch above his head at mid-off to get rid of the left-handed Darling.

Now came a crucial moment in the fortunes of the day, and therefore of the match and rubber. Robins had taken the sixth wicket by getting Sievers stumped. Hammond was temporarily off the field having stumbled when bowling and slightly injured a knee. Voce therefore was at slip. Suddenly realizing that he would have had no experience fielding there to a leg-spinner, Gubby determined to replace him at the end of the over. But before it ended Oldfield had edged a leg-break, and Voce missed the easiest of chances. The score would have been 130 for seven, with only three negligible batsmen, O'Reilly, Ward, and Fleetwood-Smith to help McCabe, and with, as it turned out, a full hour's cricket remaining. As it was, Oldfield stayed with McCabe, and with England handicapped towards the close by a wet ball following a shower, their unbroken partnership by six o'clock had added 51.

More rain meant no cricket next day until after lunch. When it was possible everyone knew what to expect. With McCabe out at once the tail had a haphazard bang or two before Bradman declared at 200 for nine, and England faced the certainty of a Melbourne glue-pot. Recalling the miraculous partnership of Hobbs and Sutcliffe in similar conditions in 1928–29, Jardine in the *Standard* quoted other such great innings by Trumper and J. T. Tyldesley. England's present answer was Walter Hammond, who played a masterly innings of 32. But, as Cardus put it, 'There was no ignominy in the collapse. The pitch was beyond the reach of any normal batting technique.' Les Ames (out for 3) says that he faced twenty-three balls from O'Reilly without getting a touch. 'Bertie Oldfield was taking quick leg-breaks head high.'

Gubby in fact declared at 76 for nine, leaving Australia a maximum of 35 minutes' batting time, and the question that has been debated for all but half a century is whether he should have done so earlier – possibly after Darling had made his two admirable catches at short-leg to dispose of first Leyland and then Hammond. England were then 68 for four, and there was a possible hour left – if the rain held off and the dull light did not deteriorate further. Bob Wyatt, while admitting what a difficult decision it was, says that he and Robins advised an earlier declaration. Ames's comment is 'I don't know whether I'd have been courageous enough to declare.'

The captain saw the situation like this:

> The next day was a Sunday and the playing conditions allowed for the pitch to be rolled at the curator's discretion at any time after the close of play including the Sabbath. It would thus probably be in perfect condition on the Monday. The moment of decision, whether to declare or not, came when with both Hammond and Leyland out we were 68 for four and there were about 50 minutes' playing time remaining. The decision rested on the weather. The clouds were very low, threatening rain at any moment or a successful appeal against the light. If play is not going to be suspended you declare: if it is, you 'stay put', hoping to reduce the arrears of 132 on the Monday. I got the decision wrong because I assessed the weather incorrectly.

There it is then, straight from the horse's mouth, so to say. In

AUSTRALIA v ENGLAND
(Third Test)

At Melbourne 1–7 January 1937

AUSTRALIA

J. H. W. Fingleton c Sims b Robins	38	– (6) c Ames b Sims	136
W. A. Brown c Ames b Voce	1	– (5) c Barnett b Voce	20
*D. G. Bradman c Robins b Verity	13	– (7) c Allen b Verity	270
K. E. Rigg c Verity b Allen	16	– lbw b Sims	47
S. J. McCabe c Worthington b Voce	63	– (8) lbw b Allen	22
L. S. Darling c Allen b Verity	20	– (9) b Allen	0
M. W. Sievers st Ames b Robins	1	– (10) not out	25
†W. A. S. Oldfield not out	27	– (11) lbw b Verity	7
W. J. O'Reilly c Sims b Hammond	4	– (1) c and b Voce	0
F. A. Ward st Ames b Hammond	7	– (3) c Hardstaff b Verity	18
L. O'B. Fleetwood-Smith did not bat	–	(2) c Verity b Voce	0
B 2, l-b 6, n-b 2	10	B 6, l-b 2, w 1, n-b 10	19

1/7 2/33 3/69 4/79   (9 wkts., dec.) 200   1/0 2/3 3/38 4/74 5/97   564
5/122 6/130 7/183 8/190 9/200   6/443 7/511 8/511 9/549 10/564

Bowling: *First Innings* – Voce 18–3–49–2; Allen 12–2–35–1; Sims 9–1–35–0; Verity 14–4–24–2; Robins 7–0–31–2; Hammond 5.3–0–16–2. *Second Innings* – Voce 29–2–120–3; Allen 23–2–84–2; Sims 23–1–109–2; Verity 37.7–9–79–3; Robins 11–2–46–0; Hammond 22–3–89–0; Worthington 4–0–18–0.

ENGLAND

T. S. Worthington c Bradman b McCabe	0	– c Sievers b Ward	16
C. J. Barnett c Darling b Sievers	11	– lbw b O'Reilly	23
W. R. Hammond c Darling b Sievers	32	– b Sievers	51
M. Leyland c Darling b O'Reilly	17	– not out	111
J. M. Sims c Brown b Sievers	3	– (10) lbw b Fleetwood-Smith	0
†L. E. G. Ames b Sievers	3	– (5) b Fleetwood-Smith	19
R. W. V. Robins c O'Reilly b Sievers	0	– (8) b O'Reilly	61
J. Hardstaff, jr b O'Reilly	3	– (6) c Ward b Fleetwood-Smith	17
*G. O. B. Allen not out	0	– (7) c Sievers b Fleetwood-Smith	11
H. Verity c Brown b O'Reilly	0	– (9) c McCabe b O'Reilly	11
W. Voce not out	0	– c Bradman b Fleetwood-Smith	0
B 5, l-b 1, n-b 1	7	L-b 3	3

1/0 2/14 3/46 4/68   (9 wkts., dec.) 76   1/29 2/65 3/117 4/155 5/179   323
5/71 6/71 7/76 8/76 9/76   6/195 7/306 8/322 9/323 10/323

Bowling: *First Innings* – McCabe 2–1–7–1; Sievers 11.2–5–21–5; O'Reilly 12–5–28–3; Fleetwood-Smith 3–1–13–0. *Second Innings* – McCabe 8–0–32–0; Sievers 12–2–39–1; O'Reilly 21–6–65–3; Fleetwood-Smith 25.6–2–124–5; Ward 12–1–60–1.

Umpires: G. Borwick and J. D. Scott.

Australia won by 365 runs.

retrospect England by a declaration *might* have got fifty minutes' bowling at Australia instead of eighteen balls. Bradman would still have sacrificed his tail-enders, and he might well then have lost three or four wickets instead of just O'Reilly's. If on the other hand an England declaration at around 68 for four had been immediately followed by rain which prevented further play their captain, having surrendered six wickets to no avail, would have looked remarkably foolish leading out his team on a sunny Monday morning to bowl on a plumb pitch. He faced a gamble either way.

In fact the weather was still uncertain on Monday. Nevertheless Friday's gate record was easily exceeded. The great arena was packed with a crowd of 87,798 – which remained a world record until 90,800 turned up to watch the final Test of the great Australia-West Indies series at Melbourne in 1960–61. They saw the score lifted from 3 for one wicket to 97 for five, at which point Fingleton, who had been held back to No 6, was joined by Bradman. The lead was thus 221, and the issue still open. But now came England's crowning misfortune in the shape of showers which were not heavy enough to affect the pitch, merely to ensure the bowlers having to bowl with a wet ball. There were three interruptions and one and a half hours' cricket lost before Fingleton (39) and Bradman (56) came in at close of play undefeated. At 194 for five Australia now led by 318, and if England's chance had not completely slipped away it certainly faded swiftly out of sight on the fourth day as the partnership proceeded remorselessly to establish all sorts of records. Gubby recalls the Don, needing at first a considerable degree of luck still, playing himself into form with all his renowned powers of concentration. He gave no chance, and Fingleton only half a one to Hammond jumping high at slip. Fingleton he regarded as 'not exciting but technically very good'. England's fielding, and the way they stuck at it, won the highest praise. Their sole reward was Fingleton's wicket to a catch behind off Jim Sims after the partnership had grown to 346. Mc Cabe must have been a cheerful prospect coming in at No 9.

Next day Gubby soon had the wickets of McCabe and Darling with successive balls, and then judged a difficult running catch the first time, it was said, that Bradman put the ball in the air. The psychological significance of his 270, coming at this precise moment, needs no emphasis. If he had failed again, and Australia had accordingly been beaten, would Bradman have been retained as captain? On this point Gubby says he was aware of the Vic Richardson clique who, on the evidence of his leadership in South Africa the previous winter, wanted him as captain. Though Don had lost twice all the odds had been against him. When they played golf together before the Third Test he expressed his sympathy that nothing had gone right for him – it was natural indeed that Gubby should have remembered this moment in the light of what followed. He thinks it would have been an unkind decision to have robbed him of the captaincy. What can be said without argument is that this innings, the longest in time he ever played – he batted without a chance for seven hours thirty-eight minutes – was one of the major milestones in his career.

England's second innings in search of 689 was just a formality to be gone through. Leyland and Robins, making 111 together in little more than an hour, gave it a certain sparkle, and it was when they were together on the fifth evening that Leyland made the crack often told of him. Walter, who always ran like a hare between the wickets, reduced Maurice to breathlessness: 'Eh oop, lad, we can't get these runs to-night.'

The margin was 365, a result which Jack Hobbs summed up thus:

> Although this sounds a handsome victory, England were by no means disgraced. In case you Australians should get conceited over this victory, or you English disconsolate, let me say that, in my opinion, England never had a chance from the word go.
>
> You can quite rightly point to the fact that rain helped England in the first two Tests, but there is this difference: in these England had placed themselves in a very strong position before rain came.

On the evening of the last day Gubby wrote home:

> We were terribly unlucky in every possible way, and I can only describe it as a tragedy. We were in an impregnable position on the Friday night and undeniably had the rubber well won but the rain fell and the wicket was the worst I have ever seen.

'Impregnable'? None of the critics were as definite as that, though in the moment of his deep disappointment Gubby's private version to his family is understandable enough. In the perspective of time, and having read and heard so much about this fateful match, I would say that, if the weather had stayed fair throughout, an English victory must have been highly probable from the point when Australia's score stood at 130 for six on the first afternoon. The rain thereafter only benefited Australia until by the end of the third day their victory was next to certain.

Gubby awarded himself a match off after the Test, missing the visit to Launceston and flying from Melbourne to Hobart in time for the second Tasmanian fixture against a combined team including several Test cricketers from the mainland. This was his first flight of any length and since the team were not allowed to fly — nor were they allowed to in South Africa two years later — Gubby was lucky that the president of MCC, Lord Somers, was on hand to give him special dispensation. Though resting from cricket the captain was burdened with correspondence ('I cleared up 55 letters ... and have just counted up 18 more to be answered!').

He also worked each day with a firm of Australian stockbrokers closely associated with his own. That trip to Kalgoorlie and the contacts he made at the highest levels on this tour were the fruitful beginnings of those Australian business interests which he was able to develop so profitably, for himself and his Stock Exchange clients, after the war. The Baillieu family had been close friends since 1932–33, and on the ship going out this time he had come to know James Darling, the chairman of

Broken Hill Proprietary. There were no more powerful names in the financial world of Australia than these two.

Flying had always been an interest of Gubby's since boyhood days when he, cousin Dick and Sydney Camm flew model aeroplanes at Datchet. So we have the exact details of the flight of the Douglas airliner from Essendon aerodrome to Hobart via Launceston: 289 miles to Launceston, a further 110 to Hobart, and the whole journey done in 2 hours 34 minutes. By boat and train it would apparently have taken 26 hours. Gubby enjoyed the experience enormously. He wrote home describing how he had been invited to the pilot's cabin for the whole trip 'being shown how to fly and navigate the machine'. There they were 'laughing away, drinking tea, and smoking at 10,000 feet doing 185 m.p.h.' It was a foretaste of things to come.

Gubby (55) took the chance in the Hobart match of some good batting practice against the leg-spin of Ward and the old fox, Grimmett. In this and the next match against South Australia at Adelaide (where Gubby against the same pair made 60) Bob Wyatt, returning to the field after two and a half months, made runs, while Kenneth Farnes, compulsorily idle for a month, bowled well enough to suggest himself for a Test place. Three days were lost to rain in these games – this was one of the wetter Australian summers.

Writing from Adelaide Gubby says he is getting anxious about the Fourth Test 'not because I think anything has happened to lessen our chances but just because I'm so desperately keen to win.' He has gone temporarily 't.t.'. He says – with premature satisfaction, as it turned out – that Fleetwood-Smith looked like being left out, also that he is confident of his batting, especially against leg-spin bowling. 'I wonder whether it is just in this country that I can now play it, or whether I shall be successful in England in my own small way.'

The injury problems which had beset the side since they set sail persisted as Voce became troubled with a bad back. The captain was for resting him in this Fourth Test to ensure his fitness for the Fifth. Fast bowlers could not be effective unless they were fully fit. But for once he did not get his way at the selection meeting. The doubt about Voce ensured the preference for Farnes over Sims, while Wyatt came in for Worthington. (Fagg was now out of action with rheumatic fever while Fishlock had broken a bone in his hand, so the batting options were limited.)

In perfect weather and with the certainty of an equally perfect pitch Gubby again lost the toss. This was a great blow. Yet early on the second day, to the surprise of all, Australia had been bowled out for 288. As the early wickets fell Cardus wrote that he could not believe his spectacles. As usual Bradman's success or otherwise determined the dimensions of the innings, and as usual drama surrounded his performance. When he had made 16 Gubby lost his run-up and bowled a slower ball which the Don first aimed to hook. The ball was old but it swung away wildly for some mysterious reason. In the end he tried to let the ball go by, but it slid along the face of the bat. There was so much deviation that Ames had to make an excellent one-handed catch in front of first slip, there was a loud appeal and to the bowler's undisguised dismay umpire Scott said not out.

When, says Gubby, he snatched his sweater at the end of the over the following exchange took place:

'I couldn't give him out, I didn't hear anything.'

'No, because the ball went off the face of the bat.'

It is safe to assume, I think, that it was not only the England captain who was unsettled by this incident which, by his own account, reached the very limit of propriety. When the Don had scored another 10 runs he made an uncharacteristically loose attempt at a hook and dragged the ball into his stumps; Bradman b. Allen 26. Forty years later Don thought this the worst decision bar one in which he was concerned. He did not say which was the worst.

At this fraught moment Ross Gregory, playing in his first Test, came in, says Gubby, with his face as white as his shirt. Nevertheless with McCabe playing admirably as usual Australia reached the 200 mark with the fifth wicket still intact. Gubby in the morning after only three overs had slightly strained his left ham-string and Voce was only half-fit, so who should share the new ball with Farnes? While the captain was wondering about this Robins was bowling to McCabe with a packed off-side field set deep. McCabe, then 88, looking for fours rather than singles, on-drove straight into the hands of Gubby, the only man near the wicket at wide mid-on. Vic Richardson described this as 'a distinct triumph for Allen's captaincy'. Leyland now made a suggestion. Young Gregory will not have had much experience of the swinging ball – the shine in those days only lasted an over or two in Australia – and the breeze is right for Hammond's out-swinger. Why not give him the new ball? Gubby agreed, and Hammond promptly did the trick.

Overnight Australia were 267 for seven, which represented, of course, an excellent English performance. Next morning Gubby was woken up by an early telephone call from a friendly reporter who thought he would prefer to break the news rather than that Ken Farnes should learn from the papers that his mother had been killed in a motor accident. So the captain had a sad, highly emotional start to his day, and the memory of poor Ken's distress is still vivid with him.

In five Test innings England had failed to make a good start, and now Gubby gave everyone something to chatter about by sending in Verity with Barnett rather than Wyatt. Verity did a steady, blunting job in both

AUSTRALIA v ENGLAND
(Fourth Test)

At Adelaide, 29 January–4 February 1937

AUSTRALIA

J. H. W. Fingleton run out	10	– lbw b Hammond	12
W. A. Brown c Allen b Farnes	42	– c Ames b Voce	32
K. E. Rigg c Ames b Farnes	20	– (5) c Hammond b Farnes	7
*D. G. Bradman b Allen	26	– (3) c and b Hammond	212
S. J. McCabe c Allen b Robins	88	– (4) Wyatt b Robins	55
R. G. Gregory lbw b Hammond	23	– run out	50
A. G. Chipperfield not out	57	– c Ames b Hammond	31
†W. A. S. Oldfield run out	5	– c Ames b Hammond	1
W. J. O'Reilly c Leyland b Allen	7	– c Hammond b Farnes	1
E. L. McCormick c Ames b Hammond	4	– b Hammond	1
L. O'B. Fleetwood-Smith b Farnes	1	– not out	4
L-b 2, n-b 3	5	B 10, l-b 15, w 1, n-b 1	27

1/26 2/72 3/73 4/136 5/206   288 1/21 2/88 3/197 4/237 5/372   433
6/226 7/249 8/271 9/283 10/288   6/422 7/426 8/427 9/429 10/433

Bowling: *First Innings* – Voce 12–0–49–0; Allen 16–0–60–2; Farnes 20.6–1–71–3; Hammond 6–0–30–2; Verity 16–4–47–0; Robins 7–1–26–1. *Second Innings* – Voce 20–2–86–1; Allen 14–1–61–0; Farnes 24–2–89–2; Hammond 15.2–1–57–5; Verity 37–17–54–0; Robins 6–0–38–1; Barnett 5–1–15–0; Leyland 2–0–6–0.

ENGLAND

H. Verity c Bradman b O'Reilly	19	– b Fleetwood-Smith	17
C. J. Barnett lbw b Fleetwood-Smith	129	– c Chipperfield b Fleetwood-Smith	21
W. R. Hammond c McCormick b O'Reilly	20	– (4) b Fleetwood-Smith	39
M. Leyland c Chipperfield b Fleetwood-Smith	45	– (5) c Chipperfield b Fleetwood-Smith	32
R. E. S. Wyatt c Fingleton b O'Reilly	3	– (6) c Oldfield b McCabe	50
†L. E. G. Ames b McCormick	52	– (7) lbw b Fleetwood-Smith	0
J. Hardstaff, jr c and b McCormick	20	– (3) b O'Reilly	43
*G. O. B. Allen lbw b Fleetwood-Smith	11	– c Gregory b McCormick	9
R. W. V. Robins c Oldfield b O'Reilly	10	– b McCormick	4
W. Voce c Rigg b Fleetwood-Smith	8	– b Fleetwood-Smith	1
K. Farnes not out	0	– not out	7
B 6, l-b 2, w 1, n-b 4	13	B 12, l-b 2, n-b 6	20

1/53 3/108 3/190 4/195 5/259   330 1/45 2/50 3/120 4/149 5/190   243
6/299 7/304 8/318 9/322 10/330   6/190 7/225 8/231 9/235 10/243

Bowling: *First Innings* – McCormick 21–2–81–2; McCabe 9–2–18–0; Fleetwood-Smith 41.4–10–129–4; O'Reilly 30–12–51–4; Chipperfield 9–1–24–0; Gregory 3–0–14–0. *Second Innings* – McCormick 13–1–43–2; McCabe 5–0–15–1; Fleetwood-Smith 30–1–110–6; O'Reilly 26–8–55–1.

Umpires: G. Borwick and J. D. Scott.

Australia won by 148 runs.

innings, and in the first Barnett's hundred earned him universal praise. By the close on Saturday England were 174 for two and extremely well-placed. After the week-end however Fleetwood-Smith's left-arm wrist-spin came into its own, and England's limitations against high-class slow bowling were exposed. Gubby was lbw to the spin of Fleetwood-Smith, the man he hoped would not be picked. In the end the lead was a mere 42, and he could truly write that evening, 'we had a really bad day today losing all our advantage, and will now have to put up a great performance tomorrow if we are going to win this blasted match.'

Alas, the great performance – or at least the rigidly disciplined, utterly patient performance that turned the scales – was contributed by Bradman. With Voce and himself only half-fit, Gubby gave the new ball to Farnes and Hammond. Farnes bowled well on his first Test appearance in Australia while Hammond, using the cross-wind at a brisk medium-pace, rose to the occasion in the way he always could as a bowler when there was a real need. On the easiest batting pitch in Australia the English tactics could only be attritional, with Verity wheeling away for hours, supremely accurately, generally at the leg-stump to a leg-side field.

In the heat of the Adelaide Oval anyone with lesser powers of concentration must have lapsed from self-discipline occasionally. The Don did not – and to their infinite credit neither did England ever for a moment relax their effort in the field. For the second Test running the Australian captain's innings extended into a third day. When he had batted for seven hours twenty minutes he hit a return catch to Hammond who clung on to a fierce hit. As with his 270 at Melbourne it was said to be the one and only time Don had hit the ball in the air. His 212 was his seventh double-hundred against England, and while it was his slowest big innings, in which he eschewed the slightest risk, he was still able to push along at 28 runs an hour. He had made, incidentally, just more than half the total runs scored from the bat.

After their ordeal in the field England, needing 392 to win, did well to reach 148 for three at the close of the fifth day with Hammond and Leyland not out. Obviously a very big innings by one or both was the only hope, and neither was forthcoming. Fleetwood-Smith in the first over of the day dropped a beauty plumb on the spot and Hammond played outside it. Victor Richardson quoted Hammond as saying 'It was too good a ball to meet so early.' Like all strong wrist-spinners Fleetwood-Smith was able to make the ball dip late in flight, and Richardson reported that it was this plus the off-break that got through Hammond's defence. Fleetwood-Smith next had Leyland caught at slip, and when Ames was lbw next ball he had taken five of the six wickets that had fallen, and 'the blasted match' was lost. Gubby stayed for three quarters of an hour with Wyatt (whose sterling 50 was one of the encouraging English features), but succumbed to McCormick with the new ball directly after lunch, and the end was not long in following. 'We undoubtedly threw the match away by our bad batting in the first innings and never really recovered from the shock,' was the captain's verdict. That was indisputable, as was the fact that Fleetwood-Smith's ten wickets – in seventy-one overs for 239 runs – had given a new cutting edge to the Australian attack. His scrap-book at this point contains a light-hearted postscript to the Fourth Test in the form of a parody by the famous Beachcomber of the *Daily Express* of C. B. Fry's column. For the Dragon read Bradman:

Archdeacon Dribble says:–

Wooloomooloo soaking in the golden sunlight, the turf as sweet as a fairy's kiss, and a long day's cricket before us. But I don't like the look of the Dragon. He comes up like thunder across the bay, and his bat is a battering-ram, you know.

Our Bert is bowling to the Dragon. Bowling like a god, I tell you. That extra flourish of the sword arm is just keenness. And now the Dragon has wafted him for a dinger. A beautiful stroke. Genuine three-ply Sèvres, this youngster. He has the root of cricket in him. May it grow into a sweet briar.

The Dragon has lifted Bert in a sedentary manner over the screen. Why? We shall see. Gubby knows. He's as keen as mustard – and doesn't lack beef. Those shoulders. Like Colin Blythe's in 1904 at Taunton.

Creative defence strokes. Pretty, but is it art? The Devil knows. Gubby is frisking like a lamb. Oh, that Gubby. And still more big stuff from the Dragon.

Gubby is scratching his head. That means business. No carpet knight, this young Apollo, but a tornado in trousers.

Johnny Morton, who produced that hilarious column of his for fifty years or so, professed to mock cricket, of which in reality he was rather fond. What he was lampooning here was Charles Fry's unique style, a blend of the expertise, wit, scholarship and amiable buffoonery of a first-rate mind.

Charles Fry would have enjoyed Beachcomber's parody. Indeed it took a lot to shake his composure, though Cardus did so around this part of the tour, speaking after Fry at a function when all the English party were present, 'We've been hearing a lot on this tour from C. B. Fry,' said Neville, 'but here it has been Fry B. C.' The great man is said not to have been amused – which is not surprising for if ever there was an interminable 'laudator temporis acti' it was Cardus!

The team had three weeks' respite for medical repairs before returning to Melbourne for the Fifth and final Test. Before they left for the next stage at Canberra Bruce Harris reported:

Allen feels the effects of his ricked thigh muscle, but he was able to golf to-day with Bradman. The two captains are becoming very close friends. They never lose an opportunity of opposing one another at golf and squash. Indeed, a feature of the tour has been the free 'fraternisation' between the players of the two sides.

At a similar stage of the tour four years earlier Gubby was the only man on the English side the Australians would even talk to, or who wished to have anything to do with them. For the fact that relationships were back on a civilized basis Gubby, with Don Bradman's cooperation, was chiefly to thank.

After a two-day game at Geelong next stop was Canberra, the federal capital, whither Gubby and Bob Wyatt motored from Melbourne in a twenty-five h.p. Morris (with a wireless set!) kindly lent by Lord Nuffield – 412 miles in a day. With six men out of action, MCC had to include their manager, Rupert Howard, both at Geelong and Canberra. Gubby, Bob and Ken Farnes stayed at Government House with the Governor-General, Lord Gowrie, who, as Sir Alexander Hore-Ruthven when Governor of South Australia, had been an important mediating factor in the Bodyline row.

The Canberra visit followed the usual demanding social pattern of the tour. There was an official lunch, followed by a tree-planting ceremony and speech to the boys at the grammar school. Gubby presented to the school a stone from the fabric and a photograph of Eton which to him was 'the greatest school in the world'. He hoped that the boys would think the same of their Alma Mater and help to make it great. There was a High Commission garden party and a visit to Parliament House with speeches at both, which caused Maurice Leyland to remark that 'It was the first time he had seen the skipper work.'

Gubby's clearest memory, though, is with one of the key figures in Australian history, the Prime Minister, Joseph Aloysius Lyons. Mr Lyons told him over a drink afterwards that he knew Bob Menzies was a considerable friend of his, and added, 'He has the best brain in Australia, and I'm determined he shall succeed me. But he's got a dangerous tongue, and the first time he won't last long. I believe he'll come back and become one of Australia's great Prime Ministers.' The forecast proved to be wholly accurate.

Thanks to Lord Nuffield's car Gubby continued to see something of the outback, staying with friends at Moss Vale en route for Sydney where Robins was leading a rather weak MCC team to defeat against New South Wales. There Gubby decided, in agreement with Howard, Robins and Wyatt, that it would be better for him 'to keep away for a few more days and miss the State match in Victoria'. Thus he wrote home, adding that he was mentally 'worn out'. Instead he took Arthur Mailey with him on the long, attractive sea coast route down to Melbourne 'and simply loved it', even if once they encountered a bush fire. The fire had brought out the snakes, but they drove over the snakes and through the smoke to safety. Altogether Gubby saw more of his native country on this trip than most cricketers used to do on several tours. Not that his missing the Victoria match went without comment. Plum Warner subsequently criticized it at second hand, pointing out that Gubby had given himself no cricket for three weeks. The Victoria match, by the way, introduced to English eyes a diminutive youngster named Lindsay Hassett, 'a beautifully free player with an attractive style' thought Hobbs, and a sure Test cricketer of the future.

The only suggestion of possible trouble on the tour, quickly scotched, immediately preceded the last Test. Victoria suddenly produced a tearaway fast bowler called Nash, who had never played for the state though as a Tasmanian, and likewise pulled out of the blue, he had shot out the South Africans on a sticky dog five years earlier. When Gubby arrived in Melbourne he learned that Nash had been very inclined to bumpers in the state match and that the Australian selectors who were deficient in fast bowling resources other than McCormick, and anticipating a pitch faster than anything hitherto, had named him among thirteen for the Test. Determined that the last Test should maintain the hard but friendly nature of those preceding it, Gubby told the Don over lunch on the eve of the match that if Bodyline tactics were introduced he would hold the Australian captain responsible and consider himself free to retaliate. Finally, before the start Dr Robertson, chairman of the Board, took the unusual course of calling the captains and umpires together, saying he sincerely hoped nothing untoward would occur, and warning the umpires of the powers they had to ban intimidatory bowling.

In the event Nash did play (he is said to be the only Australian Test cricketer never to play in a Sheffield Shield match) and got some wickets but without giving any offence.

Gubby suggested that he should stand down – more on grounds of mental exhaustion than anything else. However the selectors would not hear of it, and omitted Robins, who apart from his superb fielding and no doubt due to his finger-break, had had a poor tour, in favour of Worthington. For the third successive time the toss was lost, and England took the field in a temperature of 90° in the shade with higher to come. Gubby found his disappointment hard to disguise, and still more so when first Farnes missed Fingleton off him, and then vice-versa. Fingleton had made only two at the second escape. By early afternoon the dreaded combination of Bradman and McCabe were together and now Gubby dropped his second chance, given by McCabe to short-leg – the sort he was swallowing hitherto on the tour. With no leg-spinner to add variety – admittedly both Robins and Sims had been very expensive – England had to rely on pace plus Verity. Gubby even allowed Leyland three (very expensive) overs. England missed another chance, McCabe when 86 being dropped by Farnes off Voce.

Bradman was in his best form, and was still there with 165 to his name out of the large total of 342 for three in the day. McCabe had made 112, and Cardus decided that 'there is no batsman today better worth watching unless it is the incomparable Woolley of Kent'. The 249 made by the third wicket had taken only two and three-quarter hours, Bradman's hundred little more than two hours.

Farnes, much the best of the bowlers, had the ultimate distinction of bowling Bradman early on the second day, but this brought together in wholly favourable circumstances two of the younger school, Badcock and Gregory, who batted almost as surely if not quite as freely as their elders and betters. At the end of the second day Australia were 591 for nine, and by then Gubby must have realized that his gallant quest had failed. England went in early next day to face a score of 604 – looked at in the light of such a total Farnes's six for 96 spoke for itself.

In England's reply Hardstaff of the front-line batsmen alone pleased the critics, Barnett, Hammond and Leyland all failing. Worthington, reinstated in place of Robins, began well before overbalancing on to his stumps. Where nothing short of the heroic could avail them only 184 for four by close of play was forthcoming, three of the wickets falling, so Fry declared, to long-hops. During the lunch interval the Victorian Cricket Association presented Gubby with a handsome set of onyx and pearl waistcoat buttons, shirt studs and cuff-links which he wears today. In his speech of thanks he said he was grateful for all their kindness, even if it may have ruined his cricket, and repeated his theme that because of the demands made upon them all recent Test captains had been 'flops'. While recognizing the big extra strain involved, flop, I think, with due respect, was rather too drastic a word, whether applied to him or to several of his predecessors.

As things turned out here England were deprived of even the possibility of a fight-back by a thunderstorm on the third evening which when the game was resumed gave the Australian bowlers all the help they wanted. It was not so glutinous a sticky as Melbourne had produced for the Third Test but it was bad enough, and the extra difficulty simply added to the anti-climax. Two English wickets were left on the fifth evening after the follow-on and two balls were enough next morning to dispose of them. An innings and 200 was the verdict.

The gates being open, 14,000 people turned up to see the brief finale and to gather round the pavilion for the concluding speeches.

Bradman said:

Rain dealt England a cruel blow, but I have yet to hear one single

AUSTRALIA v ENGLAND
(Fifth Test)

At Melbourne, 26 February–3 March 1937

AUSTRALIA

J. H. W. Fingleton c Voce b Farnes.......... 17
K. E. Rigg c Ames b Farnes.................. 28
*D. G. Bradman b Farnes....................169
S. J. McCabe c Farnes b Verity..............112
C. L. Badcock c Worthington b Voce 118
R. G. Gregory c Verity b Farnes............. 80
†W. A. S. Oldfield c Ames b Voce........... 21
L. J. Nash c Ames b Farnes.................. 17
W. J. O'Reilly b Voce 1
E. L. McCormick not out.................... 17
L. O'B. Fleetwood-Smith b Farnes 13
    B 1, l-b 5, w 1, n-b 4 11

1/42 2/54 3/303 4/346 5/507   604
6/544 7/563 8/571 9/576 10/604

Bowling: Allen 17–0–99–0; Farnes 28.5–5–96–6; Voce 29–3–123–3; Hammond 16–1–62–0; Verity 41–5–127–1; Worthington 6–0–60–0; Leyland 3–0–26–0.

ENGLAND

C. J. Barnett c Oldfield b Nash 18	– lbw b O'Reilly	41
T. S. Worthington hit wkt b Fleetwood-Smith 44	– c Bradman b McCormick	6
J. Hardstaff, jr c McCormick b O'Reilly.... 83	– b Nash............................	1
W. R. Hammond c Nash b O'Reilly 14	– c Bradman b O'Reilly	56
M. Leyland b O'Reilly 7	– c McCormick b Fleetwood-Smith	28
R. E. S. Wyatt c Bradman b O'Reilly........ 38	– run out	9
†L. E. G. Ames b Nash...................... 19	– c McCabe b McCormick	11
*G. O. B. Allen c Oldfield b Nash.......... 0	– c Nash b O'Reilly................	7
H. Verity c Rigg b Nash 0	– not out	2
W. Voce st Oldfield b O'Reilly 3	– c Badcock b Fleetwood-Smith....	1
K. Farnes not out............................ 0	– c Nash b Fleetwood-Smith	0
L-b 12, n-b 1 13	L-b 3........................	3

1/33 2/96 3/130 4/140 5/202   239   1/9 2/10 3/70 4/121 5/142   165
6/236 7/236 8/236 9/239 10/239   6/142 7/153 8/162 9/165 10/165

Bowling: *First Innings* – McCormick 13–1–54–0; Nash 17.5–1–70–4; O'Reilly 23–7–51–5; Fleetwood-Smith 18–3–51–1. *Second Innings* – McCormick 9–0–33–2; Nash 7–1–34–1; O'Reilly 19–6–58–3; Fleetwood-Smith 13.2–3–36–3; McCabe 1–0–1–0.

Umpires: G. Borwick and J. D. Scott.

Australia won by an innings and 200 runs.

word of complaint from any one of them.

I should like to thank my team-mates for their support right through the series, without which we could not have won.

It will be only another year before another Australian team goes to England. I hope I shall be privileged to be with that team, and renew my acquaintanceship with the friends I have made during this tour.

The MCC captain said in response:

If I were in Bradman's position and had his ability, I should be very glad to be standing here. I make no bones about it. I am a very disappointed man.

Australia owes a great deal to a captain who has shown magnificent form first with the bat and then with that infernal coin.

Bradman says that none of the English team has complained about our luck in this game. I am not complaining, but I think you will agree that we shall not go down in history as the luckiest team ever to tour Australia.

Australia played wonderful cricket and fought out of very difficult positions. I'll only say that though we lost we live to fight again.

This is probably my last appearance at Melbourne. It has been a sad one for me, but never mind.

According to Reuter Allen's last words were greeted with cries of 'No, no.'

Instead of three cheers the crowd gave him six. The progress of the series was recapitulated in a leading article in *The Times* which ended:

Allen, himself Australian born, did more than prove himself an inspiring and astute captain; he increased good feeling wherever he went. And in that spirit English cricket will have the greatest pleasure, next time, in knocking the Australians' heads off.

It was an extraordinary rubber in several ways. It was watched by not far short of a million people, 943,000 to be more exact, the highest number to have seen a Test series anywhere, before or since. The English share of the profit, £42,000, was the highest any team had by then brought home from Australia. All five victories were won by the side winning the toss, and the aggregate of the respective margins was greater than in any other series. Heavy rain came into the reckoning in four Tests out of the five – which brought from Test cricketers of both sides pleas that in future Tests in Australia pitches should be covered.

Bradman's batting, as always during his time, was the dominating factor, and his innings in successive matches of 270, 212, and 169 dictated the result in each case. Yet once it need not have done so. In an interview on the day the series ended, after paying due tribute to the Australians and to their captain, Gubby added:

I shall always think we should have won this rubber and settled the issue at Adelaide in the Fourth Test, for surely even the moderate batting side that we are should have succeeded in scoring 700 runs in two innings on a wicket that was almost perfect throughout.

Cardus underlined the chance lost at Adelaide through 'strokeless batting', of which Hammond *in Australia* was as guilty as anyone. 'Something must be done,' wrote Cardus at the end, 'to compel English players to leave the crease now and again and jump into a half-volley.'

As to the Fifth Test, maybe if Gubby had won the toss England might have risen to one more supreme effort, but the solemn fact is that in nineteen Test series in this century in Australia England have only once won (in 1970−71) when the rubber was still at stake. Not only the captain − though he most of all − but the whole side have passed their peak by the beginning of February.

It is interesting looking back at the tour cuttings to see how universally, despite the defeat, Gubby's own performance on and off the field was lauded. His old critic, Trevor Wignall, had long ago eaten his words, but another columnist, L. V. Manning of the *Daily Sketch*, had been almost equally scathing. In his postscript to the series he told his readers:

The Captain Who Made Good
No matter how complete the Melbourne 'massacre', I think a mountain-high wave of sympathy for Allen will sweep across the seas from these islands.

If Allen's pathetic words mean he feels he has failed, he will get the right answer when he steps from the boat-train at Waterloo.

Sportsmanship is not at such a low ebb in cricketing England that the captain who, by his unceasing labours on the field and off, made a poor team into a good one − a team not one of us gave a chance of winning even one Test − will be allowed to leave the stage without some unmistakable sign of the affection he has won.

In those more spacious times the team had five days in Sydney before sailing for New Zealand on the *Wanganella*. For Gubby they were crowded days of farewells, wherein every member of the Allen family was remembered in addition to the official round. The very last thing was a football match against a New South Wales team which attracted a gate of 12,000. Playing inside-right Gubby missed a sitting goal and the Australians won 5−2. George Duckworth brought to the ship a weighty bag containing MCC's share of the gate − £15 per head, which in Gubby's case he handed over to the ship's barman for drinks all round.

Though Gubby complained often that too much was being asked of him he was apt to fill his spare moments strenuously enough. No sooner had the team got to Christchurch than he was up at six a.m. squashing Hedley Verity and Bruce Harris into a ten h.p. Austin and driving them on rough roads the 216 miles over the spine of the South Island to the snows of Mount Cook, at 12,000-odd feet the highest point in New Zealand. They lunched, climbed a little on the mountain, walked on 'the famous Tasman Glacier' and drove back next day in time for Gubby to make his fifty-third speech.

MCC played three three-day matches, the second being at Wellington against 'A New Zealand XI' which, in fact, was the pick of the New Zealand team that was due to sail directly afterwards for their tour of England. New Zealand had been elevated to Test rank seven years earlier, and this game had only not been so called because it was thought, erroneously, that the home touring team would by then be on the high seas. When it was confirmed that both teams would be representative efforts were made, both then and subsequently, to upgrade the fixture into a Test Match. The result was a draw which was within a few minutes of being an innings win for MCC, Gubby's contribution being to make 88 in one and three quarter houres and take five wickets. However not even his advocacy could later win over the Chairman of the MCC Cricket Committee, the aforesaid Stanley Jackson, to award the game Test status. It is said that Walter Hadlee, whose 82 in the second innings saved his side, is agitating the ICC to this day! Gubby recalls sleeping in the dressing-room and saying to the attendant, 'Please stop that boy rushing in here and waking me up.' 'I can't very well do that, sir,' came the answer. 'He's the New Zealand twelfth man.' It was indeed one of the most famous of left-handers and subsequently a great friend, Martin Donnelly.

There was time for a quick trip to the hot springs of Rotorua, a Maori concert, a ceremonial rubbing of noses between Rangi, the famous guide, and England's captain, and a final match, easily won, against Auckland before the party stepped aboard the *Mariposa* for the first stage of the voyage home.

Gubby's last words home from Australasia were:

> I shall definitely not play this summer as I must work and I need a
> rest from the worries of big cricket. Whether I shall ever attempt a
> come-back depends on the city, my physical condition and the wish
> to take on the job again, if asked.

He duly informed the selectors on his return that he would not be available for the series against New Zealand. Thereupon they appointed Walter Robins.

On the *Mariposa* as she sailed north to Los Angeles Gubby performed his last necessary function as captain of the MCC team of 1936–37 in the shape of his official report on the tour for the benefit of the Committee. He had seen and agreed with the longer, factual account written by Rupert Howard, and saw no need for a detailed apologia. Much of his comment I have recorded in this chapter and the last, so a précis of his main conclusions will, I think, meet the case.

He attributed the ultimate defeat to three causes, number one being an excess of cricket, number two the many batting failures, and number three the lack of accurate spin bowlers. As a consequence the extra responsibility on the leading players led to staleness 'long before the end of the tour, especially among the bowlers'.

As to the selection:

I am not in any way criticising the composition of the team as I was entirely satisfied with every selection which was made but I do think that the method of selection which was adopted was wrong. The team should not, in my opinion, be chosen in four lots. No doubt it is desirable to annouce the names of six or seven outstanding players during the month of July but in my opinion the remaining selections should be made en bloc, say four or five weeks before the date of sailing. This would prevent hasty decisions and probably produce a more balanced side.

On the always vexed matter of the umpiring he wrote:

The Board of Control were extremely helpful in all my dealings with them and actually gave me greater power with regard to the appointment of umpires than I was entitled to under the conditions laid down before the commencement of the tour. I expressed a very strong wish that a certain umpire whom they favoured should not be appointed and after some rather awkward discussions they acceded to my request.

The umpiring in both the Test and State matches was at times inaccurate but with one exception (the 1st NSW match) certainly not prejudiced.

The Australian balls used in one state match were harder than the English and not as good. He professed himself 'open-minded' about the eight-ball over — which, by the way, is no longer used in Australia. He warned that the Australian Board of Control would be raising the matter of the covering of pitches before the next MCC tour of Australia, adding:

Very briefly a rain-damaged pitch in Australia is an entirely different proposition to a rain-damaged pitch in England. In England the batting side has some chance, in Australia it has practically none. Consequently it may be claimed that rain is liable to play far too big a part in the result of a match in Australia. If and when this point is raised perhaps it would be a suitable opportunity to press home the advisability of time-limited Test Matches, an innovation which seems to have gained many supporters since we were there four years ago.

On official functions he endorsed the manager's comment that there were too many:

> I am convinced that a captain of an MCC touring team in Australia has little chance of doing himself full justice as a cricketer on the field as things stand at present. The cricketing peformances of Gilligan, Chapman, Jardine and Holmes, the last four MCC captains in Australia, confirm this view.

He finished by recording a warm tribute to the manager, thanked the MCC Committee for the honour they had done him, and paid this compliment to his team:

> To each member of the team I am most grateful for his loyalty and support. In my opinion every one of them would be a definite asset to any future touring team provided his cricket ability warranted his selection.

The note of appreciation for the entire team was no formal platitude. I have since had occasion over the years to talk over the happenings of the tour with most of them, and found that the captain's admiration for them was wholly mutual. Les Ames seemed to speak for them all when he said: 'Gubby did a great job. Despite our mishaps he kept the team together, and was more than adequate – if a bit stereotyped! – as a tactician. We all looked up to him.'

The last word – literally – comes, with gratitude to the author, from Gerald Howat's biography of Walter Hammond. Normally the least expansive of men, Hammond is quoted by the author as saying, 'Gubby Allen was worth a nip of champagne all round to any team, a popular leader whom nothing could shake.' He added, 'This was the happiest tour of my life, made up of men on the best terms with one another.' No one could wish for a more whole-hearted testimonial than that.

The sea trip up to California made the perfect recuperation for a team which since its landing at Fremantle had been on the go for all but six months. They stopped briefly at Suva and Pago Pago, had time at Honolulu to man the long surf boats on Waikiki and taste the delights of the Royal Hawaian Hotel, and after fourteen days docked on time at Los Angeles.

This was as well, for Gubby had made arrangements ahead with C. Aubrey Smith for the team to make the most of their time in Hollywood. So they met two ravishing beauties, Binnie Barnes and Eleanor Powell, and a whole galaxy of stars – Ronald Colman, David Niven, Boris Karloff, Nigel Bruce and Raymond Massey – lunched at Metro-Goldwyn-Mayer, and watched the filming of *Broadway Melody of 1938* and *The Prisoner of Zenda*. After a memorable day they bade farewell to the captain and piled on to the Santa Fé express for Chicago. Thence they took train to New York, and within an hour or two were boarding the *Queen Mary* for home. They arrived to the warmest of welcomes on 26 April, just a few days, for most of them, before the new season got under way.

To Gubby once again the lure of Hollywood cast its spell. He stayed with Nigel and Bunny Bruce in Beverly Hills, and renewed acquaintance with most of the famous names of four years before: Leslie Howard and his wife, for instance, Robert Montgomery, Ronald Colman and the inimitable Marlene Dietrich, the last, he tells his mother, 'very quiet and natural nowadays'. C. Aubrey Smith gave a dinner party for his companion of Sussex summers in the 1890s, Charles Fry, with the great P. G. Wodehouse and Gubby also present — a glamorous quartette if ever there was one. He made many new friends, notably Raymond Massey, Eleanor Powell, Gary Cooper, Constance Bennett, Frederick March and, not least, renewed boyhood bonds from Isle of Wight days — when he was apparently 'plump and ugly' — with David Niven:

> He is not at all spoilt and is extremely popular with everyone. He is earning £70 a week and they say has a big future.

Gubby played two games for Hollywood Cricket Club which on Sundays in C. Aubrey Smith's day was the social focus of the film world. The doyen, then coming up to his seventy-fourth birthday, made a good slip catch off the England captain! Gubby's host, the ever-genial Bruce, was wicket-keeper. Then there was a game of tennis with Norma Shearer, Claudette Colbert, and Carole Lombard. Carole was a decent player, but as for her language ...!

Dragging himself away at last from the bright lights, he took the train to the Grand Canyon, Arizona, marvelling at the wonder of it with the Colorado River winding its way far below. Then — the last thrill — he flew by DC3 of TWA from Albuquerque to Washington, covering the 1800 miles in thirteen hours, and stayed with the future Sir Victor Mallet, then First Consul at the embassy.

Finally came New York and 'after eight glorious months', as he wrote, all transient troubles forgotten, he boarded the *Empress of Britain* which docked at Southampton on 22 May.

The Lull

MCC celebrated its 150th anniversary in 1937, and naturally marked the occasion in a suitable manner. There was a celebratory week's cricket at Lord's in May, first a Trial Match between North and South, won convincingly by the South, and then one between the MCC Australian XI and the Rest of England, won by the touring side by 69 runs. There was a celebratory dinner, and also a book was published reprinting a special MCC number of *The Times*.

Gubby landed at Southampton on the Saturday of the first match and made straight for Lord's. He was not this time greeted by an uncomprehending secretary. Instead the twenty-one-year-old Hutton announced his promise with a hundred, followed by young Compton who marked his nineteenth birthday with an innings of 70. For both the tour had been a year too soon. Gubby went into the second match without even having had the chance of a net. Not having played an innings for a couple of months, he was dismissed for the second and last 'pair' of his life. He was lbw to Gover second ball in the second innings, 'and absolutely plumb'. However, according to Howard Marshall (who for a short while was cricket correspondent of the *Daily Telegraph*), 'Allen proceeded to bowl extremely fast and remarkably well, considering that this is his first match of the season.' Gubby bowled thirty-one overs in the two innings and took six for 115, in what Marshall considered 'a glorious match'.

The selectors were no doubt disappointed to hear straight away that he was unavailable for England that summer. With three Tests coming up against New Zealand individual performances held significance in several cases, including those of two 'near-misses' for the MCC tour, Gover and Stephenson. Gover took ten wickets while Stephenson not only bowled well and fielded brilliantly but, making 68 not out at No 9, helped Jim Langridge (80) save a disastrous situation in the Rest's first innings.

At the 150th Anniversary Dinner at the Savoy the Duke of Gloucester was the chief guest, and G. O. Allen responded to the toast of Cricket proposed by Sir Stanley Jackson.

Plum Warner in his book, *Lord's, 1787–1945*, was highly critical of the speeches, saying that 'a frightful faux-pas was committed when the names of Lord Harris and W.G. were not even mentioned'. His protégé,

Gubby, got quite a roasting for failing even to mention his interesting and exciting tour. 'He confined his remarks almost entirely to the preparation of wickets, and never said a word about the tour, or about Bradman, his opposite number, whose wonderful batting had won the rubber for Australia after England had been victorious in the first two Test Matches, or about the great hospitality of the most hospitable people in the world.' This seems fair comment, though, according to *The Times*, his plea to MCC to do something to restore the balance between bat and ball by regulating the preparation of pitches was greeted with cheers. He also observed 'as a great supporter of first-class cricket I say that a lot of it is rather slack'. Though Test cricket would always draw the crowds something must be done to make the game more attractive 'for these people who pay their shillings'.

In one of the very few articles he has ever written Gubby developed his main theme in a contribution to the 1938 *Wisden* entitled 'A Case for More Natural Wickets'. His interest in and talent for the administration of cricket had been stimulated three years earlier by his election to the MCC Committee at the almost unprecedented age of thirty-two, when the only other Committee member under the middle forties was the Derbyshire captain, Guy Jackson. He was fortifying – and perhaps attempting to guide – in this essay the thoughts of a three-man committee known as the Findlay Commission which had been appointed (one of the many!) by MCC at the request of the counties to examine and report on the first-class game.

As usual Gubby supported his arguments by facts, pointing out that in the three Old Trafford Tests of 1934 to 1936, all drawn, 3546 runs had been scored at an average of 50 per wicket taken. He said that 'too much water, liquid manure and various forms of dope' were to blame for such easy-paced pitches as gave the bowler absolutely no incentive to attack. He told how at Northampton once, on arrival at the ground, he noticed an odour which he assumed came from a neighbouring farm-yard, but in fact emanated from the pitch. As it happened, I had first-hand evidence of the powerful effect of liquid manure a few years earlier. Playing for MCC in a one-day match against the Club Cricket Conference at Brentwood I asked the then Essex secretary, Brian Castor, afterwards whether he was worried about the pitches for the inaugural Brentwood Week which was very shortly due, considering that by tea-time the ball was taking divots off the dry pitch we had been playing on. 'Oh, that'll be all right,' I was told, 'you'll see.' A week later I did see. Kent made 803 for four declared (the highest score this century in a county match) at Brentwood in seven hours. In the next match there Essex declared at 570 for eight – but only after they had bowled out poor Surrey for 115. The second time the mixture at the start cannot have quite dried out. Both pitches came literally out of a bucket.

Gubby always maintains that writing even a few lines is sweated labour to him. The fact is he has never given himself sufficient practice! This *Wisden* article is lucid and well-reasoned, and merits re-reading, as do the conclusions in the same issue of the Findlay Commission, many of which bear a startling resemblance to the ills and needs of the game today. Cricket has nearly always been on its last legs.

Middlesex as in every year from 1935 to 1939 challenged hard for the Championship, which went four times to Yorkshire, once to Derbyshire, Middlesex finishing third in 1935 and then as runners-up four times consecutively. Gubby could give no help until the end of August when Middlesex and Yorkshire were going neck and neck. Reporting this match against Kent, under the heading 'Peerless Allen', Thomas Moult wrote in the *Daily Telegraph* about his 'fiery life' and how Ames was dropped off him twice in an over. His 50 not out in the second innings had much to do with Middlesex winning a grand game which might have gone either way.

Then came the Surrey match which traditionally ended the Lord's season (and is now apparently thrown in whenever the computer pleases). As this was Pat Hendren's last appearance before retirement — he had been thirty-one seasons at Lord's including the war years — the occasion had an added significance. He marked it with a sparkling hundred, and a large crowd did so by singing 'For he's a jolly good fellow'. Gubby contributed a rapid 53. So far so good, but on the last day the game, sadly and remarkably, ended on a sour note. When it was obvious that Middlesex could get nowhere near the stiff target of 295 at the rate of 100 an hour Robins joined Allen with seven wickets down. They batted and ran for their strokes normally until when quarter of an hour remained and with the score 178 for seven Errol Holmes bowled to Robins a succession of six boundary wides and byes in order to claim the new ball. This led to an uproar from the crowd before the batsmen and the umpires jointly brought the disorderly scene to an end, Gubby appealing against the light, and Bill Reeves and E. Cooke acquiescing, and bringing the players in although it was perfectly good. In belated fairness to Errol Holmes, he maintained afterwards that in return for the declaration Robins had said they would go for the runs 'regardless'. This was unknown to Gubby when he appealed.

Though J. W. Hearne was always Gubby's favourite among the Middlesex professionals he was fond also of Pat who was amusing, with his dry Irish humour, both on the field and off. It was Plum Warner's faith in him before the First World War — and in particular his admiration of his fielding — that eventually brought Hendren into the same bracket as the younger and more gifted J. W. Gubby remembers

what an excellent player of spin he was 'because he was always prepared
to use his feet', what a fine hooker and cutter. And what a model cover-
driver he was, too, 'leading with the head' as Harry Altham used to say.

The Scarborough Festival gave his MCC side a last chance to
foregather, against H. D. G. Leveson Gower's XI, and Gubby a chance to
round off his season by taking five good wickets in a drawn match.

During the 1937–38 winter gossip in the press about the England
captaincy revolved round Gubby and Walter Robins, who had led
England in the three 1937 Tests against New Zealand. There was even a
speculative paragraph on Gubby's intentions in the *Daily Express* by his
friend Kay Stammers who gave an interesting insight when she went on
to remark that 'he is the one well-known public figure that I know who
genuinely hates publicity'. It was around this time, incidentally, when he
was seeing a lot of this glamorous lady that, however disinclined to
publicity he was, Gubby had to deny a more momentous intention
announced in the press – that they were about to become engaged.

Then in the spring came the unexpected news that Walter Hammond
had been offered a business position that would allow him to play as an
amateur. Overnight Hammond (W. R.) became W. R. Hammond and an
automatic candidate for the captaincy. Such was the order of things in
those days. Slightly before Hammond's change of status widened the
field of choice I made in the *Evening Standard* the following contribution
to the subject under discussion:

> The stupidest of all fallacies is that a Test team 'captains itself.'
> Morale is everything, and it needs a rare combination of virtues in
> an English cricketer to captain our side through a 'rubber' in
> England. In point of historical fact, it has not been achieved since
> A. C. Maclaren in 1909, and he offered to resign because of lack of
> form, but was dissuaded.
>
>   There is one man to-day who knows the Australians, and has the
> regard and confidence of our foremost players as a captain – G. O.
> Allen. I think, that an Allen in good enough form to be picked, plus
> a strong Selection Committee, is a very fair answer, even to
> Bradman, O'Reilly and Co. After all, we so nearly did it in
> Australia a year ago.

When April came round Gubby faced the usual dichotomy, his
business life pulling one way, the challenge of Test cricket against
Australia the other. He *wanted* to play: he *had* to work. And he would be
thirty-six in July. As a fast bowler it probably had to be this year or never
again.

The selectors were anxious for him to show his form – indeed to do so
in MCC's match against the Australians, which came unusually early on

14 May. Middlesex by then would have had only two matches, immediately preceding. Gubby, who was at the meeting, said he was not prepared to expose himself thus early. A fairly heated discussion followed and Plum was upset by his declining, to put it mildly.

'But, Plum, I don't think you really understand fast bowlers' problems,' Allen told Warner. 'It's something I might have put more tactfully,' he adds today, 'though there was an element of truth in it.' To the man who had twice brought home the Ashes from Australia, and had a singularly high reputation as a sympathetic as well as a tactically acute captain, it must have been a wounding thrust from one in whose career he had taken an affectionate interest for so long.

Gubby made his first appearances in successive matches at Lord's against Notts and Worcestershire between 21 and 26 May. He jumped into form, in two innings victories contributing 64 and 53 and ten wickets for 146 in forty-seven overs. He was due next to play immediately for Middlesex on Saturday 28 May against the Australians, but was stricken with back trouble and retired to bed. Simultaneously that weekend the selectors, P. Perrin, A. B. Sellers and M. J. Turnbull under Warner's chairmanship, announced their teams for the Trial Match at Lord's the following Wednesday, naming Hammond as captain of the England side, Allen as captain of the Rest. Gubby was angry that the captains' roles were not reversed. In the event he declined, saying he was not fit, and he did not again appear in first-class cricket until July. He was upset not only by the decision but by the fact that Warner had given him no prior notice of it.

It is not difficult to appreciate at this distance the selectors' dilemma: on the one hand a great cricketer completely untried in captaincy, on the other a well-proved captain who had missed almost a whole season in 1937 and had played far too little to fit himself for four-day Test cricket. On the face of it their immediate decision was indisputable. The personal sadness was that the circumstances disrupted a life-long friendship. The consequence for cricket was that England were landed with someone ill-equipped temperamentally as a leader of men, except in so far as he could inspire by example. This was manifest most clearly on tour, both in South Africa in 1938–39 and, more disastrously, in Australia directly after the war.

When Gubby returned to the fray his fortunes were mixed. At Trent Bridge, usually a lucky ground for him, he made 56 against Notts but when bowling suffered further muscular trouble in the thigh, after which he told me and I my readers: 'You may take it as certain that I shall not attempt to bowl fast again this year. In fact it is very probable I will never risk the strain of fast bowling again.'

So much for the prospect of his being able to accept, if it were offered to him, the captaincy of the MCC team to South Africa in the autumn. The treasurer of MCC, Lord Cobham (the 9th, father of Charles the captain of Worcestershire and later Governor-General of New Zealand) had approached him as to his availability.

However with Gubby one never knew – and sometimes nor did he. Within three weeks of saying 'I shall not ...' etc. the mood seized him down at Hove and there was L. V. Manning writing 'G. O. Allen stages great come-back', lauding his twenty-two overs up the hill in tropical heat, and the five for 68 which was the result of the fastest sustained spell he had seen all summer. 'Gubby Allen is unexpectedly back in the Test news.' In the second Sussex innings the first three wickets fell to him, and then – snap went another muscle, this time in the 'other leg', the left one.

Was this the end for Middlesex that summer? Not a bit: he played through the last fortnight, made some useful runs, and sent down a few overs. Then came the Scarborough Festival wherein George Hirst umpired, as he was wont to do, in the Gentlemen and Players. In what turned out to be the last appearance at Scarborough for both of them there occurred, of all unlikely things, the only brush Gubby ever had with the old patriarch.

Gubby was so fond of Hirst that he naturally recalls the occasion though he cannot begin to remember what had riled him. Anyway for some reason he let Herbert Sutcliffe, with whom he was never altogether *simpatico*, 'have a few'. I expect they were very quick and pretty short. At the end of the over Hirst, umpiring at Gubby's end, said without being asked for it, 'Here's your sweater, you're the last person I ever expected to do that.' It is significant that though the provocation altogether escapes him the rebuke after half a century or so remains clear.

So much for cricket in 1938. Gubby's most important decision that summer had nothing to do with the game – except in that he thereby retained his association with many cricketers. The *London Gazette* of 8 July 1938, among Territorial Army commissions to 2nd lieut, listed G. O. B. Allen (late cadet-sergt, Eton Coll: contingent). Along with many friends in sport and on the Stock Exchange he joined the City of London Yeomanry, nicknamed the Rough Riders and, like most Yeomanry regiments, part of the Royal Artillery. The suggestion of getting friends together came from Gubby's brother, Geoff, working now at the War Office and as a lieut-colonel, GSO1, concerned with TA expansion. He attended TA camps in both the last pre-war summers at Stiffkey, in Norfolk, and there is a press photograph showing 2nd lieutenants Allen and Enthoven, wearing battle-dress and those rather ridiculous and impractical forage caps manning an Ack-Ack two-pounder. The caption, composed perhaps by a sub-editor who remembered Old Trafford, 1934, said 'Now Lads, No Wides.' Errol Holmes and Norman McCaskie were among others recruited by Gubby into his unit.

Like all other AA and Coast Defence TA units, the City of London Yeomanry were called up in the Munich crisis. On 26 September, 'the blackest day to date in my life', the 32nd Battery of the 11th Light AA Brigade – almost untrained as they were – found themselves at Tilbury prepared with their guns to defend the docks. There is a photograph and caption which evoke those perilous, amateurish times showing 'B Group and "*the*" 2-pounder' mounted on a railway goods wagon. Alongside is berthed the *Orion* on which Gubby had sailed to Australia a couple of years before.

Who of an age to remember does not recall those six fearful days which brought us face to face at last with the stark prospect of war – and Neville Chamberlain's return with his umbrella and his promise to the crowd from the window of No 10, of 'Peace in our Time'?

Soldiering loomed larger than cricket in Gubby's life during the last pre-war summer, though the two could sometimes be combined. At camp at Stiffkey a star-studded side went off one afternoon to play a village game at Bawdeswell Hall. It was reckoned only civil to get the parson off the mark, and likewise their host, R. Q. Gurney. Bawdeswell's score of 55 looked surely just about right. But the toffs from London reckoned without one considerable difficulty. After tea the sun shone dead into the batsmen's eyes at one end. The Territorials were all out for 44 – which no doubt set the villagers chuckling over their beer-mugs.

There was a grander two-day occasion at Aldershot which strangely escaped mention in *Wisden*, an official fixture between the Army and the TA. Gubby came away full of runs and wickets and the TA, consisting wholly of Test and county cricketers, scored a resounding victory.

Gubby made only four Middlesex appearances that summer, the first in mid-July against Yorkshire at Bradford in a rain-ruined match for Arthur Wood's Benefit. The most notable was in Canterbury Week wherein he was instrumental in Kent following on to an innings defeat by taking six for 46. This performance called forth two spoof wires. One said, 'Magnificent. Horder and I standing by – Dawson of Penn'; the other read, 'Respectful Congrats. on our greatest triumph – The Masseurs Union'. With his aches and pains he was perhaps a natural candidate for practical jokes, which he greatly relished. This, I suppose, as history ordained, was Gubby's last truly fast bowling performance.

It was, incidentally, the game in which Jim Smith made his one and only hundred, 98 of them in company with his captain and the No 11 batsman, Ian Peebles. Smith batted – or, rather, smote and cleaved and edged – for eighty-one minutes, several of his seven sixes being, according to the *Middlesex History*, 'the biggest hits ever seen at Canterbury'. Gerry Weigall stigmatized it as 'a prostitution of the art of batting, sir.'

Gubby was proposing to play a last game against Surrey at Lord's when on the afternoon of 24 August he was called up. At four-thirty a.m. next morning the 32nd Light Ack-Ack Battery moved off in convoy to Stanmore where Lieut Allen's troop was sited on Stanmore golf course to assist as best it could in the defence of the headquarters of Fighter and AA Command. Both RAF and Army were stationed together in Bentley Priory.

The Allen family now perforce dispersed. Lady Allen departed with her daughter Pat Dickson, expecting a baby, to the country. Sir Walter remained in London, commanding the Metropolitan Special Constabulary. Geoffrey remained at the War Office until his desire for active service was answered, and he was given command of the 1st Battalion of his regiment, the Royal Fusiliers, who were part of the BEF on the Franco-Belgian border.

On 3 September we all knew the worst.

13

Intelligence Officer

Picture now 2nd Lieut G. O. Allen, always craving activity, easily bored, stuck with his gun troop on Stanmore golf course. Having done his daily inspection and no doubt supervised some gun-drill, what next? The prevailing idea when war was declared that England would at once be subjected to heavy air attack proved 100% wide of the mark. Throughout that mild and sunny autumn all was quiet on the home front. As usual Gubby was in luck. He might have been stuck anywhere, but he was on a golf course, so he played, notably with two excellent women players, Pam Barton, a former British champion soon to be killed in a flying accident, and Jacqueline Gordon.

But Gubby, with the other officers of his Battery, was attached to the AA Command mess wherein he soon got to know the GOC, General Sir Timothy Pile. The general, seeing talent kicking its heels, brought him into the Operations Room, plotting aircraft in liaison with Fighter Command. Such was the beginning of Gubby's contact with the RAF.

During that winter of the phoney war he got to know Tim Pile pretty well, and among other things gathered that the general had no intention of allowing all the potential officer material of the City of London Yeomanry to hang together. When Gubby enquired when they were going to be allowed to see some action he was told there were 250 potential officers and that 'I won't let you go until I've milked you dry.' Knowing now that he was to be divorced from his friends Gubby shaped his ambitions accordingly.

He spent the exceptionally cold winter of 1939–40 at Stanmore, during which never a shot was fired in anger, and according to its commander couldn't have got anywhere near the target if it had. But perhaps this comment needs very slightly qualifying. Gubby and his troop were moved temporarily to Canvey Island off the Essex coast where one day they espied a slow-moving balloon. There were orders that stray barrage balloons were to be brought down, and such this seemed to be. So it was 'action stations' at last, and with the *fifth* shot the balloon was hit. Whereupon it transpired that it was not a stray which had escaped its moorings, but was being towed by a barge on its lawful business!

The most rigorous part of the troop's training routine was Bofors trials by night, and it was this nocturnal activity that produced Gubby's only scare of the winter. He went down with pneumonia and registered a temperature of 105°. (Gubby never did anything by halves.) The doctor alarmed him somewhat by saying, 'You're the first chap I've ever given these pills to.' However the pneumonia cleared up in a week – it sounds as though he may have been an early penicillin guinea-pig.

By the time the war took active form in the spring it had been decided to appoint flak liaison officers from AA Command to each Bomber Group in England and one to the Advanced Air Striking Force of the BEF. They were to be responsible for disseminating information about German AA equipment and its location, about which little was known. In the light of what these specialist officers could discover they were to advise air-crews about taking avoiding action. They were to be administered by the War Office Intelligence branch known as MI14E. This obviously was to be an important job, and when Gubby was offered the appointment with the BEF he accepted with alacrity.

Events however, luckily for him, moved too fast – though only fractionally so – to allow him even to report for duty. The Battle of France began with the German offensive on 10 May. Capt (Acting-Major) Allen was ordered to report to Hendon aerodrome for take-off at 1000 hours on 20 May, by which time the German armoured break-throughs had already determined the fate of the allied armies. That very morning the cabinet were approving provisional plans for the evacuation of the BEF. Gubby and his gear were aboard the aircraft when at 0950 over the tannoy came word that he was to report to control. There he was given orders that he was not to fly and to report instead to the War Office.

It was understood, though not confirmed, that the plane was bound for Amiens. Later the flight was cancelled. If it had left according to plan at 1000 hours it was estimated that its arrival at Amiens and that of the German tanks would have synchronized almost exactly. By nightfall on 20 May the Germans had not only swept through Amiens but had entered Abbéville some twenty-five miles to the north-west and only a few from the sea, having utterly cut the communications of the French and British armies to the north. If that plane had landed, says Gubby, 'I'd have run damned quick – but would it have been in the right direction?' In my considered opinion few men were less suited than Gubby to life as a prisoner-of-war.

A week later, on 27 May, he was sent to Hawkinge, the RAF station that lies behind Folkestone where had been established the Control Room for the Dunkirk evacuation. There in the Air Component, as it was called, he spent his 'most exciting moments of the war', and perhaps his most hard-working and difficult. He, who had been a 2nd lieutenant a few weeks before, and another officer, George Everett, a TA gunner major, were instructed by Brigadier 'Frankie' Festing, the senior soldier present, to select targets for bombing to cover the BEF retreat. Knowing nothing of such matters when he arrived, Gubby and his comrade leant heavily for advice on this friendly brigadier, and were considered, when the post-mortems were being held years later, to have made a good job of it. That was the less surprising seeing that the brig. subsequently ascended to the very top of the tree as CIGS.

The memory stands out in those fraught days of Air Chief Marshal Dowding, at the head of Fighter Command, being called on constantly to provide aircraft to cover the evacuation, and of his extreme reluctance to risk his precious Hurricanes; the tugs-of-war between the various brass-hats, and of the soldier who, on getting a refusal of aid from 'Stuffy' Dowding, picked up the telephone, ordered: 'Get me Downing Street,' and was actually put through to the Prime Minister.

Gubby was able to make a flying visit or two to Folkestone to try and get news of his brother, and on Saturday 1 June he heard the news he dreaded from Geoff's second in command. He had been seriously wounded by a sniper — in the head. Gubby's reaction and his capacity to fulfil what he set out to do were surely characteristic of several elements in his character, his determination, his ingenuity and his powers of persuasion.

His new Hawkinge friend Everett, extraordinary to relate, had on hand a light aeroplane of which with fair justice he claimed the ownership. Everett had been sent with a party to destroy aircraft of the BEF on a Belgian airfield to save them falling into enemy hands. While thus engaged a Belgian told him the Germans were only half a mile up the road. The rest of the British on the job had beaten a retreat. In this extremity Everett, who held a pilot's licence, saw a light aircraft, pulled it out of the hangar, started it and flew off under the noses of the advancing tanks. He landed at Hawkinge. It was a private plane on which the owner had painted Belgian markings and, incidentally, got the red, yellow and black rings in the wrong order, so that they might equally have been taken for the German colours.

Gubby's preoccupation was to give his mother at Datchet the news about Geoff before she might learn about it from official sources. Everett said he would fly Gubby to tell her, and Gubby managed to get permission for him to do so. No one thought of getting clearance from Fighter Command. Gubby knew of an airfield near Datchet, and off they went. Approaching Windsor they thought it would be interesting to take a close look at the Castle and went low to do so. When it was seen that the airfield was surrounded by barrage balloons — it had become an assembly plant for Hawker's — what more natural than to make for the chief Eton cricket ground, Agar's Plough? Certainly there were some spikes driven into the outfield that needed to be avoided, but that was safely done, and down they came. By good luck there was the Datchet bus, coming up the Slough road. They caught the bus, and while Everett waited in the garden Gubby told his mother and sister the sad news, preparing them for the worst.

When they returned to Agar's Plough they found the plane surrounded by a guard from the Eton Corps. There were also two policemen who had had orders from Fighter Command to take them into custody. So it was a case of 'Cum along o'me,' and the next couple of hours being spent in Slough Police Station. Luckily, when a call was made to Fighter Command, Gubby knew the duty officer, and explained things as best he could. Orders were given to the police for their release, and they were given a strict flight plan home *avoiding the Castle*. Assuming there was AA defence of the Castle presumably Gubby might possibly have been shot down by one of his own Rough Riders!

B. J. W. Hill, the Eton historian, who was the master in charge of the guard, describes the affair in his as yet unpublished memoirs, *Eton Remembered*. He records that:

> Allen could not imagine what all the fuss was about. The police were sympathetic and brought the two aeronauts back to Agar's where I was the sulky commander of the LDV guard. I was furious at having my Sunday ruined by turning out for guard duty. I was not in a saluting mood and I fear I behaved in a curmudgeonly fashion, but now I am glad I witnessed the pair take off from Agar's dodging the posts and staggering through a gap in the young lime trees bordering Dutchman's because this was the nearest the Eton OTC ever came to earning a battle honour.

The good Everett was apparently – and with good reason – 'a bit windy' about the take-off. When they measured the gap there was only a wing clearance of a few yards. The last word must come from William Bowles, the celebrated Eton groundsman: 'Fancy you of all people, Mr Allen, landing on our wickets.'

The miracle of the Dunkirk evacuation having been completed by 4 June, the Air Component at Hawkinge was disbanded, and its staff were told to await orders. The events of the fateful days that followed were briefly noted with comical bathos in Gubby's diary along with more personal appointments, thus:

4 June Air Component disbanded
7 „ Saw 'Gone with the Wind'
8 „ Eton Ramblers v XL Club at Lord's – took nine for 23

Gubby received his next posting on 26 June, by which time a brief *Times* obituary had announced that Lt-Col G. T. M. Allen, MBE had died of wounds received in action in Flanders. The MBE dated from his brief First World War service. The course Geoff Allen's military career had taken suggested the probability of high command coming his way if he had survived.

Gubby was sent to Grantham, headquarters of Five Group, Bomber Command, as flak liaison officer. The Directorate of Military Intelligence at the War Office was the collecting centre for reports of enemy AA defences. The flak liaison officers' job was two-fold, to disseminate this information and also to pass on data obtained from crews. This involved Gubby in making regular visits to the stations in the Group, notably Scampton, Waddington and Hemswell, briefing the pilots and getting to know them. The late Marshal of the RAF, Sir Arthur Harris — the redoubtable 'Bomber' Harris — commanded Five Group and Gubby came to know and admire both him and his very nice wife, Jill. The friendship that arose with 'Bomber' Harris survived until his death in 1984.

Gubby decided that he should accompany one of the regular sorties over Germany in order to give himself a first-hand look at the aircrews' problems. On the night of 6–7 September therefore at Scampton (permission obtained this time!) he climbed aboard a Hampden with its crew of three bound for a target in the Ruhr. Gubby took over the gunner's seat, but did not man the gun. It was a good aircraft but not exactly comfortable! They took off at 1930 hours. Visibility was bad, but not too bad to deter the German air-defences. Gubby says that 'You saw the tracer coming, thought it must all hit, but they generally missed by plenty.' Bob Allen, the pilot, never found his target, but eventually saw a light, unloaded his bombs and turned (up-wind) for home. Maybe this was reported as yet another bombing of the fabled 'Marshalling Yards at Ham'. Gubby inclined to think that this phrase was a euphemism for 'Conditions made it impossible to locate our target so we did our best to find something useful'. They were subjected to tracer attack both ways.

Towards the end of the long journey home ground control instructed them, to the pilot's annoyance and surprise, not to land at Scampton, nor at Waddington. They were so short of fuel that he ordered 'prepare to bail out'. Eventually defying ground control, they did land (at 0320) at Waddington, and as they came in the reason for the difficulty became all too clear. Tracer passed near, fired by an intruding ME111. As they landed, Gubby's namesake stalled his engine, giving the Messerschmitt a sitting duck target. The German came at them straight down the runway. Gubby threw himself on the floor, and the burst mercifully missed by twenty yards on the starboard side. On the face of it, it was a lucky escape. His emotions, he says on enquiry, were roughly akin to those of Jim Sims, who, batting for Middlesex when the Notts flak was flying around, on being asked by his partner, Pat Hendren, whether he was frightened, made the oft-quoted, laconic comment out of the side of his mouth: 'Not exactly frightened, just a trifle apprehensive.'

This was apparently the first time the Germans had lain in wait for returning bombers in this way. The pilot 'got ticked off', the official drill in such circumstances, when the tanks were almost dry, laying down the grim alternatives, in the hours of darkness – either to land on the sea shore or in shallow water, or to bail out with the consequent loss of the aircraft.

The whole experience must have been of value to Gubby in his liaison work, and the fact of its having been voluntarily undertaken, entirely on his own initiative, can only have lifted his prestige with the RAF.

In December 1940 Gubby was posted to the War Office to become GSO2 in charge of the sub-section MI14E responsible for the collation and dissemination of information about the air defences of Germany. With everyone out of London who was not obliged to stay, he rented a ground-floor flat in Palace Gate for a fiver a week. While Gubby was building up his department his father was busy at Scotland Yard directing the vital work of the Metropolitan Special Constabulary. Sir Walter moved in to Palace Gate, and they endured the bombing together. Once Gubby, hearing a stick of bombs on the way, made for the passage. One fell near enough to deposit glass and a chunk of paving-stone in the sitting-room where Gubby found his father still smoking his pipe in a high-backed chair. 'Old boy,' he replied, on Gubby asking why he had not sought a safer spot, 'when you're over seventy bombs are of absolutely no consequence.'

Let Gubby tell this crucial part of his war activity in his own words:

When I took charge of my sub-section it had not long been in existence and information regarding enemy A.A. equipment and its siting was sparse. Gradually through various sources of intelligence, and in particular photographic reconnaissance, a clearer picture evolved. Once established, my sub-section started to receive the most secret source of information available to the Allies, known as Ultra. Briefly, Ultra was the information obtained by breaking enciphered signals sent out on their highly complicated Enigma machines. Such was the tremendous importance attached to Ultra that all recipients had to sign fairly regularly a terrifying document which included the following: 'No recipient of Ultra may voluntarily place himself in a position where he could be captured'.

One of my memories, when information started to come in about the weapons later to be known as the V1 and the V2, is of reading an alarming agent's report that the warhead of the latter could be as much as twenty tons. In the event it was less than one ton.

The flak liaison officers (FLO) attached to the Bomber Groups were all appointed by me and it was through them and Bomber Command that all MI14E information was disseminated. We had some anxious moments as on one or two occasions Air Intelligence suggested that we should be transferred to the Air Ministry on the grounds that the information was of far more value to them than to the War Office. I suspect I may have won the day partly because I was known to be 'Dickie' Dickson's* brother-in-law, a popular and rising star in the RAF, and partly to my friendship with 'Bomber' Harris.

I would not have relished the change as I had made many friends in the War Office and by attending the DMI's regular weekly meetings was well informed as to the course of the war. I've never forgotten the occasion, I think it was in July 1943, when the DMI opened his address by saying something like 'Gentlemen, the war is won but I cannot forecast the date.' He had made this assessment on the Ultra information of the enormous German losses of tanks and troops when failing to penetrate what was known at the time as 'the Kiev bulge'.

Gubby much relished being 'in the know' — who, if he is honest about it, does not? — and in the spring of 1941 his arduous days at the War Office were compensated by diverting evenings with his old Australian friend Robert Menzies, who, following visits to Singapore and to the Middle East, came to London as Australia's Prime Minister with the chief purpose of alerting the British government to the grim threat overhanging his country and the whole Far East by the military and naval power of Japan.

Bob Menzies had a suite on the first floor of the Dorchester, choosing that position on the assumption that in the event of a direct hit the bomb wouldn't penetrate so far down and he would escape the worst of the blast of a near-miss. He attended cabinet meetings and spent his weekends at Chequers — and since Gubby was on the secret list certain things at least could properly be revealed over dinners à deux.

* Dickson became Chief of Air Staff in 1953 and the first-ever Chief of Defence in 1958.

In the First World War all cricket ceased. Not so this time, for with England – and London in particular – in the front line, some sort of relaxation was accepted as not only permissible but to a degree necessary. Gubby accordingly got in a little cricket. After his nine for 23 against the XL Club at Lord's the previous year for Eton Ramblers, in the same fixture in 1941 he demolished a side containing Percy Chapman, Bob Wyatt and Hubert Ashton with eight for 28. He played, too, for MCC at Rugby in the Centenary celebrating the match in *Tom Brown's Schooldays*.

It must have seemed more than a little odd to those thousands in England from overseas – though assuredly not to Bob Menzies – that in the height of war *The Times* should have marked the occasion with a leader measuring twelve and a quarter inches, in addition to a full report and scores. The secretary of MCC, Lieut-Col R. S. Rait Kerr, appropriately enough an Old Rugbeian, taking a day's leave from military duties, led his team on to the field, as his predecessor, Benjamin Aislabie, had done in 1841. Rugby played in the light blue shirts traditional in Tom Brown's day and still, happily, worn today. If the boys did conspicuously less well than those of a century before old Mr Aislabie cannot have brought down quite so lethal a pair of bowlers as Gubby and Jim Smith (who unfortunately took six for 8).

During the months and years of the bombing of London, cricket, it was reckoned, was good for morale. One recalls how players beyond combatant age, after nights of Home Guard duty or on fire-watching, would hump their cricket-bags long distances in order to play. At the foot of the Lord's score-cards, printed, as usual, for all matches during the war, was the following advice:

> In the event of an Air Raid good cover from shrapnel and splinters should be obtained under the concrete stands. Public shelters will be found in St John's Wood Church; Wellington Court, Wellington Road; South Lodge, Circus Road. Spectators are advised not to loiter in the streets.

In the autumn of 1941 Lady Allen, like other old ladies preferring the perils of London to the boredom of the country, returned from Datchet, and Gubby and his parents lived for the following years at St George's Court. His mother had not picked a good moment for her change of abode for at first London was being attacked nightly. When Gubby worked very late, and when the bombing was particularly severe, he bedded down in the bowels of the War Office.

His work brought him in touch with Professor R. V. Jones, the brilliant scientist who as assistant director of Intelligence at the Air Ministry was concerned among other things to counter the German technique of 'beam bombing' whereby the aircraft could locate their targets by a system of intercepting radio beams. Jones and his team became able to identify the beams and give advance warning to the defences. They could not 'bend' the beams, as has been alleged, but they could and did make them difficult for the Germans to pick up and follow. Our Intelligence learned that the Germans had slackened their London attacks somewhat because they were building up a force to pulverize some of the great industrial cities such as Coventry, Birmingham, Wolverhampton and the major ports.

Gubby remembers the raid which almost demolished the centre of Coventry for a special reason since it was later charged against Churchill that he knew of the target in advance, and 'betrayed' Coventry. What Churchill had to guard against was to take such special precautions against attack on a provincial target — in the form of increased Ack-Ack and Fighter defence, and ancillary services — as to risk making the enemy suspect the existence of Ultra. The secrets of Enigma and Ultra were marvellously well kept. They were not indeed made public until the 1970s. The fact about the Coventry raid, as told to Gubby, was completely the opposite. Churchill was discouraged by the cabinet from spending his working week-ends at Chequers when the moon was high because of the risk of air attack, or, as he put it in volume 2 of *The Second World War*, 'in case the enemy should pay me special attention'. He used to go instead to Ditchley, a house near Oxford (and Blenheim, the home of his ancestors) which had been put at his disposal by the rich Anglo-American MP, Ronald Tree. The moon was full, and on the fateful Friday evening of 14 November Churchill was being motored to Ditchley when, reading his papers as he went, he learned that a heavy raid was expected that night on London. He always wanted to be present when London was attacked, and so ordered the driver to return to Downing Street. This time, however, Intelligence had misread the beams and the target for nearly 500 aircraft was Coventry. (The following night it was London again.)

The Japanese attack on Pearl Harbor which brought the United States into the war occurred on 8 December 1941, and Gubby vividly recalls the news of it. He had taken a few days' leave and was staying with Lady Ann Hunloke, who was living on the Chatsworth estate. He knew from secret sources that the Jap fleet was out, and that Whitehall had sent to Washington an estimation of the situation, which suggested that they *would* attack Malaysia and *might* also go simultaneously for Pearl Harbor.

On that Sunday evening Gubby and his hostess were due to dine with her mother, the Duchess of Devonshire, in another house on the estate, the great house being in use as a hospital. After dinner they were late tuning in to the nine o'clock BBC News – which, of course, during the war was required listening for everyone. All they heard was the tail-end of the final summary: '... and considerable damage was done to the American fleet'. The old lady naturally wanted to know more, and asked Gubby to attach the wireless set to a plug in her bedroom. While he was doing so she turned on the set, there was a flash and a shock strong enough to knock Gubby off his feet. She had blown a fuse and put the machine completely out of action though not, happily, the officer commanding MI14E. For him the snatch of news was enough. The American fleet had been attacked, and what with the electric shock and overwhelming relief at the realization that the Americans were now committed to the conflict his reaction, as he and Ann Hunloke drove home, was one of hysteria. He reckoned that however long victory might take to achieve the war would be won.

Gubby's diary around now contains a poignant entry of a date that was never fufilled. Two charming Aussie cricketers serving with the RAAF, Sgt Observer Ross Gregory and F-O C. W. Walker, of both of whom Gubby was fond, called in on him one day at the War Office, and said they wanted 'to hear the Bodyline story'. Gubby arranged time and place for a dinner-party, but both were posted away, each, as it proved, to his death in the air. Charlie Walker was the reserve wicket-keeper for two Test series in England in the 1930s: as for Gregory, Gubby always thought he might have had the stuff of greatness in him until he was passed over for the 1938 tour of England because of eye-trouble.

As soon as the United States' bomber force came into action in Europe several Americans were sent to learn and liaise in Gubby's office. Sub-section MI14E was promoted to become Section MI15, and Gubby was appointed GSO1 with the rank of lieut-colonel. The Americans' arrival caused some re-arrangement since they were not to be privy to the secrets of Ultra. They were, of course, introduced to the flak liaison officer techniques, as these had been built up by British experience. Gubby appointed Errol Holmes to be one of the British FLOs to the Americans.

For many months now Gubby continued his work from the War Office, in the summer taking his hours off duty playing cricket in and around London, whenever possible at Lord's. Captaining Sir Pelham Warner's XI against the RAAF he had one of his last tilts against a side of Australians. The score book shows that he and a certain Sgt Keith Miller took one another's wicket, and that although Keith made 45 not out of his team's total of 100 before Gubby bowled him the RAAF were comfortably beaten. He was to have led England v The Dominions in the star game of the summer but pulled a muscle at practice and withdrew.

Early in 1943 his father's health began to fail and after twenty-nine years' service, eighteen of them as Commandant-in-Chief, he retired from the Metropolitan Special Constabulary. Sir Walter underwent a prostate operation from which he never fully recovered, and he died aged seventy-three, peacefully, on 27 November. Plum Warner followed up the *Times* obituary with a personal appreciation. 'His pleasant manner and smile radiated friendship, and he was gentle and kind in all he said and did.' Recalling that one of Sir Walter's elder brothers, R. C., had played for Australia, Warner went on: 'I only saw him bat once in a net in his garden at Datchet, and he had a very pretty style. He was also a good lawn-tennis player and golfer, and here too his style was built on sound lines.' Like father like son: no one could seriously fault Gubby's method whether batting, bowling or hitting a golf ball.

Plum quoted an amusing exchange between Walter Allen and A. C. MacLaren on top of Lord's pavilion during Don Bradman's great innings of 254. 'Yes, I know he's pretty good,' the arch-pundit kept remarking, 'but he's got a lot to learn.' A bit sensitive perhaps, seeing that his son, like all the other England bowlers, was taking a good deal of punishment, Walter Allen said, 'Look here, Archie, if he learns much more, he will ruin the game.'

Gubby's War Office routine was welcomely interrupted in February 1944 when the Commander-in-Chief of the American bomber squadrons requested his presence at Allied Headquarters at Caserta (just north of Naples) because they were beginning to attack Germany by air from Italian bases. The journey, in an American bomber on a cargo mission, was not without its hazards, starting with three abortive take-offs not calculated to breed confidence, due to engine trouble. They flew perforce by night and low, out over the Atlantic, as a safeguard against intercepting fighters. When the dawn came up, far from being where the navigator supposed, they were flying just off Lisbon, recognized by Gubby (the only passenger) from a pre-war visit when on his way to South America with MCC. They should have been 200 miles westward over the Atlantic, and 100 miles further south. At Algiers, reached with only five minutes fuel left, the pilot sacked the navigator saying he could do better himself. They landed – despite prohibiting signs – at Bari. Thence in another aircraft Lieut-Colonel Allen was flown to Caserta.

In a Headquarters passage who should Gubby bump into but the C-in-C himself, Field-Marshal Alexander! They had met playing cricket before the war and become friends, especially after he had married Margaret Bingham, a close friend of Gubby's. 'Alex', after Gubby had explained his mission, said, 'I'll take you tomorrow up to Anzio.' But the chief Intelligence officer said, 'Sorry, sir, but you can't.' Colonel Allen, the C-in-C was informed, was on the top secret list. Never mind, next day it was to be Cassino. So to Monte Cassino they went and there followed the tête-à-tête alfresco lunch on the white tablecloth. Gubby did not like the idea of the tablecloth attracting enemy aircraft, exposed, as it was, on a hill: ' "Alex" did not know what fear was. I did.'

This fortuitous meeting was the prelude to a riper friendship after the war. Gubby when playing golf at Ashdown Forest stayed with 'Alex' who was living nearby, and would listen for hours to the reminiscences of almost the only great war leader who never wrote a book. As Lord Home observed, Gubby is a very good listener – once he starts. In 1955 they were brought close when within a few weeks Gubby became chairman of selectors and Earl Alexander was named president of MCC, on the Committee of which Gubby, of course, served.

The summer of 1944 followed its established pattern – hard graft at the War Office and some cricket relief. He went to Eton for the Fourth of June and made a hundred for the Ramblers against the boys. *The Times* reported:

> There was a rumour that Allen had pulled a muscle, but this fortunately proved to be unfounded, for there was no apparent lack of mobility and he gave a masterful display.

Gubby led England to victory v Australia in a bank holiday one-day match for the Red Cross, taking the wickets of both opening batsmen. Len Hutton, invalided out of the Army by then because of the gymnasium accident which permanently shortened his left fore-arm, gave welcome evidence that he could still bat pretty well with an innings of 84, England's last 70 runs being knocked off against time by Squadron Leaders Ames and Robins.

While on the subject of Gubby's war-time cricket one incident which created some palaver at the time must not go unrecorded. Leading a South of England side against the RAAF at Lord's he was given out in the most unusual of all ways – 'handled the ball'. Some of a crowd of 11,000 showed noisy disapproval. The victim had best tell the story in his own words:

> I played on to a ball from Mick Roper. Sismey, the wicket-keeper, who was standing up, and I had a good look at the bails and when we found them firmly in their grooves I threw the ball back to Roper as a friendly gesture saying 'bad luck'. He then appealed to the umpire, Archie Fowler, a great friend of mine, and I was given out. Later Roper insisted he had appealed for bowled which I found totally unacceptable because of the careful check his own wicket-keeper and I had made. Frankly I think it was a silly decision as, in light of the long delay whilst the inspection was taking place, the ball must have become 'dead'. The Australians subsequently stated that they had called me back but the only one who came near me

was Keith Miller and he was not captain.

When the war in Europe was clearly nearing its end Gubby more than suspected that the Americans, with whom he had worked in such close contact and harmony for so long, were keen that he should be posted to their forces in the Far East to continue the work he had been doing in charge of MI15. Naturally enough, this prospect did not appeal to him at all. He knew he was due for an early release on account of his age and service, and felt he had 'done his bit'. With the idea of getting out of the way for a while he therefore talked the War Office into letting him go to Washington. He was to see a General Somebody-or-other about some-thing-or-other, and the fact that he scarcely remembers more suggests the mission cannot have been specially important.

Anyway, on 4 April 1945 he left Prestwick in a British aircraft carrying back to the States and Canada a batch of the ferry pilots whose job was to fly across the Atlantic supplies of new aeroplanes. They touched down at Goose Bay ('I had the best breakfast for years') and Gubby finally reached Washington. The Flak Conference with the general at the Pentagon was over in an hour, after which Gubby was shown around. His hosts readily cooperated in his flying to New York where he found his old friend Adrienne Allen. No sooner had he arrived than the news came of the death of President Roosevelt. Gubby thought that this would mean the theatres closing and entertainments coming to a halt, but he was quickly corrected. 'It's not like the King, you know,' said Adrienne Allen. She took him to Beatrice Lillie's birthday party, after which he found himself in Central Park in highly enviable company at five o'clock of a warm spring morning listening to talk of the early days of those three delightful celebrities, 'Bee', Adrienne, and the fabulous Gertrude Law-rence. Was anyone else present? No, the dashing colonel had them all to himself.

He was away a fortnight, and on his return there was no more talk of the Far East. On 8 May came the celebration of VE day. A certain amount of winding-up remained to be done at the War Office before on 29 July, two days before his forty-third birthday, Gubby was a free man. He received a parting letter from the Director of Military Intelligence which anyone would be gratified to have:

24 July 45

My dear Gubby,

   A line to wish you good-bye and to congratulate you on building up and then running a first-class show.

   Your reward is that you satisfied RAF and US Air Forces and your chaps, and you must have saved countless lives.

   I am sure that General Davidson would join me in saying that

MI15 was a damned good integrated inter-service show with a grand GSO1.

Alec Sinclair

One other relic of his war service came Gubby's way. At a ceremony at the American Embassy in 1946 he was invested with the Legion of Merit (Degree of Officer) 'for the performance of outstanding services for the United States Air Forces in Europe from August 1943 to May 1945.' The GSO1 of MI15 recommended his second-in-command for an award, and he received the MBE. It would have been inappropriate surely if one of the two countries chiefly concerned had not made some tangible recognition of his talent for liaison – for getting a diverse assortment of people to work harmoniously together.

A final, flippant parenthesis for those who find Gubby's medical history a source of fascination: he had survived the incessant bombing of London, including a near miss of his flat, and much air travel within the enemy's reach, notably one direct attack when his aircraft was on the run-way, without sustaining a scratch. Within a week of being demobbed he was on crutches, having pulled a muscle playing at the Guard's Depot at Caterham and so putting himself out of action for the rest of the season.

14
A Tour Too Much

The war over, and with the passing of six years Gubby's personal cricket ambitions with it, he got down to business with a will. Having learned to work during the war, as he candidly observes, he saw the Stock Exchange as a renewed challenge, especially after David Bevan and Co. had made him a partner. 'As a half-commission man before the war I was fairly idle.'

It so happened that a further unexpected demand on his cricket leadership lay ahead – hence the heading of this chapter – but was two years away. His immediate sporting preoccupations were with golf and squash. Leonard Crawley, his contemporary and friend since Cambridge days, was his golf mentor, this after an early encounter with Henry Cotton had got master and pupil off to a disconcerting start. Gubby had played with the great Cotton at Ashridge against Crawley and another shortly before the war, after which the following conversation is remembered:

'Henry, do you think we can make Gubby into a golfer?'

'Well, you see, Leonard, *everything* is just wrong.'

One can well imagine that remark sticking – plus, maybe, a certain determination to invalidate it! Leonard and his dear wife, Elspeth, lived and dispensed flowing hospitality at their Coastguard Cottage at Rye. Leonard was a keen theorist both on golf and cricket, and, of course, with his beautifully slow and rhythmic swing a perfect model. And at Rye, too, was another good teacher, the amiable, easy-going Scots professional, Willie Anderson. Soon Gubby was playing down to a handicap of four, and was gratified to be elected to membership of the Oxford and Cambridge Golfing Society, the spiritual home of which was Rye. He tells the story of Bernard Darwin, the doyen of the society and of amateur golf, expressing concern at a General Meeting lest playing standards be allowed to slip, the usual qualification having always been to win a blue or come very near it. 'It's no good,' came a voice, 'Gubby's in.' In fact he generally held his own, with a bit to spare, on the golf course for the next twenty years and more (when he was not undergoing operations to his hips) for the Society, for the Moles, the County Cricketers, and in match club contests, and on one notable occasion for

Eton in the Halford-Hewitt Cup.

In the summer of 1946 he turned out only twice, for Jim Sims's Benefit at Whitsuntide against Sussex, and at Bramall Lane, Sheffield, in mid-August when, as usual before the war, Middlesex were going hard with Yorkshire for the Championship. Rain interfered with the Benefit – which, as it happened, was Gubby's last first-class appearance at Lord's.

A young Middlesex cricketer recalls the Yorkshire match and its preliminaries. On putting his bag down in a corner he was advised to choose somewhere else as that would be Mr Allen's perch. He soon saw why, there being convenient ledges on which Gubby arrayed a selection of bottles and tins, and from which he hung several different widths and lengths of elastoplast. In the pavilion he had seen his old friend, Maurice Leyland, who greeted him warmly, adding, 'But you shouldn't come up here bowling against us chaps at your age.' Gubby didn't need reminding he had just turned forty-four, but hoped he might be able to make them hustle a bit. 'But, Maurice, I'm not too bad for an over or two.'

Middlesex lost the toss, the right (bowling) boots were selected, a suspect muscle or two was strapped up, and, thus carefully accoutred, Gubby took the field and the new ball. Leyland received it, a full-pitch (since Gubby had forgotten the hill, picked the wrong end, and got in a muddle with his run-up) to which Maurice ducked too low and was bowled – behind his back! Leyland, said the evening paper, 'stood there stupefied', having 'misjudged the height of the ball'.

Gubby then produced, from the other end, 'some of the best fast bowling of the summer' according to *The Times*, twenty-five overs of it for a return of five for 26. Had not Brian Sellers come to the rescue of Yorkshire they would have been bowled out for a handful.

The game, in that liquid summer, was likewise drawn, and Middlesex had to wait another year before, at long last, they finished on top. But their captain came back with a story, that notorious leg-puller vouching solemnly for the truth of it. In the hotel bar before dinner, in a nearby group, Robins heard a Yorkshireman declaiming that he'd just been up at Bramall Lane and seen a young fast bowler by the name of Allen, and if he didn't play for England in a couple of years he'd eat his hat!

In the summer of 1946 the British Army of the Rhine were keen to get English clubs to visit them, to play on the 'Dutch' artificial pitches which had been laid down soon after the fighting stopped. Gubby, going out with MCC, remembers an occurrence involving a remarkable coincidence. A British officer called on the MCC side of which Gubby was a member and asked for J. C. W. MacBryan. He then presented Jack MacBryan with a sword, on which his initials were inscribed, and which its owner had had to hand over to his captors when taken prisoner in the First World War. The officer, luckily a cricket enthusiast, had recognized the initials on the sword which was hanging over the mantelpiece in a house on the German side of the border with Holland: a remarkable coincidence and an emotional moment.

Gubby, who had played for Middlesex, if only for a match or two, in every summer since 1921, did not make a single appearance in their Championship-winning year of 1947. Instead he was more humbly – and perhaps more valuably – engaged captaining the 2nd XI and Club and Ground sides, helping to bring on the young. His sole first-class exploit was, when playing for the Free Foresters at Oxford, to have Martin Donnelly missed twice in an over before he went on to make one of those felicitous hundreds which used to attract crowds measured in thousands to the university Parks.

Gubby went two or three times, around now, to talk to the prisoners at Wormwood Scrubs. He recalls, as I did similarly at Pentonville, an acute sense of depression on entering the massive iron-studded gates, but also the sharp, lively audiences. It was Stephen Leacock who observed when doing the same thing: 'You have the pleasant feeling that you're not trespassing on their time.'

When Gubby told a story about Eddie Paynter one of the prisoners called out: 'Next time you see him, give him my love.' However, this earned the man a rebuke, and Gubby was not encouraged to discover his name. So the message Eddie got was merely one of anonymous affection!

Lifting the social scene more than somewhat, Gubby with Willie Hill-Wood and the Queen's brother, David Bowes Lyon, at the Eton and Harrow Match in July was co-host to the King and Queen, their daughters and Princess Elizabeth's fiancé, Prince Philip of Greece. Their engagement had been announced only the day before. 'Let me see, Gubby, when did you and Willie play in this match?' asked the King. In answer Gubby drew his attention to the string of Eton victories immediately after the First World War listed on the back of the score-card. 'Ah yes,' the King laughed, 'I see I shouldn't have asked.'

Prince Philip in the photographs on this, his first visit to Lord's, looks very young and very shy. Happily for the game, however, he was a cricketer, had been captain of the XI at Gordonstoun, and was to prove a keen patron of cricket. The first of his two presidencies of MCC lay only two years ahead.

During the glorious summer of 1947 the Test selectors and the MCC Committee were exercising themselves in trying to find a side, from which it was decided that most of the top players must be excluded, that could worthily undertake a tour of the West Indies in the winter. Karl Nunes, the first West Indian Test captain in 1928, had come over as president of the West Indies Board to plead that an MCC side should be sent, since, because of the war, no one had visited them for thirteen years, and their cricket was badly in need of such a stimulus. Not much in the way of outstanding talent, he said, had recently come to flower. Nunes's appeal struck a ready chord in the Committee, and in particular with Plum Warner, Trinidad born and part-educated in Barbados, with whom the West Indians in his sentimental moments were always 'my country-men'.

It is Gubby's view that Plum was hoodwinked by Nunes, with the result that too many unproved young cricketers were chosen, too many of the best left at home, most of them on the grounds that, in addition to the two English seasons, they had had a hard tour of Australia and New Zealand the preceding winter, and that the Australians were due here in 1948, with a tour to South Africa immediately following. Thus Hutton, Compton, Edrich, Washbrook, Yardley, Simpson and Gimblett of the batsmen were not invited, nor Bedser, Wright, Pollard and Hollies among the bowlers. All-rounders were as scarce as bowlers – Bailey was at Cambridge and so unavailable.

The choice of captain was little less taxing than that of the side was sure to be. Tom Pearce, the much-respected Essex captain, was an early favourite for the job, while another candidate was Kenneth Cranston, an all-rounder who in 1947 had taken over the Lancashire leadership. Gubby says that the first time his name was mentioned was in early August at one of Ian Peebles's splendid lunches, attended, among others, by Ronny Stanyforth and myself. (Ian and Hans Siegel were partners in the wine firm of Walter Siegel, in whose offices selected members of the cricket fraternity were handsomely entertained.) Gubby's recollection is that no one took the idea seriously, but that is not strictly the case. In the *Daily Telegraph* I expressed the view that if an unavoidably experimental side were to be sent, it would need an experienced captain, versed in Test cricket. My suggestions were either Robins or Holmes or Valentine or Allen. In the event MCC approached Gubby.

When, not without considerable qualms, he accepted the dual post of captain and manager, he kept to himself a plan to lead the side off the field, and if possible to delegate the Test captaincy. No one knew better that, at 45, he was well over the top. In fact he was to be the oldest England captain since W.G. gave up in 1899. Peterborough in the *Daily Telegraph* assessed his role, reasonably enough, as a 'trainer of troops'.

The following fourteen others were chosen to go with the venerable captain: S. C. Griffith (assistant manager), K. Cranston, D. Brookes, H. J. Butler, T. G. Evans, J. Hardstaff, R. Howorth, J. T. Ikin, J. C. Laker, W. Place, J. D. Robertson, G. A. Smithson, M. F. Tremlett, and J. H. Wardle. Of these only three, Evans, Hardstaff and Ikin, had sailed to Australia the previous year. Of the others Cranston, Butler,

Howorth and Robertson had had the briefest Test experience against South Africa the previous summer – six games between the four of them. Of the others only Laker and Wardle, both raw in 1947–48, accomplished very much of note for England several years later. Gerald Smithson, a 'Bevin Boy', given special leave from the mines by the Ministry of Labour, was chosen on the strength of one innings, Maurice Tremlett by virtue of one piece of bowling. Apart, of course, from his friend, Griffith, Jack Robertson of Middlesex, and Joe Hardstaff, who had been with him in Australia, the captain knew virtually none of the team. But as the tour progressed he got to know and like many of them.

The fact was that England's resources, so soon after the war, would have been insufficient even if the side had by a merciful Providence escaped injuries. Alas, they happened in profusion, starting with the captain himself who, after nine days of horribly rough weather tossing about in an empty banana boat, called the *Tetela*, as soon as the sun came out called for a skipping-rope and promptly pulled the first muscle of the tour.

It would be tedious to recite more than the most momentous of the divers troubles that beset the team: the captain's injury prevented his playing at all in Barbados, the first port of call and the strongest of the colonies, and he pulled muscles also in Trinidad and British Guiana; Brookes, after showing good form as a No 3 bat, soon broke a finger, and had to be sent home; Butler, the chief 'strike bowler', what with malaria and later muscular injuries was wholly fit for only one match on the tour; first a blow on the head and then a carbuncle put Ikin out of action at Trinidad; Hardstaff, the star bat on reputation, tore a hamstring.

Out of action in Barbados, Gubby had the mortification of seeing his raw side, led by Cranston, fresh to the taxing demands of West Indian conditions, fielding out to vast scores, and unknown youngsters such as Walcott and Weekes laying the foundations of their fame. Luckily, pitches were not yet covered once the game started, and rain at convenient moments helped MCC to come the better out of the return game with Barbados, and England to save the First Test when it would surely have been lost.

After a few days in Barbados Billy Griffith had found his captain with his head in his hands. He had seen enough to realize he had several passengers to carry, thus putting an added burden on the few essential men, most of whom were due to suffer aches and pains of varying severity. There were also two senior members whose attitude to the tour depressed him. However in public the captain invariably showed a cheerful face, and, of course, there was plenty to enjoy, especially the friendly, sandy beach-fringed, Trade-wind cooled island of Barbados. Moreover the best aspects of the tour were invariably presented to their readers at home by the English travelling press. As I have written elsewhere, Gubby was the best captain from a cricket-writer's point of view that could be imagined. He was amiable, understanding and communicative, the result being that our small party were naturally sympathetic towards his difficulties. There were Charles Bray of the *Daily Herald* (and formerly of Essex); Brian Chapman (who wrote for many papers in his long life in Fleet Street but now was the *Daily Express* man); Crawford White of the *News Chronicle*; Norman Preston of Reuter's; and myself. Two of us, Crawford White and I, were even able to give a little practical help. The team were generally looking for net bowlers, and the two of us spent many happy hours giving batting practice to men either recovering from injury or out of form.

In the West Indies, as in South Africa, it was the friendly custom to appoint a local manager to help with the hundred-and-one things that need to be attended to on a touring side's progress, and in Barbados we were lucky in finding J. M. Kidney, manager of the West Indian sides to England of 1933, 1939 and 1950. This was all the more welcome since Gubby officially combined both captaincy and managership. When we got to the metropolitan city of Port-of-Spain, Trinidad, our deputed manager was said to be a chap with an intriguing nickname which perhaps I should not disclose. There was no sign of him until on the second afternoon he was pointed out to Gubby at the Union Club playing bridge. 'I believe,' said Gubby, going up to him, 'that you are our manager.' For once Gubby was at a loss for words when the reply came: 'Oh, no, I've resigned. The job was going to be too much for me.'

This sally did not pre-dispose the captain in favour of Trinidad where however he was able to lead his side on the field. In the first match (the one in which Butler was fully fit until, having taken five for 36, he went down with malaria) MCC had the better of a draw, Gubby making top score of 77 in the first innings while that most whole-hearted of triers, Winston Place, came good with a hundred in the second. MCC were obliged to field four substitutes in the second innings, and it was now that Gubby made an SOS for help. With Brookes already on his way home, Hardstaff's injury proved the last straw.

There was sympathy both in London and the Caribbean when the captain telephoned urgently for a distinguished replacement. Compton, the first choice, was ruled out, much to Gubby's chagrin. He was said not to have fully recovered from the first of the several subsequent operations on his knee. Yet he was on the football field. However, Yorkshire in the crisis reversed their previous veto on Hutton, who flew out in time to boost morale and performance in British Guiana and Jamaica.

Meanwhile the Second Test was upon them and with the field of choice much reduced. Who should go in first with Robertson? Ikin with his experience was the easy choice, but with the limited batting available Gubby was not prepared to risk him. He therefore organized the final net practice so that Butler and he, each using a new ball, bowled to Griffith, Laker and Tremlett. On this evidence Gubby voted for Griffith, who went in laughing with his captain's words in his ears, 'This must be the blackest day in English cricket history.'

As is now history Griffith responded, at the age of thirty-three, with his maiden first-class hundred: 140 in all in six hours of dedicated effort that ran an hour into the second day. It has also been generally believed (though not by his captain) that his innings was something of an expiation of guilt for the running-out of Robertson. Let me therefore take the opportunity of quoting my report in next day's *Telegraph*:

> Griffith played the ball about ten yards on the off-side towards deep cover, calling as he made the stroke. Robertson seemed to start a little late and certainly did not ground his bat as Gaskin, the bowler, who had had a long way to go, picked the ball up, changed hands and threw down the wicket. It should have been a perfectly safe run.

Among many messages Billy had, one came from his old friend, Austin Matthews, the briefest wire on record, containing the one word, 'Really!'

On the extremely easy jute mat at Port-of-Spain both sets of bowlers had a hard job. Gubby contributed 36 to England's first innings, joining Griffith at the crux of 54 for three and being out 72 runs later attempting, for the one and only time in his life, an upper-cut. England's 362 was eclipsed by the West Indies with 497. Before 'the three Ws' could get in, the opening bats, Carew and Ganteaume, made 173 for the first wicket. Both were new to Test cricket, both got hundreds, and it was illustrative of West Indian batting strength that George Carew, who played a dashing innings well in keeping with his jaunty homburg hat, was chosen only once more in the series, while for the pedestrian Andy Ganteaume this proved to be his only-ever Test! The most significant and elegant innings was that of Frank Worrell who in his first Test missed his hundred by three.

Gubby found it hard going in the steamy heat of Queen's Park Oval, keeping up a brisk pace, and taking two for 82 in sixteen overs. Harold Butler, despite his having just lost a stone and a half from malaria, got through thirty-two overs, and the side stuck to the job splendidly. Fighting to secure a draw England then made 275, Robertson (133) in a polished effort contributing half the runs made from the bat. When the West Indies went in again they needed 141 in fifty-seven minutes. They changed the order, indicating that they were at least going to make the effort, but Allen and Butler bowled extremely well while England showed

WEST INDIES v ENGLAND
(Second Test)

At Port-of-Spain, 11–16 February 1948

ENGLAND

J. D. B. Robertson run out	2	– c Christiani b Ferguson	133
S. C. Griffith lbw b Worrell	140	– c Ferguson b Gomez	4
J. T. Ikin b Ferguson	21	– lbw b Ferguson	19
K. Cranston c and b Ferguson	7	– Christiani b Williams	6
*G. O. B. Allen c Walcott b Gaskin	36	– (6) c Walcott b Williams	2
R. Howorth b Ferguson	14	– (7) b Ferguson	14
†T. G. Evans c Walcott b Williams	30	– (8) st Walcott b Ferguson	21
G. A. Smithson c Goddard b Ferguson	35	– (9) b Ferguson	35
J. C. Laker c Gaskin b Goddard	55	– (5) c Carew b Williams	24
J. H. Wardle c Worrell b Ferguson	4	– not out	2
H. J. Butler not out	15	– b Ferguson	0
L-b 1, n-b 2	3	B 5, l-b 3, n-b 7	15

1/5 2/42 3/54 4/126 5/158   362   1/18 2/53 3/62 4/97 5/122   275
6/201 7/288 8/296 9/306 10/362   6/149 7/196 8/270 9/275 10/275

Bowling: *First Innings* – Gaskin 37–14–72–1; Williams 21–8–31–1; Ferguson 39–5–137–5; Goddard 23.3–6–64–1; Worrell 23–4–55–1. *Second Innings* – Gaskin 21–6–41–0; Williams 27–7–64–3; Ferguson 34.2–4–92–6; Goddard 9–4–11–0; Worrell 14–2–30–0; Gomez 8–2–22–1.

WEST INDIES

G. M. Carew lbw b Laker	107	– (5) not out	18
A. G. Ganteaume c Ikin b Howorth	112		
E. de C. Weekes b Butler	36	– (1) c Evans b Butler	20
F. M. M. Worrell c Evans b Cranston	97	– not out	28
†C. L. Walcott c Butler b Howorth	20	– (2) lbw b Allen	2
*G. E. Gomez lbw b Laker	62		
R. J. Christiani c Robertson b Allen	7		
J. D. C. Goddard not out	9		
E. A. V. Williams c and b Allen	31	– (3) b Butler	0
W. Ferguson b Butler	5		
B. B. M. Gaskin b Butler	0		
B 2, l-b 4, w 1, n-b 4	11	L-b 2, w 1, n-b 1	4

1/173 2/226 3/306 4/341 5/440   497 1/3 2/8 3/41   (3 wkts.) 72
6/447 7/454 8/488 9/497 10/497

Bowling: *First Innings* – Butler 32–4–122–3; Allen 16–0–82–2; Laker 36–10–108–2; Cranston 7–1–29–1; Ikin 20–5–60–0; Howorth 32–3–76–2; Wardle 3–0–9–0. *Second Innings* – Butler 8–2–27–2; Allen 5–0–21–1; Cranston 3–0–18–0; Howorth 1–0–2–0.

Umpires: B. Henderson and V. Guillen.

Match drawn.

'some of the most brilliant fielding I remember seeing anywhere' (E.W.S.).

After eight overs England had saved the game for sure, and Godfrey Evans urged Gubby to take himself off, as we in the press-box were all hoping he would. But the captain was not so sure, and giving himself a fifth over, trying to save a single in the follow-through, sure enough he pulled up lame.

Len Hutton, joining the team in British Guiana, naturally had a great welcome, to which he responded by batting all day for a masterly 138. The MCC side against the colony perforce contained five invalids or semi-invalids. It might therefore well have perforce included me had I not lingered inadvisedly for a day in Port-of-Spain.

As in all the centres there was to be a second colony match preceding the Test, but after MCC had shown a sad lack of initiative in not trying to force a victory on the last day of the first of them the second, in which Gubby was due to play, had to be abandoned without a ball bowled. The party enjoyed the traditionally warm Guyanese hospitality, but golf on a course reduced to a paddy-field was no substitute for cricket.

The Third Test on the trim Bourda ground (arguably the best in the West Indies) was the most interesting game of the series, from which England came with reasonable credit. However, the issue was determined by the luck of the toss which allowed the West Indies to make 284 for five on the first day on a plumb wicket. Thereafter rain obliged the batsmen of both sides at various times to struggle against the turning and lifting ball. This match was as good an illustration as any in support of Gubby's view, frequently expressed after his Australian experiences, that pitches abroad should be completely covered. In England rain often made pitches difficult – and the cricket correspondingly more compelling to watch. In both Australia and the West Indies especially, batting after rain was apt to be reduced almost to a lottery.

Gubby, taking the new ball on the first morning, bowled his opposite number, Goddard, in his second over but in his third 'Allen was hopping on his right leg, having strained the tendon above the left knee. The spirit indeed was willing but at forty-five such exertions bring their punishment sooner or later.' I went on to describe 'a really beautiful innings by Worrell. He has gifts exceeding those of any modern player, Bradman and Compton excepted.' His 131 not out was the first – and, incidentally, the lowest – of his six hundreds against England as distinct from the four of Walcott and the three of Weekes.

Hutton and Robertson batted admirably in an opening stand of 59 when England replied to the West Indies' 297 for eight declared. Thereafter the conditions did not altogether excuse some paltry play which suddenly left Gubby – who had held himself back in the interests of his injury – bereft of partners at No 11. All out 111, England redeemed themselves, partly at least, in the follow-on.

Batting with a runner, Gubby helped Joe Hardstaff to put on 85 for the fourth wicket, and one way and another England scratched together 263, leaving the West Indies 78 runs to win. After more rain had refreshed the pitch England had three out for 26, at which point Gomez joined Walcott. If they could have been quickly separated hope was not lost, and while the tall Walcott countered lift and turn marvellously Gomez, a

WEST INDIES v ENGLAND
(Third Test)

At Georgetown, 3–6 March 1948

WEST INDIES

G. M. Carew b Cranston	17	– c Allen b Laker ... 8
*J. D. C. Goddard b Allen	1	– lbw b Laker ... 3
†C. L. Walcott lbw b Cranston	11	– not out ... 31
R. J. Christiani c Hardstaff b Tremlett	51	– lbw b Howorth ... 3
F. M. M. Worrell not out	131	
G. E. Gomez c Evans b Cranston	36	– (5) not out ... 25
E. de C. Weekes b Cranston	36	
E. A. V. Williams b Laker	7	
W. Ferguson c Allen b Laker	2	
L-b 1, w 3, n-b 1	5	L-b 7, n-b 1 ... 8

1/7 2/26 3/48   (8 wkts., dec.) 297   1/10 2/23 3/26   (3 wkts.) 78
4/127 5/224 6/284 7/295 8/297

J. Trim and L. R. Pierre did not bat.

Bowling: *First Innings* – Allen 2.4–0–5–1; Tremlett 14–4–35–1; Cranston 25–5–78–4; Laker 36–11–94–2; Howorth 23–4–58–0; Ikin 5–2–22–0. *Second Innings* – Cranston 2–0–11–0; Laker 9–1–34–2; Howorth 9–0–25–1.

ENGLAND

L. Hutton c Williams b Goddard	31	– b Ferguson ... 24
J. D. B. Robertson c Ferguson b Goddard	23	– lbw b Ferguson ... 9
W. Place c Christian b Goddard	1	– b Ferguson ... 15
J. Hardstaff, jr b Ferguson	3	– c Christiani b Trim ... 63
J. T. Ikin c Ferguson b Goddard	7	– (8) run out ... 24
K. Cranston st Walcott b Ferguson	24	– c Christiani b Goddard ... 32
R. Howorth c Ferguson b Goddard	4	– (9) lbw b Ferguson ... 2
J. C. Laker c Walcott b Ferguson	10	– (10) c Goddard b Williams ... 6
†T. G. Evans b Trim	1	– (7) c Goddard b Williams ... 37
M. F. Tremlett c Christiani b Trim	0	– (11) not out ... 18
*G. O. B. Allen not out	0	– (5) lbw b Ferguson ... 20
B 4, l-b 1, n-b 2	7	B 4, l-b 5, w 1, n-b 3 ... 13

1/59 2/61 3/64 4/64 5/94   111   1/21 2/51 3/52 4/137 5/145   263
6/96 7/109 8/110 9/110 10/111   6/185 7/226 8/233 9/249 10/263

Bowling: *First Innings* – Trim 10–6–6–2; Pierre 2–0–9–0; Williams 6–0–21–0; Goddard 14.2–5–31–5; Worrell 2–0–5–0; Ferguson 15–5–23–3; Gomez 1–0–9–0. *Second Innings* – Trim 13–2–38–1; Pierre 5–0–19–0; Williams 24.4–12–34–2; Goddard 24–8–43–1; Ferguson 40–6–116–5.

Umpires: E. S. Gillette and J. Da Silva.

West Indies won by 7 wickets.

game fighter if ever there was one, died a hundred deaths but – miraculously – remained until victory came.

At Kingston, Jamaica, the last port of call, England, though stronger on paper than hitherto, were no match for a side much fortified by success and with a cohesion that had grown as the series developed. Moreover they unearthed a large thirty-seven-year-old fast bowler called Hines Johnson whose pace and lift brought him ten wickets in the match for 96 runs.

Gubby was able to get through twenty overs in the West Indies' first innings. He had a theory, as I recall, that Worrell might be susceptible to the bouncer and bravely, and without physical mishap, tried him out with a few before having him lbw. It was in this Fourth Test that Weekes established himself firmly in the 'W' trilogy, with a masterly innings of 141 – which, as it turned out, was the first of five Test hundreds in succession, a sequence (continued in India) which no other man has ever achieved. The start of the succession at Kingston is one of the classic illustrations of the part of luck, in life and sport. He was not chosen for this last Test against England, coming into the team only when Headley dropped out. It must have been this innings which led Gubby at the end of the tour, when asked to place the three 'Ws' in order of merit, to put Weekes narrowly first, Worrell a shade behind him (though with the potential to be the best), and by an equally small margin Walcott third. He recalls, after all the intervening years, a six of awesome power hit straight over the sight-screen by Walcott off the back foot against the fast-medium pace of Cranston.

Another memory: in the second Colony match against Jamaica MCC found two Burkes umpiring, father, S. C. and son, P. The latter's name was put forward to stand in the Test, but he was only twenty-one and Gubby thought him too young. The West Indies Board respected the view of the England captain, replacing the son with the father. However it was the latter who in England's second innings gave Gubby out lbw to a ball which, viewed from the Sabina Park pavilion at square-leg, was going over the top of the stumps by a foot. Gubby's evidence, readily open to view on request, was a nasty bruise at the top of the thigh. It was the son who went on to become one of the most reliable West Indian umpires.

So ended without a victory a tour bedevilled by misfortune from the first. I have known Gubby to say he was 'a silly old man' to go to the West Indies. Yet he enjoyed the trip, even though the injuries made it a hopelessly up-hill job from the start. The tour – of what was little better than an England 2nd XI – had a positive value for several of the less experienced players. One of them, Jack Ikin, shortly before his sudden death, contributed on request the following thoughts:

> Never really fit himself and as a front-line attacking bowler with time against him I marvelled at the courage the skipper displayed against overwhelming odds. He set a great example on the field in all departments of the game and, perhaps most important, we learned much in the after-dinner talks and conversations from which I and most of my colleagues were to benefit. He was greatly respected by us all and his concern and welfare for the individual was a quality which was appreciated when things were most trying. In spite of our mishaps, shortcomings, call it what you will, the tour

WEST INDIES v ENGLAND
(Fourth Test)

At Kingston, 27 March–1 April 1948

ENGLAND

L. Hutton b Johnson	56	– c sub (J. K. Holt) b Goddard	60
J. D. B. Robertson lbw b Johnson	64	– b Johnson	28
W. Place st Walcott b Ferguson	8	– st Walcott b Stollmeyer	107
J. Hardstaff, jr c Gomez b Ferguson	9	– b Johnson	64
K. Cranston c Walcott b Johnson	13	– b Kentish	36
*G. O. B. Allen c Walcott b Kentish	23	– lbw b Johnson	13
J. T. Ikin run out	5	– c Worrell b Stollmeyer	3
†T. G. Evans c Weekes b Kentish	9	– b Johnson	4
R. Howorth not out	12	– st Walcott b Stollmeyer	1
J. C. Laker c Walcott b Johnson	6	– not out	6
M. F. Tremlett b Johnson	0	– c Walcott b Johnson	2
B 12, l-b 8, n-b 2	22	B 8, l-b 2, n-b 2	12

1/129 2/132 3/147 4/150 5/173   227   1/69 2/101 3/214 4/291 5/316   336
6/185 7/200 8/205 9/221 10/227   6/316 7/327 8/327 9/329 10/336

Bowling: *First Innings* – Johnson 34.5–13–41–5; Kentish 21–8–38–2; Goddard 19–7–33–0; Ferguson 38–14–53–2; Worrell 11–1–25–0; Stollmeyer 5–1–15–0. *Second Innings* – Johnson 31–11–55–5; Kentish 26–7–68–1; Goddard 25–9–38–1; Ferguson 32–7–90–0; Worrell 20–3–41–0; Stollmeyer 19–7–32–3.

WEST INDIES

*J. D. C. Goddard c Hutton b Howorth	17	– not out	46
J. B. Stollmeyer lbw b Howorth	30	– not out	25
E. de C. Weekes c Hutton b Ikin	141		
F. M. M. Worrell lbw b Allen	38		
G. E. Gomez b Tremlett	23		
K. R. Rickards b Laker	67		
R. J. Christiani c and b Laker	14		
†C. L. Walcott c Hutton b Tremlett	45		
W. Ferguson c Hardstaff b Laker	75		
H. H. H. Johnson b Howorth	8		
E. S. M. Kentish not out	1		
B 11, l-b 17, n-b 3	31	L-b 4, w 1	5

1/39 2/62 3/144 4/204 5/320   490   (0 wkts.)   76
6/351 7/358 8/455 9/482 10/490

Bowling: *First Innings* – Allen 20–1–83–1; Tremlett 31–1–98–2; Howorth 40–10–106–3; Laker 36.4–5–103–3; Ikin 19–0–69–1. *Second Innings* – Allen 2–0–14–0; Tremlett 1–0–4–0; Howorth 4–0–27–0; Laker 2–0–11–0; Ikin 2–0–15–0.

Umpires: S. C. Burke and T. A. Ewart.

West Indies won by 10 wickets.

of the West Indies was a happy tour which I and my colleagues would not have missed. This was due entirely to leadership of the highest class. There was never any panic. I doubt if any touring captain had a more difficult task.

One thing this captain certainly brought home was a conviction of the big future in Test cricket that undoubtedly lay ahead of the West Indies. In the long term this asset to the game as a whole was the biggest benefit of the MCC West Indies tour of 1947–48.

15
Mellow Years

The years of Gubby's life between early manhood and his sixties tend to have divided themselves – give or take a month or two and excluding the war and the periods immediately before and after it – into cycles of seven. From his entry into the City in 1923 to this first appearance for England in 1930 was one such span. The years of his prime as a Test cricketer then lasted seven years, until 1936–37. From the end of the MCC West Indies tour in the spring of 1948 to his taking on the chairmanship of the selectors in the spring of 1955, the period at which we have arrived, was likewise seven years. And it was for the seven following seasons that he and his colleagues were responsible for the choice of England's teams, at home and abroad.

The seven years, 1948 to 1955, were mellow ones and, I would judge, among his happiest. As a partner in David Bevan (which during this period was enlarged to become Bevan, Simpson) he had increasing responsibility, both to his Stock Exchange partners and his clients, and a greater financial incentive. In the councils of MCC he played a bigger and more important rôle. As to his games, he remained a good enough cricketer to enjoy playing in the summer whenever he could, and in particular, giving a series of practical lessons to the undergraduates, especially those of Cambridge. Out of the cricket season he got vast pleasure from his golf – which, incidentally, introduced him to a widening circle of friends. To the fellowship of cricket was added the fellowship of golf. He was, in general, remarkably fit. The first of all those hip operations, the legacy of all that fast bowling, was a long way into the future.

In the summer of 1948 he played four away matches for Middlesex, stiffening the batting when Compton and Edrich were playing for England against Australia and Robins was on his selection duties. On one of the rare occasions that he captained Middlesex he led them to a handsome win at Leicester, putting himself in last and not being required to get his pads on. At Bradford he (76 not out) and Sims (57), ninety years old in the aggregate, scored 111 together after six men were out for 92. He made useful contributions with bat and ball at Worcester and his favourite Old Trafford.

Above, Hollywood Interlude 1937 – With Marlene Dietrich 'very quiet and natural nowadays' and Herbert Marshall

Right With Sir Aubrey Smith, doyen of the English colony. Aged 73, the old Cambridge and Sussex cricketer took a fine slip catch off GOA

Below A golf 5-ball at the Riviera Club, with David Niven, Raymond Massey, Nigel Bruce and Basil Rathbone

War-time at Lord's and a useful side: standing, Capt. Griffith, Sub-Lt. Stevens, Flt.-Lt. Robins, Maj. Allen, P/O R. M. Taylor, Sgt. Hutton; sitting, G. F. H. Heane, O-Cadet Valentine, Lt Brown, L. N. Constantine

Royal Box: the scene is the Eton and Harrow match of July 1946. From the left, Mrs. David Bowes Lyon, Princess Elizabeth, The Queen, Lord Harcourt, Lt. Philip Mountbatten, R.N., W. W. Hill-Wood, The King, Miss Sharman Douglas, Princess Margaret, Mr. Hugh Wyld, Sir Pelham Warner, Miss Davina Bowes Lyon, Hon. L. H. White, Mrs. Hugh Wyld. The royal engagement had been announced the previous day. Co-host GOA is out of the picture

Above Free Foresters v. Cambridge, 1948: GOA off-drives W. H. Griffiths during his innings of 180, the highest of his life. Trevor Bailey is at first slip. In six seasons between the ages of forty-five and fifty he made four hundreds in this fixture and averaged 84

Left Billy Griffith not out 110: Having gone in first in the Second Test in a team much weakened by injury he batted all day, scoring his maiden first-class hundred. Next morning he was out for 140, made in six hours, the highest English innings of the tour

MCC West Indies Team 1947–48. Standing, G. A. Smithson, W. Place, H. J. Butler, M. F. Tremlett, J. C. Laker, J. H. Wardle, D. Brookes, J. D. Robertson; sitting, T. G. Evans, J. Hardstaff, S. C. Griffith (Assistant Manager), G. O. Allen (Captain and Manager), K. Cranston (Vice-Captain), R. Howorth, J. T. Ikin

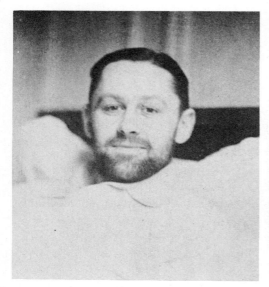

Hospital Beard: GOA endured 5 hip operations between 1965 and 1979. During a long stay in hospital in the 1960s he dispensed for a while with his razor. More Gatting than Grace perhaps?

Convalescence at last. In December 1967 with Mrs. Mary Hill-Wood at a coming-out dance

The MCC Committee 1963–64: clockwise from GOA (President), S. C. Griffith (Secretary), J. G. Dunbar (Asst. Sec.), M. J. C. Allom, J. S. O. Haslewood, H. S. Altham, Marshal of the R.A.F. Viscount Portal, W. W. Hill-Wood, F. G. Mann, G. C. Newman, Lt.-Gen. Sir Oliver Leese, Lord Nugent, T. N. Pearce, C. C. Paris, T. E. Burrows, G. O. Shelmerdine, D. B. Carr (Asst. Sec.), R. H. Twining (President-designate)

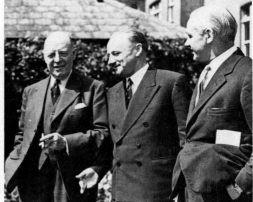

Above H. S. Altham, Sir Donald Bradman and GOA: Sir Donald had flown over for the momentous ICC meeting of 1960 as an indirect result of which the Throwing Crisis was resolved

Above left Vizianagram Palace: as Chairman and Secretary of ICC, GOA and Billy Griffith visited India in early 1964. They stayed as guests of 'Vizzy', as the Maharajah of Vizianagram was popularly known

Below The Taj Mahal was seen in wonder, during MCC's visit to India in February, 1964, by Michael Melford and John Woodcock, standing, Billy Griffith, GOA and Colin Cowdrey.

Opening of the MCC Indoor School: GOA performing the ceremony in November, 1977, supported by
D. G. Clark, J. A. Bailey (Secretary), Sir Cyril Hawker, F. R. Brown, R. Aird, J. G. W. Davies (Treasurer) and
C. G. A. Paris

Before the 80th birthday dinner, fourteen of the thirty Test cricketers present take the field once more: from the l
George Mann, Mike Smith, Godfrey Evans, Ted Dexter, Denis Compton, Tom Graveney, Sir Leonard Hutton,
GOA, Alec Bedser, Leslie Ames, Freddie Brown, Peter May, Basil D'Oliveira, Jim Laker.

Toast of Honour in the Long Room on 9 August 1982: from the left, GOA, Hubert Doggart, Lord Home, and Ronnie Aird

Golf at the Berkshire: with Keith Miller and Sir Douglas Bader, shortly before the latter died in 1983

The painting by John Ward, R.A. which hangs in the Long Room

Author and Subject in the Harris Garden, 1984

At Old Trafford, off Jack Young's bowling, he dropped a gaping catch at mid-off and was sure he detected a great laugh in the pavilion as coming from Ernest Tyldesley. When the lunch interval arrived there was his old friend at the gate having thoughtfully brought down his blazer, laughing again and saying 'You were never catching it – you were never catching it.' Ernest is likely to fill one of the pictures in Gubby's mind when it dwells on past deeds, for when he took all ten Lancashire wickets at Lord's Tyldesley (E.) played what *Wisden* called a 'masterly' innings of 102 before becoming one of the seven who were b. Allen. But this modest, whimsical Lancastrian is remembered with a special fondness by Gubby's generation – he embodied all that was best in the professional cricketers of his day.

This year saw the start of what became the annual ritual of Gubby's highly successful inspection of his old university's bowling talent. Seven successive years he played for the Free Foresters in the May Week match which brought the Fenner's season to an end prior to the university tour. He batted in them twelve times, made four hundreds, and averaged 84.50 – this between the ages of forty-five and fifty-one. It is a record which says much for the quality of Cyril Coote's pitches. It may suggest that with some members of the opposition there was a degree of celebration in the aftermath of examinations. Yet, allowing for such possible qualifications, it remains a notable statistic pointing both to that rare degree of concentration and a purity of style and method which defied the years. The 180 which Gubby made in 1948 against Trevor Bailey and Hugh (now Mr Justice) Griffiths etc was in fact the highest score of his life, and it landed him, as a result of eight first-class innings, at the top of the English batting averages, with 384 runs and an average of 76.

Gubby went with George Newman's MCC side to Holland on a tour which was remembered by the survivors for a somewhat macabre reason. The Dutch had a bowler named Molenaar who on the matting surface and when his tail was up was disagreeably hasty. Against All Holland in a match celebrating the Diamond Jubilee of the Hague Cricket Club Gubby, going in No 3, was still picking his bat up when the first ball flew by. There was some chaffing later on the grounds that he then stuck at the safer end, but, as he points out, there was nothing he could do but watch as Aird, Newman and K. A. Sellar ('Monkey', the great full-back, who also played cricket for Sussex) were all clean bowled in the course of four balls. Molenaar struck his opponents as a somewhat sinister fellow, but they scarcely expected to hear that he was subsequently convicted, and given a sentence of ten years, for complicity in a murder committed during the war. Ramsbottom, the Lancashire League club, who had signed him on as a professional for the 1949 season, were obliged to look elsewhere.

The strength of Gubby's influence on the MCC Committee, still much in evidence at the moment of writing, dates from these early post-war years although he had served a previous term starting in 1935. Those Committees of the late 1940s were inclined to be both elderly and reactionary. Though both Hawke and Jackson were dead, their spirits still seemed to Gubby and some others to overhang their deliberations. He has always had scant respect for those he dubs as 'Yes men', and was therefore in the forefront of a ginger group who saw their duty as bringing in some livelier minds. Dick Twining, Ronny Stanyforth and George Newman (though he in later years was to outlive his value) were associated with Gubby in this.

One of his first successes was to suggest and steer through the election of famous retired professional cricketers as honorary members of MCC. The idea had come to him as a result of a talk with Len Hutton in the West Indies. The proposal was not at first accepted unopposed in the Committee, but when in July 1949 the Committee put it to a Special General Meeting chaired by the Duke of Edinburgh as president the members' decision was unanimous. The first list of twenty-six (the names of almost all of whom, I think, have been mentioned in these pages) were: S. F. Barnes, C. J. Barnett, W. E. Bowes, L. C. Braund, G. Duckworth, A. P. Freeman, G. Geary, G. Gunn, sr., J. W. Hearne, E. Hendren, G. H. Hirst, J. B. Hobbs, H. Larwood, M. Leyland, C. P. Mead, E. Paynter, W. Rhodes, A. C. Russell, A. Sandham, E. J. Smith, H. Strudwick, H. Sutcliffe, M. W. Tate, E. Tyldesley, W. Voce and F. E. Woolley.

The gesture of gratitude and goodwill was, of course, well received both by those so honoured and by the public at large, and today the list is regularly refreshed with other distinguished cricketers after their retirement. It is now also extended to outstanding players, and a select few administrators, from overseas.

The MCC Committee, however, had next to face a sharper issue, wherein Gubby was decisively involved. The treasurership has always been the key position in the administration of MCC, a then permanent post which carries with it automatic membership of all sub-committees and the duty of understudy to the president. In July 1949 Viscount Cobham, who had succeeded Lord Hawke as treasurer in 1939, died at the age of sixty-seven, and the identity of his successor was plainly of the first importance. The MCC minutes, as was in those days the custom, dealt only briefly and factually with the matter, but happily Gubby's memory of events that really matter is thoroughly clear.

The August Committee merely 'stood in silence in memory of an old friend'. The next reference is in the December minutes which announced that the vacancy would be considered at the January meeting. The minutes of that occasion record the conclusion thus:

Treasurership
It was decided by a ballot to ask Mr H. S. Altham to allow his name
to be submitted in the Annual Report as the Committee recommendation to fill the office of Treasurer.

Allowing for the fact that the Committee is in recession in September, the
delay in dealing with the matter suggests there seemed to be no
universally acceptable successor, and that a certain amount of lobbying
therefore took place. When the item came up on the January agenda
Plum Warner proposed Sir Eric Gore Browne. This surprising nomination was at once opposed by Gubby, who pointed out that Sir Eric had
no connection with the playing side of the club and was an only recent
recruit to the Committee. He was in fact a distinguished banker and
chairman of the Great Western Railway, and had only been appointed to
the Committee the previous year. Gubby then proposed Harry Altham.
Plum's response was to say that if a cricket qualification were required he
would propose Mr Findlay. Since all three nominees were present the
situation was, inevitably, embarrassing. After discussion the issue was
put to the vote, and H. S. A.'s name was narrowly approved. There were
seventeen out of twenty-one members of the Committee present under
the chairmanship of Lord Gowrie, standing in for the Duke of Edinburgh. Gubby thinks that the margin *may* have been as close as a single
vote. What he vividly recalls is the extreme good nature of Gore Browne,
whom he much liked, when after the meeting he told him how sorry he
was to have had to say what he did. 'You were quite right,' was the reply.

It was a case of the old *eminence* instinctively resenting the growing
influence of the new. The relationship between Plum and Gubby had
never been quite the same since the way in which the England captaincy
question had been resolved caused the breach in 1938. Even allowing for
this, Warner's attempt to install Gore Browne to follow in the shoes of
Ponsonby-Fane, Harris, Hawke and Cobham suggests that at seventy-six
his judgement was faltering. Likewise to have backed his great friend,
Billy Findlay, then coming up to seventy, against Harry Altham, with
whom also he was on the warmest terms, was scarcely less extraordinary.
Altham had retired from the teaching staff at Winchester the previous
summer. He was sixty-one, and his experience had touched cricket at
every point. In the next thirteen years as treasurer he completed a lifetime
of service to cricket. Yet but for G. O. A. this crowning contribution
would almost certainly have been either lost or greatly curtailed.

The first match of Gubby's 1950 season had a significance beyond its
intrinsic importance. Playing at Cambridge for the Arabs which I
founded in 1935 – which still, I am happy to say, goes strong, and for
which he played a good deal in his last years before the selection job

brought his cricket to a halt – he met a certain J. J. Warr, a fastish bowler and a freshman who had come into our side as a substitute at the last minute.

After dinner on the first evening John Warr had the good sense to sit at the feet of the old master who, having just made the first of his season's hundreds, was no doubt even more benignly inclined than usual to a young bowler looking for guidance. Gubby discovered that Warr, who with a good sideways-on action had taken two or three Crusader wickets during the day, had actually been taught at Ealing County Grammar School to grasp the ball across the seam, and almost in the palm at that.

Warr went away having been shown how to hold the ball in order to swing it, was given a trial for the university in the next match, and in the following one (just a week after ours) took six Lancashire wickets for 35 runs. From this start Warr scarcely looked back. He and John Wait, another tall freshman of no mean pace, topped the bowling averages and had much to do with a surprise victory over Oxford. The case of John Warr is a good example of a man who seized his luck intelligently and made the most of it thereafter.

Gubby had three matches for Middlesex in 1949, all when they were weakened by other calls and each in its way notable. Against the champions, Glamorgan on a moderate pitch at Swansea, concentrating on accuracy and a full length, rather than pace, within a few weeks of his forty-seventh birthday, he got through forty-eight overs in the two innings and took nine for 65. He also had a brusque altercation with one of the Glamorgan side whose fairness was not above suspicion. Wilfred Wooller said he wasn't going to have one of his players spoken to like that. An argument followed, but as with Gubby in other cases disagreement proved to be the prelude to a warm friendship. (Wilf was to serve all seven years on his Selection Committees.)

Gubby had noticed in the Lord's nets a youngster on the staff who bowled medium pace and showed promise with the bat. His name was Fred Titmus, and he was sixteen and a half. As Gubby finished practice before going down to play against Somerset at Bath, he told Walter Robins – due to lead the side because George Mann was captaining England – when he went out for a net to cast an eye over him. To Gubby's astonishment Robins returned and said, 'I've picked young Titmus to come to Bath.' This typically precipitate decision caused a quick return by Fred to Kentish Town, a rare flutter in the Titmus household, and his reputed arrival at Bath with the minimum of cricket clothes in a brown-paper parcel. He was given only two overs, but with 13 and 4 not out had some share in a narrow victory. (He did not play again for the 1st XI that summer, but made his place secure in the following one.)

The chief agent of the victory at Bath was Gubby, who made 91 in the first innings out of 193, being last out having a crack at Bertie Buse. He and young Titmus had put on 34 together. Before he batted a second time there arrived on the ground his old friends, Jack White and John Daniell, who said they'd come to see how he did it. Thereupon he promptly hit over a half-volley and was again bowled by Buse, this time for a duck. 'Flattered out' he called it. However with the new ball he took the first three Somerset wickets, and when it was all over there was a highly sociable evening in the tent with the Farmer and the Prophet, as a result of which Gubby stayed the night – a rare departure from routine and in this case certainly a wise one.

The following month when Middlesex went up to Worcester Jack Robertson made history by scoring 331 in the day. Needless to say the pitch was a beauty, and soon after Gubby got in, in mid-afternoon, at 274 for three he ran back to the dressing-room window and called out to Robins, 'Throw me my cap. It's a lovely day – I think I'll make a hundred.' 'You make me sick,' was the reply of one candid friend to the other, who had to find his cap himself – and in fact made 98 before, according to *The Times*, he 'unaccountably missed a straight ball from Palmer'.

Robertson, need I say, was a classical player of the Lord's school. Substituting for Washbrook as Hutton's partner in the Lord's Test three weeks earlier, he had made 121 and was then dropped! Middlesex declared at close of play with 623 for five, and Robertson's innings was, and remains, a Middlesex record. Only three men, Macartney, Ponsford and Duleepsinhji by name, have ever made more runs in a day.

The Forester match at Cambridge brought another hundred in the second innings after a much-quoted scene in the Allen saga in the first. When Bryan Valentine joined Gubby he said, in passing, that he hadn't been very well, and didn't want any short runs. The first thing that happened (says G. O. A.) is that Bryan called for an impossible single and somehow they got away with it. Then bad went to worse, so that after a bit the university captain, D. J. Insole, called his side together, and said words to this effect: 'Look here, lads, we've got two famous cricketers in, and if you want a good lesson in how not to run between wickets don't miss it.' Shortly afterwards Valentine was run out for 11. This comment tickled Gubby so much that he decided there were distinct possibilities about the future captain and chairman of Essex, Test cricketer, tour manager and chairman of the Cricket Committee of the TCCB.

The 1949 averages show G. O. Allen prominently for the last time, eleventh in the batting with 378 runs, average 54, and second in the bowling with fourteen wickets at 15 apiece.

In this year of the Duke of Edinburgh's presidency of MCC his cricket association was enhanced by his appearance in September as captain of his own side against Hampshire in aid of the Silver Jubilee appeal of the National Playing Fields. Gubby was invited to join him in some net practice at Windsor. When asked by HRH whether he could 'get away' with playing himself, he replied that he could.

On a warm, sunny day the match went off very well, the Royal contribution consisting of some respectable off-breaks which brought a wicket and 12 well-made runs. I reported that 'he stayed long enough to make it clear, as his bowling and zestful fielding had suggested, that he would always hold his own in the company of good cricketers if he could contrive the time to practice'. Gubby had the pleasure of returning with the Duke's party flying from Hurn airport in a Viking of the King's Flight. Noble patronage of the game was never higher than around this time, with several publicly supported charity matches in which the Duke and Gubby were involved, at Arundel and Badminton, associated, respectively, with the Dukes of Norfolk and Beaufort.

Gubby played his last matches for Middlesex in 1950, leading the side at Birmingham, Leeds, Cheltenham and Weston-super-Mare in the absence of Walter Robins. The Yorkshire match was for Len Hutton's Benefit and was badly affected by rain, which ruined both the subsequent games in the West country. His 420th and last wicket for Middlesex was that of M. M. Walford, Somerset's leading batsman that summer, caught in the slips off the new ball for 8.

At Cambridge for the Free Foresters he was not intending to bowl, but got cross at what he considered a very bad lbw decision, went and bought some elastoplast and in the first of his eighteen overs had the much-heralded David Sheppard caught behind for a duck. Then he and Bryan Valentine put on a brisk 147 together in the second innings – so that honour, if not the match, was saved.

21 September 1950 was a red-letter day, for on it he played St Andrew's for the first time. Jim Sims was with him, and since it was considered that so august an occasion demanded a distinguished match G. H. Micklem and R. H. Oppenheimer, Internationals both, selectors and commanding figures in the world of amateur golf, took a cricketer each as partner. The result is not recorded but it can safely be said that the talk must have been pretty good. Gubby was elected to the Royal and Ancient in the following year.

A health note must be the first entry for 1951, and the jaundice which confined Gubby to his bed for a full month in April and May had a distinct cricket significance since while he was thus imprisoned he and Harry Altham toiled hard together on the MCC Coaching Book, an integral part of the Club's country-wide drive towards better cricket facilities for the young. But for the jaundice Gubby's collaborator thought that the book might never have been finished. Broadly speaking, Gubby's influence predominated on the technical aspects, Harry's in the writing.

Medical advice was that he should play no cricket until July. Translating this none too literally, Gubby played for the 2nd XI of Eton Ramblers at the school on the Fourth of June, and duly fulfilled his annual rôle at Cambridge the following week-end. One wonders what his doctor thought when he saw that his patient's scores were 103 and 55 – thanks to which John Warr's university side came very close to being beaten. The inimitable Jim Sims addressed his wire of congratulations to the Advanced Dressing Station, Fenner's Ground.

The coaching programme in which Gubby was immersed contained not only the MCC Coaching Book but a film on the basic bowling action for the script of which he was helped by Alf Gover. John Arlott spoke the words. Ian Peebles and Walter Robins assisted with the spin portion of the manuscript. The best part of a dozen visits to Wardour Street, made after his day's work in the City was done, were necessary before the perfectionist was satisfied. But now came the one hiccup in his cordial partnership with H. S. A. He decided that the artist J. A. Board's drawing for the book of the forward defensive stroke was not quite right and, late in the evening, rang Harry at Winchester. The latter was not cooperative. The printers had to have the illustrations next morning. It was too late to change anything.

But where did the artist live? At Kingston apparently. Gubby therefore dressed, got out his car, and drove through (light!) snow from Kensington out to Kingston, posed the forward defensive stroke for about an hour and a half and got home, tired but satisfied, around two a.m. What episode could tell more of Gubby than this? I wonder how pleased the artist was!

A Special General Meeting of MCC in the autumn unanimously voted a sum of £15,000 in order to found the MCC Youth Cricket Association. H. S. Altham was the first chairman, G. O. Allen one of the MCC representatives in a national Council. In December at the Council of Physical Recreation's headquarters at Lilleshall, Shropshire, the first Coaching Conference was held. Under the spell of the chairman's personality those who had doubted the worth of the system of group coaching were won over. There were a dozen and more Test cricketers, amateur and professional, in a company of sixty which covered all the chief centres of cricket in the country.

When the MCC Coaching Book appeared in the spring the *Daily Express* serialized it, and the first printing was sold out in a week. It has been selling ever since, and is today in its fourth edition. There have been all but a dozen reprints. In this, as in other later cricket matters, the firm of Allen and Altham were the perfect combination. After publication Harry wrote in a characteristically generous spirit: 'I want you to know that I regard your share in it as decisive.' He thought that Gubby's break-down of the basic bowling action 'the most important advance in bowling technique in my life-time ... Your "relentless" criticism was absolutely invaluable.' He ends on a note of regret that his days of practical coaching — he was sixty-three — were almost over.

In his fiftieth year Gubby slipped somewhat at Cambridge, scoring only 61 and 4, but made amends at Oxford — up to a point. Following rain on the first day Errol Holmes announced that he would have to declare, come what may, on the second at lunch, which found Gubby looking helplessly on at the non-striker's end, not out 99. His birthday however coincided with the annual match, always contested with the utmost Yorkshire keenness, against Sir William Worsley's XI at Hov-ingham Hall on the Arabs' Northern Tour. Brian Sellers captained the opposition, which maybe gave yet an added savour to his celebrating the occasion on that lovely ground with a chanceless innings of 108. The Arabs declared at 224 for seven, Sir William's side replied with 223 for nine, and over dinner, as the old accounts used to put it, 'many toasts were drunk'.

Many a schoolboy and club cricketer will have taken profit from watching Gubby's batting that summer of 1952 — and they had plenty of leisure to do so seeing that his figures worked out like this: 29 innings, 5 times not out, 1593 runs, average 66.38.

Talking of schools, all through his career he enjoyed playing against them, especially Eton. David Macindoe, now Vice-Provost, writes that :

> Gubby used to play against the School for IZ etc on two or three occasions a year; he made a lot of runs against us, but did not always bowl — being more subject than most, as we all recall, to pulled muscles, inflamed toe-nails etc! (His bag was always stuffed with elastoplast and other medicaments.) He continued to play against Eton after the war, when Claude Taylor and I ran the cricket. He was always most generous in his attitude to boy cricketers and full of helpful advice to the young, especially his friends' children, the Eckersleys, Robins and so on.

Only one thing irritated Gubby when playing against boys — the extreme reluctance of umpires, who were often the school professionals, to give boys out when they should have done. At Harrow once he remonstrated quietly about this with the great J. T. Hearne, who said, 'But the boy's plumb out of form.' To this came what is surely the best practical answer, 'If you'd told me that I wouldn't have appealed.'

We both recall an occasion at Eton when Claude Taylor pleaded with the MCC side to give a start to a young left-hander who clearly had much promise but couldn't get a run. It so happened I had quite a long bowl, and forebore – not without effort! – to ask for lbws and even a catch at the wicket. At the other end Bob Wyatt made a slip catch and then in the same movement almost flung the ball on the grass. The left-hander – who when nowadays taxed with his good luck that day said he had a vague suspicion that something might have been going on – was Colin Ingleby-Mackenzie, then just short of his sixteenth birthday. It had probably been his last chance that summer. He went on to make a hundred, and to top the averages!

Gubby recalls his first sight of the slim, tall Peter May at Charterhouse and finding no difficulty in even going beyond the high estimate of George Geary as the latter, umpiring at square-leg, and he swapped opinions. He played against Colin Cowdrey at Tonbridge when, playing at the age of thirteen, he had the first of his five years in the XI. 'He won't be a bowler's boot-lace, but he will be a very, very good batsman,' was, it seems, the verdict. As to the youthful Ted Dexter at Radley, he told his Eton contemporary Vaughan Wilkes, then Warden, that 'He's got immense talent.'

His last first-class hundred came at Fenner's in 1953 (143 not out and 17) and elicited the usual spoof telegrams purporting to come from the chairman of selectors, Freddie Brown, asking about his Test availability, from Leveson Gower saying he was expected without fail for all matches at Scarborough, and from 'Home and Lady' saying 'Next thing you'll be getting married'. Altham sent a genuine wire in Latin, to which Gubby replied that he couldn't understand a word but it was all in the Coaching Book.

Robin Marlar, if I recall aright, was not going to be beaten by a fifty-year-old and, being the university captain, bowled and bowled. He had his reward in the second innings when Gubby was stumped by Gerry Alexander – in about the sixtieth over!

In what proved to be his last summer of cricket, 1954, he made a few runs at Cambridge, playing as by custom for the Free Foresters and also at Oxford, where his three wickets included that of the man who within a couple of months he was urging should be sent to Australia – Colin Cowdrey, caught behind for 2.

There was also the sentimental occasion of his last appearance at Lord's against the official touring Canadian side, whose first visit there it was. On his fifty-second birthday Gubby led quite a distinguished side including, among those of riper years, in addition to himself, Bob Wyatt, Freddie Brown and Bill Voce. Despite a gallant 48 not out from that admirable wicket-keeper, Adam Powell, the Canadians won by 13 runs on the second evening a few minutes before time.

Late in July Gubby, representing MCC along with Charlie Palmer, joined the 1954 Test selectors (Altham, Yardley, Robins, Ames and the captain, Hutton) in order to pick the team for the tour of Australia in the winter. They spent most of the day on the job and at the end of it came up with several surprises, both in the way of inclusions and omissions. On the face of it, the preference of Tyson over Trueman among the fast bowlers came into this category, as did that of Cowdrey over several who could show better figures. At this distance it may seem odd that McConnon, of Glamorgan, got the vote over Laker, and perhaps that no room could be found for Lock. The selectors on the other hand could argue that on the West Indian pitches the previous winter Laker's fourteen Test wickets had cost 33 runs each while Trueman had nine, averaging 46, and Lock fourteen, averaging 57.

The choices among these which Gubby successfully pressed for – and this has been since confirmed by all present – were for Tyson and Cowdrey. In Tyson's case he went for his sheer pace and strength, as against others who on English pitches did more with the ball. The shine does not last long in Australia, as he knew too well. As for Cowdrey he remembered his two fifties on a Lord's wicket with some pace in it for the Gentlemen against what *Wisden* called 'all out attacks by Miller and Lindwall' for the Australians the previous year. He liked Cowdrey's classic method, and thought his exceptional facility of timing would serve him well on Australian pitches.

When as an extra insurance against Compton's knee trouble Vic Wilson, of Yorkshire, was later added to bring the party up to eighteen, the captain made a bet of £1 with Gubby that Wilson would average more on the tour than Cowdrey.

In the winter Gubby took advantage of the fact that his firm was showing increasing interest in the Australian stock market to propose taking his holiday out there, chiefly for business reasons but likewise to see some of the Tests. This was a fruitful move from the business point of view, because he was able to extend the important contacts he already had in Australia and, of course, to gather knowledge at first hand. As a result of this and several further visits he became one of the leading Stock Exchange authorities on Australian investment. He flew out in early December with stops at Cairo, Beirut and Singapore, and was able to see, with what pleasure may be imagined, England's three successive victories at Sydney, Melbourne and Adelaide, the last of which ensured the keeping of the Ashes. He saw the partnership of 116 for the fourth wicket in the second innings of the Second Test at Sydney between May and Cowdrey which gave England glimmers of hope in the face of otherwise sure defeat. He saw Tyson, with his shortened run and by sheer speed and stamina, take ten wickets in that match to level the series.

At Melbourne he saw the twenty-two-year-old Cowdrey – the youngest Englishman to have made a hundred against Australia since J. W. Hearne on the same ground in 1911–12 – make 102 out of England's total of 191 on the first day and Tyson taking his decisive seven for 27 on the last, to put England one up. And he was in the dressing-room to see the triumphal conclusion at Adelaide which the captain could not bear to watch. Before the finish Len Hutton took the wallet out of his pocket. 'I don't want an Australian pound,' said Gubby jokily. 'No, no,' was the reply, 'I've got an English one for you.' And, no doubt with one of those enigmatic smiles of his, the captain of England paid up.

Also on the cricket front he saw one less admirable aspect, the bowling by England at Melbourne of 54 eight-ball overs in five hours, latterly to the constant booing of the crowd. It was the first time that Gubby was conscious of the slow over-rate being used, as it has so commonly been manipulated for years now, as a tactical ploy. Gubby raised the matter of over-rates on his return home at the March meeting of the Board of Control, which fully supported his view that action should be taken.

2 February 1955 at Adelaide, where England won a rubber in Australia for the first time since he had helped them to do so more than twenty years before, was one red-letter day in Gubby's third visit back to his homeland. Another more personal one, as the score-card attests, was 13 January when he played what he reckons to be the best round of his life – a 70 on the East course at Royal Melbourne. He was playing what started as a three-ball against the Governor of Victoria, Sir Dallas Brooks, a notable cricketer and golfer in his day, and another. At the 18th the Governor told Gubby he had a 4 for a 69. Visions of glory! But Gubby had driven the line that would give him a safe 5, thinking that that was all he needed to break 70. He duly took 5, so 70 it was. Thus he bettered the standard scratch score for this magnificent course by four strokes. It is incidental to the story and became of significance only a decade or so later that early in the round they found one Lindsay Clarke playing alone and asked him to join them. He was chairman of a small company Gubby had not even heard of called Western Mining – which was in years ahead to prove Gubby's most successful investment.

A less testing game of golf, with Clarrie Grimmett and Tim Wall on the Kooyonga course at Adelaide, is remembered for an amusing reason. There had often been speculation about Clarrie's real age, and it was thought that if a stroke were offered for each year's difference in their ages the little man would have to come clean. He promised faithfully that he was born on Christmas Day 1892, as *Wisden* then proclaimed. He therefore received nine strokes from Gubby who duly beat him. However as researchers can discover, three years before his death in May 1980 *Wisden* changed his year of birth to 1891. I expect he may have long ago lost his birth certificate, and that one of those inquisitive 'statisticians' nosed the truth out of the parish registers of his birth-place, Dunedin, New Zealand. (Parenthetically, Bill O'Reilly's obituary notice in the 1981 *Wisden* makes rewarding reading.)

Gubby flew home via New Zealand with Ronny and Viola Aird, Ronny having been the first MCC secretary to have seen when in office Test cricket in Australia – which he had done by courtesy of an invitation from the New Zealand Cricket Council. There was the expected pile of mail awaiting him, and near the bottom of it Gubby was astonished to find a letter from Middlesex informing him that he had been nominated as Chairman of Selectors for the coming summer. He had refused to stand more than once in the past, and no one had asked him now. His reaction was that he did not want the job and that Johnny Bevan, his senior partner, would be against his taking it anyway.

However – a further surprise – Bevan's reaction was that, if he was wanted, the firm ought not to stand in the way. This cut Gubby's legs from under him, so to say. Without the excuse of business, and knowing that Altham definitely did not want to serve again and that Robins was unavailable, he reluctantly accepted. Reluctantly, yes – but in retrospect he is delighted. It was going to mean the end of his cricket – but he was against old men hanging on and becoming a nuisance. In fact he never played another match. The job was going to be restricting in lots of ways, but – well, he wouldn't have missed it!

16
Selector-in-Chief

Like practically everything else in Gubby's life, the work of the seven Selection Committees of which he was chairman from the summer of 1955 to 1961 inclusive is precisely recorded. There being no secretary present, the minutes of every meeting were written by the chairman without delay. Likewise he has filed important letters and also the reports made at the summer's end – to give it its full name – to the Board of Control of 'Test' Matches at Home. Until the transformation of cricket authority in 1968, which resulted in the formation of the Test and County Cricket Board, the Board of Control made all decisions affecting home Tests. They were made up of the president of MCC, five nominees from the MCC Committee, one representative each from the first ten counties in the previous year's Championship and one from each county staging a Test Match if not already represented. It was this Board which appointed the selectors, and to which they were responsible.

Gubby in 1955 had no say whatever in the choice of his colleagues since he himself had been appointed along with Leslie Ames, Brian Sellers, and Wilfred Wooller simultaneously. However there is no doubt that all who were appointed – plus the captain once he was selected – worked very amiably together. There were four selectors appointed each year, of whom Wooller in addition to the chairman was in office for the seven summers. In the other places were Sellers for one year, Washbrook and Tom Dollery for two, and Ames, Herbert Sutcliffe and Doug Insole for three. There was always one current county captain and sometimes two. Geographically and in terms of experience the four usually made a reasonable balance, though to the critic looking in it seemed that Sutcliffe was too far from the modern scene both in years and in the amount of cricket he was able to see to be perhaps an ideal representative of the north. Gubby was happy with all of them, and only if pressed will he give the palm by a narrow margin to Les Ames.

The new chairman of selectors took up his post in the spring of 1955, and in view of all the travel that lay ahead treated himself to a second-hand Bentley (and has never been without one since). He assumed office with English cricket dominant against Australia, and the general mood euphoric after the struggles and difficulties of the years after the war.

Gubby was confident — he told the Northern Cricket Society that the Ashes should remain here 'from five to eight years' — but he was by no means starry-eyed. We were strong in bowling, but the batting depended on just two or three men of outstanding talent — as indeed it had done since the palmy days of 1930 when Gubby's Test career had begun. To ensure the attractiveness of Test cricket he wanted to see rather more enterprise among the batsmen, a higher standard of fielding, and, in particular, he was determined to implement the Board of Control's request to pass on to the captain their concern about the recent over-rate.

He had said as much in a letter to Sir Donald Bradman following discussions they had had on the subject in Australia, Don in reply having sent him the figures for the first four Tests. They made gloomy reading. Translated into six-ball over terms from the Australian eight-ball, they showed that whereas Australia had bowled the equivalent of 19.6 six-ball overs per hour over the four Tests England's rate had been 14.74. Maybe England had used their faster bowlers a shade more than Australia, but there was not much to choose, as regards the speed of bowling overs to be expected, as between an attack of Lindwall, Miller, Johnston, Davidson, Benaud and Johnson on one side and that of Tyson, Statham, Bailey, Appleyard and Wardle on the other.

At the first meeting of his new Committee on 27 April — with Ames, Sellers, and Wooller present — he passed on the Board of Control's request, and at the second meeting on 21 May the minute of the first item on the agenda spoke for itself:

> It was decided to appoint L. Hutton captain for the series but before doing so obtain from him a definite undertaking that he would do his utmost to prevent 'time-wasting' and generally to speed up the team in the field in accordance with the wishes of the Board of Control expressed at their meeting in March of this year.

When Len Hutton thereupon joined the meeting he was told of the determination of the selectors to implement the Board's request:

> even to the extent, in any extreme case, of omitting a player who after being warned had not given his full cooperation; furthermore the reason for the omission would probably be given to the press.

The chairman told Len that it would be preferable for him to explain the position to the team. He agreed with the views expressed, and undertook to speak to them before the First Test. It was then decided to announce his appointment two days later.

This duly happened — and, incidentally, it was the first time the captain had been appointed in advance for a whole series since C. B. Fry in the case of the Triangular Tournament in 1912. But the news was still-born.

Hutton, leading MCC against the South Africans, had had a hero's reception on coming in to bat on the first evening. On the Monday he failed to appear, stricken with lumbago, and when the selectors met to choose the team for the First Test he persuaded them he was not fit to play. The selectors therefore chose Peter May, who undertook to fulfil the talk to the team about time-wasting that Hutton had agreed to do.

The selectors naturally relied as far as possible on the men who had won the Ashes, replacing Hutton with Don Kenyon and Cowdrey (called up for National Service and an RAF recruit) with Barrington. England beat South Africa at Trent Bridge by an innings, and two days later the following letter landed on Gubby's mat:

Dear Mr. Allen,

It is with a sad heart that I have to write this letter to you.

For some considerable time now when playing in England I have suffered from rheumatic pains. During the past three weeks I have been far worse than ever before.

On my return home from Australia I felt fit, and well, but after a few days cricket in this climate my pains returned.

I therefore feel, in the interest of cricket, that it would be the right thing for me to retire from International Cricket.

Unless my health improves I do not see how I can play another season in first class cricket, there are indeed times when I can hardly move without pain.

The Australians are here next year, and I feel some of our young players should be given the opportunity to gain experience.

I will make no statement to the press until I hear from you, or see that you have given the information to the public.

I have kept this matter very quiet, and will do so until I hear from you.

With kindest regards,
Yours sincerely,
Len.

Len's letter was more of a disappointment than a surprise. He had played a few Yorkshire matches without finding form and in obvious discomfort. The fact was, both physically and mentally, he had 'had enough'. The selectors could only express their deep regret, invite him to join them as a co-opted member for the remainder of the season, and appoint May – also for the remainder of the season – in his place.

So began the close and happy association between chairman and captain which, except for 1960 during which May was unfit, lasted until both retired from their respective jobs simultaneously after the summer of 1961. It is the longest chairman-captain partnership English cricket has known, and certainly one of the more successful.

Temperamentally the two were well suited. May was twenty-five when he was first appointed, old enough to be able to form his opinions from experience, and yet, as one new to the job, sensible enough to make use of the immense reserve of knowledge that was available at his elbow if and when he needed it. Gubby's reassuring comment at the outset was that 'If I possibly can I'll back you to the hilt on selection — but there *may* have to be exceptions.' There were a few, of course, but Peter says, 'We were generally able to talk a decision through to agreement without needing to go to the vote.'

The first side chosen by the new committee was, in batting order, Kenyon, Graveney, May, Compton, Barrington, Bailey, Evans, Wardle, Tyson, Appleyard and Statham. It differed unavoidably from that which finished the series in Australia, in that replacements had to be found not only for Hutton but for Cowdrey. The reserves for the various positions (which often took longer to decide on than the Test side) were Milton, Watson, Watkins, Andrew, Lock, Trueman and Titmus.

May had started with a comfortable win at Trent Bridge, but could not be given quite the same side for Lord's because Appleyard had been rated unfit. The replacement, chosen on a vote and in face of the chairman's opinion, was Titmus rather than Laker. Gubby's view, borne out by events, was that his protégé, still only twenty-two, was not yet ready. In fact after two Tests he had to wait seven whole years before playing again. The case of Barrington was likewise unfortunate for after being tried twice he was not called on again until 1959.

England won also at Lord's but only after a hard fight which might have gone the other way, by 71 runs. When South Africa needed 183 to win May bowled Brian Statham, most willing of horses, unchanged through the innings of three and three quarter hours. Seven for 39 he took in twenty-nine overs, firing away straight, tireless, getting movement off the ground and setting a thoroughly stiff examination. Gubby rates him as one of the greatest triers ever — and also, in the dressing-room, as one of the soundest and most consistent sleepers.

Roy McLean's 142 in the first innings was one of the most admirable exhibitions seen at Lord's for a long while, and South Africa were plainly capable of winning at least one Test if not more. In fact they won the next two, at Old Trafford and Headingley, and fully extended England in the decider.

The selectors, taking the summer through, had more than a fair share of worries. Graveney and Kenyon never quite looked the part as an opening partnership, May and Compton having to make most of the runs. Cowdrey, though unexpectedly released from the RAF because they were nervous — of all strange things — of having to provide compensation because of some malformation of his feet, could play in only one Test; Appleyard was bothered by injury; Statham, Tyson and Evans were also at times out of action.

A fast and lively Old Trafford pitch led to several injuries and a magnificent match, South Africa getting home by only three wickets and with three minutes to spare. Gubby recalls it, among other things, for an entertaining encounter with the great Sydney Barnes. He has not been greatly interested in the game as played before his own time, but he has much enjoyed the friendship of some of the famous players of the Golden Age who just preceded him or were in their last years when he was starting. J. T. Hearne, Joe Murrell and 'Young Jack' Hearne come to mind with other names, the two Bills, Reeves and Bestwick, Fielder and, of course, George Hirst.

One such was Barnes, whom he had first spotted bowling at Lord's, strangely enough, for Wales against MCC. (He was Staffordshire through and through, but as pro at Colwyn Bay had a loose qualification for Wales.) Gubby on his way from the nets one day years before saw this tall, spare fellow with a high arm and wonderfully fluid approach and delivery. The year was 1930, and so the greatest of all English bowlers, (in the estimation of most historians) was fifty-seven. 'That's a pretty good action,' said Gubby to the pro who had been bowling to him. 'So it should be, it's Sydney Barnes,' came the answer. Gubby never again saw him bowl, but in his years as a selector came to know 'Barney' when they met at Test Matches.

During the match at Old Trafford Gubby joined a few old Lancashire croneys. Young Fred Titmus was bowling and Alec Bedser, whose hands were usually as safe as most, dropped an easy catch at mid-on which would have given him his first wicket for England. Gubby said to old Syd, with malice aforethought: 'What would you have said to the fielder, Syd, if you had been the bowler?' The gist of the reply was that he'd have just said, 'Bad luck, old chap, we'll get him soon.' Whereat there was a gale of laughter, because all knew — and Barnes knew that they knew — he was apt to be a difficult colleague and was at all times the sternest of cricketers. Though he mellowed in old age, you could still see it in the set of his jaw. Woe betide the fielder who gave away a run, let alone spilt a catch when he was bowling, one felt. He continued to watch Test Matches with a critical, discerning eye, until a few years before his death at ninety-four.

For the Headingley Test the selectors had to announce five key men on the injured list, and South Africa scored a resounding victory. The selectors were so concerned about England's chances when it came to picking the team for the Oval Test that they considered asking the counties to rest those chosen for the three preceding days, but decided, no doubt rightly, that the counties would not comply, even though they were going to enjoy a good share-out from the series – it turned out to be £97,000. Laker was brought back on his home pitch to join Lock, May had the good luck to win the toss, rain came to end the drought, the ball turned, England had two high-class spinners to South Africa's one (Tayfield), and that was that. It was a hard-fought series and the only major one in England of five matches without a draw. The selectors finally sent to the Board of Control a number of recommendations for future Tests, interesting at this range of time only as evidence of how thoroughly they did the job.

Their conscientiousness extended to some concern about Lock's action. Though the crisis about illegal actions was several years away this was natural enough seeing he had been no-balled for throwing in one match in England in 1952 and one in Barbados two years later. Ames indeed had been one of the selectors who had chosen Lock for England against India in 1952 only a few weeks after he had become the first English bowler to be called for throwing in more than forty years. Accordingly, before Lock was brought in for the Third Test of 1955 Gubby and Les Ames decided to make a clandestine inspection of their own, from all angles and without anyone else's knowledge. The chairman therefore left the tell-tale Bentley in a Blackheath side-street, wore an unfamiliar hat, paid at the gate, and with Les prowled about incognito amid a crowd of 12,000 – making a thorough inspection. It was the annual battle at the Rectory Field against Kent, and Lock took five for 43 in eighteen overs. They thought that at times his action looked 'a little bit funny', but neither could see that his elbow was bent just prior to delivery. These being the days before photography was brought into use as evidence, Lock passed the examination – and, in fact, was not again called until 1959.

In the close season two things worthy of record happened to Gubby. He spent a week in hospital having a toe joint of his right foot removed – a legacy of his having stubbed it badly thirty years before. The operation occasioned several newspaper bulletins. More significantly for the game, he was appointed chairman of the MCC Cricket Sub-Committee which until the establishment of the TCCB twelve years later was the most important post of all. The press at this announcement coined the phrase, 'Mr Cricket', which has stuck ever since.

'Mr Cricket' was always 'newsworthy'. With the 1956 Australians on their way over, 'Emmwood' of the *Daily Mail* cartooned him wearing city clothes and a bowler hat, with bat and pads defending a wicket comprising a ticker-tape machine.

Cyril Washbrook having replaced Brian Sellers as compared with 1955, the selectors at their first meeting in April had a long discussion about possible opening batsmen. The chairman agreed to ask his county captain if he would try Willie Watson, the best Yorkshire bat at this time, as an opener. However Billy Sutcliffe did not see his way to comply, and in fact the selectors eventually fixed on a pair which saw them successfully through the series in Cowdrey and the left-handed Peter Richardson, the new young captain of Worcestershire. The selectors at the outset decided that 'more attention should be paid to discipline' – not that there had been any 'serious breaches'. They appointed May as captain for the First Test, and, after that had taken place, for the remaining four.

As the chairman had confidently predicted before the season began, England retained the Ashes and no doubt deserved to do so, though Australia's wholesale victory at Lord's was gained on the only pitch of the five unaffected by rain. England would in all probability have won the drawn Test at Trent Bridge and the Oval, and of course, they won by an innings on both the turning pitches of Headingley and Old Trafford. This, need it be said, was 'Laker's series', his bag of forty-six wickets being larger than anyone has achieved in the history of England v Australia. Yes, he took nineteen wickets in the unforgettable Old Trafford Test, but he got wickets in all the others, and it remains a strange fact – well beyond the scope of this book to examine – that though he took part in eleven Test rubbers in England this was the only one in which he played throughout.

England's batting in the Second Test emphasized the vast onus now on the shoulders of Peter May following Hutton's retirement and with Compton recovering from an operation. The meeting at the Bath Club on Sunday before the Headingley Test, with England one down, was accordingly extra-important. It proved to be momentous.

The appropriate minute reads:

> When it was agreed to omit Graveney and Watson and to include five batsmen instead of six, it was decided that one of the three must be a player with Test match experience. When it was appreciated that the choice lay between Washbrook and Simpson, Washbrook was asked to leave the room.

After a discussion prolonged by the captain's 'rather luke-warm' reaction to the prospect of his return, Washbrook was chosen, to Gubby's great satisfaction, with Simpson held in reserve. It is easy to understand May's reservations, likewise those of some of the critics. Washbrook had not played Test cricket since Australia in 1950–51 when he averaged 17 over the series. He was forty-one (though still a high-class cover-point). His dignified reaction, so typical of the man, was to say that 'One does not decline to play for England. One will do one's best, but it will not be easy.'

As every cricket historian knows, Washbrook walked out at Headingley to join his captain on that first morning with the score showing 17
for three, his chest pressed forward 'like a pouter-pigeon'. Together they
made 187, May being out for 101 just before close of play. Washbrook
was not out 90, and when Gubby went to the dressing-room to con
gratulate them May, oblivious to his own achievement, said, 'Wasn't
Cyril magnificent? Thank God I listened to you on Sunday.' Gubby
recorded this 'typically modest and generous comment in a moment of
triumph' as 'a wonderful finish to a day I shall not easily forget' in the
article which he contributed to the 1962 *Wisden* after his retirement from
the chairmanship.

It was entitled 'My Seven Year "Stretch"', and, incidentally, like his
other two articles in the *Wisdens* of 1938 and 1981, it refutes the
author's own poor estimation of his writing. It maintains that Washbrook's selection was entirely logical. He wrote:

> I have often been asked whether selection committees are some-
> times guided by intuition. I think the answer is that an occasional
> choice looks strange because all the facts have not been known or
> the motive behind it has not been fully understood.

He then cited the circumstances surrounding Washbrook's case. Cyril
was out next day two short of his hundred, but the job had been done,
since the pitch was responding generously to spin on the second evening.
Thereafter Australia, with 81 for six on the board before the close, could
only pray for rain, rain, rain. It came all right but not enough to save
them.

The Headingley pitch certainly had not the lasting properties that all
concerned had a right to expect, but what the Australians thought about
it was mild compared with their feelings at Old Trafford. I must now
tread carefully over ground as delicate as the pitch for the Fourth Test
which turned out to be unexpectedly and reprehensibly brittle.

When the selectors met on the Sunday preceding the Fourth Test they
considered first, as usual, the best evidence available as to what sort of
pitch to expect. They had it this time at first hand from Washbrook, who
had seen it on the preceding Tuesday and reported, according to the
minutes, that in his opinion it would, 'barring further rain be a good one
and very similar to the Test Match wicket in 1955' – which had yielded
more than 1300 runs and a splendid match.

The selectors had other news before they got down to the selection,
this from the chairman who happened to see David Sheppard, now a
London curate, at the University Match. When David told him he was
going to take his annual holiday playing cricket Gubby suggested he

might advance his plans by a few days in case he should run quickly into form and England stand in need of him. In fact he had batted twice with success by the time of the selection meeting, Gubby having seen one of the two innings. The only other form to go on was a 97 against the Australians in the relaxed atmosphere of a pre-season match at Arundel. These credentials were enough to decide the selectors to pick 'the Rev' – the first parson to play, as such, in Test cricket – in preference to Insole. Graveney also got the vote over Oakman, capped at Headingley for the first time.

In view of Washbrook's report the selectors thought it unsafe to pick only four bowlers, as at Headingley, and so named five in their twelve names. You never know till you get there, the chairman thought. How right he was! At the last minute Graveney cried off unfit and the hunt was on to find Oakman. Someone said 'try the police', who replied that if he was in his native Hastings they'd find him in ten minutes – and did!

A vast surprise awaited the chairman and Washbrook when they went to look at the pitch on the afternoon before the game. The latter says that he was astounded by its appearance compared with when he had last seen it eight days before. It wore a pinkish tinge, and Gubby, rubbing his finger on the surface in the traditional fashion, found that it was not firm. The only explanation was that Bert Flack, the groundsman, had applied a dressing after Washbrook had seen it, and that, for some mysterious reason, had been prevented from 'washing it in'. Thus it had been allowed to 'cake' on the top.

Was there, at some point, direction from the Lancashire Committee? Flack was a capable groundsman, and if he had dressed the pitch at so late a stage would surely have watered sufficiently to allow the dressing to sink in. When the two selectors were looking at the pitch they were approached by a member of the Lancashire Committee who asked Gubby if he would like a further mowing. To this his reply was: 'It wouldn't break my heart, but I must remind you that responsibility for the preparation of the pitch before the match starts is in the hands of the ground authority.' This, of course, is the case according to what was then and still is No 7 of the laws of cricket.

Gubby readily admits today that he was unwise to make the remark he did, but firmly maintains that by that stage it would have made no difference whether there had been a mowing or not. He believes that the condition of the pitch at Old Trafford was the result of an honest mistake, deriving maybe from a not-very-knowledgeable member of the Ground Committee who may have prevented watering in the belief that it would decrease its pace.

I wish I were so sure. I am inclined to believe that there were some in authority, certainly at Headingley and probably at Old Trafford, who misguidedly aimed to provide pitches that would be helpful to spin, though no doubt they would not have hoped to see the dust rising and the ball turning extravagantly by the second day, as happened in both cases before rain came to give a different sort of aid to the bowling side. To this extent the Australians had every cause to think they had been hard done by. The press in both countries strongly condemned both pitches.

However in their attempts to find scapegoats some Australian cricket-writers alleged that the pitches had been prepared either at the behest of 'Lord's' or of the chairman and his fellow selectors. In these suggestions I am satisfied there is neither evidence nor truth. Naturally enough Gubby deeply resented the slur on his reputation, not least since the story was widely circulated in Australia.

Peter May, who took the next MCC side to Australia two years later, cannot recall Gubby's name being associated with the drama of the two pitches but he adds, significantly enough:

> I always felt that the Australians took no action regarding the complaints Freddie Brown and I made against their chuckers because they thought they had been 'done' by us over the pitches at Headingley and Old Trafford.

To an extent the furore about the pitch obscured the merit of the admirable hundred made on the first day by Sheppard, and the subsequent phenomenal achievement of Jim Laker who exposed the Australians' extreme fallibility to off-spin by taking nineteen of their twenty wickets in sixty-eight overs for 90 runs. He bowled marvellously well, of course, and the close fielders held every catch that they could get a finger to.

When the selectors met to pick the team for the last Test the Ashes were safe but at 2−1 the rubber was still undecided. They now made the third of their successful gambits, reinforcing the batting further by bringing back Denis Compton, still only thirty-eight but as a result of his latest operation lacking a knee-cap. He had been fit for only eight Middlesex matches, but the selectors for the third time backed class and character, and for the third time the recipe worked. After May had won his fourth toss out of five Compton joined him at the cross-roads of the innings, 66 for three. This time the partnership of youth and maturity was worth 156, before Denis's last Test innings in England ended with 94. The pitch, it should be added, started true and easy-paced, but rain later made it difficult and in the end Australia were grateful enough to snatch a draw.

The 1956–57 winter was marked by the tragic adventure of Suez. During the preliminary weeks of uncertainty it was additionally tantalizing for Gubby that he had as brother-in-law an Air Chief Marshal (as he was then) who was Chairman of the Chiefs of Staff Committee. 'Dickie' Dickson knew all, could say nowt. On 22 October Gubby remarked, 'Don't say we're going to have another war?' Dickson looked at his watch which showed 5.59. He said, 'The bombers are going in in one minute.'

Gubby was closely involved during the winter in a special enquiry into the welfare of county cricket. A strong Committee under Harry Altham, formed, as all such bodies always have been, with the object of reinvigorating first-class cricket, struck one blow for sanity by proposing that leg-side fielders be reduced to five with only two behind the wicket. Everyone round the world approved of that. There were other more debatable measures designed to encourage batsmen to attack. The Chairman of Selectors marked the occasion with a devastating pronouncement, saying:

> I believe that batting is at its lowest standard of all time. Batsmen have the ability but lack the will to attack. That makes it difficult to assess the strength of the bowling.

The Advisory County Committee, who had first been urged to stage a Knock-Out Competition by the comparable enquiry of 1944, now again 'referred back' a similar scheme – which, need it be added, was finally adopted in 1963. The mills of cricket have usually ground slowly! This was the meeting at which special powers were given to umpires to prevent time-wasting. In the intervening twenty-eight years the ultimate penalty of ordering that the offending bowler be taken off has never once been applied!

The new selectors met in anticipation of the 1957 series against the West Indies – Tom Dollery for Ames was the only change – in the wake of one of the slowest and dullest series ever played. (England in South Africa had averaged 32 runs an hour, South Africa 29!) Their first decision was not to use Bailey as an opening bat with Richardson, as had happened through the rubber in South Africa. They tried (but in vain) to recruit Sheppard for the First Test as Richardson's partner, and decided to watch Close, D. V. Smith of Sussex – both of whom played in the series – Tom Clark of Surrey and Alan Wharton of Lancashire.

No doubt as a mark of their continuing confidence – the extraordinary fact was he had averaged only 15 against South Africa – they forthwith named May as captain for all five Tests. Dollery reported that the Edgbaston pitch would be easy and would last – a prediction that was amply justified by events. This was the astonishing match wherein England began their second innings 288 runs behind, and, thanks to May and Cowdrey, came close to winning. Their partnership of 411 (still the highest ever for England) came after England had been thoroughly outplayed and the chairman correspondingly depressed.

He was slightly cheered by his captain coming in, 20 not out, at the end of the third day saying, 'Chairman, I've rumbled him' — him being the wily Ramadhin who with seven for 49 in the first innings had tied England in knots. What May and Cowdrey had decided was not that they had detected from the action which way he was aiming to turn the ball but simply to play him as off-spinner. To the good length ball they went full forward, bat and pad together. Ramadhin bowled and bowled and bowled, ninety-eight overs in all, the most ever in an innings by anyone. He was met by unwavering concentration. May made 285, Cowdrey 154, and little 'Ram' was never the same bowler afterwards.

Nor were the West Indies, after this extraordinary turning of the tables, half the side they should have been considering the talent at John Goddard's command. Of the remaining four Tests England won three by an innings, and in the fourth declared at 619 for six. In the Second Test at Lord's, on a fast pitch too uncertain to be deemed satisfactory, England had much the stronger attack for the conditions and actually won inside three days, as they subsequently did at Headingley and the Oval. What strange reading this makes today!

While the West Indies never 'gelled', England for the one and only time against them since the war dominated match after match. The selectors went conscientiously through the motions, modifying their attack to the likely behaviour of the pitch, and, for a change, finding that their chosen batsmen were more than good enough to master what on paper looked an adequate bowling side. They went through the series, ringing the changes around Statham, Trueman, Loader, Bailey, Laker and Lock, scarcely needing to call upon two such well-proven Test bowlers as Tyson and Wardle.

There was little opportunity for experiment, though the Cambridge undergraduate, Dexter, was called up at Headingley as a replacement and would probably have played if he had been fit. When they still found themselves looking for an opening bat in the last two Tests they opted for the short-term expedient of bringing back Sheppard, who duly obliged.

As usual during Gubby's time in the chair the selectors kept a strict eye open for behaviour. Thus after the Headingley Test it was agreed that the chairman should give one member of the side 'advice rather than a rebuke'. Though his manners on the field had improved, 'his mistakes were generally made when he was "showing-off"'. The minutes of the Selection Committee recording this item was at the time, of course, confidential to its members and to the Board of Control. There was no question of such a matter being given to the press. The fact of its being recorded, however, by a body of selectors two of whom were former amateurs and two professionals, indicates how equally concerned were they all to maintain standards, for the benefit of the millions now viewing on television as well as spectators on the spot.

Talking of the now long-abandoned distinction, it must be noted that the report of the strong committee examining amateur status, chaired by the just retired president of the MCC, Lord Monckton, and of which Gubby was a member, was published during the close season. It came down strongly in favour of a retention of the distinction though acknowledging current economic necessities. It approved some 'broken time' payment – in other words compensation for lost earnings – in the case of amateurs touring overseas, who hitherto had always ended up out of pocket. Gubby was fully in accord with this decision, and had indeed in a reported after-dinner speech advocated broken-time payments for amateurs several years earlier.

During the 1957–58 winter Gubby chaired the twenty-first anniversary dinner of the XL Club, of which he had been made president the previous year. Sir Pelham Warner and Sir Jack Hobbs, his predecessors in office, had not been expected to be more than titular figures. However Henry Grierson, the founder, who had had the original idea behind the Club's formation (in 1936) of bringing amateurs and professionals together on the field and off, was now, in his later sixties, looking for a more active personality at the top, and Gubby brought his characteristic zest to the job, attending all the meetings and seeing a great expansion during his nine years in office. With its 3500 members the XL Club of today owes much to his leadership as its president.

MCC were due in Australia in the autumn of 1958, and England ideally needed a searching series to give the selectors the chance to separate the wheat from the chaff. Unfortunately New Zealand, who had stretched England to the full nine years earlier, could not do so this time. One of the wettest summers on record gave England a vast advantage over an inexperienced side – and Lock thirty-four wickets, Laker seventeen, each at negligible cost. England easily won the first four Tests, three of them by an innings. The selectors met in late July during the Old Trafford Test, and announced a team for Australia which was acclaimed at the time by some – on what evidence it is hard to fathom – as the stongest ever to be sent.

Considering what Gubby had said about the batting standard not long before, it goes without saying that he did not hold with any such view. His disappointment at the choice was confined to regret that no place had been found for the twenty-three-year-old Dexter. I not only shared this regret but thought that the tour selectors were palpably at fault in not having delayed their final decision until Dexter, playing in his first Test and therefore clearly on trial for a place, had gone to the wicket. Rain had so delayed the match that by the time he joined his captain on the Monday morning and made 52 on an awkward pitch while May ran to yet another Test hundred the touring party had been published.

Within a few days of the announcement came drama wholly unexpected which put the selectors in a rare dilemma. Having told MCC on their enquiry that Wardle would be available for the tour, and he having been chosen, Yorkshire announced that they were dispensing with his services. Thereupon Wardle gave his name to some scurrilous writing critical both of the county club and its captain, Ronny Burnet. Yorkshire promptly decided he had broken his contract, and was no longer a Yorkshire player, whereupon MCC, having been put in an impossible position, determined that in the interests of cricket they must withdraw their invitation. Gubby concurred with this, but also went along with May's outspoken comment that if he could not have Wardle he did not want a third spinner at all. It would all be left to Laker and Lock. Apart from the risk of injury, since both would need sometimes to be rested, May would necessarily be left with only one slow bowler – a self-imposed disability which none of his predecessors in Australia had had to contend with. This was surely a wrong decision for which a share of the responsibility rested with the chairman. During the tour both Dexter and John Mortimore, the Gloucestershire off-spinner, were called for, the latter's departure bringing forth the well-known crack in a London club:

'I hear they've sent for Mortimore.'

'What – forty more?'

Gubby opposed in vain the request in mid-tour for Dexter who was working at the time in Paris – this was no way, he thought, to blood a young cricketer of high potential.

After the heavy defeats of 1958–59 in Australia the new selectors recognized that, with an MCC tour of the West Indies coming up in the following winter, some team reconstruction was called for in the summer of 1959. Sutcliffe (aged sixty-four) has been brought on to join Wooller of Glamorgan. Les Ames was not available, having taken on the managership of Kent, and Gubby missed both his wisdom and his companionship.

The first selection meeting stressed an old story – the need of 'a more aggressive and enthusiastic approach', including an increase in the over-rate. They agreed on a list of seventeen batsmen, ten bowlers, and four wicket-keepers, scarcely any of whom were yet England cricketers, to be watched, over and above the eighteen who had toured Australia.

When it came to naming the side for the First Test against India they chose five fresh men in Ken Taylor, Barrington, M. J. Horton, Moss and Greenhough. The minutes spelt out the selectors' feelings for the benefit of the Board of Control with unusual emphasis:

Before formally inviting Mr P. B. H. May to be captain, the chairman informed him of the committee's determination to instil into the team, through the captain, a more aggressive approach to the game. Particular reference was made to the number of overs bowled per hour, fielding, and the tempo generally. In the light of Mr May's undertaking to do his best to achieve improvement in these departments of the game, he was invited to captain England for the whole series.

It was, however, agreed to record in the minutes that, in the opinion of the present selection committee, whilst it was on occasions desirable to appoint a captain for the whole series, it was contrary to custom.

They also tackled the question of whether to consider for selection the West Indian, Roy Marshall of Hampshire, who on the face of it had good claims to be chosen as an opening bat:

It was unanimously agreed not to invite R. E. Marshall to play for England. It was felt that it was undesirable to invite a cricketer to play for England who had been born abroad and had learned all his cricket in, and had played for, the country of his birth before coming to England.

Unhappily India were almost less successful in stretching England at home than New Zealand had been. For the one and only time all five Tests were won, the closest margin being 171 runs! Performance was accordingly difficult to evaluate. Nevertheless these batsmen established themselves who were to do excellent service for England – Ken Barrington, M. J. K. Smith and Geoff Pullar.

At the end of the season these three with Ray Illingworth, Jim Parks and David Allen found themselves sailing to the West Indies for their first tour. Of the older hands who had gone to Australia Bailey, Laker, Tyson and Watson were not again chosen for England while after the first two Tests a press statement said that, 'Evans has been omitted from the team so that another wicket-keeper may be tried in the interests of team building.' For Godfrey it was the top or nothing. At the end of the summer he retired, as also did Jim Laker whose over-sized arthritic finger had been impeding him for some years.

What was a much greater handicap to the selectors than anything was that after the Third Test the captain dropped out for an internal illness which required an operation. Though May was considered fit enough to take the side to the West Indies he played there, at first unknown to all, under considerable handicap, and in mid-tour had to be flown home, where a renewal of his illness cost him the whole of the summer of 1960.

Though he resumed the England captaincy for the last three Tests of 1961 he was not quite the great batsman of his prime. The chairman-captain alliance of Allen and May had meanwhile been succeeded by the thoroughly friendly but less intimate association of Allen and Cowdrey.

From now on Colin Cowdrey saw fully enough of Gubby as chairman to retain a clear impression of his methods. For Sunday meetings in the provinces Colin would drive up from Kent to Gubby's flat in Queen's Gate for a seven a.m. breakfast cooked by his host, who always remembered that Colin preferred to start with grapefruit, Peter with orange juice (or vice-versa). This close attention to detail characterized the entire proceedings. Colin was struck by the 'complete dedication. Nothing deflected him. The chairman had done his home-work on all the possibles, with reports on their fitness where that might be in doubt. He was totally engrossed.' When men had to be dropped, such was the climate of benevolence inspired by the chairman that there were no hard feelings. He did not over-press his own opinions, and there was not the slightest suggestion of favouritism. The evidence was all that counted.

In Gubby's time Cowdrey only led when May was out of action or – in the case of Lord's in 1961 – after the latter was just returning to the fray. Whereas neither was a leader of the dashing cavalier type, Cowdrey generally seemed the more defensively-minded of the two. What perhaps we critics may not have sufficiently appreciated is that whereas (until Australia in 1958–59) May, of Surrey, scarcely knew what it was to play on or lead a losing side, Cowdrey, of Oxford and Kent, other than when playing for England, had practically no experience, until the mid-1960s, with a winning one.

The English summer of 1960 was the fourth in succession wherein England won a rubber hands down. South Africa were the visitors in a season made unhappy by the no-balling of G. Griffin for throwing. Gubby had wanted a year's rest from selection, but had been persuaded otherwise. He must have been sorry before the end that he had not stood firm.

After the last MCC Australian tour throwing was the issue of the moment, due to be debated in July at what was still called the Imperial Cricket Conference, and of which South Africa was still a member. In his capacity as chairman of the MCC Cricket Sub-Committee Gubby was very much on the war-path against illegal actions, and if ever there was a blatant case it was that of Griffin, who had twice been no-balled in South Africa. In the MCC-South Africans match at Lord's in May Gubby and Wilf Wooller went around Lord's looking at him from every angle. As a result of this Gubby arranged with Leslie Deakins, the secretary of Warwickshire, that Griffin, and also all the other fast bowlers engaged in the First Test, should be secretly filmed – and he himself paid the cameraman's fee of £22 since MCC had declined to authorize the matter!

By the time of the Lord's Test Gubby had his evidence which amply supported the six umpires who, between them, had already no-balled Griffin seventeen times in three matches. At Lord's he was no-balled eleven times, whereupon it was announced he would not bowl again on the tour – a thoroughly unhappy business for all concerned. Gubby, though it was distasteful to do so, invited Geoff Chubb, president of the South African Cricket Association, and the manager, Dudley Nourse, to see the film but they declined.

Gubby presented his film to Lord's, where it now reposes with a number of subsequent shots of suspect actions in what he calls 'The Rogues' Gallery'. Incidentally, Gubby rates Griffin as second to Meckiff as the most blatant offender. It is a nice point which of them deserves the dubious distinction.

It is one of the stranger features of sport that it is so often the offender who attracts the sympathy. This was the case with Griffin among followers in both countries. Even the solid *Rand Daily Mail* printed the headline 'It's victory for persecutor Gubby Allen'. But then knowledge of the finer points of cricket (unlike rugby football) has always been rather limited among South Africans.

By mid-July England, with victories in the first three Tests, had the rubber well and truly won, and the chairman could devote himself to the throwing dispute which was due to make this the most momentous of all ICC meetings before the intervention in cricket affairs of Kerry Packer. (I write subsequently of Gubby's part in the throwing issue.)

Australia came to England in 1961 as holders of the Ashes and also surrounded more immediately with the glamour attaching equally to both sides from surely the best of all Test series against the West Indies in Australia the previous winter. As a captain Richie Benaud was at the pinnacle of his career. Since England had emerged narrowly successful from the MCC tour of the West Indies in 1959–60 there were all the makings of a memorable Test series.

The selectors' first pre-season response to the challenge was to make up their lists of twenty probables and eighteen possibles to be watched, from whom fourteen of the sixteen were subsequently chosen for the Tests. (The other two were those doughty Midland bowlers, Flavell and Jackson.) They had an initial set-back when May asked not to be considered for the First Test. After his long absence he had started the season well but was then put out of action by a groin strain. This meant the prospect of a divided captaincy, with Cowdrey's leadership continuing at least for a while.

The selectors chose a well-seasoned side for the First Test wherein J. T. Murray behind the wicket was the only new cap. After Australia had had all the best of it, hundreds by Dexter (180) and Subba Row (112) saved the match.

The Australians having purged their ranks of throwers following the ICC meeting, the choice of Lock for the Lord's Test was accompanied by the following minute:

> It was agreed that the Chairman should speak to Lock on the eve of the match and obtain from him an assurance that he would not bowl his 'away swinger' or 'chinaman' as both were regarded as 'suspect' and, in the circumstances, no possible causes for concern can be given.

Lock in fact played in three of the Tests and took only three wickets for 250 runs!

May was pronounced fit only at the last minute for the Lord's Test, Cowdrey retaining the captaincy. Despite Cowdrey winning his ninth Test toss in succession England's batting failed them twice on a pitch allegedly marred by what was known as the Lord's ridge. At all events it was friendly to fast bowling, Australia winning by five wickets. The selectors thereupon transferred the captaincy to May 'by three votes to one' – almost the only vote recorded in the minutes during Gubby's seven years as chairman.

This was the year of the 'piebald' pitch at Headingley, a strange dull green and white strip in an emerald field. Fred Trueman, who cut down his run and took eleven for 88, had a field-day, and as in 1956 the Australians were not pleased. They had better luck, though, this time at Old Trafford where the fate of the Ashes was decided. The pitch was reported as likely to be a good one with pace, and this time prediction proved correct.

This in the end was a malign match for England, though for the first four days and a bit longer they had all the better of it. Cowdrey went down with 'flu on the first morning of the match – which meant the substitution of Close and the weakening of England's already suspect batting. Gubby will still shake his head over that final day which began with Australia, batting third and with the score 331 for six, only 154 runs on. Three of the last four wickets promptly fell to David Allen, who was turning the ball by now, for the addition of 3 runs, so that only Davidson and McKenzie stood between England and almost certain victory. 'In our long association,' says the chairman of selectors, 'this was Peter's only black day. On that last morning he never seemed to try to give Davidson a single to get McKenzie to Allen's end. He took off Allen, his match-winner, after he had been punished for only a single over.' Suddenly England lost control, and the last wicket added 98, Davidson taking out his bat for

77 while the twenty-year-old McKenzie scored a priceless 32.

Though England's job was now a daunting one Dexter batted so brilliantly in the afternoon that England saw their lost chance coming swiftly back to view. When captain and chairman had talked the matter over soon after lunch May had either agreed with or himself made the suggestion that at the fall of the second wicket he should change places in the order with Close in the hope of the latter's unorthodox aggression coming off and leaving May then to dictate the tactics at No 5 – or even at No 6 – in the light of the circumstances.

With Subba Row and Dexter together and going well, Gubby in mid-afternoon began the long drive to London, listening, of course, as he went. Thus he heard of Dexter's fall at last (for 76, made in eighty-four minutes), of May's entry at No 4 as usual and his departure first ball, and of Close's feverish, cross-batted contribution, foredoomed to failure, and finally the end of Subba Row's anchor part. England, having scored 150 before the second wicket fell, now took tea at 163 for five, with 93 needed in eighty-five minutes and only Barrington and the tail to do either one job or the other, to win if all went well and otherwise to deny Australia victory and the retention of the Ashes. Bowling his leg-breaks round the wicket Benaud had taken all four wickets.

Now if not before Gubby must surely have wished that he was back at Old Trafford, at the captain's call if needed. From the proceedings after tea England's policy could not be deduced. Barrington and Murray went quickly and from this point England never looked like saving the game. They were beaten by 54 runs – or twenty minutes, according to taste.

The series at least could have been saved, of course, at the Oval, but in fact England were always on the defensive after a poor start: Australia looked the better side. In his last letter of thanks to his fellow selectors for their services Gubby said:

> We seem to lack a spirit of aggression: consequently we sometimes fail to seize our opportunities and, when something goes wrong, we get bogged down or ragged.

It was much the same point he had made about English Test cricket back in the spring of 1955 and had reiterated regularly ever since.

17

Gubby in Committee

I near the end of this review of Gubby's life in cricket by noting the part he has played and the influence he has exercised off the field. The greater part of this activity followed his retirement as chairman of Test selectors in 1961 and his elevation first to the presidency of MCC in 1963–64 and to the treasurership directly following. As we have seen he had however been a substantial figure in the councils of cricket for quarter of a century before that, beginning in times when young cricketers, however distinguished, were not always encouraged to air their views.

Soon after Gubby's election to the MCC Committee in 1935 a particular matter came up on which he proceeded to express his opinion. The scene was the cosy atmosphere of the Junior Carlton Club where the Committee's winter business was in those days conducted – and generally concluded conveniently around tea-time. As the young recruit warmed to his argument he was slightly put off by the chairman, Lord Hawke, slowly shaking his head – and still more disconcerted when he heard him saying, 'No, no, Gubby, we can't do that.' As he finished Hawke asked his neighbour in a stage whisper: 'What was he saying, Jacker? I couldn't quite hear.' At this Gubby might well have thought, if he did not say, as Disraeli did in his maiden speech: 'Though I sit down now the time will come when you will hear me.' And indeed they have!

His first major crusade came after returning to London from a round of golf and stopping to watch a game of cricket on Putney Common. The standard depressed him, and he therefore put the need for coaching, and especially the encouragement of the young, squarely to the MCC Committee. The inevitable upshot was the appointment of an MCC Cricket Enquiry. This enquiry however, under the chairmanship of Harry Altham, bore more ample fruit than most. Less than two years later what became the MCC Youth Cricket Association was called into being, the counties were bidden to Lord's and urged to form Area Councils and a central coaching committee was formed under a director of coaching. Soon afterward MCC made a first capital grant of £15,000, and in 1951 MCC staged the first national Coaching Conference at Lilleshall.

Without going into further detail one need only add that the strong lead from the top was what got the National Coaching Scheme which was the outcome of Lilleshall so smoothly under way. The opening paragraph of the handbook produced last year by the NCA pays due tribute:

> Surprisingly, one might think that whilst cricket has been played in its various forms for some four hundred years, a National Coaching Scheme only came into being in 1952 – and only then through the combined purpose and love for the game of two great men of cricket – the late Mr H. S. (Harry) Altham and Mr G. O. (Gubby) Allen. It is right that a tribute should be paid to them in any discourse on the history of cricket coaching, as when the time comes to look back, their foresight, knowledge, eloquence and enthusiasm will be recognised as the flames that lit the torch and made possible the standard of cricket coaching we know today. Of course, there were others, not least being Mr H. P. (Harry) Crabtree, who originally developed the techniques of Group Coaching and was, in fact, the first practical leader of the National Coaching Scheme.

It was on a visit to Scotland connected with his committee work that Gubby learned that he was due to meet a redoubtable Scottish lady golf champion of times past, Miss Elsie Grant-Suttie. As a boy on holiday in the Isle of Wight, he had won a juvenile one-club competition – by five strokes. When he went up to collect his prize from Miss Grant-Suttie she asked him whence he got his handicap. Resenting what he took as a personal reflection, the awful boy said, to his father's anger and embarrassment, 'I'm not interested in your prize,' and walked away.

Now at North Berwick many years later he recalled the occasion to her and made a gracious apology. The old lady had remembered right enough. She said, 'Don't tell me it was you! I've always regretted I asked when I did.'

By 1956 Gubby was chairman of the Cricket Committee of MCC, which was always considering changes which might improve the game. During that year they were thinking about a slightly smaller ball, with a slightly more prominent seam, in order to help the bowler. With a new ball to this specification Ray Lindwall, on what proved his last tour, bowled in an empty Lord's net, nominating to Gubby what he was about to bowl next – the out-swinger, the in-swinger, the yorker, the straight one. Gubby was fascinated by Lindwall's precision and ability to deliver the goods time after time. The verdict of this great Australian (thirty-four at the time and destined to play his last Test at the age of thirty-eight) was enthusiastic: 'It would mean another four years' bowling for me.' The size idea was not pursued, though the seam nowadays protrudes far more than it used to.

The heavy defeat of England in Australia in 1958–59 led, as was always the case, to much post-mortemizing, much of it centring on the Throwing problem. That trenchant columnist, J. L. Manning however secured an interview with Gubby on a wider brief. Was MCC too much of a dictatorship, he wanted to know – and got a forthright reply:

What are cricket's needs, I asked. Leadership? Showmanship? Dictatorship? Sportsmanship? It was a glibly put question. Allen measured his run.

'Let's deal with dictatorship. We are often accused of it at Lord's. We are also accused of being Victorian and Colonel Blimpish. These cheap phrases are thrown at us unceasingly.

'But MCC can hardly be a dictatorship if, as is the case, cricket is run by the Advisory County Cricket Committee, who advise on all matters concerning county cricket, and by the Board of Control who have absolute power over Test Matches in this country.

'Next, just look at this list of men who are on MCC's Cricket Sub-Committee! They make recommendations to the main committee on all aspects of the game.

'Eight England Test captains and five active county captains are on the list. There are also Trevor Bailey, David Sheppard, and with men like them, Peter May and Colin Cowdrey, how can it be said that this is a die-hard committee out of touch with modern cricket? It is ridiculous.

'Far from being reactionaries I sometimes find them a bit "bolshy", but their loyalty is unquestioned.'

Could it be that because there is NO dictatorship by MCC cricket faces some of its greatest problems?

'If MCC had been able to give orders to the counties about the type of pitches they wanted, there would not now be so many slow turning wickets on which it is difficult to play strokes freely and so entertain spectators.

'With a little bit of dictatorship I also think we could have speeded up the game. Some bowlers take far too long over their business. I have examined the figures from every angle. The drop in the rate at which overs are bowled is alarming. Compared with pre-war the public is being denied forty-five minutes to an hour's cricket in EVERY DAY'S PLAY. It is one of the things which really irritate spectators.'

Gubby went on to advocate county championship cricket at weekends, including Sundays, except in the holiday season. This would allow a programme of twenty-six matches. One of the advantages would be to make it possible for more amateurs to play.

Manning's article was objective enough, and on the whole Gubby's relationship with the press continued to be generally harmonious. He was always accessible and friendly, and had learned the technique of dropping the occasional deliberate leak. He recognized, too, the inevitability of the odd side-swipe from the popular papers. An article by E. M. Wellings in the *Evening News* calling for his removal from the Selection Committee and entitled 'Allen in Blunderland' was an example.

Poor Lyn Wellings, who thought that 'Allen must go for the good of cricket,' was apt to be unlucky in his criticism. In castigating the selectors on their team for the West Indies the following winter under the title 'Dexter – Darling of the Selectors', he remarked that Dexter had been given enough rope to hang himself nine times over. Unfortunately 'the worst choice' finished the series against Wes Hall and co. away at the top of the Test averages with 65. The selectors, who had announced they were sticking to a policy of backing class and aggressive approach, could afford to smile.

In his capacities as chairman of the MCC Cricket Sub-Committee and as the senior MCC representative on the ICC Gubby was the central figure in the throwing problem which burst into the open on the 1958–59 tour when the English press reflected in colourful language the resentment of Peter May's team regarding the actions of several Australian bowlers, and of Ian Meckiff in particular. (I cannot even now recall without indignation his bowling in the New Year Test at Melbourne wherein in front of a crowd of 63,000 England were 'bowled' out for 87 on a plumb wicket, Meckiff taking six for 38.)

The fact that subsequent developments were enacted in the shadow of England's loss of the Ashes by a margin of 4–0, with the inevitable suggestion of 'sour grapes', was a misfortune rather than anyone's fault. For the facts, duly minuted, were that MCC had been much concerned about the legality of several English actions more than a year prior to the tour of Australia, and before the start of the 1958 season Gubby had addressed the first-class umpires, expressing the club's concern and that of the county captains at the current situation. He assured the umpires of the fullest support. Nevertheless the summer of 1958 went by without anyone being called, and on 7 October, before May's team had arrived in Australia, according to the relevant minutes, he 'expressed his surprise and disappointment that no action had been taken'.

During the 1958–59 winter the umpires were invited to prepare a list of suspect bowlers. This was circulated to the counties, and in the 1959 season three men were called, followed by five Englishmen in 1960, apart from Griffin of South Africa. At the 1959 ICC meeting, after a debate on the throwing law, MCC undertook to circularize all member countries with the steps they had taken over the last eighteen months in respect of its observance. The show-down came at the next ICC meeting, the historic one of 1960.

In the meanwhile the value of the camera as evidence in the case of suspect actions was being increasingly realized in England – and also, as it turned out, in Australia. Unknown to them, certain bowlers were filmed in action, before, during and after delivery, and the pictures were taken from different angles.

Before the 1960 ICC meeting, which was attended, on behalf of Australia, by Sir Donald Bradman and the president of their Board, W. J. Dowling, Hubert Ashton and Gubby on behalf of MCC had a preliminary discussion. The Don could be as tenacious in argument as he was in his occupation of the crease. In other words he and his old friend and adversary were a fair match. They had agreed to discuss throwing in principle, rather than talking about individuals. After a while to Gubby's surprise – and also, he's pretty sure, to Bradman's – Bill Dowling produced two photographs of Meckiff, one before delivery and one after. In both the left arm at shoulder height was perfectly straight. But the sharp-eyed Allen noticed a piece of paper on the turf in the first print, and that it was also there, though in a slightly different position, in the second. He therefore concluded that these were 'stills', taken from a film strip, and said, 'Ah, but I'd like to see Meckiff's position immediately prior to delivery,' indicating by himself posing with a bent elbow what he expected it to be.

Gubby believes that as a result of this discussion Don Bradman, if not Dowling, also realized that the situation had to be cleared up. At the ICC meeting all countries agreed to do all in their power to free the game of chuckers. Australia, and Bradman in particular, were as good as their word. The side they sent to England in 1961 contained no one whose action was suspect.

The year 1962 was a mixed one. It began pleasingly enough with the award of the CBE in the New Year honours 'for services to cricket'. Learie Constantine (subsequently a life peer) in the same list was awarded a knighthood – in his case the service was for community relations in addition to cricket. Richie Benaud, Australia's captain, received the OBE.

In the spring he had an unusual and expensive car crash on Constitution Hill just after rounding Hyde Park Corner. He lost consciousness, grazing first a tree and then a passing taxi before being brought to a halt by a lamp-post. Happily he was scarcely hurt although the Bentley was a write-off. Low blood pressure (which has never recurred) was diagnosed, and he did not drive for three months. When he had been to the doctor some while before he had said, 'I think you're a bit of a hypo.' Gubby couldn't take that lying down – or did he?

Then in September came the shock of his mother's death. She died quietly and painlessly in her flat after a heart-attack, at the ripe age of eighty-nine. On Lady Allen's death Gubby inherited £18,000, the third and last and much the largest legacy of his life, following the £1000 from Oswald Watt and £3000 from Uncle Reggie, the Test cricketer. Although his years of post-war stockbroking had by this time brought Gubby financial security the legacy was by no means amiss – for it was not until around 1966–67 that his Australian Western Mining shares 'took off' and his early purchase of them then assured his financial future.

He was by now accepted as an authority in the City on Australian securities, and likewise a well-known and unmistakable personality. He played cricket and golf for the Stock Exchange, and was much in demand at slack periods in the market for reminiscence and current comment on sporting affairs. 'He cast something of a spell in the City,' says a fellow dealer. 'He had his leg pulled a lot in the time-old Stock Exchange tradition, but we laughed with him, not at him.' It was not quite the same with some other sporting personalities who were regarded rather as figures of fun. Unconventional as usual, he is reputed to have been seen, at slack moments, practising his golf swing in unlikely places. He did not retire from the Stock Exchange until 1972.

A few months short of his fifty-ninth birthday Gubby had been chosen to play in the Halford-Hewitt Cup for Eton – this, for the uninitiated, is a foursomes knock-out competition, five pairs a side, competed for annually at Deal and Sandwich by the old boys of sixty-four schools. Research might well show that no one had ever before come into one of the leading sides at such an advanced age. Eton got through two rounds, and in the third, against Oundle, all depended on Gubby's match. Gubby's recollection is that Eton stood one up on the 18th tee and that Oundle holed right across the green to keep the match alive. (That's his version, and he's sticking to it!) For the play at the 19th there is the evidence of Henry Longhurst, no less, who told his readers of the *Sunday Times* how the old England captain drove into the rough on the right, how his partner, Krefting, cleared the ditch with the second stroke as did Oundle, who moreover got their 4 whereas Eton did not. An honourable exit.

There was a change in the MCC secretaryship in October 1962, Ronny Aird, Gubby's Eton contemporary and friend of all the years between, retiring and being replaced by Billy Griffith, who for the previous ten years had been his assistant. Gubby recalls how extremely courteous and popular Aird had always been with both members and staff during his time at Lord's – he had served there, excluding the war years, since 1926. The secretarial tradition of helpfulness and bonhomie was amply maintained by Billy Griffith, with whom Gubby was now to be so closely associated.

One of the major decisions of Gubby's time was made at the meeting of the Advisory County Committee of November 1962, when by a majority of eleven votes to seven they recommended the abolition of amateur status in first-class cricket. The Committee of MCC accepted the will of the counties in this respect – despite its being directly contrary to the decision recently reached by the very strong Committee, of which Gubby was a member, mentioned in the last chapter. This body had reported that 'the distinctive status of the amateur cricketer was not obsolete, was of great value to the game and should be preserved.'

This was, and remained, Gubby's view – and also, among many others, that of the editor of *Wisden*, Norman Preston, who in his 1963 Notes wrote: 'By doing away with the amateur, cricket is in danger of losing the spirit of freedom and gaiety which the best amateur players brought to the game.' Gubby preferred a system of broken time to the total loss of the independent cricketer, but he admits that by today economic necessity would have made something akin to the present system inevitable. It is merely in tune with the general perversity of things that among those who sigh most loudly for the return of the old amateur – impossible as all know it to be – are the old professionals.

In the winter of 1962–63 Gubby paid another visit to Australia wherein he again combined business and pleasure. His companions were all close friends – Lord Nugent, the reigning president of MCC, R. H. Twining, whom Gubby was due to nominate as his own successor as president two years later, and an old friend, Jerram Briggs. They spent a few nights en route in Bombay where friendships were made which were soon to prove of much value. There was a luncheon given by the president of the Indian Board of Control, M. A. Chidambaram, and Gubby gave a talk reviewing the current problems of cricket. They did the trip very much *en prince*, visiting Delhi and the Taj Mahal, flying next to Hong Kong and enjoying the best VIP hospitality before taking ship on the *Himalaya* down to Sydney.

In Australia they were able to see three Tests of contrasting fortunes: first England's magnificent victory at Melbourne, followed swiftly by the anti-climax of defeat at Sydney, and an even draw at Adelaide.

Though their day was doomed, it was the amateur contributions of the captain, Ted Dexter, of David Sheppard and of Colin Cowdrey which gave the strongest support to the leading batsman, Ken Barrington, on that MCC tour of 1962–63.

Gubby's practical contribution to the new order, incidentally, was to invite three of the leading professionals, Sir Leonard Hutton, Les Ames and Alec Bedser to join the MCC Cricket Sub-Committee, of which he was chairman.

At the MCC AGM on the first Wednesday of May, when the announcement is traditionally made, Gubby was nominated by Tim Nugent as his successor when the presidency changed hands in October. Gubby at this stage of his life must have been hoping to be made president one day, though he can have had no high expectation at this moment since during their two and a half months together in the winter Nugent never mentioned the matter. Had he not yet made up his mind, one wonders, or did he not want to put his chosen successor under a strain – which it would certainly have been – of keeping a secret for too long? The news was well received, not least on the Stock Exchange, where came the usual banter which in those circles, one gathers, has generally been a token of popularity. Peterborough in the *Daily Telegraph*, noting his appointment, quoted the latest Allen story going the rounds. When he remarked of a mutual acquaintance that he was so nice one would hardly know he was a foreigner, his partner Denis Hill-Wood replied, 'But Gubby, one would hardly know you were an Australian.' The Peterborough paragraph also noted that before he assumed the presidency Gubby was to undergo an operation in connection with an arthritic hip that had begun to be a painful inconvenience. This operation was however, according to the victim, 'a piffling thing', a mere muscular releasing by no means to be confused with the saga of major hip surgery which began in 1965.

John Warr in his *Sunday Telegraph* column commented appreciatively in his own inimitable style on the presidential appointment. He recalled how at Cambridge Gubby had first dissuaded him from grasping the ball 'as one would hold a ham roll'; how he would score his hundreds for the Foresters at Fenner's 'encased in layers of elastoplast like one of the mummified Pharaohs of ancient Egypt': how 'he enjoyed nothing better than to run over a successful round stroke by stroke'. But amid all the persiflage his readers were told that 'his dedication to cricket has been unwavering, and absolute'. His work for cricket had been 'tremendous'.

The visit of Frank Worrell's West Indies side in the summer of 1963 produced one of the historic Test series and as a by-product a diplomatic issue of importance and long-lasting consequence. The West Indians of the early 1960s following their momentous tour of Australia (wherein occurred the 'Tied Test') were the most attractive side in the world. Yet according to a Test programme sketched out in 1960 and at that time bespoke up to the dim mists of 1972 it would be eight years before they were next due in England. On the morning after the thrilling Test at Lord's the *Daily Telegraph* printed a letter from a well-known sportsman, T. J. R. Dashwood by name, deploring the long gap between visits and advocating the system of 'twin tours' whereby in certain English summers two Test countries should come on shorter visits.

Jack Dashwood's letter, which appeared on 26 June, was widely approved, but time was against the prospect of any quick result since the six countries of the Imperial Cricket Conference were due to meet at Lord's under the chairmanship of the president of MCC on 17 July. Nor were they as a body exactly renowned for speed of action. I did my best with a leader-page article in the *Daily Telegraph* of July 13 entitled 'Diplomatic Cricket' and illustrated by a photograph of Lord Nugent looking every inch a statesman.

At the meeting the West Indian representatives, J. St F. Dare, president of their Board, and Worrell himself put their case for more frequent tours, and found a sympathetic response both from Tim Nugent and G. O. Allen. Wonderful to relate, the Conference agreed 'twin tours' to England in principle leaving the ticklish details to MCC. It was going to be a matter both of prestige and of cash, and Gubby was the man into whose lap the job would fall.

In the autumn Gubby lost two fond friends in C. M. Wells and Sir Jack Hobbs, both 'masters' in their different fashion. The *Eton Chronicle* obituary of the man who 'was so utterly unlike anyone else', lightened the recital of his virtues with some illustrations of a style that made a boy's inattention impossible. The writer overheard Wells expounding history. 'So they went on this expedition, and they were all killed – killed, and if I wemember wight, eaten.'

Jack had spent his last years at Hove tending his invalid wife. When she died, his friends thought they might now see more of him for he was still apparently fit. But with her death life seemed to lose its purpose for him, and he passed on a few days after his eighty-first birthday. Gubby went down to Hove for the funeral, and heard Harry Altham's memorable eulogy at the Memorial Service in Southwark Cathedral, culminating in the thought:

> that for him the far country had become the beckoning shore, and that, as for Mr Valiant-for-Truth, 'when he passed over, all the trumpets sounded for him on the other side'.

MCC toured India in the winter of 1963–64 and Gubby, who had assumed the presidency in October, was invited out with the secretary, Billy Griffith, by the Indian Board both to see some cricket and to discuss future tours. MCC sent out a paper ahead of them to both India and Pakistan pointing out the advantages of shorter tours to England at more frequent intervals. On arrival they were duly garlanded and hospitably received, but were discouraged to hear that most of the Board opposed the idea strongly. Gubby accordingly put on his pads for his meeting with the Indian Board in the knowledge that the wicket would be difficult. According to Billy the situation brought the best out of Gubby. He was understanding, sympathetic, persuasive – so much so that when the two English representatives suggested they withdraw while the matter was debated they were asked to stay, and to their delight saw the proposal passed by twenty-one votes to one.

There was just one thing the Indians much wanted, and that was to be invited for the first half of the summer of 1967, and not the second. Gubby's secret fear had been that both India and Pakistan would opt for the second half of the English summer with the likelihood of more congenial weather. Much relieved, he said he could promise nothing, but would do his best.

And so by air to Pakistan – in fact via Karachi to Rawalpindi; more garlands, more warm Oriental hospitality, and this time less persuasion called for. However, there was just one thing the Pakistanis much wanted, and that was to be invited for the second half of the summer of 1967. Gubby, relieved once more, said he could promise nothing but would do his best. Thus both these uneasy neighbours were satisfied, and the president and secretary of MCC could turn their attention to the Third and Fourth Tests (both unexcitingly drawn, along with the remaining three), and to three memorable visits, one to Agra, the others to stay with the Maharajahs of Vizianagram and Jaipur.

Gubby took Colin Cowdrey, Johnny Woodcock, Michael Melford, and Billy to see the Taj Mahal, and was again thunderstruck, as were they all, by its ethereal beauty. At Benares 'Vizzy', Gubby's opposing captain in the Test series of 1936, gave them a great dinner, and also laid on a trip down the Ganges in the princely barge. Down the sacred river they flowed with the current, but so close at first to the bank that the aroma of the funeral pyres was such that the chief guest tactfully suggested a change of course. The journey lasted three hours during which a lavish luncheon was served on board before the return journey was made by car. On enquiry it emerged that it took two men two days to pull the barge back to its starting point.

There is a photograph of Gubby sitting with Prime Minister Nehru at the Delhi Test Match, the latter looking preoccupied and hollow-cheeked. Gubby opined that the co-architect with Gandhi of modern India was not long for this world, and sure enough within a few months he was dead.

The summer of Gubby's presidency, 1964, was full of sunshine except, sadly enough, during the Tests against Australia when rain interfered three times out of five. Only one was finished, and that in favour of Bobby Simpson's side, who thus retained the Ashes. The high point of the season, the Lord's Test, was graced as usual by the Queen, but the loss of the first two days meant an almost certain draw. A more satisfactory game there was that between the President's XI and the Australians – a new fixture this, for which Gubby chose an Under Twenty-five side captained by the twenty-two-year-old J. M. Brearley which held its own pretty well, Brearley making top score and youngsters such as Colin Milburn, Keith Fletcher, David Brown and Richard Hutton giving an idea of their potential.

Gubby chaired an ICC meeting which neither attempted nor achieved very much. He presented the Gillette Cup, now in its second year, and still more or less on probation, to Ted Dexter, whose Sussex side retained it easily against Warwickshire.

The event of the year was the celebration at a dinner in the Long Room in May of the 150th anniversary of Lord's Ground. The Prime Minister, Sir Alec Douglas-Home as he was at the time, headed a distinguished company which heard one of the most memorable speeches surely ever delivered on the theme of cricket, by Harry Altham. He took the guests nostalgically, often humorously, sonorously, impeccably through the history of the ground from 1814 to the present. Those lucky enough to possess the *Memoir* of H. S. A. edited by his old pupil, Hubert Doggart, will need no reminding of this speech which is reprinted there in full. From the concluding words may be caught perhaps a hint of its oracular flavour:

> But surely our last and most grateful memory tonight must be of Thomas Lord himself. How little can his father, when he rode north from Yorkshire to stake life and fortune for Prince Charlie at Culloden, how little can his son, as he bowled away in the open fields at Islington at the members of the White Conduit Club – how little can either of them have imagined what the family name and the ground that bears it would come to mean to all the world today: a focus of tradition and history for a game that like Ariel has fetched a girdle round the earth, a cement of loyalties and of friendships, and a symbol of values constant and unchallengeable in a changing and a challenging world.

Gubby remembers how when he afterwards congratulated Harry and suggested that such things came easily to him he replied with some indignation that he had retired to the West Country for ten days with his reference books in order to prepare it. Harry never spared himself in his labours for cricket, and indeed it was after speaking to the Sheffield Cricket Lovers' Society that, less than a year later, he died suddenly at the age of seventy-six.

Harry Altham had retired from the MCC treasurership on Gubby's assumption of the presidency on 1 October 1963. Lord Cobham, whose father had been treasurer of MCC from 1939–49, succeeded him, but after only a year resigned on accepting the Lord Lieutenancy of

Worcestershire. Who now was to take over the key office of treasurer? Gubby was not at first keen, preferring to revert to his chairmanship of the Cricket Sub-Committee, but allowed himself to be persuaded, chiefly by Tim Nugent and his own nomination as the new president, Dick Twining. So on 1 October 1964 he hopped from one perch to the other.

Twining and he represented MCC on a five-week trip to South Africa and Rhodesia at the turn of the year. Along with Briggs and another old friend, John Haslewood, they saw the Second Test at Johannesburg, and the Third at the Cape – in neither of which was a result ever in sight – and travelled the glamorous Garden Route to Durban. There they met Walter Hammond at dinner, cheerful but showing grave signs, both mental and physical, of the terrible road accident which it was said that no one with a lesser frame could have survived. 'I was fond of Wally,' says Gubby, 'and perhaps I was lucky enough always to see the better side of him.' He died at sixty-two a few months later.

Finally came a week in Rhodesia as guests of Sir Humphrey Gibbs, an Eton contemporary of Gubby's, all too soon under Ian Smith's UDI regime to be beleaguered in his own Government House at Salisbury. The Rhodesian Cricket Union just had time to celebrate their seventy-fifth anniversary in the company of the president and treasurer of MCC before the shutters came down. Both of them underlined Gubby's persistent theme of the need to speed up the game. Dick congratulated his hosts on producing the best fielder in the world, as then he certainly was, Colin Bland.

In 1965 Gubby suffered a political defeat at Lord's when he unsuccessfully opposed the admission of associate members to the ICC. It was a development about which, as we shall see, he subsequently changed his mind. In that year the rules were amended to allow of the election of countries outside the Commonwealth. Accordingly the USA, Ceylon (now Sri Lanka), and Fiji were admitted, to be followed in later years by sixteen more. At the same time the old outmoded 'Imperial' in the title was changed to 'International'. Under the new wording South Africa were eligible for readmission, but though their team was engaged in a Test series in England at the time of the Conference they were not brought back, and, of course, never have been.

Gubby's view regarding the position of South African cricket today is pragmatic and clear-cut. Though he resents the intrusion of politics into sport he accepts it as a fact of life. Thus he believes that so long as the Commonwealth countries maintain the Gleneagles Agreement it is up to sporting bodies to conform to it. This means in practice that while cricket authorities should not attempt to dissuade a man from playing and coaching in South Africa they should not countenance an English team playing a representative South African team.

In the autumn Gubby endured the first of what turned out to be five major operations on his hips. They were spread over fourteen years but let me dispose of his sufferings once for all. In November 1965 the left leg was 'done', in August 1967 the right. This second time the bone failed to join, so the whole business had to be repeated a few months later. Twelve years now elapsed before in January 1978 the left and in December 1979 the right were operated on again. Gubby's experience with his hips illustrates the surgical advances made over the period. After the first three operations he hobbled painfully about on crutches for three or four months and needed a stick for two more. Following ops four and five he had no pain after the first week and was hitting some gentle iron shots after six. Does he think the cause of this dramatic saga was half a lifetime of fast bowling? Possibly — but then his sister is also a sufferer from arthritis, and she never bowled a ball in her life. One thing is sure — he must be today the leading lay expert on all that appertains to hip surgery!

This perhaps is a convenient moment to note some of the new things at Lord's which over the years he pioneered, or was associated with. There was, for instance, the tenure put on the posts of trustee and of the treasurer. Hitherto both had been life appointments, and there was at least one case of a noble trustee who in the last decade or more of his life had never been seen on the ground. Trusteeships henceforth came up for re-election or otherwise after three years, the treasurership after five. Before Altham, there had been only four treasurers since Sir Spencer Ponsonby-Fane assumed office in 1879. All rendered great service, and all carried on until death.

Finance and general purposes were handled by one sub-committee, mostly comprising old buffers who could attend in the mornings before the General Committee met after lunch. Gubby, after becoming treasurer, divided the work between two sub-committees, and helped to recruit some lively City brains to deal with finance.

Re-arrangement of the north end of the pavilion made possible a bar with a view of the cricket in what had been the professionals' quarters. This cleverly pre-empted pressure to allow drinks in the Long Room.

What Gubby takes no credit for is the building in 1977 of the Indoor School. In fact he opposed it, not at all on principle but because he thought its position on the southern side of the Nursery Ground might prejudice future development on the St John's Wood Road frontage. But for a change in the tax law a major building scheme in that area had been in train two or three years before which would have been worth a million pounds to the Club. Despite his original attitude, such was his prestige in the cricket world that he was chosen by the Committee to perform the opening ceremony of a project which was always likely to be the great success it has become. A first-class Indoor School at the game's headquarters for the coaching of the young and winter practice for cricketers of all ages and sorts had been envisaged by some for quarter of a century or more.

On the first-class scene Gubby, in association with his old comrade and supporter, Walter Robins, pushed hard and at last in 1954 successfully for the covering of pitches in Tests *overseas* – an obvious reform, as anyone who has watched cricket after rain in the hot countries will agree. There the batsman as a rule scarcely has a chance. In England he has – and both subject and author wish to go on record as regretting total covering in county cricket at home.

The duration of Test Matches was a point of contention for years. Gubby was for a uniform maximum of thirty hours, and this the ICC eventually ordained – with an optional extension if a rubber depends on the last match. Haunted maybe by his experience at Old Trafford in 1934 he campaigned for the filling in of foot-holes – now incorporated in Law 10. As a bowler, incidentally, he wanted twenty minutes for tea instead of fifteen, and got it.

On another important matter he voted in 1967 against the immediate registration of overseas players, believing that they might come to dominate the English game, and that we should stand on our own feet. The fact was that the counties urgently wanted to recruit great stars like Sobers, Procter and others to add glamour to their sides and so attract one-day sponsorship. I am on record as welcoming at any rate a limited blood-transfusion. But who shall say that Gubby has not, in the long term, been proved right?

1968 was a momentous year for cricket in general and MCC in particular and accordingly an especially active one for Gubby in the central position of the treasurership. For one thing, Lord's itself had had, over the winter, something of a face-lift with the new Tavern Stand, built during the winter, now curving round from the St John's Wood Road score-box to the Q enclosure, and flanking the Grace Gates on one side, as the new Tavern itself now did on the other. Kenneth Peacock was the architect, as he had been of the Warner Stand on the other side of the great pavilion built nearly twenty years before. The treasurer's deep regret today about the Tavern Stand is that the members in Special General Meeting decreased the original concept to the extent of approving only one row of boxes instead of two. This decision has turned out a major disaster, for the boxes are always heavily subscribed for the big matches, and the second row might have been there today but for a trifling saving of £36,000.

But the major change was in the modified role to be played in future by MCC in the English game, a devolution of power and responsibility proposed and carried through by the Club itself. Looking back from this distance it seems fairly clear that in an increasingly commercial sporting world cricket would soon have needed in any case tighter administrative machinery than the advisory guidance that had been available down the years to cricketers of all degrees from Test and county to club and school. Gubby felt strongly that a more democratic structure was now called for. When the change was in the offing an article in the *Telegraph Sunday Magazine* entitled 'The Captains of Cricket' contained the comment that 'MCC try very hard not to throw their weight about. This has often meant that they have not given a firm enough lead in the game.' From now onwards, the writer went on, they would have no excuse for being reticent in the new governing Cricket Council, which was to have three component parts, a Test and County Cricket Board, a National Cricket Association, and MCC itself.

The immediate reason for the new governance was the formation four years earlier of the Sports Council with funds at its disposal provided by government. As Denis Howell, the newly-created Minister of Sport, who emerged as a thoroughly friendly figure in the transition period, remarked at the outset: 'You are the only sport without a governing body.' Gubby as treasurer and Billy Griffith as secretary were the men chiefly involved in setting up a system which would allow cricket to benefit financially out of the resources of the Sports Council. In their visits to Whitehall Gubby did not find himself altogether *en rapport* with the Civil Service mind. However a Cricket Council wherein none of the three constituent bodies had sufficient voting power to defeat the other two was satisfactory to the Minister, and on 20 May the changes were announced.

While all this was happening the prospect of trouble looming in connection with the forthcoming tour of South Africa by MCC in the following winter was very much in the minds of Gubby and the rest of the Committee. Anti-apartheid feeling in England was much stronger in 1968 than when the South Africans had come on a short tour three years earlier, and there was a body of liberal opinion that opposed any further sporting contact. The MCC Committee were not going to be deflected from fulfilling their fixture in South Africa, but they were naturally aware that the presence of Basil d'Oliveira, the Cape Coloured South African, who was playing for England in the West Indies in the early months of 1968, was a potential flash-point if he should be selected to tour in the land of his birth. Indeed South Africa's Minister of the Interior had indicated a year earlier that d'Oliveira's presence would be unacceptable.

In January MCC accordingly wrote to the SACA asking for an assurance that no restrictive preconditions would be imposed on their selection. They got no immediate answer, but it so happened that ex-president and Committee member Home, at that time Shadow Foreign

Secretary, was in that capacity visiting Rhodesia and South Africa and he was asked by the Committee to give an assessment of the d'Oliveira situation on his return.

When he did so, having seen Mr Vorster, the South African Prime Minister, on this and, of course, the Rhodesian matter, and also tested the ground with other sections of society including the cricketers, his advice was not to press for an answer to a hypothetical question. Alec Home told the MCC Committee that in his view if d'Oliveira were to be chosen the odds were 5/4 on his being allowed in. This advice was accepted by Gubby and the rest of the Committee, though the private view of the secretary (who had been sent out by the Committee on a liaison mission at the New Year of 1966–67) was that MCC should have pressed the SACA for a reply to their letter.

Five to four were indeed short odds, but the Committee were not unconscious of the fact that d'Oliveira had met with only moderate success in the West Indies. Nor did he strike any great form as the season progressed. There seemed the likelihood throughout the summer therefore that he would not make the touring side. Then came d'Oliveira's unexpected recall as a substitute after the team for the final Test against Australia had been chosen and his admirable response to the occasion with an innings of 158 which was one of the chief factors in the victory by England that squared the rubber. (Before reaching his hundred, in the fast time of three and a quarter hours, he had given only one chance, at 31, to the wicket-keeper. It proved perhaps the most fateful drop in cricket history.) He also had a bowling analysis for the match of 9–6–4–1. (Personally I thought that d'Oliveira's performance in such a tense situation should and would have tilted the selection for South Africa in his favour.)

Unknown at the time, except to four men, was that another distinguished ex-president of MCC, Lord Cobham, at the end of a visit to South Africa had seen Vorster at the latter's invitation shortly after Sir Alec, and the Prime Minister had indicated firmly that d'Oliveira would not be acceptable.

This meeting had been in March, before the English season opened, and Cobham passed on the information to Lord's in an unusual and, as I have always thought, uncharacteristic way, in the form of a letter not to any officer of the Club but to a senior member of the Committee. Furthermore the letter was marked 'Private and Confidential'. Notwithstanding this, the receiver passed it on to the secretary, Billy Griffith, and he in turn gave the information therein to the president, Arthur Gilligan, and the treasurer, Gubby.

These three key figures had now to make the decision, whether or not to inform the Committee of this evidence, unwelcome as it was and in conflict with Sir Alec's assessment. Gubby has always made two points in defence of their policy of silence. In the first place was the fact that Sir Alec was a former Prime Minister, a statesman with the broadest experience of Commonwealth and Foreign Affairs. They had asked him for his advice, he had given it, and it had been accepted. Secondly there was a practical difficulty from which there was no escape. Two of the four Test selectors, Messrs Insole (the chairman) and May, were on the MCC Committee. Their job was to pick the sides against Australia without any other consideration. The knowledge of Cobham's talk with Vorster would be an unfair extra burden to put upon them, if it could be avoided. Such was the decision, and it was this difficulty which the chief officers gave for their silence when news of the Cobham warning was revealed in the press in April 1969.

The only other contact with Lord Cobham on the matter during the summer was a hurried talk between himself and Griffith at a big match at Lord's wherein the former was content with satisfying himself that the gist of his letter had been passed on.

The d'Oliveira story is a sombre one, and probably all too well known to many readers of this book, but Gubby's part in it cannot be told without giving something of the general picture. Imagine then the MCC tour selectors as they gathered at Lord's at eight o'clock on the evening that the last Test ended. They comprised the four TCCB selectors, Messrs Insole, Bedser, May and Kenyon; Cowdrey and Ames, the appointed captain and manager; along with the president and treasurer of MCC. Griffith acted, of course, as secretary. The convention was that the senior officers of the Club were present since the team travelled under the flag and auspices of MCC. They did not as a rule however give technical opinions. They were present primarily to oversee the acceptability as tourists of those chosen.

The meeting took place in the Committee Dining Room, and it lasted with a short informal interval or two from eight o'clock until after one thirty a.m. It was anything but an easy side to pick if only for the dearth of good-class all-rounders. No one had taken on the mantle of Trevor Bailey. Above all considerations was the question of d'Oliveira. There had been much press speculation about the likelihood of the effect of his inclusion. Cobham letter apart, everyone knew that his presence must put the tour in jeopardy — also that this was a factor that they were instructed to ignore. Their position was unenviable indeed. No vote is recorded, and memories at this range of time must be accepted with reserve. Gubby is clear that he did not exercise his vote, and believes that Gilligan did not do so either. Other evidence on this point is more dubious. One thing at least is surely clear. On the face of it, all but six hours, and at night at that, is far too long a session for anyone to be at their best at the end of it, least of all a captain who has come straight off the field at the end of a Test series. They must have been better advised to adjourn until the morning.

Gubby thought, prior to the meeting, that the selectors probably would choose d'Oliveira, but he did not himself rate his claims for a place particularly high. Nor did he take any great account of the Cobham letter – which, incidentally, he never saw. Not until much later did Cobham tell him of his visit to Vorster. He stuck throughout to the Home line.

When next day the full Committee approved the chosen team he thought the omission would cause a stir, but no more. He was no more prepared for the national upheaval, the resignation of members, and the call for censure motions by members of the Club, than other members of the Committee – which d'Oliveira's subsequent bringing into the team as a replacement for Tom Cartwright, the rejection of his inclusion by Vorster, and the consequent cancellation of the tour by MCC, did little to abate.

There is no need to cover much further the details of the d'Oliveira affair which culminated in the Special General Meeting at Church House, Westminster wherein the Committee comfortably, if not unscathed, survived the three motions put. Despite that members could vote by post a thousand took part in a meeting which, under the chairmanship of the new president, Ronny Aird, lasted almost four hours.

Unfortunately in view of their official positions – Lord Cobham was now Lord Steward of the Household as well as a Lord Lieutenant – neither he nor Sir Alec Home thought it appropriate to speak, and the standard of much of the debate was unworthy of the occasion. Gubby took no active part, believing that as the president's deputy he should remain outwardly neutral.

When the secret of the Cobham-Vorster interview was disclosed in April 1969 by the *Daily Mail* the subject received a fresh and lively ventilation, with a call by one newspaper for the resignations of Gilligan, Allen and Griffith. The secretary in fact considered resigning but was dissuaded by a unanimous vote of the Committee's confidence. All in all, it was in an unhappy atmosphere, in strong contrast to their normally benign conduct of affairs, that MCC relinquished their direct responsibility for Test tours overseas.

On a more congenial note the Club made it known that players contracted with counties – in other words professionals under the old order – would be welcome as members and promptly elected the first five names put up.

At the end of 1968, after twelve years in his Queen's Gate flat, Gubby moved to his present ideal house in Grove End Road, behind Lord's pavilion and separated only by a wall from the Harris Garden. His eye on the proceedings of MCC was henceforward to be, literally at least, closer than ever. However that winter he departed on one of his short business trips to Australia — and was promptly burgled.

When the question came up as to whether, in the circumstances, the visit of a South African team to England should go forward as arranged in the summer of 1970, the decision was of concern to MCC no longer exclusively but in that they were the members with the biggest voice in the new Cricket Council. Gubby, as treasurer of MCC, was at first, and over this crisis, vice-chairman of the Council, the president of MCC being chairman. Opposition to the tour grew in intensity, fuelled by the tour of a South African Rugby Union team which attracted disrupting protesters everywhere they played, and police counter-action. The size of the police presence and the violence engendered were in places akin to that seen in the miners' strike of 1984. On one night in mid-January a dozen county grounds were attacked and damaged.

Soon after this sinister threat Gubby, among others, went to see Mr Callaghan, in charge of the Home Office, and Mr Howell, the Minister for Sport. The Council maintained their attitude that encouragement, not isolation, was needed to further progress towards multi-racial cricket in South Africa, and that they had a duty towards 'a traditional, lawful pursuit supported by the majority of people in this country'. Mr Callaghan made it clear to the delegation that no help was to be expected from the government. They would be responsible for policing outside the grounds, but the cost of the necessary large police presence inside the grounds would fall on the counties concerned.

Gubby's tactics were to make the government decide what, after all, was a political matter. He was beginning now to think the tour was simply impracticable. Still, however, preparations went on. The projected tour was reduced in time and to be confined to a dozen grounds. The Prime Minister, Mr Wilson, in April gave open encouragement to the Cricket Council's opponents when he denounced the tour as 'a big mistake' and expressed the hope that 'everyone should be free to demonstrate against apartheid — I hope they will do so.'

South Africa were expelled by the International Olympic Committee. Opposition to the tour was being voiced by organizations and individuals in a gathering flood. Still, however, with the season now started, the Cricket Council stood firm on the issue of principle, determined that if the tour were not to take place it was the government who would have to make the decision. With an election due in June this they were highly reluctant to do.

However on 21 May after a full Commons debate on the issue and the South African arrival date only a few days away the chairman of the Cricket Council, now the new president, M. J. C. Allom, and the secretary, were called to Whitehall and requested by Mr Callaghan on grounds of broad public policy to withdraw their invitation. To this, with feelings mixed but without a dissentient voice, the Council agreed next day, confirming at the same time that, as had already been agreed with the TCCB, 'an alternative programme, comprising of five Test Matches between England and the Rest of the World' should be held instead.

Gubby and all closely concerned with cricket in every department, in the words of *Wisden*, 'had been subjected to pressure never experienced in the game before. Let us hope', added the author, Irving Rosenwater, 'that cricket will never know such conflict again.'

Cricket did, in fact, know a conflict just as momentous in its way, and even wider in its repercussions, when the Australian tycoon, Kerry Packer, irrupted rudely onto the scene seven years later. However for the present we may move gratefully into calmer waters, indeed to the shores of Italy whither Gubby in the spring of 1971 travelled on a care-free holiday with Willie and Diana Hill-Wood.

A late recruit to culture, might it be thought? It is truer perhaps to suggest that, as it came his way, he recognized and admired perfection in many forms, whether in an innings by Hobbs, or Lindwall at practice, or the reminiscences of a Menzies or an Alexander. (Gubby would say with Lord Houghton that 'The intimate conversation of important men is the cream of life.') He had marvelled at the beauty of the Taj Mahal. Now it was the Sistine Chapel and the transcendent frescoes of Michelangelo. The picture in a museum of a woman with a baby in her arms held him in wonder, irrespective almost of the fact that what he was looking at was the Virgin and Child. He insisted on trying to find the scene of the al-fresco lunch with 'Alex' on the hill-side overlooking Cassino, and was delighted with himself at locating it. The Mediterranean attracted him again in 1983, this time to admire the Parthenon, Ephesus, Sounion and other Greek glories on a Swan's Hellenic Cruise.

An unexpected call on his services was made in the spring of 1971. The TCCB Cricket Sub-Committee nominated him, ten years after his retirement as chairman, to serve again as a selector. Gubby, while far from enthusiastic, said he would do the job if there was a very strong wish that he should. However, the 1970 selectors, under Alec Bedser, the sitting chairman, had picked the side which under Ray Illingworth had just won back the Ashes in Australia. As soon as Gubby learned that the wisdom of a change was disputed and that Alec was keen to carry on, he saw to it that his nomination was withdrawn.

As the new bodies formed in 1968, TCCB and NCA, grew in experience it was reasonable that their responsibilities should be reflected by some reorganization within the Cricket Council. In 1974 Gubby and the secretary successfully proposed a revised distribution of five members apiece for MCC, TCCB and NCA, and also the appointment of a chairman other than the president of MCC, who had been combining the chairmanship of the Council and of the ICC.

As it happened he himself in 1974–75 was, in effect, usually in the driving seat at Lord's, for when the Duke of Edinburgh had taken on the presidency of MCC for the second time it was accepted that except on special occasions he would have to be represented by the treasurer.

Since Gubby had been appointed treasurer one-day cricket had proliferated in response to public demand. In 1968 the John Player League on Sundays had followed the Gillette Cup. In 1972 came the counties' Benson and Hedges Cup. In 1975 the first Prudential World Cup was launched, involving the six Test countries and also Sri Lanka and East Africa. In perfect weather the event came to a triumphal climax at Lord's with the presentation of the Cup by the Duke to Clive Lloyd.

His Royal Highness presided on the opening day of the International Cricket Conference, but on the second the chair was taken by Gubby on what in fact, after more than twenty years, was his last appearance, apart from his attendance at the emergency meeting called at the onset of the Packer troubles. He and Philip Snow, the Fiji representative, were the only survivors of the meeting ten years before when Gubby had opposed the idea of associate membership. Mr Snow recalled to me how on this final day he:

> magnanimously stated that he had made a mistake in opposing their being allowed to join. He had seen, he said, much evidence of the value of their contributions to ICC, and he was pleased to acknowledge the historical fact ... I thought you would like to have this record as showing part of a no doubt complex character which could be so likeable amid the strength and force of his convictions.

18
'A Touchy, Testy, Pleasant Fellow'

The occasion of his giving up the MCC treasurership, at the 1976 AGM, seemed to Gubby a proper moment to compare the game as it was at his retirement with what it had been when he took the post in 1964. After presenting the annual accounts with his usual thoroughness, this is what he had to say about the broader aspects of cricket:

> Now, looking back over my twelve years, I see many changes, some I am in no doubt were wise, some I would classify as necessary, and one or two which cause me concern. Though not in the traditional role of the Treasurer at an Annual General Meeting I hope you will bear with me on this occasion if I start by saying a few words about the game and its administration. In this field there have, of course, been many significant changes such as the front-foot law, leg-side limitation, bonus points and the influx of overseas players but I feel the formation of the Cricket Council and the introduction of limited-over cricket have been the most far-reaching.
>
> The formation of the Cricket Council was, in my opinion, a sound and necessary step. In these days I believe all sports require a democratic and broadly based governing body. Whilst this has inevitably meant some lessening of MCC's influence, I am happy to think it has in no way impaired the prestige of, or respect for, this great club. Remember, our President is President of the Cricket Council, our Treasurer its Vice-Chairman and we are represented in equal numbers with the other two constituent bodies, the Test and County Cricket Board and the National Cricket Association.
>
> As regards limited-over cricket, some may not approve of the forty over matches but it cannot be disputed that they, together with the sixty and fifty-five over matches, have done much to alleviate the financial stresses. They have not only brought to the game a new, albeit at times rather unruly, category of supporter but also additional television coverage, which in turn has attracted very valuable sponsorship and advertising.
>
> I cannot leave the subject of the game without expressing one

great and deep-rooted regret. It applies particularly to first-class cricket and it is this. I have failed to convince the authorities in this country and overseas of the evils of the LBW Law introduced in 1935. And as I retire along with others of my generation who had the experience of playing under both Laws, I fear the cause is as good as lost.

I am now more than ever convinced that this change in the Laws, to which in my infancy and to my everlasting shame I was in some small degree party, was the most disastrous piece of cricket legislation in my life-time. The 1935 Law was designed to prevent batsmen 'padding up' to balls pitching just outside the off-stump. Well, this it has done to some exent but the administrators of the day clearly failed to examine in depth the possible by-products of their brain-child. It was argued that it would help all types of bowlers equally and increase off-side play. In the event it has done precisely the opposite, as looking back it was surely going to. As it has helped disproportionately the bowlers who bring the ball in to the batsmen, it has in fact reduced off-side play, has contributed in no small degree to the demise of the leg-spinner and orthodox left-armer and, perhaps worst of all, it has bred a race of front-foot batsmen for safety reasons.

So what have we now got as a general pattern: 'seamers' bowling endlessly at a funereal over-rate, off-spinners and an occasional left-armer pushing the ball through flat, to batsmen pushing endlessly forward. Containment is the theme. Efficient it is, backed by brilliant fielding, but variety and a sense of urgency, once amongst the charms of our game, are no longer there.

The treasurer's last words — even more emphatically true today than they were then — were fully reported in the more serious papers. John Arlott in the *Guardian* took occasion to sketch the history of the LBW Law and to remind his readers of the experimental law of 1972 (now Law 36 of the new 1980 code) whereby the batsman could be lbw to a ball pitching outside the off-stump, even though he had not been struck 'between wicket and wicket', if he had offered no stroke. Having referred to Gubby's relationship with Robert Browning, the poet, Arlott concluded that

his argument comes from the head as well as the heart; from experience as well as emotion; and his ancestor could hardly have faulted its expression.

From such a source, quite a compliment! John Woodcock thought that 'he has exerted as massive an influence at Lord's as Sir Pelham Warner did before him and Lord Harris and Lord Hawke before that', and made the point that two men would henceforth share the treasurer's functions, J. G. W. Davies, a fine cricketer and until recently an executive director of the Bank of England, and the merchant banker, E. W. Phillips, who would be designated chairman of finance. The Committee subscribed to present him with a Royal Worcester coffee service, which they did at a dinner attended by present and past members of the Committee.

As a trustee Gubby retained his position on the MCC Committee, and continued to serve on the Finance and Cricket Sub-Committees and also on the Cricket and Overseas Tours Sub-Committee of the TCCB. He remained a member of the NCA Coaching Committee, as he had been from its beginning. Add to that his ever-close involvement in the affairs of Middlesex, of which he was president for three years from 1977, and his presidency of the Association of Cricket Umpires (assumed, strangely enough, on the death of Douglas Jardine back in 1958), and it is evident that he was still busy enough, to say the least.

The question why the name of Allen does not figure among those whose services to sport have been rewarded with a knighthood is often asked. The Honours system, naturally, is a closed book to those outside the corridors of Whitehall, and one can only note that the approaches on his behalf of several within the cricket hierarchy have not, so far, borne fruit. The last of cricket's six English knighthoods was Sir Leonard Hutton's in 1956.

Pondering the problems of cricket as Gubby never ceased to do, he and Les Ames began to crystallize their thoughts on some novel way of curbing the over-use of the bouncer, which both recognized as a fetish which from its example at the top was affecting all cricket. Apart from the increased physical danger to batsmen they saw the balance and variety of the game being undermined. The umpires had always been highly reluctant to exercise their powers – indeed their duty – under the Unfair Play Law ever since intimidation was recognized as a threat and legislated against directly after the Bodyline tour more than forty years earlier. Both, of course, still had the clearest memories of that tour. The umpires, they knew, had *never once* applied the final sanction of ordering that an offending bowler be taken off and debarred for the remainder of the innings.

They accordingly came up with the idea that bouncers should be restricted to a maximum of one per over, and found that the MCC Cricket Committee were prepared to propose to the TCCB the drafting of an experimental law to this effect. In the summer of 1978 the TCCB adopted the plan, which they then put to the ICC. Here again – and more surprisingly – on 26 July 1978 it was approved for recommendation to all member countries.

In the autumn of that year the then editor of *The Cricketer*, Reg Hayter, published an interview with Gubby and Les in which they spelt out at length the factors already mentioned which had guided their plan and also answered a string of questions about Bodyline. Ames thought that 'cricket is still paying for that tour'. Neither wanted to ban the bouncer, Gubby stressing that they aimed at 'reducing not eliminating' the number of bouncers being bowled. He picked out the last hour's play at Old Trafford in 1976 when three West Indian fast bowlers assailed Edrich and Close as 'the most ghastly exhibition of cricket I have ever seen'.

The experimental law, as promulgated by the ICC, was as follows:

(i) A bowler shall be entitled to deliver one fast, short pitched ball, as currently defined, in any over. When such a ball has been delivered the umpire should make it clear to the bowler that he has accepted it as a fast, short pitched ball.
(ii) If a bowler delivers a second fast, short pitched ball in an over, the umpire should call and signal 'no ball' and the signal should make it clear that the 'no ball' has been called for this reason.
(iii) If a bowler is 'no balled' a second time for this offence he should receive his first official 'caution' under Law 46, Note 4 (vi). The further caution and subsequent suspension procedure laid down in the Law should apply to any subsequent breach of this regulation.
Their guide to umpires reads:
'BOUNCER': A short pitched ball is one that pitches short and passes or would have passed above shoulder height of the batsman standing normally at the crease.

The snag, so far as cooperation from the other Test-playing contries was concerned, is inherent in the constitution of the ICC, which has executive powers only in the fixing of the International tours programme. Sadly, it has no teeth.

In practice the experiment was pursued with reasonably satisfactory effect in English first-class cricket for five summers – but was suspended in 1984 because the top players thought it put them at a disadvantage when playing other countries (in this case the West Indies) who did not subscribe to it. Back, in fact, to square one.

It is worth observing here that whereas in the old days bouncers were usually intended to disturb the batsman and were aimed to pass over the stumps today they are often aimed to intimidate, on the line of the body. The evil still defies solution.

It was as well for Gubby that he vacated the treasurership when he did, for less than a year later, out of a clear blue sky and closely following the nostalgic triumph of the Centenary Test at Melbourne, came the threat to the established game which became known as the Packer Affair – or, more expressively, the Packer Intrusion. For at least the chief responsibility for the MCC policy was no longer his. He was all but seventy-five when the news broke – and there was the awkward circumstance that two further hip operations lay in the near future. One way or another he might have worried himself into a decline.

As one of the five MCC members on the Cricket Council however Gubby attended the emergency meeting at Lord's called a few days after the news that thirty-five of the world's leading players, including four Englishmen, had signed up with the company controlled by Packer which owned his television Channel 9. They were to play in Australia in matches outside the control of the Australian Cricket Board and in competition with its Test and Shield programme.

The Council at this meeting instructed the selectors not to nominate Tony Greig, one of the four, to continue as England's captain but otherwise to pick their sides for the forthcoming series against Australia on merit pending an emergency meeting of the ICC. Gubby was present also at this one dramatic ICC confrontation with Packer whom he remembers as comparing unfavourably, in looks and demeanour, with his father, Sir Frank, an old friend of cousin Dick Allen.

When ICC put to Packer its compromise proposal which acknowledged his 'World Series Cricket' and made concessions in the cause of peace as regards dates in the Australian forthcoming Test programme with India, Gubby felt that in his words 'we might have got a deal'. Packer, with three advisers including Richie Benaud, left the committee room to think it over but, as history relates, returned to demand exclusive television rights for his channel as soon as the Australian Broadcasting Commission's contract ended two years later. This the ICC would not in principle accept as a condition of agreement. From that moment the war was on, the most damaging affliction ever to hit the world of cricket. For two years cricket had to endure the devaluation of Test Matches and deep rifts in the fellowship of the game before the Australians came to their accommodation with Packer.

Other international troubles followed, notably the clandestine departure of English and West Indies teams to South Africa, in contravention of official policy and with suspensions as a predictable result. The cricket world was utterly different in so many ways from Gubby's first recollections of it sixty-odd years before.

Yet Lord's pavilion still stood four-square to the old ground laid 150 years before, the embodiment of the Golden Age of Gubby's boyhood and a reminder, with all its relics and treasures, of the evolution of cricket down the centuries. It was Lord's which enshrined so many of his own memories and the Long Room was the perfect setting for the dinner that

MCC offered for his eightieth birthday celebration.

Twelve fellow presidents sat down to dinner under Hubert Doggart's chairmanship, nine fellow captains of England and in all thirty fellow Test cricketers, plus several old stalwarts of the MCC staff. And, filling the Long Room to a comfortable capacity, were friends of all ages, cricketers, golfers, men of the City, and of the professions. The Queen Mother headed those who sent messages. MCC's royal ex-president in his wire of good wishes reminded all present that:

> No man has done more for the MCC and for cricket over a long period when things have been far from easy. He deserves all the tributes he is going to get.
>
> Philip

The *Daily Mail* led the publicity field with a 'centre-spread' showing a group of dinner-jacketed heroes of days past framed in the background of the Father Time stand and surrounded by a nostalgic pen-picture by Ian Wooldridge.

Characteristically enough, the sentimental accompaniments to his eightieth birthday did not deflect Gubby's eye from the ball. The TCCB had been pressing for some while for a redistribution of the voting strengths of the component parts of the Cricket Council. Five representatives each, from NCA, MCC and themselves, along with one from the Minor Counties, no longer satisfied them. Though the NCA was set up by MCC and at first financed largely by them, they were now chiefly beholden to the TCCB. As the principal money-earners for the English game the TCCB claimed the right to an equality of votes – which, in effect, with the chairman of their choice, would give them a majority.

Gubby maintained that it was wrong that a national game should be virtually controlled by a body that is chiefly concerned with its professional side, and when the Council reconstituted itself to include eight representatives from the TCCB, five from the NCA, and three from the MCC (the Minor Counties, incidentally, losing their place) he resigned as a matter of principle.

It should be added that Gubby's decision, which both surprised and disappointed his friends on the TCCB, reflected the strongly held view of the MCC Committee. The editor of *Wisden* expressed the feelings of many thinking cricketers when he wrote in the 1983 edition:

> If, besides running its own show, namely English Test and county cricket, the TCCB is now to have, should it wish, the final word in matters affecting the 25,000 clubs and 150,000 players who form the heart and soul of cricket in these islands,

Mr Allen may have been right to sound a warning. He and MCC stand for cricket with a capital 'C'; the TCCB, as it has to be, is more commercialistic.

John Woodcock went on to say how the marketing people have 'quite drastically changed' the character of the game in Australia:

> With sponsorship taking an ever firmer hold, it is not impossible to imagine something similar happening in England. I hardly think it will – but it could. Beware the small, executive sub-committee of businessmen, to whom the charm of cricket is little more than a technicality; that was the burden of Mr Allen's message.

It is less what the present holders of TCCB office might do that causes concern so much as their successors in future generations.

But now for some final thoughts on my subject. An impression of G. O. Allen's place among England's all-rounders will have emerged, I hope, from these pages. A few further points from the playing side may help to round the picture. For instance, very few fast bowlers can be truly classified as Test all-rounders: Jack Gregory, of course, and Keith Miller come to mind plus a handful of marginals. The combined strain has been too much for most – which is almost sufficient in itself to explain the series of injuries which were all the more likely to affect someone who was obliged to play his first-class cricket periodically. His batting he could keep in trim in nets and club matches, but he could not bowl full out except in the middle against men of county class.

As to his speed, Fred Titmus, talking recently to Harold Larwood, says that the latter gave his opinion that he was faster than Gubby in Australia but Gubby was the faster in England. Gubby disagrees, saying that Harold was the faster in both countries. What there can be little doubt about is that they were, at their best, faster than any of their contemporaries. Larwood had considerably more control and was the greater bowler, though Allen did more with the new ball. I suppose, too, that their combined speed when they opened together was greater than that of any English pair, though Tyson and Trueman would have their advocates. (Strangely enough this latter pair only once shared the new ball in a Test Match.)

Of his twenty-five Tests, thirteen were against Australia, and of these Bradman played in twelve. He took eighty-one wickets for England at 29 runs each. He made 750 runs with an average of 24, having several times sacrificed his wicket at the end of an innings. He caught twenty catches in Tests, and could certainly be classed as an above average fielder. One thing is sure: though the reason for the omission is understandable seeing that he never played thoughout a summer, he must be the best English cricketer not to have been given the accolade of inclusion as one of *Wisden*'s Cricketers of the Year.

An estimation of his service to the game off the field is easier to make if only because few men have interested themselves to the point of close involvement in so many aspects of it. First a player of distinction, he turned while still active on the field to administration, and not only in routine matters. We have seen the directions in which he was an innovator and reformer, beginning with the organization of cricket for the young. This led in turn to the coaching side wherein he and Harry Altham made so knowledgeable a partnership.

Simultaneously came the labours of selection, and, following this episode in the story, all that went with the treasurership of MCC. The presidency involved, of course, the chairmanship of ICC, whereon he represented English interests for more than twenty years.

No one had as much to do with the (at first) quiet revolution in the governance of English cricket that began with MCC voluntarily delegating part of its historic role as the parliament of the game to the TCCB and the Cricket Council. In most of the international and domestic crises of the post-war period his has been a dominant voice.

Inevitably there are those who suspect his voice has been too dominant for too long. They may say, with truth, that it has not become exactly less insistent with age. Having known his mind on all the issues of the last forty years, and having worked with him for these last ten on the Committee of MCC, I would say, with as much impartiality as an old friend can muster, that the value of his judgement and his unique breadth of experience have far outweighed the advantages that might have accrued if posts of authority had circulated more rapidly — such, for instance, as happens in the Royal and Ancient Golf Club. There are wide dissimilarities in the worlds of Lord's and St Andrews — as members of both these venerable institutions know well enough.

Did Lord Harris wield a wider or more benevolent influence on the game in his day, or Plum Warner in his? I would doubt it.

When I told a mutual friend, not, as it happens, a cricketer, that I was embarking on this biography he came out spontaneously — after a good lunch — with this: 'Ah, Gubby! Like Dr Johnson, difficult, utterly independent, incorruptible, irascible, attractive ...'

This not inapposite summary has points in common with Addison's lines applied once in a book review by Alan Gibson to me but more fittingly ascribable, I would suggest, to Gubby:

> In all thy humours, whether grave or mellow
> Thou'rt such a touchy, testy, pleasant fellow,

Hast so much wit, and mirth, and spleen about thee,
There is no living with thee or without thee.

Cricket and Gubby have been living together in reasonable accord for most of his eighty-two years, and it is difficult indeed to imagine Lord's and the game without him.

Index